JUILLIARD: *A History*

Music in

American Life

A LIST OF BOOKS IN THE SERIES

APPEARS AT THE END OF THIS BOOK.

Andrea Olmstead

*University
of Illinois
Press*

URBANA
AND
CHICAGO

Juilliard

A HISTORY

Publication of this book was supported by grants from the
Henry and Edna Binkele Classical Music Fund and the
Sonneck Society for American Music.

Library of Congress Cataloging-in-Publication Data
Olmstead, Andrea.
Julliard : a history / Andrea Olmstead.
p.   cm. — (Music in American Life)
Includes bibliographic references and index.
ISBN 0-252-02487-7 (cloth)
1. Juilliard School.
2. Conservatories of music—New York (State)—New York.
I. Title.
II. Series.
MT4.N5J846   1999
780'.71'17471—dc21   98-58043
CIP

C 5 4 3 2 1

To Juilliard students, past, present, and future

CONTENTS

ILLUSTRATIONS

ACKNOWLEDGMENTS

FIRST AND FOREMOST, thanks must go to librarian Jane Gottlieb and former archivist Stephen Novak of the Lila Acheson Wallace Library and The Juilliard School Archives. Their *Guide to the Juilliard Archives* saved months of work, and their knowledge of the archives and of bibliography was invaluable. Others gave access to published and unpublished materials. Gideon Waldrop lent materials commissioned but not published by the School. Allan Kozinn gave me copies of *New York Times* articles pertaining to Juilliard. Jeremy Warburg Russo lent unpublished materials about the Loeb and Warburg families. Cindy (Liou) Chen gave copies of letters by parents of students. Georganne Mennin kindly provided access to her private files.

Music librarians who were so helpful to me in work on my books on Roger Sessions have again been unstinting and should be thanked. Judith Johnson, the Lincoln Center archivist; Wayne D. Shirley at the Library of Congress; Millard Irion at the Eda Kuhn Loeb Music Library of Harvard University; Diane Ota and her staff at the Boston Public Library; Barbara Haws, the New York Philharmonic archivist; and Bridget Carr of the Boston Symphony Archives have all been helpful.

Thanks must also go to people interviewed for this book; all were generous with their recollections. Interviewees include the current president of Juilliard, Joseph Polisi; former deans Mark Schubart, Gideon Waldrop, Gordon Hardy, and James Sloan Allen; and the current dean, Stephen Clapp. I also talked with the widows of two former presidents, Frances Schuman and Georganne Mennin. In addition, Janet Kessin (in communications), Mary Gray (admissions), Laura Drake (archives), and Lynne Rutkin (development) were helpful. Faculty interviewed included Michael Kahn (director of the Drama Division), Muriel Topaz (former director of the Dance Division), Olegna Fuschi (former director of the Pre-College Division), Stanley Wolfe (former head of the Extension Divison), Joseph Fuchs (violin), Michael White (Literature and Materials [L&M]), Viola Peters (vocal coach), Margot Harley (former Drama Division faculty), and Jacob Druckman (a former L&M faculty member). Board members were not exempt, and Mary Ellin Barrett, Mary

Rodgers Guettel, and Anna Crouse were all generous with their time. I have talked with numerous former and current students, whose special perspectives have enriched this history. Finally, I extend my deepest gratitude to all those with ties to Juilliard who provided valuable insights but asked not to be named. They spoke from their own experiences, just as I have brought to this work my own direct observations before, during, and after the eight years I taught at Juilliard.

Wayne Shirley read the entire manuscript and made valuable suggestions. David Perkins's input was valuable. Several people also read individual chapters. Thanks go to George Martin (chapters 1 through 4), Edgar Young (chapter 7), Muriel Topaz and Marcia Siegel (chapter 8), Mary Olmstead, who proofread the manuscript, and Mary Giles, who copyedited it.

During the summers of 1993 and 1994, fellowships at the Virginia Center for the Creative Arts supplied me with a studio in which to work and a climate necessary for a writer. During the summer of 1995 at the Aspen Music Festival, I not only wrote five chapters but also heard concerts by many Juilliard alumni and students.

Larry Bell, who received his master's and DMA at Juilliard in composition (and was a student of Vincent Persichetti) and who taught in the Regular and Pre-College Divisions, was, as ever, patient and supportive. We met at Juilliard during the 1970s, and—flying in the face of the chronic lack of social life at the School—we married.

Acknowl-
edgments

JUILLIARD: *A History*

INTRODUCTION

THE WORD *Juilliard* arouses passionate reactions. Many regard it with awe as the ultimate training school for the performing arts. Others dismiss it with hostility for its a reputation for competitiveness. Some graduates react with a grimace: Their experience was unpleasant.

"Juilliard is generally regarded as the leading conservatory of music in North America," *The Encyclopedia of New York City* declares.[1] Many performers would agree. In music, drama, and dance the word has become synonymous with quality, talent, and polish. What made Juilliard the most famous performing arts school in the country, if not the world? How has it achieved and sustained success since 1905? The answers to these questions lie in a complex history in which talent, money, location, publicity, and vision all play crucial roles. But negative elements also contribute to a legend: Notoriety is also fame.

The continual tug of new ideas was felt on this fundamentally conservative—that is what the word *conservatory* means—institution. Tried, true, and traditional technical instruction and adherence to repertoire have been challenged by the influence of money, new pedagogical ideas, multiculturalism, and a desire to improve students' social lives. An almost continuous struggle took place at Juilliard between 'traditional' and 'progressive' viewpoints. That struggle continues today.

Henry Kingsbury, an anthropologist, has written of the conservatory environment (his example is the New England Conservatory): "A conservatory is probably more appropriately compared with a seminary than with a professional school, in that the concentrated focus of a conservatory training seems more an inculcation of devotion than a preparation for a career."[2] Nevertheless, careerism is a factor. What were—and are—Juilliard's entrance requirements? How many students were admitted, against how much competition, and how many fulfilled the requirements and graduated? What was it like to be a student or a faculty member? What did it cost to attend, and how much were faculty paid? What were the relationships among key administrators, faculty, and students? I hope to convey the internal conservatory culture, that is, the changing atmosphere of the School. This is shown in part by discussion of the students' social environment, or lack of it, as well as descriptions and photographs of the School's six buildings. To give a sense of what lessons were like, I quote students describing the teaching of certain faculty.

What effect did changing musical and cultural values have on this institution? For example, how did the two world wars and the Vietnam War dent its cloistered walls? How did a pervasive sexism in professional musical life—orchestras were all male—affect the majority of students seriously pursuing music? And what were the effects of racism and nativism on black, Asian, and foreign-born students? To what degree did the School create and disseminate contemporary music, choreography, and drama?

Juilliard's story is about both the people and the institution. Each lent the other prestige, thereby mutually amplifying their fame. The personalities who contributed make up a cast of characters that could not have been concocted by a novelist. They include Frank Damrosch, James Loeb, Augustus Juilliard, Eugene Noble, Olga Samaroff Stokowski, Ernest Hutcheson, John Erskine, Albert Stoessel, William Schuman, Jean Morel, Renée Longy, Martha Hill, John Houseman, Peter Mennin, Vincent Persichetti, and Joseph Polisi, as well as numerous others discussed here.

An adage relates, You don't go to Juilliard to get an education, you go to Juilliard to be discovered. Nevertheless, among the many who attended and received an education were Arthur Loesser, Wallingford Riegger, Richard Rodgers, Meredith Willson, Henry Brant, Louise Talma, Kay Swift, Irving Kolodin, Joseph and Lillian Fuchs, William Kroll, Robert Mann, Van Cliburn, Billy Strayhorn, Philip Glass, Steve Reich, James Levine, Leontyne Price, Ned Rorem, Miles Davis, Wynton Marsalis, Yo-Yo Ma, Itzhak Perlman, Barbara Hendricks, Myung-Whun Chung, Nigel Kennedy, Renée Fleming, James Conlon, Midori, Ellen Zwilich, and many others.

The dance faculty, which reads like a who's who of the dance world, once included José Limón, Doris Humphrey, Martha Graham, Anna Sokolow, Antony Tudor, and Martha Hill. Graduates such as Bruce Marks and Paul Taylor have headed their own companies, and many others populate major dance companies.

Some graduates of the youngest department in the School, the Drama Division, have achieved a celebrity not attainable by those in the music or dance worlds. Their appearances in movies and on television magnify their talents and fame. Juilliard-trained actors include Robin Williams, Kevin Kline, David Ogden Stiers, Christopher Reeve, Val Kilmer, William Hurt, Kelly McGillis, Christine Baranski, Mandy Patinkin, and Kelsey Grammer. Others continued work on the stage, for which they were trained at Juilliard, for example, Michael Stuhlbarg, Gerald Guttierez, and Patti LuPone.

The path to institutional fame involves positive values such as the hard work, talent, and determination of a Frank Damrosch as well as negative ones. One need not be a cynic to acknowledge the role human failings play. Pride and envy as well as the lesser sins of snobbery, secrecy, arrogance, intimidation, and self-interest are part of the School's history. Any one of these traits, once visible, could lead to a reaction against the School—and increased name recognition.

For example, in chapter 3 I investigate the Juilliard Musical Foundation, the result of Augustus Juilliard's $12.5 million bequest. Eugene Noble, who controlled this money, indulged in xenophobia, bigotry, and self-interest that ultimately engulfed the Foundation and blackened the name of Juilliard. Paradoxically, the negative publicity this generated ultimately contributed to the School's fame. In some ways the School never recovered from the nativism and notoriety of the 1920s. Although it is hard now to imagine a music school so short-sighted as to exclude all but American-citizen applicants, that is precisely what happened at Juilliard. Bigotry barred foreign students from the Juilliard Graduate School for twenty years at a time when the faculty was predominantly foreign-born.

Later controversies took place over a theory program called Literature and Materials (L&M), in disputes with the National Association of Schools of Music and with unions, in moving the Dance Department to Lincoln Center, and in the founding of the Drama Division. The higher the price, the higher the publicity stakes: The move to the expensive complex at Lincoln Center embroiled the School in still more controversy.

Envy over the endowments of three schools—Juilliard, Eastman, and Curtis—made them all highly desirable and also targets of criticism. (Envy over Juilliard's early faculty and administrative salaries was solidified by the publicized extravagant life-style in the depression years of president John Erskine.) In addition, an elitism spawned from mastering a technique is inevitable inside the classical music world. Much time, personal effort, psychological stress, and money are invested in making the best performance possible, a "struggle for perfection" as Judith Kogan has described it.[3] Faculty and students who have an enormous amount at stake tend to be defensive. Their defensiveness and clannishness leads to a social separation that is easily mistaken for snobbery. Two consequences flow immediately from this: sour grapes from those excluded and a closing of the ranks by those on the inside—an us-against-them feeling within the School's community.

The role of journalism in both criticizing and praising the School was important in bringing it to the attention of a wider audience. From its beginning the School co-opted the press by inviting prominent music critics to become faculty members or deans, to translate libretti for opera productions, and even to sit on entrance exam committees (and be paid very well for this service). In what today would be seen as a conflict of interest, the press then praised the School in return.

As the story unfolds it becomes clear that the German authoritarianism of Frank Damrosch, the arrogance and bigotry of Eugene Noble, the rash, bull-in-a-china-shop leadership of William Schuman, and the aloofness and enigma of Peter Mennin all produced the same result: People were intimidated by these presidents. This fear was a powerful source of the School's mystique. (Damrosch and Schuman were both revered as well, but in part because people were afraid of them.)

Powerful presidents aside, true authority rests in the faculty, an authority their pedagogical lineage grants them. An ethnomusicologist remarks, "The separation between administrator and teacher is greater in the field of music, and the association of teacher and student closer than that found in higher education at large."[4] For example, a student's commitment to solo technique, as opposed to frequently expressed anti-orchestra sentiment, is in effect a commitment to a relationship with an individual mentor. Kingsbury writes, "A powerful centralized structure of authority—whether in a dean's office or on the orchestra podium—would tend to undermine the strength of the 'studio' social organization of the conservatory, the primacy of the artistic individuality of the faculty members, and in turn the aural tradition of musical performance that these faculty members serve to maintain."[5] Although to the outside world it is enough to say that someone went to Juilliard, within the School it is more important to observe that he or she is a student of Harvey Shapiro or of Ania Dorfmann. In this book, therefore, when a music student is named, the major teacher is also identified, and a list of students will often be given for faculty.

The publication in 1992 of the *Guide to the Juilliard Archives* speaks to a more open-minded attitude toward research into the School's history than was previously the case. Peter Mennin and William Schuman had closed the archives and prohibited those interested in writing a history access to the School's records. Their restrictions on scholarly research lasted forty years (1945–85). Such behavior begs a question, What did they wish to hide? For their part, the current administration and board have shown a strong desire to control the School's image.

The secrecy on the part of presidents Schuman and Mennin combines fatally with the attitude toward music schools in the academic world, a point of view that is either condescending or oblivious. Musicology has all but ignored conservatories. The stories of American conservatories are found mostly in old pamphlets, in dated masters' theses, and a single doctoral dissertation.[6] There are no histories of the Curtis Institute of Music, Manhattan School of Music, Peabody Institute, Eastman School of Music, Oberlin Conservatory, and other U.S. music schools. A history of the New England Conservatory was produced by the school itself as a public relations document in 1995, a "glossy, coffee table book."[7] There are no separate entries for any of these schools, or for Lincoln Center, in *The New Grove Dictionary of American Music*, nor will there be in the forthcoming revised *Grove*. Conservatories are therefore wide open for study on two fronts: historical research and cultural analysis.

Since 1969 I have had firsthand knowledge of conservatories, initially as a violin and music history student at the Hartt College of Music (now The Hartt School), then as a music history teacher at Juilliard (1972–80) and at The Boston Conservatory (1981 to the present). I also taught theory and ear training at the Aspen Music School. I identify deeply with the goals of music students and seek to explain something of their world.

History necessarily follows a narrative journey dictated by what actually occurred. Certain choices, once made, determine the route. This path becomes solidified in such a way as to make it appear later to have been inevitable. Nevertheless, I shall occasionally highlight other possible paths that, if pursued, would have altered the course of events. We can only speculate how differently things might have turned out if a Lincoln Center–like plan in the 1920s had not fallen through, if the School had been able to secure Nadia Boulanger or Arnold Schoenberg (after two attempts) as teachers, if Erskine had not been injured in an automobile accident or Alan Schneider not killed in one, or if Mennin had not gotten cancer. Some of Juilliard's best-laid plans, like the attempt to take control of the Metropolitan Opera, fell apart. Sometimes fate intervenes.

The eminence that attaches to a few conservatories can be explained by three factors: the endowment in the absence of government support, the goals of the founders and subsequent directors, and the achievements of the faculty and students. All three factors need to be treated in detail. I shall trace the histories of the Institute of Musical Art (IMA) from 1905 to 1946, the Juilliard Musical Foundation (JMF) from 1920 to 1992, the Juilliard Graduate School (JGS) from 1924 to 1946, the Juilliard School of Music (JSM) from 1946 to 1969, and The Juilliard School from 1969 to 1998. I shall also profile the IMA's two founders and all the School's subsequent presidents as well as (necessarily) selected faculty and students. The story of Juilliard is almost entirely a story of these people, whose backgrounds, talents, ambitions, prejudices, pathologies, and cultural assumptions contributed to the renown of the institution and helped develop the performing arts in America.

Having weathered storms of controversy and having achieved many positive goals it set out to accomplish, The Juilliard School has become an institution whose name recognition and fame are practically indestructible. The mystique surrounding Juilliard is larger than any one individual's ability to affect or alter it; for better or worse it has entered the realm of legend. This is the story of how that legend was created.

I

The Founding Fathers:

FRANK DAMROSCH
& JAMES LOEB

IN 1906 A MUSIC MAGAZINE predicted that the
Institute of Musical Art (IMA) "will certainly have a most powerful effect, not only upon the art development of America, but a direct effect,
no matter how slight, upon the business of every individual teacher on
this side of the Atlantic."[1] To trace the events leading to this "powerful
effect" we must begin by briefly outlining the history of conservatories
in Europe and in the United States prior to the IMA's founding the year
before this prediction was made.

The first secular music conservatory, Santa Maria di Loreto, opened
in 1537 in Naples. The word comes from the Italian *conservare*, referring both to the preservation of music and to the foundling children
(*conservati*) whom the schools instructed in music. Conservatories were
orphanages, and by definition they were conservative. A state music
school in Lisbon was founded in the seventeenth century, in 1771 one
was begun in Stockholm, and the Paris Conservatory opened its doors
in 1796. The nineteenth century produced conservatories in Prague
(1808), Brussels (1813), Vienna (1817), Berlin (1822), Leipzig (1843),
Munich (1846), St. Petersburg (1865), Moscow (1866), and numerous

other privately endowed or state-supported schools. The oldest music school in the United States is the Oberlin Conservatory of Music (1865). The Cincinnati Conservatory of Music, the Boston Conservatory of Music, and the New England Conservatory were all founded in 1867, and the Peabody Conservatory of Music opened the following year. These American schools were influenced mostly by the German conservatories.

New York City at the turn of the century was strewn with failed conservatories that had been stricken by decades of sharp competition and mounting debt. There once had existed the Columbia Conservatory of Music (founded in 1872); the Mason-Thomas Conservatory (1873); the Grand Conservatory of Music (1874); the New York Conservatory (ca. 1875); the New York College of Music (1878), which absorbed the German Conservatory in 1920 and the American Conservatory in 1923; the William G. Vogt Conservatory (1880); the Metropolitan Conservatory of Music, which became the Metropolitan College of Music and, in 1900, the American Institute of Applied Music; and the Synthetic Piano School (1887).

The National Conservatory of Music in America, founded by Jeannette Thurber in 1885 to encourage an indigenous musical culture, was a special case. Antonín Dvořák directed the Conservatory from 1892 to 1895, Andrew Carnegie acted as president of a thirty-nine-member board, and Theodore Thomas contributed $20,000 annually to its American Opera Company. Talented students—under the age of twenty-four and of any race—paid no tuition, and those charged paid very little. Thurber appealed to Congress for $200,000 but received the same response that New England Conservatory had gotten when it applied to the state of Massachusetts for aid. In both cases the bills died: It was considered un-American for the government to support the arts. (Thurber pointedly noted that the government supported the U.S. Naval Academy and the U.S. Military Academy, both private schools.) The contrast between state support of conservatories in Europe and U.S. hostility to public funding for the arts remains the largest single difference between music schools on the two continents.

The year 1905, when the IMA opened its doors, marked changes in the directorships of three important European music schools. Gabriel Fauré became director of the Paris Conservatory, at which post he remained until deafness forced him to resign in 1920. The St. Petersburg Conservatory was profoundly affected by the 1905 revolution, and Alexander Glazunov was elected director. At the Moscow Conservatory a separate dramatic power struggle unfolded in 1905. Vassili Safonov was succeeded by composer Mikhail Ippolitov-Ivanov, who remained director until 1922. In America, the Yale School of Music (founded in 1890) elevated Horatio Parker to dean in 1904, a position he held until his death in 1919. Composer George Chadwick had taken over the New England Conservatory in 1897, remaining president until his death in 1931. Schools on both continents continued the tradition of asking well-known composers to serve as directors.

The year 1905 also marked the founding of the International Workers of the World (IWW), the publication of Einstein's theory, and the appearance of nickelodeons, the forerunners of the movie industry. America experienced a period of progressivism that lasted until 1920, when women won the right to vote.

In the 1890s, in an atmosphere of competition among music schools, few musical philanthropists, and lack of government support for the arts, Frank Damrosch dreamed of founding his own music school in New York.

Franz Heino Damrosch was born in 1859 in Breslau, Germany, into what has been called "America's First Family of Music."[2] The eldest of five and named for his godfather Franz Liszt, Franz was renamed Frank in a U.S. public school. "Damrosch" in Hebrew means "red-headed," and indeed his younger brother Walter did have blond-red hair. Their father was the famous conductor Leopold Damrosch, and their mother, Helene von Heimburg, was a prominent singer. Walter Damrosch also became a renowned conductor and radio personality. Their sister Clara married David Mannes, and together the two founded the Mannes

Frank Damrosch.
(Photo from The Juilliard School Archives)

9

School of Music in 1916. Although the Damrosches were half Jewish—
Helene was a Lutheran—music was the family's true religion. Frank
Damrosch regarded teaching with a missionary zeal: His goal was to
bring music, like a religion, into people's lives.[3]

As a youngster in Breslau, Damrosch had been a pupil of the eminent
pedagogue and piano virtuoso Rafael Joseffy (1852–1915), a Hungarian pianist who had studied with Liszt but who owed more to Tausig as
a teacher and was known for his pianissimos. Joseffy taught at Thurber's
National Conservatory from 1888 to 1906.[4]

Frank Damrosch's personality was molded by a love of music, a strong
desire to communicate that music, and by a close-knit German family
who valued hard work. For decades the extended family lived in the same
apartment or building in New York. In the realm of composition, he did
not compete with his father or with other composers. (Virtuosi in his
day all tried their hands at composition.) In conducting, although successful, he did not compete with his more famous brother, whom he
never openly envied. But he outdid both in a role in which the entire
family strongly believed, that of pedagogue. As a conductor and a teacher
he was patriarchal, kindly, demanding, and devoted.

Damrosch was influenced by Felix Adler's Society for Ethical Culture,
where he played the organ on Sundays. Adler advocated the ethics of
the Jewish and Christian religions without their dogma. His aim was to
assert the supreme importance of the moral factor in all the relationships of life. His society also was devoted to the elevation of the working classes, and Damrosch conceived the idea of teaching music to the
poor. In 1892, after receiving the support of trade unions, he wrote an
open letter to working people, met with some at the Cooper Union hall
for the first class (filled to capacity while outside another thousand gathered), and donated his services to the People's Singing Classes. Most
students were from diverse backgrounds and were either women of German descent or African Americans. The People's Choral Union, drawn
from the Singing Classes and conducted by Damrosch, performed annually in Carnegie Hall. Five separate courses were organized, headed
by Damrosch's assistants. Nonplussed, critics asked whether the classes
were music or social service. Such questions went unanswered, however;
Damrosch's Singing Classes were a popular triumph and a highly original contribution to musical life in New York for twenty-five years.

In the fall of 1893 Damrosch founded the Musical Art Society with
the help and financial support of several prominent Newport, Rhode
Island, society women. Their aim was to present works of Palestrina and
other composers of a cappella polyphonic music of the sixteenth and
seventeenth centuries. Fifty to sixty professional singers were hired.

Their performances were the first to revive early music on a large scale in the United States. Damrosch edited the scores from manuscript into modern editions and succeeded, partly through the force of his personality, in nearly filling Carnegie Hall for the concerts. The Musical Art Society gave these concerts for twenty-six seasons.

When the New York City Board of Education created a position of supervisor of music for public schools in 1897, Damrosch was appointed and stayed until 1905 at a salary of $4,000 a year. He and twenty-six assistants dealt with seven thousand teachers and three hundred thousand pupils. Damrosch intended to revolutionize the public schools' methods of music education. To combat a general ignorance of music, in October 1898 he began a series called Symphony Concerts for Young People, which were performed on six Saturday afternoons a season in Carnegie Hall. He persuaded Andrew Carnegie to pay the hall's rental fee of $1,500 for the first year, and the series ran for thirteen more years under Damrosch's direction.

Damrosch's greatest success still lay ahead: the founding of the Institute of Musical Art. To achieve this, he needed vision, considerable skills as a pedagogue, a great deal of money, and even more luck. Like many pedagogues, Damrosch had his own theories about teaching music, which relied heavily on ear training and dictation. He had experimented with a four-year-old student, teaching her ear training for three years before he allowed her to touch a piano. When she did finally play the instrument, she was able to correct herself because she could "hear" the right note in her mind; she could also play a piece in any key because of her foundation in intervals. Later she entered the IMA as a student of Sigismond Stojowski and was graduated with the first class of eighteen musicians in 1907.[5]

Damrosch realized that musical training in America, unlike that in Europe, was not government-supported. In addition, many U.S. conservatories taught only instruments and not music history, theory, ear training, orchestration, counterpoint, or harmony. They were "schools" of private lessons only. The cost of private lessons for each study was prohibitive. In Europe, at the Berlin Hochschule, for example, students paid only 300 marks of the 1,000 that their education cost per year. In Brussels gifted students paid nothing at all, and in Paris they received not only free tuition but also a stipend from the government. Damrosch envisioned a school able to provide all these courses in which the tuition would represent the cost of instrumental lessons only.

As early as 1892 Damrosch had wanted to found a music school but could find no one to back him. For more than a decade his dream was unfulfilled. In the summer of 1901 he went to Scotland, hoping to gain

Andrew Carnegie's support. After a month, however, he left empty-handed, partly because, as he wrote to his wife Hetty, "I am, as you know, a poor hand at pushing anything in which I am personally interested and besides am a poor conversationalist."[6] Carnegie had nevertheless told Damrosch that he was "the best man in America to organize and direct a large educational musical institution."[7] Hetty Damrosch tried a year later to approach Carnegie but received a firm rejection, probably based on his unhappy experience with Thurber's National Conservatory.[8] Carnegie did tell Frank Damrosch, however, that he could have Carnegie Hall (which Walter Damrosch had convinced him to build) to use as the school's building if he raised an endowment of $1 million. But where would Damrosch get that kind of money?

Matters stood at an impasse until May 1903, when, on a steamer bound from Atlantic City to New York, an accidental meeting changed Damrosch's life and the course of American conservatories. On that trip the Damrosches met an acquaintance he had not seen in a while, James Loeb.[9]

Handsome, brilliant, cultivated, a talented 'cellist, fluent in French and German, James Loeb, although born (in 1867) into an extremely rich family, was not permitted to live the life he would have chosen for himself. To please his father, Solomon Loeb, founder of the famous Wall Street firm of Kuhn, Loeb and Company, he gave up a career in arche-

James Loeb.
(Harvard University Archives)

ology and classics (for which he showed genuine aptitude) for a career in banking (for which he had little interest). Equally important, he was forbidden to marry the woman he loved. Marriage at Kuhn, Loeb was as serious as business. Indeed, marriage was business. Solomon had married Kuhn's sister, and Kuhn married Solomon's sister. Jacob Schiff married Solomon's daughter, Theresa, and their daughter Frieda married Felix Warburg, the Florestan (à la Schumann) of the well-known Warburg family. Felix's brother Paul, the Eusebius, married Solomon's daughter Nina.[10] Partner Otto Kahn married another partner's daughter. For forty-four years all partners at Kuhn, Loeb, and Company were related by blood or marriage. Despite being thwarted in two important areas and having suffered heavy psychological burdens, James Loeb managed to make significant contributions to the arts and humanities.

Anita Warburg, a relative, described James as one who "lived for beauty in all his senses, a Renaissance man."[11] Frieda Schiff Warburg wrote, "Of all [five of] my grandparent's children, my Uncle Jim was the most vivid, brilliant personality. As handsome as a Greek god, he charmed everyone, was an excellent scholar, a fine musician and an esthete." While at Kuhn, Loeb, "He took part in political reform, collected early Greek figures, played his favorite cello as well as the piano and organ—and had several love affairs."[12] Frank Damrosch later observed, "James Loeb, although intended for a career as banker, had the nature of an artist [and] a highly trained intellect, a love of beauty, a fine character, and a sympathy with any work that tended towards ideal conditions in the development of higher culture."[13]

Loeb's mother, Betty Gallenberg, was the daughter of Simon Gallenberg, the first violinist at the grand duke's opera in Mannheim. Betty had been brought up to be a musician, and a prosperous uncle in Paris had enabled her to get the "finishing touches" on the piano at the Paris Conservatory. She also played the violin. Her marriage to the widowed Solomon Loeb had been arranged before they met.[14]

In addition to formal schooling, all five Loeb children were educated in numerous subjects at home. What is more important, they learned the cultural lessons of Jewish philanthropy in New York.[15] Solomon set a high standard in generosity to the poor. To promote her children's musical talents, Betty Loeb populated Sunday dinners with visiting conductors, singers, composers, dancers, and musicians. Undoubtedly that included Damrosch's parents.

James was the only one in his family who had any real musical talent.[16] When he attended Harvard University (1884–88) he studied with the American composer John Knowles Paine and with Charles Eliot Norton, professor of the history of art. Loeb and future art critic Bernard Berenson were classmates under Norton. Loeb's musical education may have also been amplified by trips to hear the newly founded (1881) Boston Symphony Orchestra. In 1885–86 he was vice president of Harvard's music club and orchestra, the Pierian Sodality, and sat in the small 'cello section with Walter Naumberg. Walter Spalding described both as "unusually gifted players."[17]

After Loeb's graduation from Harvard came the decision as to a career. His older brother Morris had escaped a life at Kuhn, Loeb by becoming a chemist, and James was the only remaining son. (Unfortunately for Solomon Loeb, neither son produced children, even after Morris Loeb dutifully married Samuel Kuhn's daughter, Eda.) James Loeb wrote of his career decision:

> [I] had received a tempting offer, through the good offices of [my] teacher and friend Charles Eliot Norton—an offer which meant a number of years of study in Egyptology in Paris and London, opportunity to excavate in Egypt itself, with a fair assurance of a curatorship at the Boston Museum of Fine Arts and a teacher's post at Harvard. Though it is natural to suppose that father had a secret hope that his second son would ultimately enter the family firm, he by no word or sign placed an obstacle in the way of the son's choosing the career for which he had a decided preference. When after a long inward struggle the decision to become a banker was finally reached, father silently smiled his approval.[18]

Stephen Birmingham, however, the chronicler of New York's Jewish banking families, gives a different, less stoic, and more plausible version of this story: "For months Jim Loeb begged his father to let him take this study offer, but Solomon was adamant. One of his seed line had to join the bank, and there was no alternative."[19]

Giving up his chosen career was one result of family obligation, but in 1891 Loeb was asked to sacrifice the love of his life as well. A generous sum of money was given him—after the threat that he would be disinherited—if he agreed not to marry a woman whose identity still remains a family secret. It is known that she was a Gentile. Loeb's powerful, manipulative, and sternly Jewish brother-in-law Jacob Schiff rewrote his will to stipulate that his own unmarried children would be disinherited if either married a non-Jew.

The sacrifices James Loeb made in his choices of career and whether to marry, combined with emotional problems he shared with his brother and one of his three sisters, affected his mental health. He has been described as both schizophrenic and epileptic, although the diagnosis is not entirely clear. In agony, he went abroad to consult a neurologist, possibly Siegmund Freud; the story has it that he lived in Freud's house. It is likely that Freud's advice to Loeb consisted of the suggestion to get away from his family, specifically Jacob Schiff.

To escape New York's financial world, Loeb attended concerts. There he met Frank Damrosch. In March 1900 he wrote to Damrosch, "I feel impelled to tell you what unbounded delight I got from your concert last night. It was indeed a rare treat; such masterly handling of a choir as you presented, in the performance of the Chorales of the [Palestrina] Stabat mater cannot fail to move a person who has a heart and his five senses. It was very, very beautiful and I feel that it is no more than due to you that I should express to you in this way my thanks and appreciation."[20] In the same letter Loeb agreed to serve as a trustee of Damrosch's one institutional failure, the ill-fated American Institute of Music, and volunteered $25,000.

A shock awaited. Although his mother was a diabetic, the amiable Betty Loeb's appetite frequently got the better of her. On September 2, 1902, Solomon saw her reach for another serving of Nesselrode pie, which was forbidden by her diet. He cried, "Betty, don't!" "I don't care if it costs me ten years of my life," she said. "I'll take a second helping." With a smile she did and was dead within hours.[21] James Loeb was devastated.

Months later, Loeb encountered Frank and Hetty Damrosch on the ferry to New York and consulted Damrosch about a memorial for his mother; he had thought of establishing a fellowship in music at Columbia University. Damrosch reported that President Nicholas Murray Butler of Columbia had told him that the university had several such gifts and they lay idle, wanting applicants. The two may have noted the coincidence of their mothers sharing the same birthday, January 16 (1834 for Betty Loeb, 1836 for Helene Damrosch). For twelve years Damrosch had sought support for a conservatory. While in the millionaire's stateroom, he thought to ask whether Loeb would favor a plan of endowing a music school in his mother's memory. He finally found hope: Loeb asked for written particulars.

On the surface the forty-four-year-old Damrosch and Loeb, thirty-six, seem an unlikely pair to embark together on a lifelong commitment to found and sustain a music school; indeed, their personalities could hardly have been more different. Damrosch had a systematic, stolid, stable manner, whereas Loeb was fragile, mercurial, and depressive. Still, similarities of background may help explain their mutual devotion. Each was raised in a German-speaking home and was fluent in French; each had a musical mother, a brother, and three sisters; and each had a father involved in a highly publicized rivalry, Damrosch with Theodore Thomas, Loeb with J. P. Morgan.[22] Reacting to the publicity swirling about their fathers, each had sought to escape New York: Damrosch had gone to Denver, and Loeb would soon move to Europe. Loeb's mother had recently died, and Damrosch's mother would die soon after their shipboard meeting. Finally, each brought to the founding of a music school a sense of duty and idealism—in part reflected in their shared concern for the poor—whose strength cannot be underestimated.

At the school's first commencement ceremony Damrosch described his quest for a sympathetic patron: "I always found a kind of respectful attention, but no understanding, no real appreciation, until I spoke to James Loeb, and to him I had but to say a word and he understood."[23] Loeb could not have chosen more wisely than to invest his money with Damrosch, an excellent musician, pedagogue, and administrator. After decades of continued search for other such patrons, Damrosch never found a second Loeb. More than twenty years later, Loeb's brother-in-law and IMA board member Paul Warburg reminisced:

> To me Frank Damrosch's and Jim Loeb's association in the concep-
> tion, organization and building up of our Institute of Musical Art has
> always been something unique and peculiarly moving. For both of
> them music meant more than mere art or science. To them it was, and
> always has remained, something like a sacred heritage, something like
> the subtle influence of early religious impressions and traditions that
> one received from the background of one's parents' home. Frank in-
> herited that from his father. Jim from his mother, and, whether they
> know it or not, I believe that neither of them has ever been able, con-
> sciously or subconsciously, to divorce his love and devotion for music
> from these memories. That is why they have been so keen and anxious
> to keep musical standards high and pure, and that is why—each in his
> own way—they were willing to bring sacrifices for it.
>
> Of the two, Frank contributed the infinitely larger share. For while
> Jim furnished the material foundation and, what is more, his warm,
> and unceasing sympathy and moral support, Frank gave to the task his
> entire life.
>
> It is a beautiful thing and a rare one, to have a real ideal. It is rarer
> still to find it possible to make this ideal a living thing, and still rarer
> to convert it into one that will continue to live when all of us will be
> gone. But the rarest of them all is to find two people united in such an
> ideal, united in their flight toward a common star.[24]

Loeb had asked Damrosch to meet with him and two other interested friends, music publisher Rudolph Schirmer and Charles Eliot Norton's eldest son, Eliot Norton, at the Lotos Club to discuss the new music school. Damrosch already knew Schirmer, who had published his *Popular Method of Sight Singing* in 1894. The four decided to raise an endowment of $500,000 during the summer of 1903, securing nine subscriptions of $50,000. (Loeb had already volunteered $50,000.) The plan was to open the school in the fall of 1904, but Damrosch, worried about raising his one-tenth share, could not imagine where he would find the others. He wrote:

> In October [1903], I was called to the telephone one day by Rudolph Schirmer, who told me that he had just had a long conversation with James Loeb in which he told him that he was afraid it would take too long to raise the necessary endowment, and that therefore he would donate the entire sum of $500,000 in order to get the work started as soon as possible. One can imagine the sensations which came over me when this message reached me over the phone. I was stunned and could hardly believe what I heard. However, the message was confirmed by a letter from James Loeb, and it was arranged that I should resign from my position with the public schools and go to Europe in the spring of 1904 in order to look over the field as it then existed in the European conservatories.[25]

But two months after the call, in December 1903, Solomon Loeb suddenly died, and Loeb slid into another depression, lasting until spring 1904. When he recovered, he still wanted the music school dedicated to his mother. The money Loeb now inherited (which he would not have received had he married the woman he wanted) would be spent in part on Damrosch's music school. A condition in Loeb's liberal-minded endowment decreed that students of both sexes be admitted, irrespective of race, color, or creed. These conditions were by no means universal: The Cincinnati Conservatory's founder, for example, restricted black students from attending, a condition that lasted well into the twentieth century. In April 1904, about a month after receiving Loeb's confirmation letter, Damrosch sailed for Europe to study the conservatories there.

For several months he visited conservatories in Paris, Brussels, Amsterdam, Berlin, Leipzig, Vienna, Stettin, Cologne, and London to familiarize himself with their pedagogical and administrative methods. He did not visit the St. Petersburg, Moscow, or the Italian conservatories. "Few American students really know anything of the dilapidated condition in which some of the great European schools are to be found," he wrote. "The general fault with all European music schools is the lack of eclectic individualism in the instruction of pupils, together with the almost complete absence of a unified pedagogic scheme.... Artistic temperament has been beaten into hopeless submission by the relent-less machinery of the 'music factory.'"[26]

He found an example of poor cooperation at the Royal Music School in Brussels. The school, noted for its string department, had no string quartet in residence because no leading teacher would play second vio-lin. "Each teacher is interested only in his own specialty," Damrosch wrote, "and neither knows nor cares what is being done by other teachers or students. The student soon learns to take the same narrow point of view and the result is the sensation-seeking, highly specialized, self-cen-tered, egotistical virtuoso, not the really great artist whose complete mastery of the technique of his art is joined to the most thorough mu-sicianship, artistic perception and general culture, and to whom virtu-osity is but a means to a higher end."[27]

At the Paris Conservatory he found nothing to praise except the li-brary. In Leipzig, whose conservatory had been founded by Felix Mendelssohn and whose titular head was Artur Nikisch, he was shocked to find discipline so lax that students could cut a theory class or orches-tra rehearsal if they liked. There was no coordination among the de-partments. In Berlin he found a splendid catalog describing all that he wanted to do in his own conservatory; Joseph Joachim's Hochschule, however, conspicuously failed to live up to its prospectus. Further shocks were in store at the Vienna Conservatory. The level of teaching and students was very high, but every teacher Damrosch met was financially strapped, and all—including the director—begged for a job at his new conservatory in New York. The German schools operated on a semi-penal system of discipline, a holdover from the medieval university that could never be introduced in the United States because it would vio-late students' civil rights.

As late as 1962, student-teacher relations in some European conser-vatories still contrasted sharply with those in the United States. Pianist Irwin Freundlich, a student at the IMA and later a faculty member, described it:

> [In Europe] the master teacher is more formal, more distant in man-ner, more removed from his students. In general, his opinions and be-liefs permit of little discussion. He is inclined to hand down the Word, and his students are inclined to accept it as Gospel. He is likely to demand deference in outward behavior as well. When your maestro enters the room at the Accademia Chigiana in Siena, you and your fellow students rise until permitted to resume seats by the maestro. You would not, by and large, have individual lessons if you were a pia-nist or instrumentalist. You would meet, let us say, from four to seven o'clock in the early evening with all students present, and you would

have your lesson in the presence of your colleagues, submitting to the criticism of the master, whether it be kind or cutting, in the semi-public atmosphere.[28]

The one example of a successful school in Damrosch's opinion was the Royal College of Music in London, run by Sir Hubert Parry. Its faculty members cooperated fully with each other in developing thorough musicians. It also had an endowed dormitory and dining room, which vastly improved the students' social environment. One reason why the IMA's eventual building, Lenox House, seemed so desirable to Damrosch was its homelike atmosphere.

Damrosch did not note the inequality between the sexes in the European conservatories. Women were admitted, but their education was separate from and not equal to men's. Women were mostly limited to voice, piano, and harp. In Paris for most of the nineteenth century, courses in harmony, counterpoint, and fugue, as well as composition, were for men only. In Munich no women were admitted into score reading until 1902. At the Paris Conservatory women faculty were routinely paid less than men. At the Berlin Hochschule in 1881 the deputy director wrote to Joachim, "We have to make sure that orchestras will not have men and women playing together in the future."[29]

Given Damrosch's already strong views on musical education, it is not surprising to discover that nothing he met with in Europe altered his opinions about how music should be taught. He concluded disparagingly that these conservatories were first of all trade schools and furthermore lacked a unity of pedagogical effort among their faculties:

> We need an institution, not alone for the training of professional musicians, but for the development of true musical culture among all classes. . . . Another important duty of the school would be the thorough training of teachers. Present conditions in this respect are bad beyond belief and demand improvement. I believe that ninety per cent of the music teachers in the United States have neither the natural ability nor the necessary pedagogical preparation and, in consequence, millions of dollars are annually wasted in musical studies which amount to nothing. Our institution will create proper standards and establish correct methods of instruction and in this way will teach the public what to expect of music teachers.[30]

When Damrosch returned to the United States he received an honorary doctor of music from Yale University. From then on, he was referred to as "Doctor Damrosch" or merely "the Doc."

The school was scheduled to open in October 1904. In August, however, yet another tragedy beset Loeb. Olga Warburg, once in love with

Loeb, was pushed into an unhappy marriage when her family prevented her from marrying him. She committed suicide at age thirty-one. Olga's brothers had married into Loeb's family—Paul to Loeb's sister Nina and Felix to Loeb's niece Frieda Schiff. Loeb did not rebound easily from this third death in less than two years. The opening of the school was delayed indefinitely, leaving Damrosch on tenterhooks to wonder whether his dream of establishing a conservatory would really come true.

Damrosch reminded Andrew Carnegie that he had promised to provide a home for the school in Carnegie Hall if Damrosch could raise $1 million. Carnegie asked where the money was, and Damrosch, controlling his impatience, said that Jacob Schiff would vouch for half of it, Loeb's endowment. Satisfied, Carnegie offered an apartment house called the Rembrandt next door to Carnegie Hall that would, however, cost $100,000 to soundproof and bring up to the building code. Damrosch cabled Loeb, in Rome, who asked Paul Warburg for advice. "Though so far no further money raised," Warburg cabled back. "Carnegie agrees endlich [finally] to give us Rembrandt, provided your money turned over to conservatory now."[31] For whatever reason, Loeb did not oblige, and ultimately Damrosch had to refuse Carnegie's offer. The school was never associated with Andrew Carnegie or with the hall that bears his name.

The winter of 1904–5 was spent trying to find a suitable home for the school and hiring competent teachers. Damrosch and the board decided in March 1905 to lease the old Lenox Mansion at 53 Fifth Avenue, the northeast corner of Fifth Avenue and Twelfth Street. The address was prestigious. In the mid-1840s William Lenox had built the $100,000 Gothic Revival brownstone mansion, and in 1870 James Lenox incorporated a famous library that eventually became part of the New York Public Library. Across the street, at the northwest corner, in 1905 stood the home of wealthy Metropolitan Opera patron August Belmont. Lenox House was owned by the aptly named Thomas Fortune Ryan, whose $50 million soon would be worth twice that and who controlled the Equitable Insurance Company. He had bought the Lenox property to protect his own house on the southeast corner.

With a hundred feet on Fifth Avenue and seventy-five feet on Twelfth Street, the home had nearly twenty rooms. It had "a large, long hall on one side which used to house the Lenox Library [and was converted into an assembly hall], and . . . a spacious interior hall and staircase, large light rooms, stuccoed [high] ceilings, and wonderful old Italian marble fireplaces. It was a millionaire's palace, but in a frightful state of disrepair."[32] The rear of the hall was flooded, and it would cost $11,000 to repair the building, plus yearly taxes of $6,000. Damrosch's friend Otto Eidlitz promised to have the mansion ready for occupancy in October. James Loeb agreed to pay for equipment at a cost of $19,000, and with that money Damrosch shopped for instruments, including Mason and Hamlin and Steinway pianos and a pipe organ.

Students could reach the school by taking the city's first subway, which had opened in 1904 and ran from City Hall to Union Square and then under Park Avenue to Grand Central. Or they could take the private Fifth Avenue Coach Company trolleys or the cross-town streetcars on Fourteenth Street. The els ran up and down Second, Third, Sixth, and Ninth Streets. The cost of riding the new subways—a nickel—was politically sacrosanct until after World War II, but the experience of doing so is reflected by the term *subway crush* from 1904.

The original charter for the school was granted by the University of the State of New York Board of Regents on June 27, 1904. Its first name, "The School of Musical Art of the City of New York," turned out to be already in use. "Institute of Musical Art" appears on a second charter,

Lenox Mansion.
(United States History, Local History and Genealogy Division, New York Public Library, Astor, Lenox and Tilden Foundations)

dated June 28, 1905, and the School was frequently referred to as "the IMA" or simply the "Damrosch school." Conservatories such as Eastman, Curtis, and Peabody were named after their patrons, but Loeb's modesty prevented the obvious choice: the Loeb School of Music. Article VII of its bylaws gave the director full administrative freedom, including complete responsibility for policies, curriculum, and faculty, conditions that few conservatory directors in the United States had been able to obtain. (In Chicago, for example, Theodore Thomas was frustrated by the limited range of his control.)

The first board consisted of James Loeb, Frank Damrosch, Charles O. Brewster, Eliot Norton, Rudolph Schirmer, and Paul Warburg. The board elected seven more members, including another brother-in-law of Loeb's, Isaac N. Seligman. Apart from Damrosch, the board did not have a musician on it for years, and not until after World War I did women sit on the board of a school, even if students were disproportionately female. Rudolph Schirmer offered to donate a music library, and Loeb's brother Morris, president of the Betty Loeb Memorial Foundation, offered 4 percent annual income on the $100,000 fund. Damrosch's salary was set at $10,000 per year until 1910. He hired as his secretary Helen Frank, who would work at the school for forty years.

James Loeb's only request in return for his extreme generosity was to be allowed to commission an artist to design the school's seal. He chose Gutzon Borglum (1867–1941), who had established himself in New York in 1901, was the first American sculptor whose work was bought by the Metropolitan Museum of Art, and would later carve Mount Rushmore. The seal included a motto in Greek suggested by

The seal of
the Institute of
Musical Art.
*(Photo from The Juilliard
School Archives)*

D. E. K. Dunham and approved of by Loeb: "Prothumeomeltia tà kálà" Translated it means "let us devote ourselves to noble and beautiful works" or "let us devote ourselves with ardor to noble and valiant works." The figure of Orpheus and his lyre was struck into silver medals that were awarded to graduating students. A raised reproduction of the seal graced the cover of IMA catalogs, and the figure can still be seen in stained glass on the inside, as well as carved on the outside, of the 120 Claremont Avenue building.

The first four meetings of the board, in March 1905, were held at Loeb's house. By April, however, he had gone to Europe to enter a sanitarium for his depression and seek a cure for his epilepsy. Although holding the position of second vice president and even president of the board of trustees, Loeb appeared only once again at a board meeting and never attended any ceremony connected with the school. Except for two trips home, in 1907 and 1910, he never again returned to the United States. He had helped to launch the school; he trusted Damrosch to run it. Increasingly reclusive, Loeb was kept informed of it by letters and visits from Damrosch for the next twenty-eight years.

In April 1905 Damrosch once more returned to Europe (probably funded by Loeb) to seek instructors for the school. His first object was to secure the Hungarian coloratura soprano Etelka Gerster (1855–1920), who had an internationally known school for singers in Berlin and experienced meteoric success in Europe and America. Damrosch attended a musicale of her students in her apartment in Berlin. "I heard eight or ten fine voices beautifully trained—notable particularly for the velvety quality which had been developed by Mme. Gerster. I therefore had no hesitation in entering into negotiations with her."[33] Because Gerster would not leave her own students for the school year, she suggested that her assistant, Madeleine Walther, teach from October. In January, Gerster would arrive, remain for three months, and teach Walther's pupils. Damrosch agreed, but after the three months Gerster returned to teach in Berlin, leaving the French-born Walther to carry on. Forty years later she was still teaching at the IMA.

While in Paris Damrosch received a telegram from Ferruccio Busoni's agent saying that the most prominent pianist and composer in Germany would be available to teach. Busoni had previously taught at the New England Conservatory (1891–94) and had been teaching in Berlin for the past decade. Damrosch met with Busoni in Bonn but dismissed him, writing unrevealingly, "I came to the conclusion, however, that he would not be a suitable teacher for us."[34] Inherent conservatism may had led Damrosch to choose Percy Goetschius over the more radical Busoni. It also appears that Damrosch would not tolerate Busoni's drinking.[35]

His next stop in Paris was to see the Polish pianist Sigismond Stojowksi (1869–1946), a pupil and friend of Paderewski whom Harold Bauer and Pablo Casals had recommended. Stojowski, who had studied piano and composition with Delibes at the Paris Conservatory, played Schumann's Sonata in f-sharp minor to impress Damrosch. He succeeded: Damrosch had "a pianist in [his] pocket." Stojowski remained at the IMA until 1912, when he left to teach at the Von Ende School of Music in New York.

Next came Georg Henschel (1850–1934), a singer and the first conductor of the Boston Symphony Orchestra. Damrosch had known him since childhood in Breslau, and James Loeb had also twice recommended him.[36] Although Damrosch needed him only as a vocal coach of lieder, after a day with him in Aviemore, Scotland, he hired Henschel as a teacher of advanced students. Henschel, who had studied at the Leipzig Conservatory and had the unusual experience of having sung professionally roles in all ranges from boy soprano to basso profundo, taught at the IMA from 1905 to 1908.

For opera, Damrosch secured the sixty-year-old French bass Alfred Giraudet (1845–1911), who had taught both at the Paris Conservatory and privately in Boston. Loeb had recommended Humperdinck for composition, Hugo Becker for 'cello, and Carl Friedberg for piano, as well as Oscar Sonneck for lecturer in history and aesthetics of music, but for whatever reasons none of those musicians was hired although Friedberg joined the faculty later.

Damrosch did not have to look in Europe for string teachers as he had done for voice and piano. The United States possessed an ideal teacher, Franz Kneisel (1865–1926). The Kneisel Quartette came with him; Julius Theodorowicz (1877–1964) played second violin; Louis Svecenski (1862–1926), the viola; and Alwin Schroeder (1855–1928), the 'cello. Schroeder had played both violin and viola professionally in Europe. Kneisel and his colleagues played in the Boston Symphony, where he had been made concertmaster at nineteen. When they resigned to further their quartet career Damrosch immediately entered into negotiations to secure all four for the new school. He justifiably congratulated himself on such prescience: "I may say now that this association of Franz Kneisel with the Institute of Musical Art was of more value and better results than that of any other teacher which the Institute had during the past twenty-eight years."[37]

The complete faculty list appeared in the prospectus of the new school as follows:

VOICE CULTURE AND REPERTORY

Mme. Etelka Gerster
Mons. Alfred Giraudet
Mr. Georg Henschel
Mme. Hess-Burr

Mr. Wilfried Oswald Klamroth
Miss Emma C. Thursby
Mrs. Theodore [Ella] Toedt
Mlle. Madeleine Walther

EAR-TRAINING, SIGHT-SINGING AND CHORUS

Mr. Frank Damrosch and assistants

PIANOFORTE

Miss Helena Augustin
Miss Carolyn H. Beebe
Miss E. L. Gallagher
Mrs. J. R. Herreshoff, Jr.
Mr. Arthur Hochmann
Miss Anna G. Lockwood
Miss Virginia Lucy
Mr. Wesley Weyman

Miss Stella Newmark
Miss Ellen Ransom
Mme. Lillie Sang-Collins
Mr. Sigismond Stojowski
Mrs. H. A. Seymour
Mrs. Thomas [Bertha] Tapper
Mr. Albert Weinstein

STRINGED INSTRUMENTS

Mr. Arthur Argiewicz, violin
Mr. Franz Kneisel, violin
Mr. Ludwig E. Manoly, double bass
Mr. David Robinson, violin
Mr. Alwin Schroeder, violoncello
Mr. Louis Svecenski, viola
Mr. Julius Theodorowicz, violin
Mme. Adelina Rossini, harp

ORGAN

Mons. Gaston M. Dethier

THEORY AND COMPOSITION

Mr. Percy Goetschius
Mr. Louis V. Saar

ORCHESTRAL INSTRUMENTS

Mons. Georges Barrère, flute
Mr. Caesare Addimando, oboe
Mr. Leon Leroy, clarinet
Mr. August Mesnard, bassoon
Mr. Herrman Hand, horn
Mr. Adolphe DuBois, trumpet
Mr. Abraham Tilken, trombone

LANGUAGES

Mme. Merlin Albro, French
Miss Bertha Firgau, German
Mr. Edoardo Petri, Italian

LECTURES

Mr. Walter Damrosch   Mr. Henry E. Krehbiel
Mr. William J. Henderson   Mr. Waldo S. Pratt
Mr. Thomas Tapper

PEDAGOGY

Mr. Frank Damrosch

Most of the faculty were European, and American students addressed them using the titles monsieur, madame, and mademoiselle, a formality that obtained through the 1970s. Remarkably, Frank Damrosch not only taught the ear-training, sight-singing, and pedagogy courses and conducted the chorus and orchestra but also personally auditioned every student applying to the school, which he both directed and administered. No wonder it was called the Damrosch School.

The director had hoped to attract 150 students, although his less sanguine trustees guessed only about fifty would apply. The New England Conservatory, which in the 1880s was reputed to be the largest music school in the world, had an enrollment of 2,603 in 1905 and 1906. The Institute attracted 281 students during the first week of October 1905. By March, Damrosch reported that every day the school had to turn students away because it could only hold about four hundred. In the first year 467 students enrolled. Most were not high school graduates. By 1920 only 16.8 percent of the Institute's seventeen-year-olds had graduated from high school.

Most music schools in New York were tuition-driven. Students paid for and received only lessons on an instrument. That usually meant that no one advised them on their entire musical education. It also meant that the student-teacher relationship could be corrupted by financial considerations. Printed in the first catalog and issued by the trustees but doubtless written by Damrosch, the IMA prospectus stated:

> A school has always been needed which shall not be obliged, by pecuniary considerations, to adapt its standards and requirements to the demands of every student seeking its aid. . . . Four things are essential to a school of music which has for its aim the uplifting of artistic standards. The faculty must consist of teachers of the highest ability and sincerity, each a specialist in his department and also grounded in the principles of pedagogics; every student must pursue a course of study intelligently designed and adapted to his needs; founders, directors, and teachers must be beyond the sway of merely mercenary considerations; [and] the environment of the school must be such as to afford contact with high manifestations of the art, so that ambition may be stimulated, judgment directed and steadied, good taste cultivated, and industry and zeal inspired and rewarded.[38]

The prospectus also hailed the location of the school in New York, where it claimed musical activities were greater than those of any other American city and rivaled three or four musical capitals of Europe. The Damrosches, Loebs, and Warburgs were lifelong New Yorkers who contributed their efforts and finances toward the improvement of art in their home city.

Coursework ran for three terms a year (October to December, January to March, and March to June) for a three-year (in 1912 expanded to a four-year) span in order to obtain a certificate. (Degrees were issued only in the 1930s.) Tuition was $150 a year for instrumentalists and $200 a year for singers. The Special Course in Theory and Composition, one of several special courses, was $100 a year. Students typically attended the IMA two mornings or two afternoons a week, plus concerts.

A regular course of study for, say, piano, consisted, in the first year, of courses in technics of the instrument, ear training, dictation, sight singing, elements of music, notation, attendance at lectures, rehearsals, recitals, and concerts; in the second year of technics of the instrument, dictation, sight singing, harmony, sight playing, and the required attendance; and, in the third year, of technics, dictation, sight playing, ensemble playing, counterpoint, musical form, musical analysis, and lecture attendance. The curriculum and the three-term organization lasted, with remarkably little alteration, for twenty-eight years.

The school opened on October 11, although the opening ceremony was not held until October 31, 1905. Woodrow Wilson, then president of Princeton University, spoke, as did Felix Adler and Cornelius C. Cuyler, president of the IMA board. Damrosch remarked to the audience that because other schools rely on tuition they "must always give the pupil what he asks for and not what he should have." Because of the Loeb endowment, Damrosch was able to say, "Thou shalt learn these things." He continued, "The best interests of the students shall be considered first in all things. Then we shall ultimately produce true musicians, not necessarily those who play faster or sing higher than anybody else, but musicians of thoroughness, of wide horizon, musicians who place sincerity above sensationalism, who place the work of art before the personality of the performer, in other words, musicians who are true devotees of the art of music. Then shall we feel that this school has accomplished its purposes."[39] As he did on most public occasions, here as well as in almost three decades of commencement addresses, Damrosch pleaded for financial support.

Adler's opening ceremony speech showed his own agenda clearly: "I find myself in entire sympathy with Mr. Damrosch's plan, which is not yet fully developed, to make this a Culture Institute, instead of one merely for music lessons."[40] Faculty member Lillie Sang-Collins had studied at the Paris Conservatory and taught piano at the IMA from 1905 to 1912 and voice from 1925 until her retirement in 1943. She recalled the opening ceremonies held in the Recital Hall:

> The splendid enthusiasm, the marvelous magnetism of Woodrow Wilson and Felix Adler speaking in that lovely old library recital hall at the opening ceremonies; our unforgettable visit with Paderewski; dear George Henschel with the child-like enthusiasm and simplicity of the great artist: but, above all, I remember the *esprit de corps*, the working together of all of us, interested in each other's work, and the attitude of the students—the sweetness, the enthusiasm and reverence for the beautiful, the crowded recital hall, the deep desire to learn and the loyalty to the school and its working members.[41]

For decades annual recitals were held on January 16 in commemoration of Betty Loeb's birthday. In their mother's honor, her children wished to continue her custom of inviting friends to concerts in the Loebs' music room. Morris Loeb, who gave eight lectures on acoustics during the first year of the school, and his brother James had kept the list of the guests she had invited, and these old friends were the first to be asked to the recitals; the remaining places were given to students. Possibly Frank Damrosch privately thought of these concerts as partly in memory of his own mother. The first annual concert included student performances of Beethoven's Trio, Opus 1, no. 3; Brahms's two vocal quartets, Opus 92, nos. 1 and 3; Beethoven's Piano Sonata in A-flat major, Opus 26; Brahms's Volkslieder; and Saint-Saëns's Variations for Two Pianos on a Theme by Beethoven.

At the first commencement exercises, on June 5, 1906, which included a concert, eight students—all female—of the 467 enrolled were sufficiently advanced to graduate after only one year's study.[42] The sexual demographics of the school are clearly apparent in this class. Females, in full-length dresses, button-up shoes, and mandatory hats, constituted the vast majority of the student body. The reasons for that were social. Although 20.4 percent of the female population worked for a living in the early 1900s, the only respectable careers for which women could hope were in teaching or nursing. Even within these limited options they faced an uphill struggle. The New York Musical Union, for example, would not admit females, although in 1904 it was compelled to revise its rule. The Musical Union enrolled 4,500 members in New York City, thirty-one of them women. Sexism in professional orchestras was based on the notion that women did not have the stamina to play woodwind or brass instruments, nor was it considered "feminine" to play other instruments except occasionally harp. "Prejudices against women players were rationalized to protect the limited job market against competition," one author has concluded.[43]

The announcement of the Loeb endowment had engendered great interest in the musical world, as seen in a two-part article published in *The Etude* during the spring of 1906. In every particular forecast (except in accuracy of names) its author was uncannily prescient:

> At last the endowed conservatory on a large scale has made its appearance upon our shores. Through the executive ability of Dr. Frank Damrosch and the public spirit of Mr. James Loeb, the United States now has a music school with an endowment fund of $500,000 equal to and, in the majority of cases, greater than most European music schools. An endowment of 2,000,000 marks for a music school would create an uproar in musical circles in Germany; but in America the great plethora of money has so minimized the real importance of the event that musicians seem to have taken little cognizance of the element which will certainly have a most powerful effect, not only upon the art development of America, but a direct effect, no matter how slight, upon the business of every individual teacher on this side of the Atlantic. Not many years can pass before the rivalry of other cities in America will lead to the foundation of music schools with substantial endowments. The munificence of Mr. James Loeb in founding the "Betsy Loeb Fund" and the resultant Institute for Musical Art of the City of New York will have an influence more far-reaching than it is safe to predict.[44]

2

The Institute of Musical Art:

A EUROPEAN
TRADITION

DAMROSCH BROUGHT not only his musical skills to the task of running the Institute of Musical Art but also a German authoritarianism. An old world paternalism was reenforced by his demeanor, the authority the IMA bylaws granted him, and the standing conferred by the name Damrosch. He never questioned the justness of his actions: He was certain he knew what was best for students.

The *Rules for the Guidance and Instruction of Students* (1907) outlined his regulations. Attendance was not credited for those who came late, and the door was closed for the first fifteen minutes of the lecture to prevent latecomers from entering. Absences resulted in lowered grades. Students were not permitted to wear hats in classes, lectures, or recitals, and recital programs requested that audiences also "kindly conform to this custom." All coats had to be checked in a coatroom upon entering the building. The rules also directed that "students are not permitted to linger in the upper or basement halls, but may wait between lessons on the first floor only, unless they desire to study in the library. . . . Students should rise when the Director or any member of the Faculty appears in the foyer or waiting rooms." The rule about quiet was stated loudly: *"Students are requested to refrain from loud conversation in all parts of the building."*[1] Joseph Fuchs (1900–1997), who entered the IMA in 1906, remembered the quiet rule being enforced. "Emma Brazier was the secretary. If you didn't step on the rubber mat, she knew. She had those ears, and out she came."[2] The rule was abandoned only in the 1940s, although students were then still expected to check their coats.

More significant, the 1926 handbook restricted musical activities outside the school: "No student may take part in any public or semi-public performance, either as a soloist or as a member of an ensemble, [chorus, or] opera orchestra, without the special permission in writing of the Director." He gently told students the hard truth regarding their musical potential; for example, he discouraged Blanche Yurka, who later had an acting career, from becoming a singer.[3] Damrosch also made recommendations about the use of free time and for outside reading. The fifteenth-year catalog (1919–20) spelled out Damrosch's power and paternalism: "The Director, as musical and educational expert, is charged with the proper assignment of each student to teachers suitable to his special needs. He keeps in touch with every stage of progress and guides the student in the pursuit of the studies required to fit him for professional work."[4]

Teachers' handbooks, which appeared in 1920, were just as precise in their guidance. "Teachers should have the sanction of the Director before inviting the students of the Institute to take part in private studio Recitals." When they did, "Students who perform at recitals and lectures are entitled to the kindly consideration of their fellow students. Audible unfavorable criticism is unkind and uncalled for, and should never be indulged in, in view of the fact that to many of the performers the occasion is a severe ordeal." Teachers were also to "insist upon the practice of good order and good manners at all points of contact with the students." Faculty had to obey a code of honor: "The[y] are in honor bound not to accept as personal private students any of the students of the Institute within a period of two years after such student [or the teacher] has left the school, excepting with the knowledge and consent of the Director."[5] How that was enforced is anyone's guess, but Damrosch's moral authority may have been sufficient.

Lectures were an important and required part of the course study: A certificate-holder had to have three years of these courses. Lecture courses, held in the Recital Hall, frequently included live performances as illustrations. The 1906–7 lecture courses included "Music as a Culture Study" by Thomas Tapper, four lectures by Dr. H. Holbrook Curtis on "The Physiology and Dynamics of Singing," and one by Walter Damrosch on Beethoven's Sixth Symphony. Waldo Selden Pratt (1857–

1939) gave the three-term "History of Music" lectures. He also compiled the American supplement to *Grove's Dictionary*. Pratt's teaching at the IMA from 1905 to 1920 was characterized by his modesty, reserve, and humility.[6] To call the IMA to inquire about concerts or applications in 1907, one dialed "4488 Styvesant." Concerts included those by the Kneisel Quartette, one by the Flonzaley Quartette, as well as a sonata recital by David and Clara Mannes. Recital attendance was encouraged, but at the first commencement address in 1906 Damrosch admonished students for not going to concerts.

From the beginning, the school co-opted the press by hiring major critics. Henry E. Krehbiel's (1854–1923) lecture series, which began in 1905 and continued yearly until his death, was called "How to Listen to Music," also the title of his most popular book, reprinted thirty times between 1896 and 1924. Krehbiel, a critic for the *New York Tribune*, extolled Wagner but deprecated contemporary composers such as Stravinsky, Prokofiev, and Schoenberg. He urged American composers to study the music of blacks and Indians, about which he wrote an influential study, and advocated opera in English.

Another important critic and longtime IMA faculty member was William J. Henderson (1855–1937), who yearly taught "The Development of Vocal Art." Henderson, a singer and pianist, was a music critic for the *New York Times* (1887–1902) and the *New York Sun* (1902–37). Like Krehbiel, he was a brilliant writer and shared many of his mentor's biases. Charles Ives disparagingly dubbed him "Rollo Henderson."[7] After Krehbiel's death Henderson replaced him as the "dean of American music critics." During the 1930s Henderson took up the cause of female musicians, pointing out that although the Philadelphia Orchestra had only two (the harpists), the IMA's orchestras were filled with women. IMA students were inevitably subjected to Krehbiel's and Henderson's biases and opinions; their courses were required.[8]

In 1915 Damrosch spoke of the students' initial reactions to taking required courses: "At first there were many requests by students to whom our discipline was unaccustomed to be excused from one or another subject, such as Ear-training, Theory, Languages or Lectures, but as each class progressed in these subjects and the students began to feel the power they gained and the aid these studies gave to real musical work, these requests grew less and less until to-day I could not if I would remove them from the curriculum without protest."[9]

The IMA always had an orchestra, at first a small group primarily of string players. Because the majority of students were women, and women almost never played woodwind or brass instruments, wind players were scarce. It was often necessary to engage them from outside the school for performances. The orchestra debuted at the first commencement, June 5, 1906, with a movement from Mozart's "Jupiter" Symphony, Damrosch conducting.

The second year, 1906–7, Damrosch organized a department close to his heart, the Department of Public School Music. It drew on the IMA's faculty and offered a music supervisor's course of two years; there were also courses for elementary school teachers. The particularly strong department had a separate catalog, and its students heard biweekly lectures by featured speakers such as Booker T. Washington, Horatio Parker, and Hollis Dann. Also in 1907 the Auxiliary Society was formed. In addition to raising money for scholarships and housing for students, the socially prominent women of the Auxiliary Society sponsored an annual series of reception recitals for distinguished musicians. Guests in the early years included Ignace Paderewski, Teresa Carreño, Xaver Scharwenka, Mischa Elman, Harold Bauer, Carl Flesch, Frances Alda, Percy Grainger, and Alfred Cortot. Not only did IMA students have a chance to play for the artists, but at the teas auxiliary members also instructed them in the all-important subject of manners and comportment. Talent in music provided students exposure to a society to which they were not necessarily born and for which they needed to be prepared.

Guests of the IMA during the 1920s included Elly Ney, Vincent D'Indy, Artur Schnabel, William Bachaus, Nadia Boulanger, Otto Klemperer, Alexander Glazunov, and Sergei Rachmaninoff. A student described the 1925 visit by Rachmaninoff:

> Long before the appointed hour, it seemed as though the whole audience had arrived. The opening of the doors was no ordinary event. There followed a surge for some vantage point or favorite seat with no little excitement. Suddenly an expectant hush spread over the Recital Hall—Dr. and Mrs. Damrosch appeared and with them the great guest of the afternoon, Mr. Sergei Rachmaninoff escorting Miss Rachmaninoff. After the reception and greeting of Mr. and Miss Rachmaninoff, Dr. Damrosch spoke in a delightfully informal manner.[10]

At the second commencement address, in 1907, board president Cornelius C. Cuyler claimed the IMA "to be the first Institute of its kind in this country."[11] Its uniqueness lay in the fact that it alone was free of commercial objectives. The school was also unique in its course requirements. Some of its competitors could hardly qualify as serious music schools. In the absence of a National Association of Schools of Music, any self-appointed school teaching only private lessons could confer a certificate or a diploma. Few great schools of music in the country could give both a sound technical training and a thorough musical education.[12]

At the end of the third year, 1908, a tradition began: a comic presentation given by students the day after their graduation. The first year's play was a send-up of the recently premiered, ultramodern *Pelléas et Mélisande* by "Bore-us Batterlinck" with notes by "Perseus Goetschius." The program requested the audience "to remain to the bitter end." The Class Day play in 1909, by a "Female Bluffragette Club," called the school the "Reformatory of Musical Art" and gave as its classes "Frightsinging," "Sticktation" (taught by "Dam-rush" in "Choral Clash"), with lectures by "Mr. Baldo-Seldom-Fat Craybill Tapper." The graduating students had earned the right to poke fun of the school.[13] As in other conservatories of the time, the percentage of enrolled students who completed the requirements was extremely small.

Two of the original teachers, each of whom taught for twenty years, stand out as having stamped the Institute with its particular character—

The Kneisel Quartette, 1913: Franz Kneisel, Willem Willeke, Louis Svecenski, and Hans Letz.
(Kneisel Hall Archives)

violinist Franz Kneisel (1865–1926) and composer Percy Goetschius (1853–1943).

Romanian-born Franz Kneisel had become a friend of Brahms by substituting for Joseph Hellmesberger, his teacher at the Vienna Conservatory, playing the Quintet, Opus 88, for the first time. Kneisel first came to the United States in 1885 at the age of nineteen, invited by Wilhelm Gericke to be concertmaster of the Boston Symphony Orchestra; he also conducted the orchestra during Artur Nikisch's absences. Major Henry L. Higginson, who founded the Boston Symphony Orchestra, started and supported the Kneisel Quartette in 1885. The qroup pioneered the presentation of chamber music in the United States and for many years was also chamber music's leading ensemble. Noted for precise ensemble-playing and evenness of tone, the group performed cycles of quartets of Haydn, Mozart, and Beethoven and also played new works by an impressive list of contemporary American composers, including Paine, Chadwick, and Loeffler.

At the end of its second year at the IMA, a crisis threatened to dissolve the quartette. In the spring of 1907 their 'cellist, Alwin Schroeder, decided to return to Germany, and the second violinist, Julius Theodorowicz, went back to Boston.[14] When it became known that the Kneisel Quartette would be disbanded, the Philadelphia Orchestra offered Franz Kneisel the position of conductor for $12,000 a year. The best interests of the school foremost in his mind, Damrosch appealed to vanity: "When [Kneisel] informed me of this offer I told him frankly that whereas he was easily first among the players of chamber music, he would be only one of several good conductors if he went to Philadelphia."[15] Damrosch scrambled for a solution; he asked Kneisel to delay a week before replying to Philadelphia and approached his friends Edwin T. Rice, Lillie (Lizzie) Bliss, and Mrs. Christian Herter (Susan Dakin) for money to send Kneisel to Europe to find two congenial and well-trained new members. He presented Kneisel with this carrot, but in his history of the IMA Damrosch neglected to mention the stick. At a special board meeting hurriedly held in May 1907, it was voted not to grant Kneisel's request to be released from his contract.[16] Bliss guaranteed $35,000 a year to the quartette, of which Kneisel received $9,000, the 'cellist and violist $6,000 each, and the second violinist $5,000. The rest went toward expenses.[17]

Kneisel, faced with little choice and genuinely more interested in quartet-playing than in conducting, traveled to Europe, where he engaged the violinist Julius Roentgen (1855–1932) of Amsterdam and Willem Willeke (1879–1950), principal 'cellist under Mahler of the Vienna opera orchestra. The situation was saved, and the quartet played together successfully until 1917. Happy in his new quartet, Kneisel had little difficulty in declining the position of New York Philharmonic conductor in 1911 after Mahler's death.

The Dutch Willeke married Kneisel's daughter, Victoria, in 1911 and in the 1920s took over conducting the IMA's orchestra from Damrosch. His 'cello students included Marie Roemaet Rosanoff, Phyllis Kraeuter, Harvey Shapiro, and many others who won major competitions and had successful careers. Damrosch later described Kneisel's teaching:

> When he came to the Institute as teacher, he tried to imbue his pupils with the same principles for beauty of tone, phrasing, style and inter-pretation which had governed his own playing ever since he emerged from the [Vienna] Conservatory. He would illustrate on his own violin how a phrase should be turned in order that it should have its right quality and style, and the pupils eagerly accepted the model not only for this particular phrase but for the principle which was applicable to all other parts of the composition.[18]

Kneisel also listened once a year to the students in the other departments and when they had advanced enough admitted them to his own class. "Needless to say that it was the ambition of every student to attain this goal."[19] (One wonders what their teachers thought of this ambition.) Joseph Fuchs, who started studying with Kneisel in 1911 and received an artists' diploma in 1920, remembered the pedagogue vividly. All the lessons were group lessons in which Kneisel—violin in hand, cigar in mouth, and no score in sight—might go to the piano and analyze the piece. He knew all the Beethoven quartets by memory, and so did Fuchs when he finished. Kneisel could take a four-measure rubato phrase and demonstrate how it could be played persuasively in five different ways.[20]

Kneisel's summer place in Blue Hill, Maine, where he gathered students to play chamber music, is now the location of an important summer music festival and has a hall built in the 1920s that was named after him. His students included Sascha Jacobsen; Elias Breeskin; Jacques Gordon, the concertmaster of the Chicago Symphony Orchestra; Michel Gusikoff, concertmaster of the St. Louis Symphony Orchestra; Helen Jeffrey; Amy Neil; A. William Kroll of the Kroll Quartet; Cyril Towgin; and Karl Kraeuter. In 1922 Kneisel remarked, "The Institute is as good, if not better, than the foreign schools. . . . The drawback in music in this country is to be attributed to the large part business plays. In European countries, where commercialism is not so much stressed, Art is held in greater esteem. Nevertheless, music in the United States has advanced tremendously in the past thirty years."[21] Some of the advance was due to Kneisel himself. "We have had many fine teachers at the Institute," Damrosch wrote in 1937, "but I do not think that there has been any one who has so thoroughly devoted himself, body and soul, to the task of training young artists as Franz Kneisel."[22]

Of Percy Goetschius, Damrosch wrote that he "had a remarkable gift for systematizing the work in harmony, counterpoint, and musical form in such a way that every student, even those with small gifts in this direction, was able to lay the foundations of good musicianship."[23] The American Goetschius had spent seventeen years teaching in Germany. In 1892 he headed the composition department at the New England Conservatory, where he taught until he came to the IMA in 1905 to head the theory department. In his first year there, which Goetschius told Damrosch was the happiest of his life, he had 450 students. Virtually every graduate of the IMA had at least one year of study with him. In his fifties Goetschius married Pauline Julie Gaiser, a graduate of the class of 1908. He lived to ninety but retired from teaching in 1926.

Students referred to him as "Daddy Goetschius" or "Papa Goetschius." "The cacophony of the ultra-modernist is not music to this man," one wrote. "But that he is a conservative is not true."[24] "An Imaginary Interview with Dr. Goetschius on the Subject of the 'Moderns'" from the student magazine attributes to "Daddy Goetschius" the likely not-so-fictional dictum "God's law—tonic and dominant." Included in the "interview" is a message for IMA students: "If they don't want to get their Grand'dad mad, let them not extol such 'moderns' in my presence, nor emulate them when out of my sight."[25] With such a composition teacher it is easy to understand why at least one student, the modernist Henry Cowell, who registered at the IMA as a pianist in 1916, became impatient with its stultifying academicism and returned to California after one term.[26]

Other students braved considerable hardship in order to study at the IMA. The catalog projected a cost of $8 to $10 a week to live in New York and warned, "The attempt to live and study under an extreme economy is not to be recommended. It is physically unsafe for any but the physically strong, and even when the health endures it is doubtful that the quality of the work will be high. . . . no young student, and most emphatically no young girl student, should come to New York without the safe provision for a full year's maintenance and tuition."[27] The need for such a warning encourages the suspicion that some female students suffered unpleasant fates.

When his family moved to New York in 1900, composer Wallingford Riegger (1885–1961) took up the 'cello to complete a family string quartet. He studied 'cello at the IMA with Alvin Schroeder and composition with Goetschius and graduated with the first class of eighteen that completed the three-year program. Leo Ornstein received his diploma in 1910, having studied piano with Bertha Tapper. Ornstein, who had previously attended the St. Petersburg Conservatory, credited Tapper as "the strongest single influence on [my] life in music."[28] Ornstein taught at the IMA for the year 1925–26. Considered a radical composer of "futuristic music," he founded the Ornstein School of Music in Philadelphia in 1940.

Also in the 1907 graduating class, along with Riegger and Damrosch's private dictation student, were violinist Henriette Bach and pianist Helen Elise Smith. In 1909 Bach was the first and only graduate of the Artists' Course. She sought out Morris and James Loeb, possibly visiting him in Munich, and convinced him to help launch her in London. (Eventually Loeb felt he had done enough to help her.)[29] During the 1915–16 year she attended Kneisel's postgraduate class, but by 1920 the standard-bearer for the Artists' Diploma was listed as "deceased." Possibly she succumbed to the virulent 1918 influenza epidemic. Smith, the first African American to graduate, married composer Nathaniel Dett.

Pianist Arthur Loesser (1894–1969) graduated as one of the thirteen men in the 1908 class of fifty-two students. Loesser's half-brother was the popular composer Frank Loesser. Arthur later became head of the piano department at the Cleveland Institute of Music and was author of the popular book *Men, Women and Pianos—A Social History.*[30] The next year, fifty-six students were graduated, including the conductor Alexander Smallens and Kneisel's daughter Victoria. By 1911 there were forty-five graduates, including singer Franklin Converse and violinist-composer Samuel Gardner (1891–1984), who taught violin at the IMA from 1924 to 1941. A bust of Gardner is found in Juilliard's Lila Acheson Wallace Library.

Damrosch reported to the board in 1910 that the number of male students, as a percentage of the total, was nearly 22 percent compared with approximately 18 percent during the previous four years.[31] The percentages of male students were later calculated to a fraction of a percentage point. Of the fifty-two graduates of the class of 1912, only eight were men. IMA catalogs acknowledged the discrimination toward women pervasive in professional employment—all the major orchestras in Europe and American were populated exclusively by men—by stressing the special opportunities for male woodwind players. According to a 1910 census study, women musicians accounted for 15,695 of the 54,858 musicians in the United States. Of the larger group of teachers of music (84,452), women constituted the vast majority—68,783.[32] In his many speeches and writings Damrosch never referred to the limited professional opportunities for the majority of the students at his school.

Having weathered for four years the vicissitudes of faculty, students, co-founder, and board, Damrosch now faced a crisis on an unexpected front. In the spring of 1909 Thomas Fortune Ryan invoked his year's notice on Lenox House, telling the board that he wanted to sell his own home on the opposite corner of Fifth Avenue and Twelfth Street. In 1908 J. P. Morgan had coerced "that Irish upstart" Ryan into selling control of the Equitable Life Assurance Society.[33] The lovely home the IMA had occupied would be put up for sale, torn down, and replaced by a new seventeen-story loft building. A search began immediately for other quarters. After looking citywide to rent similar property, the board discovered nothing suitable. The expensive solution was to build their own school. Damrosch outlined the requisites governing selection of a site that closely resembled Lenox House:

> 1st. A size of plot to be approximately 100' x 100'. 2nd. It must be corner property, in order to afford plenty of light and in order to avoid objections on the part of neighbors. 3rd. Accessibility to subway and cross-town lines. 4th. Expense not to exceed $150,000 and 5th. The environment must be such as not to interfere with the work of the school through noise or other objectionable features, and the approach must be of such a character that young women can pass from the [street]cars to the school without discomfort or annoyance.[34]

Paul Warburg selected an empty lot measuring 200' x 300' at the northeast corner of 122nd Street and Claremont Avenue that met most of Damrosch's criteria and whose cost was $77,500. The IRT subway ran up Broadway to 145th Street and stopped at 125th Street. The 125th Street cross-town trolley was also near, further meeting Damrosch's specifications. The streetcars were replaced by city buses during the 1930s.

Loeb considered buying the four adjoining lots for dormitories, but the land was not purchased. The Betty Loeb Memorial Fund loaned the IMA $150,000, a loan that was forgiven. The board wanted to keep construction costs under $285,000, and Loeb chose the building plans of architect Donn Barber over two other proposals. As for a contractor, Damrosch wrote to Loeb to recommend his childhood friend Otto Eidlitz (1860–1928), who had built the Academy of Music, the Metropolitan Opera, and estates for the Astors. Eidlitz also constructed such New York landmarks as the Stock Exchange, and, later, two IMA neighbors, Riverside Church (1930), and International House (1924).

The IMA property faced Grant's Tomb, Claremont Park, and the river beyond it. Across 122nd Street was the Union Theological Seminary and behind the building, across Broadway, were Charles F. McKim's buildings for Columbia University. The northwestern corner of 122nd Street and Broadway was an eyesore, however, containing as it did an "awful liquor saloon" (illustration, p. 81.)[35]

In some respects the move to 122nd Street in 1910 was a brave one. Until the advent of Robert Moses in the 1930s, the west side waterfront was a wasteland scarred by the railroad tracks, rotting timbers, mounds of untreated garbage, and tarpaper squatter settlements. By 1940 a metamorphosis had taken place, however. Riverside Park, designed by Frederick Law Olmsted in the 1870s, had tennis courts, lawns, promenades, playgrounds, and the nation's first controlled-access parkway in a major city—the West Side Highway.

Loeb suggested the new Recital Hall be named the Cuyler Memorial Recital Hall after the board's president, who had been killed in a car accident in France in July 1909. (Cuyler's widow, Mary T. Nicoll, married Thomas Fortune Ryan in 1917.) James Loeb, however, "could not agree to [Hetty's] wish to name the building the 'Loeb-Cuyler Building.'"[36] He surreptitiously contributed a student subsidy fund but demanded of Damrosch, "The beneficiaries are, I trust, not told that the money comes from me!"[37] Loeb's modesty regarding his financial generosity toward the IMA's building fund (whose cost was largely met by donations from him and his relatives) is reflected in the admonition: "By the way, in making the program for the Dedication Exercises at the new building I count on your leaving me out of sight as completely as though I were there *or even more so!*"[38]

The ceremony for laying the cornerstone at 120 Claremont Avenue was held March 26, 1910. Loeb's sister, Nina Warburg, represented him at the ceremony. She buried in the cornerstone a hermetically sealed box containing the deed of gift from James Loeb to the IMA; the Institute's catalogs for the years 1905 to 1909; the constitution, bylaws, and reports of the Auxiliary Society; copies of the students' and teachers' books of rules and regulations; a historical sketch of the organization and development of the Institute; a program of that day's ceremony; a copy of the silver medal awarded to students graduating with the highest honors (the seal with the Greek motto and Borglum's figure of Orpheus); silver coins minted in the year 1910; one Lincoln cent; copies of that day's daily newspapers; and textbooks and programs of recitals and commencement exercises.

Eidlitz completed the structure in an astonishing twenty-one weeks, and it cost $14,000 less that the lowest estimate on which the contract was based. Barber's building, designed for a maximum capacity of six

The 1910 Institute of Musical Art building.
(Photo from The Juilliard School Archives)

hundred students, faced west onto Claremont Avenue. Its exterior was limestone, and its style was freely adapted from the Adams architecture in Bath, England, treated in a French Renaissance manner.

The basement student entrance on 122nd Street—the main door on Claremont was for faculty and guests only—led to coatrooms and to large classrooms for theory, ear training, and languages. The circulating library and music store, open to the public, were also located on this floor, as were storerooms for musical instruments, the alumni clubroom, and a waiting room.

The Claremont Street entrance above led into a spacious central hall, on the right of which was the director's room and the secretary and bookkeeper's office; to the left was a large reception room that opened into the auditorium seating four hundred. An oval-shaped assembly room for students faced the main entrance and was down a short flight of steps, a location that made it equally accessible from the ground and first floors—a Damrosch request that echoed the students' area behind the stairs of the Fifth Avenue building. In stained glass the Orpheus figure and motto in Greek appeared.

The second and third floors contained the individual teaching rooms, practice rooms, classrooms, the laboratory, the large reading room and reference library with glassed-in bookshelves, and two organ practice rooms. On the top floor was a large lunchroom for students, a lunchroom for teachers, a kitchen and pantry, the teachers' retiring room, and a lecture room. The roof contained the janitor's quarters and a large, flat area that students could use as a promenade.[39]

At the dedication of the new building at 3 P.M. on Saturday, November 5, 1910, Loeb's brother-in-law Isaac N. Seligman presided.[40] The student orchestra played Beethoven's overture "Consecration of the House," Arthur Loesser played Beethoven's Sonata, Opus 101, and Samuel Gardner performed the Tchaikowsky Violin Concerto with the orchestra. Then the president of the borough of Manhattan, George McAneny, representing the mayor, spoke: "The institution was primarily endowed by my very good friend, James Loeb; and among all the men I have known in public or private life I have known no gentler spirit, no finer type of man, than this." The Rev. Francis Brown, president of the nearby Union Theological Seminary, spoke of neighborliness. Next came Edmund B. Wilson of Columbia University, who referred to Morningside Heights as the "Acropolis of our city."[41]

Walter Spalding from Harvard University then addressed the crowd: "I cannot refrain from testifying publicly that Harvard also has seldom if ever had more intelligently generous alumni than Morris Loeb of the class of '83 and James Loeb of the class of '88." He also praised Betty Loeb. Because Harvard did not accept female students, it is hard to view his proposed affiliation as serious:

> There must automatically in the due course of things exist a real affiliation between Harvard University and this institution. Harvard . . . has been devoted to the theoretical side of music in its historical, biographical and literary aspects; and from time to time there will be graduates of Harvard who will supplement their theoretical work by technical studies made here in New York; and also, vice versa, your boys and *girls* who beginning here with the pianoforte or violin or the voice, wishing to gain a broader education, *to be something more than musicians*, will we hope possibly study at Harvard University. So we feel that we are working shoulder to shoulder in this common cause for the advancement of a real musical life in our country.[42]

Max Friedländer, professor of music at Berlin University and an admirer of Leopold Damrosch, spoke next. "I need not tell you that the wonderful progress that has been made during the last few decades in the conservatories of America has aroused the greatest interest, sympathy and some feeling not far from envy among our liberal and progressive minds in Germany, since some of our best and most esteemed artists have been active and are active here as teachers, as conductors, as directors."[43] He then lost many in his audience by launching into German.

Seligman read a cable from Hamburg, Germany, that garnered applause: "I send congratulations and greetings to the trustees, teachers and students. Let us continue together to strive for the beautiful and shun no sacrifice in our endeavor to attain it. James Loeb."[44] It was an echo of the motto in Greek that Loeb had chosen.

Loeb began a third major philanthropic project in 1910; in addition to funding Harvard's music building, he founded the Loeb Classical Library, the series of translations of ancient Greek and Latin authors that still continues and numbers almost five hundred volumes.[45] His celebrated Loeb Classical Library earned him an honorary degree from Cambridge University.[46]

Concerning the possibility of an opera and dramatic school associated with Otto Kahn's Metropolitan Opera, Loeb wrote, "Only be sure to maintain the *absolute autonomy* of the Institute. We have enough to take care of and unenlightened interference on the part of the Metropolitan director [Giulio Gatti-Casazza] can hurt our work immeasurably. 'From little acorns mighty oaks do grow.' But our oak must beware of the 'clinging ivy'!"[47] Loeb was interested in one potential relationship with the Met, however: "To what extent have our students the entrée to rehearsals at the Met, the Manhattan and the more prominent concerts?"[48] To pursue that goal, IMA trustees approached Gatti-Casazza, who directed the Met extremely successfully from 1908 until 1935, to suggest that the opera might cooperate with the IMA in developing singer-students. In 1911 the *New York Tribune* gave Gatti-Casazza's response.

> Signor Gatti-Casazza placed himself on record as not favorable to the establishment of a conservatory in connection with the opera house; but he has taken a step which shows that he favors the development of singers at home rather than abroad. He and Mr. [Alfred] Hertz have joined the Board of Directors of the Institute of Musical Art in an advisory capacity, and an agreement has been entered into between the opera house and the Institute whereby pupils of the opera class of the latter institution are to have the privilege of attending dress rehearsals at the former and of beginning their careers there when found capable. With so great an operatic artist as Madame [Milka] Ternina and so capable and experienced a dramatic teacher as M. [Alfred] Giraudet in charge of the opera class at the Institute, it is expected that there will soon be a number of pupils ready for the invaluable practical experience which this working arrangement between the two establishments means.[49]

This promising situation for IMA singers nevertheless resulted in disappointment, Damrosch wrote obliquely, "because of the conditions under which opera at the Metropolitan had to be conducted."[50] Some IMA students were accepted for small parts, but they were cast so infrequently that they did not benefit from their association with the opera. The episode was the beginning of an intermittent and frustrating relationship between the school and the Met.

May 1909 cables between Damrosch and Loeb show their excitement when Damrosch contracted the soprano Milka Ternina (1863–1941). Ternina had made a successful debut at the Met as Elizabeth in *Tannhäuser* in January 1900. Her short-lived career continued with portrayals of Isolde and Brünnhilde, which won such accolades from the *Times* as "glorious" and "an overwhelming plentitude of warm, mellow tone."[51] She was still a young woman when a voice condition forced her into retirement after the 1903–4 season, during which she sang Kundry. Acquiring her, Damrosch felt "as though the Institute were [now] equipped to do its work equal—if not superior—to the best schools of Europe."[52] As the 1909–10 IMA catalog put it, "The engagement of Frl. Milka Ternina as teacher of Singing at this Institute may be looked upon as an epoch-making event."[53]

The expense of the high salaries of both Milka Ternina (Loeb had wondered whether they could afford her a second year) and Alfred Giraudet, plus scheduling difficulties (and possibly some prima donna–like behavior) led the board not to renew Ternina's contract the next year. Giraudet was reengaged to teach, but he died suddenly in October 1911 before school started (IMA classes always began during the second week in October). Meanwhile, Ternina settled in Munich, where Loeb was living, but did not inform him of her whereabouts, and so he did "not feel called upon to visit her."[54] She subsequently had an important career as a teacher in Zagreb, where one pupil was Zinka Milanov.

At the November 1909 board meeting, a letter was read from Morris Loeb (who had declined to serve on the board), in which he registered what can be considered a complaint from the Loeb family about the fulfillment of their single request from the school. The Betty Loeb anniversary concert "[should] be devoted to the adequate performance of music of artistic, educational or historic interest, rather than to the display of individual proficiency of certain students, as is customary at so-called students' concerts."[55] Two months later the Betty Loeb concert was played in Mendelssohn Hall. The Kneisel Quartette played Schumann's Quartet in F major, Opus 41, no. 2; three songs were sung by Matja von Neissen-Stone; and Sigismond Stojowski played Schumann's Fantasie, Opus 17 (it was the centennial of Schumann's birth). During the second half came Brahms songs and the Piano Quartet in

A major, Opus 26. The program was clearly meant to smooth the Loeb family feathers.

Loeb's advice concerning the Institute varied as erratically as his moods. In one letter he suggested that the IMA limit itself to no more than 650 students to give it "cachet." In another, he wanted the Institute to house three hundred for some years to come. "More than ever I am persuaded that we must keep the number of students small. Rather make it a privilege to be admitted than glory in the large number of students or yearly graduates."[56] In this respect Loeb was more elitist than Damrosch, whose missionary approach was to reach as many as possible.

Morris Loeb died at the age of forty-nine in October 1912. A memorial fund of $20,000 was established at the IMA, the interest on which would provide an annual prize of $1,000 to a graduating student for "a year of European life and experience." In this manner students would mirror Morris Loeb's life. After graduating Phi Beta Kappa from Harvard, he had gone to Berlin, where he earned a doctorate in chemistry. The death of his brother sent James Loeb into another deep depression. In November of 1914 Paul Warburg resigned from the IMA's board to become the first head of the Federal Reserve in Washington. Devoted to his wife Nina, who was in turn devoted to her brother James, Warburg continued to work on the IMA's behalf.

The 1916–17 catalog listed the requirements for admission: "evidence of musical ability, of general intelligence and of serious purpose. The degree of an applicant's advancement does not affect his admission, but his classification as to grade."[57] There was no age restriction. Only in 1923 did the IMA require that students have a high school diploma and be at least eighteen. Candidates for admission underwent three tests: vocal or instrumental talent (a test given by the director himself), theoretical work, and musical hearing.

To graduate with a certificate, students had to pass examinations in their major instrument, as well as secondary piano, sight singing, sight reading on their instrument, ear training and dictation, two languages, and their coursework. For secondary piano, they had to demonstrate the fluent and musical playing of a Bach prelude and fugue and a piece in the style of the Mendelssohn Songs without Words, the Schumann Kinderszenen, or the easier Beethoven sonata movements. In sight singing, each candidate read difficult melodies at first sight and passed an examination in the singing of diatonic and chromatic intervals. A test of the aural recognition of intervals was demonstrated orally and in writing. She or he had to write (at dictation) moderately difficult harmonic exercises in major and minor modes, including dominant seventh chords and their inversions and also modulation to any key, in addition to writing (also at dictation) a moderately difficult melody and harmonizing it. Each certificate-holder had passed examinations representing both three years' study of Italian and two years' of German or French and had attended and passed satisfactorily examinations in three of the lecture courses.

Those attempting an artists' diploma, something like the graduate degree Henriette Bach had earned, had to pass more difficult requirements. They presented a recital, referred to as a "trial," heard and evaluated by a jury of prominent musicians invited from outside the school. (Although the word *trial* has been abandoned, the term *jury* has replaced it at most schools.)

At the 1910 commencement exercises, Damrosch addressed the graduating class: "At first, the ear-training and the theory swamped you. As I watched the other evening when eighty-five of you were taking the third year dictation examination, in which a four-part chorale was played for you and you wrote it from three hearings, I said to myself, 'Think of those children three years ago how they would have sat with open mouths!' But now only fifteen out of the eighty-five failed to receive 75 percent." In awarding the diplomas, Damrosch said, "The glittering promise of a successful virtuoso life leads many to think that the teacher's profession is but a small and contracted one, but those who know THOSE WHO KNOW realize that the highest, the noblest, the most beautiful profession of all in the world is that of teaching, and only in so far as the performing artist is a teacher does he fulfill his best and noblest mission."[58]

Commencement exercises were held in June 1911 at the hall of the Ethical Culture Society. Damrosch gave the customary commencement address:

> You are approached by people who want to lead you into paths of glory. They promise you all kinds of things if you obey, if you will allow them to lead you into a splendid career as public performers. They will promise you praise and money if only you will do as they tell you—that is, consent to the lower standards of a public to which they introduce you. The moment you do that, you have already cut the ground from under your feet. You cannot afford to compromise. Stick to your ideals, stick to your standards that you have so carefully been taught and which you have learned with such care, and you will find that, while the path may be steeper, more difficult, it will ultimately lead you higher. There must be no compromise.[59]

At the end of the ceremony, Damrosch presented two surprised graduates, pianists Arthur Loesser and Alice Shaw, a student of Helena

Augustin and Stojowski, with the medal of the IMA seal and motto given to students who receive an artists' diploma with highest honors, meaning that the student's "rating in every subject of the course [was] above ninety-five per cent." The unusually large number of recipients of artists' diplomas in 1911 included—in addition to Shaw and Loesser—Elenore Altman, Louis Bostelmann, Carl Schluer, and Abraham Shyman. Altman was born in Romania, came to America, and then studied at the Vienna Conservatory. At the IMA she studied with Stojowski and began teaching there in 1913.

The 1911 Class Day Show, *Folies Brézière*, included a Prismatic Fatasm and Fugue, supposedly by Bach, with movements such as Affatuoso Ponderoso and Hustleissimo Industrioso. Bach's Chromatic Fantasy and Fugue must have been promoted by the piano faculty; it appears frequently on student concert programs. The chorus of the class song read:

> Say good-bye, say farewell,
> Three or more years we've worked like—well
> Very much harder than we can tell.
> Say good-bye, toll the bell,
> Alma Mater, fare thee well.[60]

Damrosch's speech at commencement in June 1914 reminded them that "you have not been allowed to compete for prizes at the expense of steady, uniform progress. You have all been treated alike with absolute fairness, regardless whether you were rich or poor, black, yellow or white." Among the fifty-three 1914 graduates were Dorothy Crowthers, violinists Sascha Jacobsen and Elias Breeskin, and flutist William Kincaid. Only one student, Franklin Converse, gained the artists' diploma.[61]

In 1914 Damrosch conducted the orchestra and chorus for a production of *A Midsummer Night's Dream* with Mendelssohn's incidental music. The huge cast included Howard Hanson as Theseus, Arthur Loesser as Quince, Franklin Converse as Bottom, and Samuel Barlow as Puck.[62] The senior orchestra accompanying the production numbered seventy and included the full complement of orchestral instruments. (The junior orchestra consisted of about forty from ages ten to fifteen from the preparatory and intermediate classes.) The Class Day student play poked fun of the play and the experience of producing it.

Howard Hanson (1896–1981) received his diploma in 1915. He studied piano with Friskin and composition with Goetschius. He then went to Northwestern University and in 1921 was an early winner of the Rome Prize. He was twenty-eight in 1924 when George Eastman asked him to become director of the Eastman School of Music, a post Hanson held for forty years.

An alumni association recital helped to gather support for a concert series. In February 1914 the association managed to get the New York Symphony Society Orchestra to play with them in Aeolian Hall. The students played the Brahms and Tchaikowsky violin concertos with two performers each (one doing the first movement, the other the last two). These concerts were not the director's idea; the alumni themselves pushed for a more public venue for their talents to be showcased.

The second "Public Recital" by graduates and students of the IMA, in February 1915, was also given in Aeolian Hall. The orchestra was now from the IMA, however, rather than the New York Symphony Society. Damrosch had been converted. The concert began the tradition of presenting the Institute Symphony Orchestra, the Institute Chorus, and IMA soloists in a yearly concert in addition to their commencement performances. The Aeolian Hall program was ambitious: Raff's March from the "Lenore" Symphony, Franck's Symphonic Variations for Piano and Orchestra (with Maude Hurst), Bach's Chaconne for violin (Elias Breeskin), Liszt's Hungarian Rhapsody no. 1, Saint-Saëns's Concerto in c minor for piano (Arthur Loesser), Lalo's *Symphonie espagnole* for violin and orchestra (Helen Jeffrey and Sascha Jacobsen shared the solos), and Wagner's Entrance of the Gods into Valhalla from *Das Rheingold*.

Manfred Malkin taught piano until 1913–14; later he and his brothers established their own conservatories. Daniel Gregory Mason taught at the IMA until the 1911–12 year. That year the Kneisel Quartette underwent another personnel change when second violinist Julius Roentgen left because of personality differences. He was later appointed director of the Amsterdam Conservatory, which his father had founded. Roentgen was replaced by Hans Letz (1876–1969), for three years concertmaster of the Chicago Symphony Orchestra and the teacher of Dorothy DeLay. James Friskin (1876–1967), who joined the piano faculty in 1914, played three recitals, one devoted to the Goldberg Variations. Friskin, a Scot, had been recommended to Damrosch by Sir Charles Stanford, was educated at the Royal College of Music and had studied piano with Edward Dannreuther and composition with Stanford. In 1944 Friskin married the composer and violist Rebecca Clarke. He taught at the IMA for more than four decades.

Pianist and organist Gaston Dethier (1875–1958) and his violinist brother Edouard (1886–1962) played a recital together in April 1912. They were from Belgium, where their father had taught piano and composition in the Liège Conservatory. All seven children, of whom Gaston was the eldest, were musical. Gaston came to the United States first, and

Damrosch asked him in 1905 to head the organ department. When Carl Friedberg left the Institute during World War I, Gaston also taught piano. Dethier, who for a while also played violin, spent every spare half-hour practicing the piano. He was fascinated by the relationship of technique to art, which "is not as the frame to a picture, the stage setting to acting, or the cover to a book, a mere accessory. It is as the picture, the acting, the book itself, in so far as it gives expression, vitalizes, I might say incarnates, the conception of the artist."[63]

Edouard Dethier first studied violin with Gaston, but because of their age difference and the fact that Gaston left for America, Edouard never really knew his brother until emigrating in 1905. He began teaching at the IMA in 1907 at the age of twenty-one. Edouard Dethier had entered the Conservatory of Liège at age eight and later attended the Brussels Conservatory and also taught there. He gained valuable experience as concertmaster of the opera orchestra in Brussels. During his three years in Brussels he lived with Paul Kochanski, a Polish violinist and future colleague who would later describe Dethier as an idealist. Each competitively tried to practice more hours than the other. One of Dethier's many students was Robert Mann.[64]

Not only did the IMA faculty quartet play compositions by living composers such as Ravel and Loeffler, but the piano faculty also adhered to the tradition of composing. Friskin played two recitals in the 1915–16 season and included his own Sonata in a minor. Rudolph Ganz (1877–1972), a composer and conductor as well as a pianist, also gave a piano recital and played three short works of his own. Ganz was the conductor of the St. Louis Symphony Orchestra from 1921 to 1927, and from 1929 to 1954 he served as director of the Chicago Musical College. He continued to teach until his death at age ninety-five.

When Ganz left the faculty in 1916 to spend more time concertizing in Europe, Damrosch hired Carl Friedberg (1872–1955) as a replacement. He wrote of Friedberg: "He has proved to be one of the most remarkable teachers. He is very exacting in developing a full control of the technique of the instrument, but his chief influence is in the direction of stimulating ideal conceptions of every work his pupils undertake. In other words, he develops not only a perfection of technical proficiency, but the correct conception of style of each composer."[65] Friedberg's contract stipulated $6,000 for twenty hours a week for thirty weeks, with a restriction on the number of concert engagements he could accept (no more than thirty).[66] The normal pay for teachers was $10 an hour. In 1920 the board voted the esteemed Percy Goetschius an increase to $5,000 a year for twenty-four hours of teaching a week. Damrosch had a time clock to check on teachers' hours.

The catalog of the 1917–18 year contained a last-minute insert announcing a harp department taught by Carlos Salzedo, who gave a harp recital in November that included two works by Marcel Grandjany. Salzedo (1885–1961) had studied at the Paris Conservatory, where his father taught voice. He was first harp of the Metropolitan Opera (1909–13) and toured with flutist Georges Barrère and 'cellist Paul Kefer. In 1921 he was co-founder, with Edgard Varèse, of the International Composers Guild, an organization, considered radical, that presented many contemporary works to New York. Salzedo wrote what have become classic texts on harp technique.

American pianist Richard Buhlig (1880–1952) joined the faculty in 1918 and gave six recitals: one of Schubert-Brahms, one Schumann-Chopin, plus three of Beethoven sonatas, the Rondo in G major, Opus 51, no. 2, and the Thirty-two Variations in c minor. In a competitive gesture Friskin gave two all-Beethoven concerts, one with Opus 109, 110, and 111 (which did not duplicate Buhlig's programming). The newly formed Elshuco Trio (Richard Epstein, piano, Samuel Gardner, violin, and Willem Willeke, 'cello) presented two recitals. The group's name was an abbreviated form of that of their patroness, Elizabeth Sprague Coolidge, with her husband's middle name, Shurtleff. Edouard and Gaston Dethier gave a violin and piano recital that consisted of show pieces (except for the Brahms, Opus 108).

'Cellist Marie Roemaet Rosanoff won both the Morris Loeb Prize and the silver medal with highest honors in 1916, the year the class play was called "Suite Sixteen." She studied subsequently with Casals and was the only woman to appear in the Kneisel Quartette; later she played with the Musical Art Quartet. She had displayed facility in the upper registers when, playing quartets with Vieux, Heifetz, and Joseph Press, she read on the 'cello the second violin part of the Debussy quartet and the viola part of the Ravel.

Katherine Swift's father, Samuel, had been a music critic for the *New York World* and died when she was a teenager. She helped support her mother and brother by giving piano lessons in people's homes. Swift attended the IMA beginning in 1905 as a student of Bertha Tapper, Carl Friedberg, Anna Fyffe, and Percy Goetschius, and she received diplomas in piano (1916) and piano teaching (1917). She played in a trio with Marie Rosanoff. In 1918, when she was twenty-one, the beautiful and talented Swift married Loeb's namesake, nephew, and later board member James Paul Warburg. Richard Rodgers gave Swift a job as rehearsal pianist for *A Connecticut Yankee*. She and her husband composed songs under the names Kay Swift and Paul James; their hit was the 1929 torch song "Can't We Be Friends?" The two wrote the music and lyrics for

Fine and Dandy and, after playing for George Balanchine's rehearsals, Swift wrote *Alma Mater* for his 1934 season. That same year she and Warburg divorced, having had three daughters. At a musical evening at Walter Damrosch's Swift met George Gershwin. Their relationship was both musical and personal; Gershwin was in love with her.[67]

Competition with the IMA in New York City was beginning to get serious. In the fall of 1916, Damrosch's sister Clara and her husband David Mannes opened the David Mannes School. Their original budget, however, unlike the Loeb gift of half a million dollars, was only $8,000. The next year philanthropist Janet D. Schenck founded and directed the Neighborhood Music School on East 104th Street. Schenck hired her own piano teacher, the eminent Harold Bauer. Despite lucrative financial offers elsewhere, Bauer remained loyal to Schenck and to the Manhattan School of Music (its second name), which Schenck headed until 1956.

Because many candidates for admission at the IMA needed fundamental training in either technique or musicianship, during the fall of 1916 Damrosch instituted preparatory centers at YMCAs or YWCAs in four locations around New York. Eight students enrolled for the first year, but the next year the number jumped to forty-five and by 1919 to nearly a hundred. These students received two lessons a week in their principal subjects (piano or violin only) and instruction in the rudiments of notation and sight singing. During the first five years Anna Fyffe was director of instruction. Constance Edson Seeger, a Kneisel student from 1906 to 1911 and a friend of the Damrosches, taught violin. Her husband, musicologist Charles Seeger, took charge of the piano instruction.[68] Applicants for the IMA who had this training "stood head and shoulders above the majority of candidates for admission from other sources of preparation," Damrosch declared.[69]

Seeger joined Damrosch in teaching pedagogy, and George Wedge was hired on the theory and composition faculty. In 1921 and 1922 Charles and Constance Seeger were members of the accompaniment faculty and violin faculty, respectively, and both also taught in the preparatory centers. By the next year Seeger was giving the music history lectures as well as lectures in mythology and epic and romantic poetry. The IMA staff had also grown to include a secretary, a social secretary, a recording secretary, and two librarians. In 1922 Damrosch expressed a desire to institute noon-hour concerts, foreshadowing the Wednesday one o'clock concerts.

In August 1914 when World War I broke out Damrosch was in Europe. He wrote Loeb of the "electric tension with which all Europe is charged today." Referring to the number of immigrants from Europe to the United States, Damrosch observed, "Indeed if I had made no engagements by October 1st, I could have equipped a whole conservatory with a full teaching staff of well-known European teachers."[70] In the fall of 1914 the Kneisel Quartette's second violinist, Hans Letz, was detained in Germany for military duty. Letz was replaced for one concert by former student Samuel Gardner. Letz soon returned, and later in the same season they twice played the sextet version of *Verklärte Nacht* by forty-year-old Arnold Schoenberg.[71]

During the war years in Europe, commencement exercises took on a patriotic tinge. The exercises in 1916 were preceded by pieces played by the Recruit Military Band of Fort Jay, directed by graduates of the new Military Bandmasters' Department of the IMA. Due to the financial strain of the war Damrosch had to cut faculty salaries.

The war placed German-born musicians in difficult positions. The Damrosches were thoroughly assimilated Americans who sided with the United States. Nevertheless, during the summer of 1917 Walter Damrosch experienced the anti-German hysteria that swept the country. Complaints were registered impugning Frank Damrosch's loyalty: He had once described the "Star Spangled Banner" as "a bad poem squeezed into a drinking song."[72] The Liberty Loan Committee criticized the standard repertoire as decadent products of German "Kultur." "To the editor of *The Chronicle* [who had asked for views on a ban of German music], Frank replied, 'I refuse to believe that the American people are so unintelligent as to be unable to distinguish between the German militaristic government and Beethoven's music. . . . Nor will [Germany] be defeated by the persecution of harmless German artists.'"[73]

Damrosch and Met conductor Artur Bodanzky, however, were in the minority of those writing to the *Chronicle:* Others, including John Philip Sousa and the president of the musicians' union, endorsed just such a ban. Finally, in October 1918, Damrosch was called up to serve and was eager to begin his commission as a major. The Armistice a month later meant that the IMA director, almost sixty, would not have to fight.

President Wilson had promoted a patriotic mindset known as "100 percent Americanism." The consequences of the anti-German hysteria resulted in the arrest without formal charges in 1918 of Carl Muck, the Boston Symphony Orchestra conductor and a naturalized Swiss citizen. Muck was imprisoned for seventeen months and deported in August 1919. Twenty-nine German-born members of the BSO were also interned.[74]

This hysteria also affected the Kneisel Quartette. Although not all four were German, the quartet were treated like outcasts. Kneisel was forced off the stage "because he was a colonel in the army of Austria with which the U.S. was at war. He was therefore being held, but without restraint, by the U.S. government, though not permitted to play for personal gain."[75] The quartette, destroyed by bigotry, played only a few more concerts, with Fritz Kreisler substituting for Kneisel. The quartette was replaced in 1917 on the concert stage by the Flonzaley Quartet, composed of two Italians, a Swiss, and a Belgian. The Kneisel spokesman, violist Louis Svecenski, declared, "We are leaving chamber music in the hands of our fellow artists, and it doesn't matter what countries they come from, so long as they are loyal to King Ludwig van Beethoven."[76]

As the Great War progressed, Carl Friedberg, who had joined the faculty in 1916, felt that he was putting his friend Damrosch in the difficult position of having a German on the faculty. He resigned and left for Germany, suggesting Ernest Hutcheson, an Australian, replace him in 1917. Hutcheson gave his first recital at the Institute in February 1918, and Friedberg returned to teach in 1923.

Although living arrangements for students were never satisfactorily solved during the lifetime of the IMA, a partial solution was presented by graduate Florence McMillan. In the spring of 1919 she approached Damrosch with a plan to establish a club near the IMA to provide for the housing and care of its female students and those at other schools on Morningside Heights. McMillan took an option on 607 West 115th Street, between Broadway and Riverside Drive, which she proposed to remodel in order to house students "under good hygienic conditions and at a moderate expense."[77] Asked to suggest a name for the club, Damrosch proposed "Parnassus Club." When the club added another large apartment house on the same street, it was able in the 1930s to house some two hundred students, of whom one-third were IMA women. Sidney Homer, a trustee of the Parnassus Club, suggested in 1921 that the Institute purchase the club's first preferred stock, and Paul Warburg bought some for $11,000.

The school's reputation was growing, and Damrosch was able to boast that students came from forty states and five foreign countries. The 1919 class show was given at the "Institute of Vaudeville Art, the only school in America which offers prescribed courses in polite and artistic Vaudeville (at a nominal tuition fee) to serious students of Glittering Talent."[78] The show parodied the names and programs of the Kneisel Quartette and the Letz Quartet (the "Let's-String-em Quartette").

In May 1919 a second concert of composition class students included music by Theodore Chanler (1902–61), who played his Polyphonic Prelude for Pianoforte (the assignment) and the songs "Reeds of Innocence," "The Shepherd," "The Wild Flower's Song," and "Song."

Chanler studied composition at the IMA from 1914 to 1920 with Percy Goetschius and piano with Ethel Leginska and Richard Buhlig. He did not receive a diploma and later studied with Bloch at the Cleveland Institute and with Boulanger in Paris.

Faculty and students played their own and each others' works on recitals at the school. Albert and Edna Stoessel, for example, gave a violin and piano recital in 1919 in which they played his sonata as well as a prelude by Samuel Gardner. The next year Albert Stoessel was added to the violin faculty. Joseph Fuchs had a piece played in the composition class concert. He was the only candidate for artists' diploma that year, at which the jurors were Leopold Auer and Efrem Zimbalist. The trial included chamber music performance as well as solo violin music by Brahms, Bach, and Wieniawski. Fuchs framed the grading sheet on which Zimbalist and Auer gave him the highest marks. At commencement the orchestra performed Samuel Gardner's symphonic poem "New Russia."

The IMA mounted a second full-scale production on April 16 and 17, 1920: Karl Maria von Weber's operetta *Abu Hassan*. The first performance in English (translated by Frank and Hetty Damrosch), it was directed by Albert Reiss, had a double cast, and borrowed costumes and properties from the Met. The graduating class play, *Have One on Me*, was an "opera buffet" and a takeoff on the Baghdad opera. The sultan was named Salteen, and the conductor was listed as Mr. Hank Dammerosch.

Just before the 1917 school year began, Loeb's brother-in-law and IMA board member Isaac N. Seligman was thrown from his horse and died. The story received front-page coverage. Felix Adler gave the eulogy at the funeral and George McAneny was one of the pallbearers. An IMA prize was named after Seligman, this one in composition. Seligman's daughter Margaret, a piano student of Dethier, had been a 1916 graduate. The death, combined with the pressures of divided loyalties during the war, precipitated James Loeb's most extended nervous breakdown.

At the December 1920 meeting the board sent affectionate greetings to Loeb, still in Germany, congratulating him on the splendid results that his beneficence had produced. Loeb was beginning to recover from his longest bout with depression. This recovery was brought about by the September death of Jacob Schiff, who had prevented him from marrying. At fifty-four, Loeb was now free to marry the nurse who had taken care of him during his many illnesses, Antonie Hambuechen.[79] Loeb and Damrosch's correspondence revived after a hiatus that had lasted from October 1916 to January 1923. After Loeb recovered, he asked Damrosch to organize a concert to benefit the underfed mothers and children of Munich, but Damrosch replied (on Betty Loeb's birth-day) that the idea was not financially feasible.[80]

The Baton, the monthly magazine begun in January 1922 and edited by artists' diploma graduate Dorothy Crowthers, was financed for ten years by the board and was available to students for 10 cents an issue year (raised to 15 cents the next year). Crowthers joined the faculty in 1923 to teach ear training and theory. *The Baton* published cover articles on famous musicians, including Yehudi Menuhin, who as a young student of the IMA had studied ear training with Crowthers, harmony with Wallingford Riegger, and violin with Louis Persinger. The liveliest and funniest column, Margaret Hamilton's "Accidentals," was a page of paragraph-long anecdotes. *The Baton* also carried two regular series by students Joseph Machlis (1906–98) and Richard Rodgers (1902–79). Rodgers's column was humorously dubbed "Diary of a Prodigy."

Two girlfriends had persuaded Rodgers to drop out of Columbia University and attend the IMA. "My idea of heaven was a place where I would be surrounded by nothing but music," he wrote:

> What really excited me and made me certain that I had chosen the right educational path were the lectures and the courses I took in music theory, harmony and ear-training. . . . I was fortunate to be a member of a class in harmony taught by Percy Goetschius, who was to harmony what Gray was to anatomy. . . . One of my favorites was Henry Krehbiel. . . . Whenever he was scheduled to talk, I would leave home a half-hour earlier in order to make sure of getting a front-row seat. . . . As he spoke he would become so emotional that tears rolled down his long red beard. . . . From teachers and classmates alike I can recall nothing but an attitude of mutual help and respect, and I'm sure that's why, for the first time in my life, I was actually learning something in school. . . . [The] whole experience there was more like an adventure than going to a school. My feeling of excitement and anticipation began in the morning when I got on the subway at Eighty-sixth and Broadway for the ride up to 116th Street. By the time I reached Claremont Avenue . . . I could scarcely keep from running.[81]

With the teenaged Richard Rodgers directing, the class show—still given the day after commencement—gained national attention. The 1921 show, *Say It With Jazz*, may have influenced Georges Barrère's flute student Meredith Willson to write musicals. In 1922 *Jazz à la Carte* appeared, whose music was written jointly with Gerald Warburg. It was reviewed in the *New York Times* and the *Musical Courier*, as well mentioned in newspapers in Pennsylvania, Ohio, South Carolina, Georgia, and California.[82] In 1923 Rodgers directed *A Danish Yankee in King Tut's Court*. For the two years after Rodgers left the IMA, 1924 and 1925, no class shows were produced, possibly for fear of falling short of the Rodgers productions. Instead, graduating students attended a dinner and a show together.

Rodgers later wrote of the IMA director: "I never got to know him well, but Frank Damrosch, the founder and director of the Institute, was always sympathetic about my ambitions, and had a surprising knowledge and appreciation of the commercial musical theatre. Dr. Damrosch *was* the Institute; he set the tone, created the atmosphere and established the tradition. One of these was the ritual of the final exams; they always took place in the evening, with the entire faculty attending in formal dinner jacket and black tie."[83]

Prospects for most graduating students being able to earn their livelihoods from music were always dim. Damrosch acknowledged that by remarking to the Alumni Association, "Unlike graduates from academic colleges who develop into successful bankers, merchants, lawyers, etc., the graduates from a school of music rarely earn enough to more than pay for their bread and butter, and a little jam at high feasts. For that reason we have not been able to receive any financial support from this source."[84] Notwithstanding the uncertain financial future, in December 1925, 361 of the IMA's 1,035 students were men—"34 + $\%_{10}$ percent."

Damrosch provided lofty advice in one commencement address:

> Please note, then, that the truly successful man is usually the one who has devoted himself to a cause—to a work of general benefit—not the one who has all his life looked out only for himself. We do not call men successful because they have amassed a pile of money, but because their lives have been full of service. Money is an incident and often accompanies success in other directions, but the greater the success the less important does money become, because the accomplishment of our aims and ideals is sufficient reward.[85]

Disillusioned by war, postwar America wanted nothing more than the "normalcy" promised them by their handsome but ineffectual president Warren Harding. In 1920, the year Harding was elected, both woman's suffrage and the prohibition of alcoholic drinks went into effect. Almost unnoticed, graduated income taxes had finally made their appearance during the war. But the Progressivism of the prewar years died during the course of three successive Republican presidencies and illusory prosperity.

In 1920 Damrosch reported to the board that the IMA had thus far graduated 709 regular graduates in addition to thirty-five who received artists' diplomas, sixty-four who earned teachers' diplomas, and eighteen who held certificates in composition. During the next decade the

IMA would face challenges posed by high enrollment. The population of New York increased to 5,620,048 between 1910 and 1920 (18 percent) and would increase during the 1920s by an additional 23 percent. Between 1920 and 1930 the number of American colleges and universities rose to 1,409 (an increase of almost 400). Faculty grew in the same period, from 49,000 to 82,000, and enrollment increased from 598,000 to 1,101,000, far in excess of the country's population growth. In addition, musical philanthropists who had more money than Loeb began to endow other, competing, music schools.

The IMA offered as excellent and thorough a musical training as could be obtained anywhere in the United States or in Europe. But the zeitgeist shifted drastically during the 1920s: Progressivism was out, conservatism in, and excellence alone would not prevail. An enormous sum of money, huge publicity (mostly unfavorable but press attention nevertheless), ugly nativism, and a lack of pedagogical vision noisily elbowed into the cloistered arena of conservatory training. "The Juilliard" was about to overwhelm Damrosch's school.

3

The Juilliard Graduate School:

A SCHOOL

FOR SCANDAL

KNOWN COLLECTIVELY as the "lost generation," many young people of the 1920s felt alienated from society. Most music students, though, escaped that sentiment because of their deep devotion to their art. The patriarchal treatment they received at the IMA may have helped them keep their bearings. Xenophobia and the red scare, unleashed by the hatreds of the war years and by the Russian Revolution, heightened the anti-immigrant movement. President Calvin Coolidge favored new legislation to curtail immigration, and the National Origins Act passed in 1924. The act scaled down immigration from more than a million to a mere 150,000 per year, and quotas devoted mainly to northern and western Europe controlled who was admitted to the United States. The act remained the nation's basic immigration law for more than a quarter of a century.

Pervasive nativism also affected musical organizations. In June 1924 Clarence Mackay, president of the Philharmonic Society of New York, went before the Committee on Education of the House of Representatives to refute the charge that more than 90 percent of those who played in American symphony orchestras were foreign born. Mackay offered statistics to show that of 104 players in the Philharmonic, eighty-seven were citizens, and forty-five of that group were native born. Mackay defended Leopold Stokowski at the Philadelphia Orchestra by noting that he conducted all rehearsals in English.

Anti-Semitism led colleges to impose quotas on Jewish applicants. Even the IMA began keeping statistics on numbers of Jews and Gentiles. In 1920 there were 496 Gentiles, 161 Jews, and 15 Negroes at the Institute.[1] Music, however, was fundamentally too cosmopolitan a world to allow anti-Semitism to flourish. By December 1921 the IMA's enrollment had risen to 742, partly due to the forty-five veterans who swelled male enrollment to 42 percent of the student body.

The greatest source of competition for the IMA began on April 25, 1919, with the death of Augustus D. Juilliard, a wealthy New York textile merchant. On June 27 the musical world was surprised by the announcement of the specifics of his will on the front page of the *New York Times*.[2] No one had known its contents before then. Juilliard found music to be one of several philanthropic interests. He did not travel in musical circles, however, and had never communicated to Frank Damrosch any interest in supporting a music school. The men had likely never met; if they did, it may have been at a formal occasion at the opera.

Otto Kahn described the $5 million bequest as "worthy of the man who conceived and made it, one of the most high-minded and public-spirited as he was one of the wisest, kindliest and most unassuming men that it was my privilege to come in contact with."[3] Conductors Artur Bodanzky and Joseph Stransky also praised the gift.[4]

In reality, the gift amounted to between $12.5 and $13.5 million. First reported as $5 million, the figure was exaggerated over the years in the press to $20 million and referred to frequently as the "largest single bequest ever made for the development of music."[5] A few years later the Juilliard sum was nearly matched in Mary Louise Curtis Bok's $12.5 million bequest to the Curtis Institute; therefore, it is fair to call it the largest bequest to music before 1927. Too, between 1918 and 1932 George Eastman had spent $20 million on the Eastman School, more than both the Bok and Juilliard bequests.

Unlike Bok and Eastman, however, who had real influence in running their schools, Augustus Juilliard could not directly control how his bequest was spent—and not all the money was used as he intended. Juilliard's will had foisted a new bureaucracy upon the world: the foundation for the arts. If the Juilliard Musical Foundation (JMF) had immediately endowed the IMA, years of public embarrassment, heavy expenses, and bad publicity might have been avoided. But that was not the case.

Augustus D. Juilliard.
(Photo from The Juilliard School Archives)

Augustus D. Juilliard was the son of Jean Nicolas Juilliard, a shoe-maker, and Anna (Burlette) Juilliard, Huguenots (Protestants) from Burgundy.[6] The correct pronunciation of his name is in two syllables: "Jool´-yard." Sources conflict over whether he was Methodist, Lutheran, or Episcopalian, but he was a member of the Huguenot Society of America. The family was raised in the Lutheran faith, which may have protected it from the religious persecution that Huguenots faced.[7] Juilliard had been born at sea April 19, 1836, during his parents' three-month voyage from France to America.[8] Like Solomon Loeb, the family emigrated to Ohio to work in dry goods. Also like Loeb, Juilliard periodically made buying trips to New York, where he impressed textile merchants with his fluent French.

Juilliard settled in New York in 1866 and worked for Hoyt, Sprague and Company, manufacturers of worsted fabrics. When the firm went bankrupt in 1873 he was made receiver and wound up the affairs to everyone's satisfaction. In 1874 he created the Augustus D. Juilliard Company.[9] Juilliard remained senior partner until his death forty-six years later. A. D. Juilliard & Co. distributed textiles: wool, silk, and cotton, particularly from the Atlantic Mills in Providence, Rhode Island; the Standard Silk Company in Philadelphia, New Jersey; cotton mills in Aragon, Georgia, and Brookford, North Carolina; and from the New York Mills Corporation. "The [textile] merchant adopted the plug hat and the frock coat of the best broadcloth as a virtual uniform that set him apart from the others and contributed in no small measure to his prestige and business success."[10] Textile merchants became rich because they provided the engine power—sails—for the great clipper ships.

Juilliard has been described as "possess[ing] outstanding executive ability, high character, unusually keen business sense and a forceful, commanding personality. He had a genial and charming manner and his associates in his wide range of interests eagerly sought and valued his judgement and advice."[11] In 1877 he married Helen Marcelus Cossitt.[12] They built a house at 16 East 57th Street in the 1870s and another house 11 West 57th Street in 1905. The Juilliards had no children.

Augustus Juilliard knew the ubiquitous Otto Kahn, of Kuhn, Loeb and Company as a fellow Metropolitan Opera board member. Juilliard actively supported the Met from 1892 until his death and regularly attended its performances. When the 1907 staging of *Salome*, whose one performance gripped the audience with horror and disgust, generated controversy, Juilliard and nine other board members protested that the opera was "objectionable and detrimental to the interests of the Metropolitan Opera House." Although Kahn and four others stood up for the director Heinrich Conried, *Salome* was banned. As a history of the Met describes him, "Juilliard was one of those men who always asked questions. He could not seem to obtain enough information about opera. He would frequently chat with [Giulio] Gatti-Casazza and [Edward] Ziegler. In these talks he was constantly in search of knowledge of the lyric theatre."[13] When he learned that the Met needed a storehouse, Juilliard personally set out to find a property. He settled on a site running from 38th to 39th Street near Tenth Avenue, bought the property, and prevailed upon his friend H. C. Frick to join the undertaking. But before construction could start Juilliard died, and the Met never got its storehouse.

Juilliard's name became associated with a landmark Supreme Court case. Chief Justice Horace Gray read the decision in March 1884 of *Juilliard v. Greenman*.[14] Greenman owed Juilliard $5,100; to test the law he did not pay in gold but in two notes of U.S. paper money, which Juilliard refused to accept. The case tested the right of the government to issue paper money in time of peace and to give it legal-tender status. The Court was expected to rule with Juilliard, against the so-called inflationists and for "sound money" (the gold standard). To everyone's surprise, however, Juilliard lost in a revolutionary eight-to-one decision, a victory for inflationists that pierced the states' rights constitutional theory.

Juilliard continued to spend time in Washington, D.C., testifying on March 8, 1886, before the House Ways and Means Committee in favor of equalizing the tariff on woolens and worsteds. Colorfully, he illustrated his argument with samples of South American, Australian, and Ohio woolens and worsteds in various states of manufacture:

> The great trouble is that we importers have to have expensive lawsuits about it. Every day the question comes up as to whether goods are made of worsted or wool. The appraiser says the one thing, the importer says the other; and they have more disputes over that one point in the New York custom-house than over any other one point. It takes an expert to tell the difference. The only difference really is in twisting the thread in one case a little harder and in combing the wool instead of carding it. You can get a bale of wool and make worsted goods out of one half of it and woolen goods out of the other.[15]

He was questioned by William McKinley, a member of the committee. Juilliard became one of the businessmen who supported McKinley's "sound money" campaign in his successful 1893 presidential election.

Juilliard died in the same summer as his near-contemporary Andrew Carnegie. An original Diamond Horseshoe box-holder (number 2) at the Met, he had attended either the matinee performance of *Madama Butterfly* (with Geraldine Farrar) or the evening performance of *Il barbieri di Siviglia* on April 19, 1919—his eighty-third birthday—when he came down with the attack of pneumonia that caused his death six days later. He was buried in a mausoleum in Woodlawn Cemetery.

To the surprise of many, Augustus Juilliard's will set up a corporation to be known as the Juilliard Musical Foundation, whose objects were:

> (a) to aid worthy students of music in securing a complete and adequate musical education, either at appropriate institutions now in existence or hereafter created, or from appropriate instructors in this country or abroad; (b) to arrange for and to give without profit to it musical entertainments, concerts and recitals of a character appropriate for the education and instruction of the general public in the musical arts; and (c) . . . to aid by gift or part of such income at such times and to such extent in such amounts as the Trustees of said Foundation may in their discretion deem proper, the Metropolitan Opera Company in the city of New York, for the purpose of assisting such organization in the production of opera, provided that suitable arrangements can be made with such company so that such gifts shall in no wise inure to its monetary profit.[16]

The will was dated March 29, 1917, a year after Helen Juilliard had died. It distributed more than $2 million to other recipients.[17] But the two main beneficiaries were his nephew, Frederick, and the yet-to-be-created foundation. Frederick Juilliard inherited $3 million outright, along with the 11 West 57th Street house, another house—the largest estate in Tuxedo, New York—and its cars, as well as all jewels, personal effects, and Juilliard's box at the Metropolitan.

Frederick Juilliard was the son of Augustus's brother, Charles Frederick Juilliard. (Augustus had numerous nieces but few nephews.) Frederick was born in 1867, the same year as James Loeb, and died in 1937, the same year as Frank Damrosch. Juilliard was graduated from the University of California in 1891 and entered his uncle's textile-manufacturing firm. He lived with his uncle, eventually remaining in his house for thirty years. The childless Juilliards treated Frederick as if he were their own son.

His politics were conservative. In 1919 he turned down an appeal to aid the ratification of the peace treaty and the League of Nations Covenant, saying that he was opposed to a "vague internationalism which would menace the standing and integrity of our institutions."[18] He gave $10,000 to the Republican campaign in 1924. An admirer of Warren G. Harding, he gave $25,000 to establish a hospital in his name. Juilliard also endowed a three-year composition fellowship at the American Academy in Rome, stipulating, as did the Academy, that only unmarried men (such as himself) might be awarded the grant. In 1936 he gave another $10,000 to a Republican presidential campaign, this time to defeat Franklin D. Roosevelt, who had pushed a Wealth Tax Act in 1935 that would have reached into Juilliard's pockets.

The other major beneficiary, whose amount was not specified in the

Frederick Juilliard; note the diamond horseshoe pin.
(Music Division of the New York Public Library for the Performing Arts, Astor, Lenox and Tilden Foundations)

will, was the Juilliard Musical Foundation. Such a large sum given for the amorphous cause of music was bound to generate greed from those who thought they should have received more. One of the numerous Juilliard nieces provided for in the will, Mary Etta Fauve, had received $10,000 outright and a $100,000 trust. Her suit, charging that the execution of the will was obtained by undue influence and demanding a jury trial, was soon dropped. Two of Augustus Juilliard's tax lawyers, Charles Paul Jones and Roberto Deyer, sued for $11,191, suddenly remembering that they had been paid only $2,000 rather than 15 percent of the sum they claimed to have saved Juilliard on his 1916 income taxes.

Three JMF trustees were named in the will: Frederick Juilliard; James N. Wallace (1864–1919), president of the Central Trust Company; and Charles H. Sabin (1868–1933), president of the Guaranty Trust Company of New York.[19] In January 1919 Wallace and Sabin had been awarded the Legion of Honor by the French government. A Democrat, Sabin would later support Franklin Roosevelt and work against Prohibition. Wallace was director of the Bank of America and gave to innumerable causes, including African American charities. He was called "one of the most kind-hearted and generous men who ever came to Wall Street."[20] None of the three was a musician.

If Augustus Juilliard had followed the then-typical route of musical philanthropy, he would have emulated Andrew Carnegie, Otto Kahn, or James Loeb, who put their personal stamps on Carnegie Hall, the Metropolitan Opera, and the IMA, respectively. For unknown reasons, however, Juilliard avoided an active role in the distribution of his money. Perhaps the idea of supporting musicians' study came as late as the drawing up of a new will in 1917, after his wife's death and when he was eighty-one. He deliberately kept the bequest a secret for the final two years of his life. The absence of a donor with distinct ideas about how his money should be spent, the envy such a vast sum aroused, the power invested in non-musicians over musical matters, and the arrogance that power engenders all combined to result in chaos. Human nature in some of its more unpleasant guises was to collide with the best interests of struggling music students.

Almost immediately, the terms of Juilliard's will were discussed, misinterpreted, and even disobeyed to suit the agendas of interested parties: newspaper editorialists, potential recipients, the Metropolitan Opera, and, perhaps most significantly, the three executors. The *New York Times* weighed in early with an editorial that mentioned Loeb's IMA endowment and opened with what amounted to wishful thinking: "[The JMF] should be, the most powerful of all factors favoring artistic freedom and progress. A young singer who cannot command an adequate education, a musician or composer who cannot command a hearing, should find [the Foundation] predisposed toward every novel and truly vigorous artistic personality. . . . The spirit of such a foundation should be not that of a professor or master, but that of a friend—the enlightened lover of musical art."[21]

Only months after Juilliard's death and before the JMF was formed, fate intervened. James Wallace was speaking to his doctor when "he suddenly exclaimed, 'My God, I'm dying.' He fell from his chair to the floor and expired almost instantly."[22] The fifty-five-year-old philanthropist, a heart attack victim, was replaced on the JMF by his successor at the Central Trust Company, George W. Davison (1872–1953).[23] In a savvy move, Paul Warburg, the IMA trustee and head of the Federal Reserve, took bank president George Davison to lunch in May 1920. Warburg also invited Davison to the IMA commencement, but he declined. The three trustees—Davison, Sabin, and Frederick Juilliard—set up the JMF in March 1920 at 522 Fifth Avenue. Within a few years Sabin left the board, leaving only one of Juilliard's three hand-picked trustees to run the Foundation: Frederick. Predictably, the new JMF was besieged with requests for aid. More than four thousand aspiring musicians wrote to the Foundation.

The will specified that "these three persons select to act with them on said Board of Trustees at least two other persons, who they deem best qualified to assist them in carrying out the objects and purposes of the corporation."[24] Frederick Juilliard demonstrated bad taste in presidents; he liked Harding, frequently rated the worst president in U.S. history. Juilliard showed equally poor judgment choosing administrators. The first public action he and the trustees took, in June 1920, was their greatest mistake. They appointed only one person—rather than the two new members stipulated—as executive secretary. This person was neither a philanthropist nor a performer, composer, or music educator. He had never met Augustus Juilliard. Eugene A. Noble (1865–1948) was a fifty-five-year-old Methodist minister preaching in Schenectady, New York.

Noble had studied at Wesleyan University (class of 1891), where he had been a member of the same fraternity as George Davison (class of 1892). He served as a pastor of churches in Bridgeport, Connecticut, and in his native Brooklyn. From 1902 until 1909 he was president of the Centenary Collegiate Institute, a Methodist junior college for women, in Hackettstown, New Jersey, then of the Woman's College of Baltimore, known later as Goucher College. Noble had been the personal choice of John F. Goucher, who also let it be known that he was willing to pass his acquisition on to his own alma mater, Dickinson College, in Carlisle, Pennsylvania.

Anointed president of Dickinson with much pomp and circumstance in 1912, Noble rapidly became detested by "half the college."[25] He neglected recruitment, and the enrollment declined sharply. In addition, "He was accused of padding the student damage account to add luxuries [such as four more bathrooms] to the President's House."[26] Financially, he let debts accumulate equal to more than a third of the endowment. Professors were not being paid, and the imminence of bankruptcy and closing the school forced the trustees to drastic action. After just two years Noble was forced to resign. He could hardly continue his career in academia after so resounding a failure, and he returned to the ministry in 1914. He was preaching at the First Methodist Church in Schenectady when he used his charm and his old school ties with George Davison to secure the JMF position in 1920.

From an old family, Noble saw himself as an aristocrat. A Republican, he became an art collector and the owner of a kennel of Bedlington terriers. He later collected Rolls-Royces, rugs, and prints (paid for by his second wife's money) for his Connecticut home. In 1923 he was named to New York's Social Register, which fulfilled his social ambitions. Personally charming and delightful in conversation or as an after-dinner speaker, Noble insinuated his way into the good graces of Frederick Juilliard (a longtime member of the Social Register) and was not above subtly using blackmail to achieve his ends. "As to my own competence," the misnamed Noble was later forced to concede, "I do not pretend to know anything about music."[27]

Eugene Noble.
(Music Division of the New York Public Library for the Performing Arts, Astor, Lenox and Tilden Foundations)

Noble wrote of his new job, "This is, indeed, a unique opportunity—
'sole dictator of the disbursement of the income from the fund,' the
purpose of which is an effort to develop the cultural life in our country."[28] Musicians later wondered in print what Noble held over the
Juilliard board that allowed him such absolute control of the Foundation. The parallels between Frederick Juilliard and Noble's behavior
with that of President Harding and his attorney general, Harry
Daugherty, are striking. Harding had been criticized for appointing
political cronies to high office without regard for their qualifications.
None received more criticism than Daugherty, who often treated the
press and even members of Congress arrogantly. Daugherty was widely
suspected of graft. The Teapot Dome scandal of 1924 demonstrated that
many public officials had indeed been taking graft. The Senate investigated the attorney general, who refused to resign or open his files for
investigators; Coolidge finally asked him to resign. Harding and Coolidge themselves both came under suspicion. Corruption was rife in the
federal government and in New York City government with the Tam-
many Hall scandal. Noble had only to look around him to see that more
could be gained by not distributing Juilliard's money.

The years 1920, 1921, and 1922 passed without any discernible action on the part of Noble or the Foundation. No money was paid to
support a musical or concert organization. In December 1922 Noble
announced that students had been chosen for free musical education—
although no names or numbers of students were given. Noble, said,
however, "that such an ambitious scheme required a great deal of planning and that the doors were not yet open for all who desired to avail
themselves of the fund." Volunteer committees tested the thousands of
applicants who had applied. "We shall spend close to $100,000 for in-
dividual aid, but we haven't that much money in hand yet," he added.[29]

Even that noncommittal announcement had been forced by numerous protests. One of the earliest and most public was lodged by opera
librettist and journalist Charles Meltzer (1852–1936). Meltzer was an
assistant to Heinrich Conried at the Met and helped start the opera-in-
English movement by translating twenty-two operas. He wrote to the
Times shortly after Noble's non-news:

> Dr. Eugene Noble, had after about four years' waiting, at last an-
> swered the countless protests sent him with regard to the delay in the
> formulation of plans for the administering of that 'fairy godfather of
> American music and musicians' [a quotation from a *Times* story], the
> Juilliard Musical Foundation. . . . Dr. Noble assures us that much time
> was required for planning the right ways of helping musicians. He had
> once expressed to me his fear that 'twenty years' might be needed.

Well, thanks to these protests, he has delayed less than that. . . . And though doubtless a gentleman of unblemished integrity and reputation, Dr. Noble is not widely or generally, I think, accepted as an authority on music, American or foreign, or the crying needs of American musicians, including American composers, the most important of all factors in music. I am assured that there have been instances in which Dr. Noble has refused to assist even altruistic and worthy American musical enterprises and to help composers of exceptional gifts who needed a few of those Juilliard dollars desperately.[30]

A cynical and uncharitable view of the situation would accommodate both the facts and the behavior of the executive secretary. Frederick Juilliard stood to gain a considerable amount of money if the formation of the Foundation was stalled and if, subsequently, the funds were not given out. In December 1923 he and the other beneficiaries sued and won $1 million in interest on the Foundation's money. Because the corporation was not established until 1920, the year after Juilliard's death, the court decided that the majority of the income (vastly increased due to postwar inflation) was to go to Frederick Juilliard. He received $567,087 of the interest on the fund his uncle intended for aspiring musicians, more than the original Loeb endowment to found an entire music school.[31]

Noble's mysterious hold over Frederick Juilliard could be explained by Juilliard's desire to accumulate even more of his uncle's fortune.[32] An unholy bargain may have been struck between Noble and Juilliard. Noble stalled while Roaring Twenties' financial markets increased the estate's value. For example, an auction of the Juilliard estate was held in February 1920 and garnered $1,898,500. In one year, from 1919 to 1920, the twelve downtown buildings that Augustus Juilliard had owned had gained in value by one-third. When finally pressured to spend some of the interest on music students, Noble set tightfisted conditions that were rightly called stingy.

In February 1923 the Foundation was finally "Ready for Applicants." "Incidentally," the *New York Times* reported, "it was disclosed that for the time being only those of American birth or citizenship will be eligible to the benefits of the Foundation."[33] That requirement was nowhere to be found in Juilliard's will, but the press, cowed by the anti-immigrant atmosphere or perhaps subscribing to it, never again raised the issue.

Noble dictated another condition not found in the Juilliard will: "The purpose of the Foundation is to render a social service through music, and applications will be primarily investigated to determine the fitness of individual students to co-operate in such a service." Awards would be for only one year, and the maximum amount was $1,000 worth of instruction. The money went directly to the teachers, not to the students. In addition, the following parsimonious conditions applied:

> Reports must be rendered monthly to the office of the foundation by schools or teachers instructing beneficiaries, and such reports will be requisite and must be satisfactory for successive installment payments. A grant may be withdrawn for good and sufficient reason at any time after the first installment payment, notice to that effect being sent by mail to the beneficiary's address, and the decision of the foundation to withdraw aid must be accepted as final. The foundation will direct its beneficiaries where and with whom to study. [This too is final.] No lists or names of examiners will be issued. For the present, no applications will be considered from persons not of American birth or citizenship.[34]

The JMF, in keeping with the will, made some effort to distribute the money to music institutions "now in existence," but the conditions Noble imposed on its acceptance were onerous. Some of the conditions later imposed on the Met in return for aid may indicate what Noble required of Damrosch, who went to see Noble sometime in late 1921. As he had done with the Met's Gatti-Cassaza, Noble likely demanded seats on the IMA's board and a strong hand in policy.

It is difficult to picture a meeting between Damrosch and Noble proceeding satisfactorily from the point of view of either man. First, Damrosch, who once said he had trouble persuading Carnegie to back his plans, may have been similarly tongue-tied around another man who controlled wealth. Second, the larger-than-life Damrosch was the supplicant to someone in every way his inferior and lacking in musical vision. The two clashed in important areas. Damrosch was liberal: He directed a school endowed with the purpose of admitting students from any class, religion, color, and sex. Noble was a political conservative, and he imposed the condition that only American students would receive the Juilliard aid. Damrosch knew that many music students were not citizens because their parents were not citizens; he and his brother Walter, as boys, would not have qualified under Noble's stricture. Finally, Damrosch's "acquaintance with the methods of the best music schools abroad and with the best educators, made him feel justly enough that his school should not be tampered with by men, however admirable in their intention, who knew far less about music education than he did."[35]

For Noble's part, he must have known he was meeting with the outstanding music educator in the country and could not hand control to such a powerful figure. It was not in Noble's nature to be generous;

unlike the members of the IMA board, Noble had never given money to support any institution. His chauvinism and xenophobia may have led to difficulty in dealing with a German-born musician. Eugene Noble, with his petty attitudes and restrictive demands, was a far cry from James Loeb. Damrosch declined his proposal. Their failure to come to an agreement was to have serious consequences for both institutions, which then proceeded to make and carry out other, expensive, plans.

~

Although the IMA enrollment was high, Damrosch told the board in December 1921:

> The most highly gifted are ignorant of [the Institute's] character and standing. It is looked upon as one among many similar schools, whereas it should stand as unique as does, for instance, the Paris Conservatory. The latter attracts the best talent of France because 1) instruction is free; 2) admission is competitive . . . ; 3) the best teachers are available because of the social and professional standing conferred on the professors; and 4) the State provides maintenance subsidies for certain students and engagements in the State theatres and opera houses to graduates.[36]

He asked for the board's help in obtaining more financial backing. Inspired by the Juilliard and Eastman money, he wanted $1 million and asked each trustee to come up with $50,000 toward it. He never received that endowment, however, and at the end of his life remained slightly bitter about not being able to realize some of his vision as a result.

Damrosch presented an adumbration of a Lincoln Center–like proposal originated by the mayor, John Hylan, and the city chamberlain:

> It was proposed to set aside a site, four blocks in extent from avenue to avenue, seventeen acres in all, for the purpose of creating a park to hold an Art Center. It was to contain the Metropolitan Opera House, flanked on one side by the buildings of the Associated Fine Arts, on the other three by those of the Art of Music and in the rear was to be the home of the Industrial Arts. These buildings were to be of noble and harmonious design, each adapted to its special purposes and they were intended to become the center of the city's artistic life. . . . The Institute of Musical Art was invited to enter the proposed combination of art organizations as the representative school of music of this city. The general plan was that the city supply the site while the various organizations erect their buildings in accordance with their needs.[37]

When Damrosch presented this idea to the board, his natural tendencies toward the grandiose vision surfaced and carried him away. He saw his educational plan as a model extending to every state in the union. He proposed no fewer than ten separate schools: a master school, one for opera, a high school, an intermediate school, an astounding five hundred preparatory centers in New York, a school for supervisors of music in public schools, an orchestra school, a band school, three training schools for church musicians (Catholic, Episcopal, and Jewish), and, finally, singing classes for the people—like his own People's Singing Classes that had disbanded in 1917. "These would lead to the formation of trained choruses in the five boroughs and could be united into one great chorus available on all occasions of civic or national holidays or celebrations."[38] The proposed center would have been called the Municipal Art Center. The site, however, was so far uptown as to be useless (Hunter College's annex later occupied the area), and the plan collapsed utterly.

An affiliation with Columbia University was effected in 1924. Shortly before, the IMA and Loeb had rejected an offer to affiliate with New York University. Students in public school music at the Institute could enroll in a four-year program—the first two to be spent at the IMA and the last two at Teachers College of Columbia University—and could earn a bachelor of science degree. By 1931 it was possible to earn a bachelor of music education in the program.[39]

A new issue loomed: Because the enrollment increased to 840 in 1923, the immediate problem was to accommodate them. The solution was to build an annex to the school that would reach behind the school in the direction of Broadway. (In 1923–24 the Eastman School also built a five-story annex.) Students still had no dormitories, but the Parnassus Club in 1924–25 was charging a reasonable $13–$21 a week, which included room and board. In 1924 Eidlitz built International House, facing Grant's Tomb on the north. It served for decades as a dormitory for the IMA and Juilliard students who were over twenty-one.

Loeb continued to meet the IMA yearly deficits. Nevertheless, Damrosch contended in 1924 that "[James Loeb] did not wish the Institute to be a one-family affair."[40] Yet the IMA was clearly still just that. One example is the money raised to build the annex. The 1924 estimated cost was $128,000. The Building Fund had raised the following amounts: James Loeb, $20,000; Felix Warburg, $25,000; Mrs. Felix M. Warburg, $25,000; Paul Warburg, $25,000; Mrs. Morris Loeb, $15,000; Mrs. I. N. Seligman, $10,000; and Mrs. Jacob Schiff, $10,000—a $130,000 total. Virtually everyone on the list was a sister, sister-in-law, or brother-in-law of James Loeb. All were devoted to music, and all doted on their eccentric relative. By May 1925 the building extension was paid for.

In 1925 Damrosch wrote to Loeb that he wanted to replace their composition teacher, Percy Goetschius, who had intended to leave at the end of the year, with Nadia Boulanger, for whom a reception was held. "I feel that if we can secure her we will get an unusual personality combined with great ability in teaching."[41] Damrosch offered her the job, but she could not give him a commitment. Language was a problem with Germans, and Damrosch was "not keen about securing a Britisher."

Damrosch settled on the relatively conservative composer who ridiculed jazz—fellow Bohemians Club member Rubin Goldmark (1872–1936). The men had bonds of sympathy: Both had done pioneer work in Colorado, and both had studied with Joseffy, who, with Goldmark, had founded the Bohemians, a club that would raise money for musicians. Franz Kneisel was president and Goldmark vice president. He had been a student at the National Conservatory (1891–93), studying with Dvořák. He had also taught privately in New York, where composition pupils included George Gershwin (for three lessons), Abram Chasins, Leopold Goldowsky II, Frederick Jacobi, and Aaron Copland (who studied with him from the winter of 1916–17 to the spring of 1921). Goldmark wrote little music himself but had a success with "A Negro Rhapsody" in January 1923. He was described as "a wise earnest musician and a great idealist. He wore a walrus mustache, was stout and partly bald, and suffered for the special torment the devil devised for musicians, difficulty with his hearing. Goldmark was also a perpetual cigar-smoker, a gourmet and raconteur of the first order."[42]

～

Eugene Noble decided to distribute the JMF funds himself. Teachers were paid an astounding $100 an hour while worthy students languished in need of financial assistance. To gain some perspective on this salary, note that musicians in the Philharmonic in 1924 were paid $60 a week for five rehearsals and four concerts. The Juilliard extravagance was looked upon with suspicion and irony, even by some of its recipients.

In March 1923 the distribution of the JMF's money concerned Loeb. With considerable insight he wrote to Damrosch, "Unless Dr. Noble is a complete numskull, he ought to recognize that more can be accomplished by supporting the Institute of Musical Art, that is, by giving it a handsome endowment, than by distributing the income of the Juilliard Foundation in driblets!" In the spirit of philanthropy in which he had been reared, he wrote, "It appears the commercial conditions are improving in the U.S. The more reason that those who are getting rich should pay a toll to idealism!"[43]

Having failed to find suitable institutional recipients—from their point of view—for the Juilliard money, the Foundation embarked on a third plan. In February 1924 it purchased, rather than rented, a Vanderbilt guest house at 49 East 52nd Street in order to start yet another musical school in New York.[44] The Foundation's new home had been built in 1910 with gray and blue terra-cotta bricks in English Renaissance style. It occupied a site fifty feet wide on the north side of 52nd Street, east of Madison Avenue. In 1920 the seven-story building had become an apartment house valued at $450,000, but the JMF bought it for much more than that four years later.[45]

The appearance and ambiance of the Vanderbilt house may have reflected the Foundation and Noble's self-image. Vanderbilt had wanted interesting rooms: Many of the fifty rooms had oak-paneled walls, long mirrors, beamed ceilings, silk draperies, and scenes in silk above the wainscoting. Other rooms were elliptical or oblong, and some contained undetectable doors in silk-fabric walls. Two or three rooms between flights of stairs were entered by pressing a secret spring. One suite had a red-plush elevator. Mrs. Vanderbilt's drawing room, an enormous, oak-paneled space with a real gold-leaf ceiling, became a school office. The mansion had a magnificent ballroom and many valuable marble man-

Looking north up Madison Avenue, 1928; the Juilliard Musical Foundation, 49 East 52nd Street, is on the right side of the photograph.
(United States History, Local History and Genealogy Division, New York Public Library, Astor, Lenox, and Tilden Foundations)

telpieces for its fireplaces, including one said to have been bought in Pompeii for $7,500. Large chandeliers of hand-cut crystal hung from the ceilings. The bathrooms were unusually large, and one had black marble and gilded fixtures.

Its resplendent atmosphere did not necessarily make the building suitable for music lessons: The magnificent foyer and staircase were wasted space, the acoustics in most rooms were poor, and the teaching rooms were too small and not soundproofed.[46] The most conspicuous problem was the lack of a concert hall. The ballroom served as such but could not be used for public concerts and was unsuitable as a venue for presenting operas. When concerts and operas eventually took place, the Foundation had to rent halls. Students' practice rooms—each equipped with a Steinway upright—were in the former servants' quarters on the top floor. Racial equality existed at the school, but, in a throwback to nineteenth-century conservatory practice, students were separated by sex. Girls practiced on one side and boys on another. There was reason to worry whether everyone could get out of the building in case of fire.

In order to live in luxury and exert absolute control over the School, Eugene Noble moved from his Fifth Avenue apartment to live rent-free on the sixth floor of the Foundation's school. It would seem that Noble had used Juilliard's money to buy himself a mansion.

In June of 1924 the Foundation announced it would give advanced instruction to one hundred students in the 52nd Street building. Only voice, piano, violin, 'cello, and composition students could apply. Applicants had to be over sixteen and under thirty and have a high school equivalency. The requirement was stricter than it seems today; in 1930 fewer than a third of all seventeen-year-olds had graduated from high school. "The plan of having students trained in different localities by teachers of diverse methods and standards will be given up" and, contrary to Juilliard's will, there was no money for students to study abroad.[47] Noble predicted great success. This self-congratulation was treated with some skepticism by the editorial writer for the *New York Times:* "The hope has been expressed in some quarters that this one [of the many New York music schools] may develop into a great national conservatory. For the present, however, such a prediction is premature. Various schools here, in Boston, and elsewhere already have such well-grounded reputations that it is hard to single out one and call it supreme. It would be presumptuous to make this claim for an entirely new organization."[48]

Talented students now had several enticing options. In 1920 the Julius Hartt School of Music was founded in Hartford by Julius and Pauline Hartt, Moshe Paranov, and Samuel Berkman. The Eastman School's musical director Albert Coates, along with Eugene Goossens, had met twenty-seven-year-old Howard Hanson during his fellowship at the American Academy in Rome in 1924. The former IMA student, having conducted his Nordic Symphony in Rochester and New York, discovered upon his return to Rome a cable asking him to become director of the school.[49] In Philadelphia another endowed school was to open in 1924. Damrosch told the board in May 1924:

> The Eastman School in Rochester has already been doing active work for some years past, well housed and adequately endowed. Now Mrs. Bok is establishing the Curtis School in Philadelphia with a practically unlimited endowment enabling her to enlist the services of such stars as Marcella Sembrich and Josef Hofmann. We have the satisfaction, however, of supplying to this school its head of the Ear-Training Department—our own George Wedge—whose work at the Institute and whose textbooks have given him a national reputation.
>
> And now the Juilliard Foundation intends to establish a Graduate School for the purpose of preparing talented students for public appearances and helping them to secure such opportunities. It is greatly to be hoped that the triplication of educational advantages will not lead to competitive bidding for a few famous teachers, but rather to such friendly co-operation as will bring about the gathering of many excellent teachers from home sources and abroad.
>
> As far as we can learn no new thought will enter into the projects of these new institutions which our Institute has not already put into practice, limited only by the means at our command, and we still hope that the Trustees of the Juilliard Foundation may some day see their way to co-operate more closely with us without changing their plans in principle. Such co-operation would unquestionably lead to a very large pecuniary saving and would add to the efficiency of both institutions.[50]

In June of 1924 Damrosch wrote to Loeb, "The Juilliard Foundation's 'Graduate School' has Twelve Million Dollars to back it, but money will not buy everything and I understand that Dr. Noble, who is to be the Director, is already finding it very difficult to secure good teachers of the type he would like to have."[51] Damrosch might have added to the list of Curtis faculty three others who had been affiliated with the IMA— William Kincaid, Felix Salmond, and Carlos Salzedo. Carl Flesch reported his own salary at Curtis at $25,000 annually, Sembrich received a purported $40,000, and Josef Hofmann, when he became director in 1927, was supposedly paid $100,000.[52] In the same letter Damrosch acknowledged the importance of location: "But Philadelphia is Philadelphia, and New York is New York, so who's afraid?" Loeb comforted Damrosch by predicting, "Don't worry, Frank: Noble and Co. are going to make a dismal failure. Their action is quite in line with Juilliard's damn-fool Will and Testament!"[53]

In September 1924 Noble revealed the names of the examining board who were to decide which of the many applicants would be admitted. They were author Henry H. Bellamann, critics Richard Aldrich and Lawrence Gilman, conductor of the American Orchestral Society Chalmers Clifton, composer and associate conductor of the New York Philharmonic Henry Hadley, composer Charles M. Loeffler, and pianist Ernest Schelling.

Bellamann (1882–1945), chair of the examining board from 1924 to 1926, had studied in Europe with Isidor Philipp and Charles-Marie Widor. In 1907 he became dean of the School of Fine Arts at Chicora College for Women, in Columbia, South Carolina, where he remained until 1924. The musician, who had dark-rimmed spectacles, received his doctor of music degree from DePauw University in 1926. He wrote a series of articles for *The Musical Digest* about music in America and based on his traveling on the Juilliard Graduate School's examining board.[54] Principally known as a novelist and a poet, Bellamann was appointed professor of music at Vassar College in 1928. After a year as dean of the Curtis Institute of Music, he retired from music in 1931 to devote himself to writing.[55] He would be one of the first of several prominent people to sever his association with Noble and the JMF.

Bellamann outlined the proposed activities. "First there will be our own master classes for the Juilliard fellows here in this building; then a continuation of the Juilliard Scholarships established by the Foundation in certain schools, colleges and universities; and third, the Foundation will continue to contribute to the support of certain worthy musical undertakings, as in the past."[56] Conspicuously missing in this approach is the possibility of forming a student orchestra or chorus.

The Foundation announced its twelve star faculty members in a news release in October 1924. Applications for fellowships had closed the day before the faculty was announced. They were, for singing, Marcella Sembrich, basso Leon Rothier, and baritone Francis Rogers; for piano, Ernest Hutcheson, Josef Lhevinne, Olga Samaroff, and Erno von Dohnányi; for strings, Cesar Thomson, Paul Kochanski, Georges Enesco (all violin), and Felix Salmond ('cello); and for composition, Rubin Goldmark (who would months later also join the IMA). (Dohnányi was prevented by illness from teaching at the school.) Of these, Rogers, Goldmark, and Samaroff were the only Americans. In his announcement Noble declared, "It is probable that no organization of music teachers containing so many recognized leaders has been brought together in this country up to this time."[57]

John Erskine, Noble's successor, compared Noble's collecting famous musicians with his subsequent collecting of terriers and Rolls-Royces, "without much consideration of their fitness for their immediate purpose." The Juilliard Graduate School ended up with a piano department, for example, which for several years had too many teachers for the number of pupils. "The essence of education," Erskine continued, "the building up of a school to respond to the larger interests of society, was a secret which Heaven had concealed from him."[58]

Noble's acquisition of one faculty member illustrates his approach. Pianist Olga Samaroff (born in 1882 in Texas as Elsie Hickenlooper) had married Leopold Stokowski in 1911 and was divorced in 1923. Noble did not know Samaroff personally but burst in unannounced at her summer home in Seal Harbor, Maine. He found her in a disheveled state. Samaroff recalled:

> He had come to ask if I would consider a contract to teach piano at the new Juilliard Graduate School of Music [*sic*].
>
> I literally gasped with astonishment and then exclaimed, "But I have never taught, Dr. Noble. I am utterly inexperienced. Why did you ever think of choosing me as a teacher?"
>
> "We know you have never taught," he replied calmly, "but we know you have yourself done what we want you to teach. The Graduate School will not be like the usual conservatory of music. We want an artist faculty composed of musicians who can impart what they have learned from actual experience on the concert or operatic stage to students who are sufficiently well prepared to profit by what the artist teachers have to give. The kind of teaching that might require the experience you lack, will have been done beforehand in the case of the students who will come to you. What we believe you can impart to them from the richness of your own musical background is something many an experienced teacher might not have to give. In any case we want to sign a year's contract if you are willing."
>
> I knew that if I hesitated I would never have the courage to sign that contract, so I took the plunge at once. Before Dr. Noble left the house everything was settled.[59]

She neglected to mention the fabulous salary Noble offered. Struggling as a single mother, Samaroff was paid considerably less than male soloists. (In 1923 her appearance with the Philharmonic garnered $600, while the male pianists were routinely paid $1,000–$1,200.) Originally assigned ten students at Juilliard, Samaroff found she loved teaching and excelled at it. Her subsequent students at Juilliard and Curtis included Eugene List, Rosalyn Tureck, William Kappel, Alexis Weissenberg, and Vincent Persichetti.

Another faculty member chosen was Polish soprano Marcella Sembrich (1858–1935, born Praxede Marcelline Kochanski), who had made her debut in *Lucia di Lammermoor* during the Metropolitan's first season in 1883. At a Met gala at the end of that season she played a violin solo, a Chopin mazurka on the piano, and sang "Ah! non giunge" from *La Sonnambula.* According to one encyclopedia, Sembrich was "one of the greatest sopranos in history."[60] A star of the Metropolitan, her roles included Lucia, Violetta, Mimi, Gilda, Rosina, Susanna, Zerlina, and the Queen of the Night, as well as the Wagnerian roles of Elsa and Eva. Puccini had said of her, "You are *the* Mimi." In her first New York concert, in March 1900, Sembrich set a fashion that has prevailed ever since. Bucking the tradition that divas in concert confine themselves to operatic excerpts, she sang French, Italian, and German lieder. She was a friend of both Clara Schumann and Brahms, who said of her, "I trust you perfectly to interpret my intention in what you feel inspired to do" and that "Sembrich has a mind—a heart, and a soul."[61] Blessed with a personality utterly free of jealousy, she was loved by her associates. Widowed in 1917, she withdrew from public life and then taught at both the Curtis Institute and Juilliard until her death in 1935.[62] At $100 an hour, Sembrich was the highest paid at Juilliard; Josef Lhevinne received $40 an hour, and Rosina Lhevinne, $25.

Sembrich did the most for sopranos, while the outspoken and opinionated Anna Schoen-René (1864–1942) taught contraltos, baritones, and basses. The mannishly dressed, German-born Schoen-René, who also knew Brahms, was known as the heir and continuer of the voice teaching of Manuel Garcia and his sister, Pauline Viardot-Garcia. "Later, in 1925," she wrote, "when out of a clear sky, Dr. Eugene Noble offered me a teaching position at the Juilliard Graduate School, where Mme. Sembrich had been the leading voice teacher from its beginning [in 1924], I told him that I would accept the offer only if she wished to have me as a colleague. He assured me that she was eager that I join the vocal faculty."[63] Schoen-René taught Risë Stevens, Hallie Stiles, Charles Kullman, Kitty Carlisle, Paul Robeson, Lanny Ross, Julius Huehn, and Florence Easton. When she died in November 1943, her funeral service was held in the auditorium of the school.

Noble came up with a grandiose misnomer for his music school: the Juilliard Graduate School. Both Damrosch and Erskine referred to it as the "so-called Juilliard Graduate School."[64] The reason that educators surrounded the name with quotation marks was because the School was not designed for graduates of any undergraduate institution; only a high school equivalency was required, and few students were college graduates. Nor was the term *school* accurate, because there were no general standards applicable to all and no core curriculum. Instead it offered fellowships—students were referred to as "fellowship-holders"—to study a major instrument only. It was a school of private lessons and those only in piano, violin (or 'cello), voice, and composition. After three years students were declared graduated, but with a certificate that held no place in the American educational system. Nevertheless, free lessons from illustrious teachers attracted music students. Four to five hundred applied for the approximately fifty vacancies each year at the JGS. Exclusivity, money, and renowned faculty conferred prestige.

The JGS opened October 17, 1924, as Bellamann had predicted. In December the JMF finally released names of eighty-one music students it intended to help, culled from approximately five hundred applications.[65] Fourteen additional fellowships were awarded but not announced in the press. Two of the students were "negro women." The original winners included Abram Chasins, Ulric Cole in piano (she also won a composition fellowship), and Daniel Saidenberg in violin. Of the eighty-one, however, almost half were dropped after one year.

By way of comparison, the Eastman School was built for a capacity of two thousand students. Anticipating the day when it would need to reject students because of overcrowding, in 1924 Eastman began administering Seashore psychological tests to applicants, which appeared to give accurate predictions of failure. In contrast, the Curtis Institute, which like the JGS opened in 1924, accepted only a few students. Most of these, suspiciously contrary to music-student demographics elsewhere, were male. After 1927 Curtis students were not charged tuition.

New York Times critic Olin Downes reported on results after the first year of the Graduate School's operation. He described the JGS's reasoning, which belied its advertised intention to help secure students public performances. "The New York Philharmonic Orchestra has offered to engage ten of the most gifted of the fellowship students as soloists at its Students' Concerts next season, but the policy of the Juilliard Foundation is against such early exploiting of talents which are still, in certain respects, in the formative stages, and only three or four of the most finished students will be permitted to accept these opportunities and similar ones which have been offered by other orchestras."[66] Downes pointed out that several of the faculty did not speak English and many students did not speak the faculty's language, making instruction difficult. Privy to the examining board report (by Clifton, Gilman, Hadley, and Bellamann), Downes endorsed its suggestions regarding voice students, confident that Noble would take such advice. In return for this generally favorable article, Downes immediately was given a place on the JGS examining board, which would examine and announce fifty-one new fellowship-holders the next month.[67] Downes was paid $100 an hour, which Noble perhaps saw as protection from criticism in the press.

At least one institutional recipient of the JMF's money, the Yale School of Music, however, was not entirely satisfied with the arrangement.

> This was a rather curious episode in the story of the School's scholarships. The Juilliard Musical Foundation gave $800 to the Yale School of Music in 1924 to use as scholarships for students in 1924–25. The faculty was free to decide how many and which students would receive a share and eight were selected to receive $100 each. The Foundation repeated its offer for two more years and then the largesse ended. There is sufficient evidence in the records to show that Yale was not pleased with this arrangement and, in fact, made an effort to convince the Foundation to endow the scholarships. The Foundation refused to do so. Since this was happening precisely at the time when the Juilliard Foundation was beginning its 'graduate division' . . . one can readily infer that this gift was intended as a means of recruiting talented students for the new school.[68]

The IMA was not idle in the competition for students and standing. Its new four-story annex, designed by Donn Barber, completed in the fall of 1924, and paid for by the Loeb family, contained twenty-one rooms for teaching, administrative offices, a large room on the top floor for orchestra rehearsals and some organ practice rooms; it was almost as large as the original edifice. As Damrosch described the building:

> It contained four and a half stories. The basement had three large classrooms for Ear-training and Theory, an administration room, and a storage room. The first floor had five rooms for individual teaching, a small Green Room connecting with the stage of the Recital Hall in the main building, and a stenographer's room. The second floor— four teaching rooms and two lavatories; the third floor—one large room, occupying the entire length and width of the building, for orchestra and chorus rehearsals, Dalcroze Eurythmics, etc. The fourth floor had three organ practice rooms and one room for the teaching of wind and percussion instruments. . . . It was equipped with seventeen Steinway pianos, three practice organs, and the necessary furnishings.[69]

The enrollment of the IMA continued to climb rapidly: In 1924–25 there were 943 students (325 male, 618 female). Of the males, there were 125 string players, 83 pianists, and 48 who studied theory. Students in violin were required to play viola. That year's catalog sought woodwind players who were "talented [and] young" rather than the previously specified "men." New faculty were necessary. Margarete Dessoff became director of the chorus at the IMA. Damrosch wrote of her, "I believe that I am not overstating it when I say that no such choral singing has been heard in New York since the Musical Art Society went out of existence."[70] The theory and composition faculty's seven members included Richard Donovan, Bassett Hough, and Helen W. Whiley. By the next year (1925–26) that faculty was enlarged to ten, adding composers Bernard Wagenaar and Wallingford Riegger.

Carl Friedberg returned from Germany and began teaching again at the IMA in 1923, and Noble secured him for the JGS's piano faculty in 1926 over Damrosch's objections. Damrosch gave his consent only after the merger was announced and only if Friedberg retained his position at the IMA. (Friedberg tried unsuccessfully to persuade Noble to move the Graduate School to White Plains, cheaper for students than New York City.) Friedberg taught at his home, the Gladstone Hotel, near the Juilliard mansion. Later, when Stravinsky also lived at the Gladstone, Friedberg's piano pupils had the advantage of suggestions from the composer.

Upon hearing of the Juilliard Musical Foundation in 1920, music educator Kenneth Bradley (1872–1954) sought out Noble. Theodore Thomas and Fannie Bloomfield Ziesler had suggested Bradley to William L. Bush to head the conservatory named after him: Bradley became

The IMA annex seen from the corner of 122nd and Broadway, 1929. The IMA is at the extreme left, the two towers of International House at right.
(United States History, Local History and Genealogy Division, New York Public Library, Astor, Lenox, Tilden Foundations)

the founder and director for twenty-five years of the Bush Conservatory in Chicago. As early as 1911 he had tried to interest Chadwick, Damrosch, and other fellow conservatory directors in founding a national association of music schools.[71] The author of several books on harmony, Bradley was responsible for the creation of the National Association of Schools of Music in 1924 and was made life president.[72] He spoke at length with Noble in 1920 about his idea for a national conservatory of music, but Noble told him then the JMF could not function as a school.

Four years after Bradley had presented his plans for a school, in 1924, Noble asked him to show the plans to the board. When Bradley traveled from Chicago to do so, however, he was treated rudely by Noble, who told him that the board meeting had been canceled. When asked to return to New York a week later, Bradley found himself meeting with only two trustees, whom he discovered had been presented with his plan but under Noble's name. Bradley persisted and was appointed in October 1925 at the JGS as education director, his duties to begin the following March. Noble continually delayed giving him a contract, and Bradley found the atmosphere at the Foundation inhospitable.

On October 15, 1925, the Foundation unveiled a bronze tablet honoring Augustus Juilliard. The large tablet with a bas-relief of Juilliard was the work of Chester Beach, a member of the National Academy. It was placed first at the Vanderbilt building, later in the 130 Claremont Avenue entrance way, then stored from 1969 until 1993, when it was placed on the street level of the School at Lincoln Center. The tablet reads: "Augustus D. Juilliard 1836–1919 / A citizen of New York distinguished in commerce and charity whose devotion to the finer things in human life found expression in his magnanimous gift to the cause of music in America which established the Juilliard Musical Foundation A. D. 1920." Frederick A. Juilliard performed the ceremony, at which both Noble and Olin Downes spoke.

Also in October 1925, the Foundation exhibited American paintings, chosen from those seen in New York the previous season by artists such as George Inness, Alden Weir, George de Forest, Brush and Murphy, Albert Ryder, George Luks, Abbott Thayer, Jerome Meyer, and Theodore Robinson.[73] Remembering Noble's interest in collecting art and his pro-America stance, the exhibition is understandable. Observers may have wondered nevertheless when the public concerts specified in Juilliard's will would occur.

Negotiations between the IMA and the JGS were held in secret. Damrosch told of their affiliation tersely: "Doctor Eugene Noble of the

Juilliard Foundation had been invited to attend the meeting of the Executive Committee held on October 22, 1925, at which Mr. Felix M. Warburg presided." Noble read a memorandum, which had been tentatively agreed upon and set forth the terms—principally that the JMF would give a new, combined school a quarter of a million dollars every year. The motion to adopt was unanimously carried. Damrosch summarized the reasoning that guided the IMA board:

> When . . . three highly endowed schools of music entered the field it
> was felt that the Institute could not hope to compete with these richly
> endowed institutions who would be in a position to secure all the best
> teaching talent of Europe and America. Although both the Curtis
> School in Philadelphia and the Eastman School in Rochester were
> practically financially independent they were not looked upon as es-
> sential competitors, where the so-called Graduate School established
> by the Juilliard Foundation paralleled the higher grades of our Artists'
> Courses. . . . Doctor Noble had visited the Institute a number of times
> and had attended its recitals and concerts and no doubt formed the
> opinion that an established conservatory would provide the best
> means to meet the requirements of the Juilliard School.[74]

The merger was accomplished over Damrosch's strenuous objections, but Loeb had quietly agreed to it and still managed to keep Damrosch as a friend.

Affiliation had already begun in January 1926. At a special meeting in October the IMA board voted out fifteen of its twenty members, everyone except Paul M. Warburg, Felix Warburg, Edwin T. Rice, Felix E. Kahn, and John L. Wilkie. James Loeb and Frank Damrosch were among those asked to resign. It was voted to turn over all real and personal property of the IMA, worth $716,333.16, to the JMF.

The "Damrosch School," now unable to retain its autonomy as James Loeb had originally wanted, ceased to function as it had for twenty-one years. The agreement was entered into with the consideration of one dollar given by each party to the other party. One conciliatory gesture the Foundation allowed was that money arising from transfers be held by the IMA in a special fund to be known as the "Betty Loeb Fund." Of that fund, $500,000 was to be held for the Damrosches' lifetimes, from which Damrosch's pension was paid. After their deaths the money would be used for scholarships and IMA faculty pensions. For its part, the JMF agreed to pay annually $250,000 to the newly named Juilliard School of Music. Six of the nine board members would be selected by the Foundation, and three would be selected from the IMA. Neither Loeb nor Damrosch would serve on this board.

Four days after the IMA board meeting, forty-nine Juilliard fellow-ships were announced.[75] Recipients were chosen from a smaller field of 230 students and hailed from a more limited geographical region than the previous winners. Only half the states were represented, as opposed to all but two states the previous year; a full 40 percent of the winners were from New York. Vittorio Giannini, who later founded the North Carolina School of the Arts, and Viola Peters, who was a vocal coach at Juilliard until 1995, both won fellowships in piano during this round of examinations.[76]

The advisory committee that selected these winners was evidently overruled in certain instances. The committee had changed and now included music patrons. Money gave them more clout than musicians, and they were unafraid of bad publicity. In the fall of 1925 the five com-mittee members were Janet Schenck, Lizzie (Lillie) P. Bliss, Susan P. Dakin, Ernest Schelling, and Richard Aldrich. Janet Schenck (1883–1976) founded and directed the Manhattan School of Music from 1917 to 1956 and headed Manhattan's piano department. Bliss (1869–1931) was an accomplished pianist and a philanthropist who in 1929 founded the Museum of Modern Art, to which she donated her important col-lection of Impressionist paintings. Bliss was unmarried, the patroness of the Kneisel Quartette, and her wealthy father was secretary of the interior under McKinley. Dakin (formerly married to Christian A. Herter) had for many years established her home as a center for music. She and Bliss had underwritten the first year of the Manhattan School's existence. Ernest Schelling (1876–1939), pianist, composer, and conduc-tor of the New York Philharmonic's young people's concerts, had joined the JGS piano faculty. *New York Times* critic Richard Aldrich (1863–1937) was esteemed almost as highly as the IMA's William J. Henderson. Fi-nally, a group was powerful enough to confront Noble.

In a sensational move in November 1925 this examining committee resigned en bloc. Their protest over Noble's interference with their decisions made the front page of the *New York Times*.[77] Such was the unintended consequence of co-opting the press: Aldrich was the direct pipeline from the committee to the newspapers.

Noble dissembled: "There is nothing to the report that the commit-tee resigned. They were appointed for a year and were not reappointed." This elicited a letter to the *Times* two days later from the committee but likely written by Bliss. The committee said that they were unaware their appointments were only for a year; further, they had never been thanked for their services or given a farewell acknowledgment. They had learned about their supposedly fixed terms of office from the *Times* report. The advisory committee quoted *Alice in Wonderland:* In the trial scene Alice had said to the King of Hearts, "That's not a regular rule; you invented it just now." The committee insisted that it had resigned.[78]

Their reasons for resignation were widely conveyed in the musical press. "We have found our advice in many important instances not to have been followed," the group maintained. "Reasons have been given by the Secretary for not following our suggestions which we have found difficulty in accepting. Numerous things of grave importance have been done in the conduct of the school and have not been referred to us, things which properly might have caused our dissent." In an attack on Noble, they said, "We believe that the musical administration of a school of such magnitude as the Juilliard Foundation should be in the hands of someone well qualified by training, knowledge and experience in the art of music."[79]

Behind closed doors, the public resignation did have its effect on the Foundation's board. Involved with negotiations with the IMA, the board now found even more reason to align itself with an institution of high repute. Three of the nine directors on the new Juilliard School board, Paul Warburg, Paul Cravath, and John L. Wilkie, were trustees of the IMA, but Damrosch "had a sort of resentment against them for bringing about the merger with the Graduate School."[80]

On January 16, 1926, the date of the Betty Loeb memorial concerts and the twenty-first anniversary of the IMA, a testimonial dinner was given for Damrosch. Only he and his wife knew of the agreement, which was to be made public six days later and would forever alter the school he had founded. At the dinner the entire Damrosch family was present, as were the Loebs (minus, as always, James). Hetty Damrosch was given an ovation, and Frank Damrosch lauded the faculty, "those people who could make the stones speak and the woods sing—they are the ones to whom all credit is due."[81] He spoke of his lifelong dedication to music and closed by telling the assembled group "that [his] head buzzed with future plans; he hoped he could carry out some of them before he had to leave his bronze effigy to supervise the school."[82] A bronze bust of Damrosch by Malvina Hoffman had been presented by the board. It now sits in the library's reference room. In 1930 the trustees presented the school with Damrosch's portrait, painted by Frederick Beaumont and unveiled on October 22, 1929, Leopold Damrosch's birthday. It now hangs in the trustees' room.

On the morning Frank Damrosch was to announce the merger to students, he asked his secretary, Helen Frank, if she thought some would take it hard. She replied that many would grieve over it. "Then we must act," he said cheerfully, "as if we were all very happy about it."[83] Damrosch himself was not cheerful. To his successor, "He made no secret of his disappointment that the Institute should not continue as a separate institution all his life."[84] Students were upset over the loss of independence of their school and the fact that their highly respected director would no longer be the final authority. Damrosch continued to put a good face on the situation.

The January announcement made public the fact that the JMF board had completely regrouped, although it had not rid itself of the odious Noble. A front-page *Times* story announced, "Juilliard Trustees Plan Music Centre; Merger with School Founded by James Loeb First Step in Education Program." The residue from the advisory committee's action two months earlier stained the story: The *Times* said the committee had resigned because they "were dissatisfied with the failure to take energetic action to carry out the wishes of the founder." Noble denied that the resignations had anything to do with the merger. The JGS statement read: "After a careful survey of the entire field of music education in the United States the Juilliard Musical Foundation reached the conclusion that the Institute of Musical Art occupied a leading and distinctive position among the schools of music in this country, strongly established, well conducted, and a demonstrated success." In yet another projected plan by the Foundation, the two schools would be connected with two others, one for training teachers and supervisors and one for training children. Although "negotiations are pending with an established educational institution to cooperate in this," the plan never came to fruition aside from the IMA's Columbia Teachers College affiliation.[85]

Changes were destined for the IMA as well. After an overnight horseback ride into the Grand Canyon during the summer of 1925, Damrosch had suffered a heart attack. Although he recovered, the question of who would succeed him loomed. Other major changes also occurred to mark the end of an era and the necessity of rebuilding the violin department. Percy Goetschius had retired. Franz Kneisel's sudden death at the age of sixty in March of 1926 rocked the IMA. Kneisel's funeral was held at the IMA and a second one took place in Boston. Kneisel Quartette violist Louis Svecenski died in June.

Damrosch hired the eighty-year-old and increasingly deaf Leopold Auer (1845–1930) to teach master classes for two hours on Mondays and Thursdays. Auer told Joseph Fuchs ruefully, "Kneisel's gone and I'm still here." Auer had taught for forty-nine years at the St. Petersburg Conservatory and had been the original dedicatee of Tchaikowsky's Violin Concerto. His students had included Mischa Elman, Jascha Heifetz, and Efrem Zimbalist. Auer broadened students' horizons, made them read books, and guided their careers and behavior. Boris Schwarz writes of him:

Though he valued talent, he also demanded punctual attendance, intelligent work habits, and attention to detail. He hated absenteeism. He demanded discipline of behavior and appearance; no sloppiness was tolerated. He even told them when to speak and when not to. "Remember, you are a nitwit: don't talk, just play," he admonished one of his gifted but simple-minded students. He insisted that his students learn a foreign language if an international career was in the offing. . . . To say that his word was law is an understatement; a law can be broken, but the professor could not be contradicted. Auer was stern, severe, even harsh. . . . A lesson was like a ritual, as demanding as a concert performance.[86]

In 1928 Auer joined the Curtis Institute as well. Any eight IMA students who had advanced on a piece were sent to him for half an hour a week. Auer taught in this master class fashion at the IMA until his death in 1930, when he was replaced by Louis Persinger.

The violin faculty included Carlos Hasselbrink, concertmaster of the New York Symphony Orchestra and the Metropolitan Opera Orchestra, who taught violin from 1906 to 1932. William Kroll, a Kneisel pupil, began teaching in 1919. One of Auer's associates at the St. Petersburg Conservatory, Sergei Korgueff, turned up in New York and taught at the IMA from 1927 until his death in 1933. Elizabeth Strauss, a pupil of Leschetizky, taught piano from 1908 to 1932. Indeed, most faculty members were women.

Even the announcement of the merger—about which nothing appeared to happen for another year—did not protect the JMF from criticism. In September 1926, publisher and editor Pierre V. R. Key (1872–1945) attacked Noble in a series of six front-page articles in his New York weekly magazine, the *Musical Digest*. Key, who had already published books on John McCormack and Enrico Caruso and who later broadcast "World in Music" on Friday nights, both reinaugurated and sustained a drumbeat of criticism.[87] The *Musical Digest*, which Key had established in 1919, reached an audience of twenty thousand, "the largest circulation amongst discriminating readers any music periodical commands."[88] Key referred to the Foundation's "limited accomplishments" and charged that it was under the "absolute control of the executive secretary," who had "an autocratic and patronizing attitude." Key voiced "an expressed widespread surprise in the choice of the executive secretary, who was a stranger in musical circles throughout the land, and, so far as is known, had no activity in the field of music." His comments were reported the next day in the *New York Times*.[89]

Key discovered that the Foundation had no charter. In his October 5, 1926, issue he printed a facsimile of a letter from the secretary of state for New York that stated, "We have no record of a corporation, foreign or domestic, under the name Juilliard Musical Foundation."[90] That revelation produced immediate results: The JMF's board scurried to obtain a charter for the new entity, the Juilliard School of Music. (There was no charter for the Juilliard Graduate School either.) The board obtained a provisional charter dated October 28, 1926. John Erskine tells the story of its rushed acquisition (omitting the reason it was obtained):

> When the Juilliard . . . School was organized as an educational institution, it was necessary to have a charter. There were general laws covering the organization of all schools and educational groups, and individual charters were frowned upon by the authorities. Aware of this and fearing that there might be difficulty in obtaining a separate charter, Mr. Perry made inquiries among Albany friends. They admitted it would be difficult for Juilliard to obtain a charter. However, because of the exceptional merit of the idea back of the school, a proposed charter was eventually passed by both houses of the Legislature.
>
> When the final granting of the charter reached the desk of Al Smith, then Governor of the state of New York [and a presidential candidate], Mr. Perry paid him a visit. Present at the meeting was Judge Parsons, the Governor's legal advisor.
>
> Picking up the Juilliard documents the Governor shoved his derby hat back on his head, shifted his big black cigar, and said to Parsons, "How about this, Judge?"
>
> Parsons examined the documents. "This is asking a special charter for a matter that is already covered by the general laws, Governor."
>
> Al Smith said, "Let me see those papers, Judge."
>
> After studying them he turned to Mr. Perry. "Who was this fellow Juilliard?"
>
> "He was a woolen merchant," said Mr. Perry.
>
> "Where was his place of business?"
>
> "On Worth Street."
>
> The Governor flipped back the papers. "Give me my pen. My uncle was a truckman for that man Juilliard. He always said there was not a squarer guy in the business."
>
> After the bill was signed Mr. Perry asked the governor if he might have the pen he had used. Al Smith gave it to him. It is now a treasured possession of the Juilliard School.[91]

The charter stated that the school is open to "students of both sexes with no discrimination because of creed, race or color." It did not specify that students must be American. An absolute charter replaced the provisional one on September 18, 1930.

Another of the JMF's board, Charles A. Peabody, resigned for reasons unknown some months before the first *Musical Digest* article.[92] The trustees remaining were George Davison, James N. Jarvie, William C. Potter, and Frederick Juilliard. On October 3 the *Times* reiterated the second of Key's critical articles.[93] Pierre Key had his own press, and he turned up the heat on the board and Noble.

Key called Noble's policies and behavior into question and invited comment from readers, which he then published. In his October 5, 1926, issue, he published a list of fifty-seven inquiries directed at Noble and also handed the inquiries to each trustee; they did not respond. Question number seven was, "What had been Dr. Noble's training and experience in music activities prior to his engagement as the Foundation's Executive Secretary?" Key pointed out that, departing from the usual practice of other foundations, the JMF had not issued an annual financial report. Quoting (although slightly abridging) the Juilliard will, Key asked, "Why has the Foundation never given any, even one, 'musical entertainment or concert or recital of a character appropriate for the general public in the musical arts?'"; "Why has the Foundation done nothing to aid the creative musician?"; and "How many fellowship students were dropped during the first year of the Graduate School for failing to equal the expectations held for them by the board of examiners?" Question seventeen was "What was your authority for countermanding the specific request made by Mr. Juilliard in his will that fellowship students be permitted to study in Europe?" Number forty-eight asked, "You are quoted by an individual as having said, orally; 'I know there is much criticism going on of the Foundation, but we have money and can afford to ignore criticism.' Do you recall ever having made such a statement, in substance?" Key, however, did not confront Noble on the specious requirement that Juilliard students be American citizens.[94]

Discussing Kenneth Bradley's ineffectiveness as education director in the face of Noble's iron-handed authority, Key pointed out that Henry Bellamann had resigned around the time that Bradley took office (March 1926). Key forced Bradley to admit that to reverse the audition decisions of the board of examiners "would be ethically wrong."[95] He asked Bradley for such basics as a school catalog, a list of faculty, a set of rules and regulations, or a curriculum. The embarrassed education director was unable to supply any of these in the School's third year.

The next two issues of the *Musical Digest* recorded overwhelming support from around the country for Key's attack on the Foundation and Noble. For example, Harold L. Butler, president of the Music Teacher's National Association and director of the Department of Music at Syracuse University, defended the students against Noble's arbitrary policies:

The plans of the management have been changed practically every year since inception of the Foundation. For example: Two years ago the Foundation sent an examiner to many of the recognized schools of music. Examinations were given to advanced students and a number of scholarships awarded. The next year the schools were notified that the scholarships would be discontinued unless the students who had received them presented themselves at stated places for re-examination. For many students this was an impossibility. The result was a discontinuation of scholarships to a number of students already approved by the Foundation's examiner.[96]

Fritz Reiner, then conductor of the Cincinnati Symphony Orchestra, was incredulous: "It seems almost unbelievable that the greatest part of a donation which, so far as I am aware, is the most generous history knows, has been inoperative." The dean of the University of Kansas commented: "After some five years of waiting, there seems to be a very general feeling among musicians that something is radically wrong." The president of the American Conservatory of Music, in Chicago, wrote, "That there has been keen disappointment in musical circles is undeniable," and the music editor of the *Minneapolis Tribune* observed that the Foundation's directors "have shown little inclination to move out of the most conservative administrative rut."[97]

Several writers expressed confidence in Bradley, but those who had dealt with Noble were unstinting in their condemnation. A musician from Kansas observed, "The man at the head of the Juilliard Foundation as executive secretary, unduly inflated with his imaginary importance, seemed to resent questions coming from people truly and unselfishly interested, and to draw a cloak of repulsion, aloofness, and silence about himself and his administration of the trust fund. This attitude toward the public has created a feeling of suspicion, mistrust, and resentment."[98]

Once Key opened a fissure, the JMF cracked rapidly under the weight of relentless bad publicity, public ill-will, and the arrogance of Eugene Noble, who thought money could protect him from the consequences of his highhandedness. In November 1926 the board of the JMF was reconstituted, with nine members, three each from the JMF, the IMA, and the general public. Paul Cravath, Paul Warburg, and John L. Wilkie were those associated with the IMA; Eugene Noble, and two close friends of Augustus Juilliard—James N. Jarvie and John Morris Perry—represented the JMF; and Arthur M. Cox, Allen Wardwell, and John Erskine, who had been recommended to them by pianist Ernest Hutcheson of their faculty, represented general musical interests. Wardwell (1873–1953) was an attorney and humanitarian who had in

1923 established a fund to assist newly arrived college-age Russians in the United States. Because of his travels to Russia he had "long been known as the Bolshevik of Wall Street."[99] (In 1950 the boards of both the JMF and the Juilliard School of Music still included Erskine, Perry, and Wardwell.)

Two of the three major players in this drama were not invited to join the board. Conspicuously and significantly absent were Frank Damrosch and Frederick Juilliard. It is unclear whether Juilliard had retired willingly or was forced out. Erskine claimed that Noble was still included in order to placate him after Erskine was chosen for the board and later as its president. But Noble still represented Frederick Juilliard's interests; both resisted giving up direct control of the money. The *New York Times* reported, "Some of the [nine] incorporators are of the opinion that they are to 'administer' the funds left under the will of the late Augustus D. Juilliard to finance the school of music. But Dr. Eugene A. Noble, also an incorporator, does not share that understanding."[100]

A week later Noble was put further on the defensive when the *Times* again picked up criticism from elsewhere. Charles Meltzer resurfaced and reinstituted his criticism of the Foundation. In an article in *The Outlook*, Meltzer had called the $1,000 awards "foolish scholarships," especially when compared with those in Europe. In France, students received musical educational grants for three, four, or five years, and the Prix de Rome displayed an exemplary case of support for composers. Meltzer called the Foundation "niggardly" in its support of young musicians.[101]

In December 1926 Bradley resigned from the JGS in protest, news that caused a sensation similar to the resignations of the advisory committee the previous year. Frustrated because Frederick Juilliard invested the authority of the trustees in the secretary of the Foundation (the article in the *Musical Digest* quoted Juilliard's letter to that effect), Bradley blew the whistle.[102] He called the school "chaotic," charged Noble with discrimination against worthy students on religious grounds, and maintained that only 132 of the 165 students were receiving instruction. Despite "petty humiliations," Bradley had "hung on" for the sake of music. He told the *New York Times*, "I was told whom I must not get in touch with. I was first warned that I must not get in touch with the Damrosch crowd. Then I was instructed not to get into touch with a crowd that was anti-Damrosch. That about took in all Manhattan."[103]

Bradley had found records showing that some students who had been unanimously accepted by the examining board had been denied admission, whereas others were given fellowships but were not approved by the board.[104] He reported that the former Methodist minister had said only Protestant Gentiles were welcomed. One Catholic female pianist had been unanimously approved by the judges and turned down by the Foundation. "I asked Dr. Noble who decided on these cases. He said he did."[105]

Bradley discovered that some faculty had no written contracts, others had received contracts as late as February, and still others were teaching on verbal agreements. One told Bradley that he was paid $100 an hour and thought it an outrage to be paid five times the necessary amount. Noble refused to delegate authority to Bradley, who said, "He even wrote of giving me authority, but I wrote him in July [1926] that the freedom and authority which he suggested was like giving a man a hammer and one nail and telling him to finish, according to his own judgment, the Cathedral of St. John the Divine."[106]

Bradley's most serious charge concerned the mismanagement of the money. Noble had lied to him about where the books were—repeatedly saying they were located at what turned out to be a mythical downtown office—and assured Bradley that he did not have to worry about such things. He later learned that Noble's secretary, the woman who had informed Bradley that only Protestant Gentile help was desired in the office, was the only person keeping the books of the multi-million-dollar Foundation.

His many suggestions defeated, Bradley was forced to conclude that "there is not enough help in the Juilliard Foundation to conduct the smallest music school known to me in the United States. There are many obvious things that the Foundation could do with its vast resources to be of national benefit, and any further discussion of them is at this time useless. As long as Dr. Noble has anything to do with the activities I feel that chaotic and unwholesome conditions will prevail. I remember one day hearing him say that musicians were illogical and unsound in judgement; that, in fact, music seemed to breed a sort of degeneracy. I told him I couldn't agree."[107]

Noble treated Bradley's resignation just as he had the previous round of resignations. He lied, saying the position was being terminated anyway. By January 1927 Noble felt a need to respond to Key's charges, one of which was that $175,000 had been wasted. Noble denied that little had been done. He attacked his critics, arguing that they were unable to get the Foundation to pay for advertising in their musical journals—a reference to Pierre Key. To the question of whether he was paying rent to live on the sixth floor of the Foundation's mansion, Noble responded, "If the trustees do not object, why should anyone else do so?" Ignoring the inconsistency with his claim a month earlier that Bradley's position would be terminated, he announced, "We are now trying to obtain the services of a competent person as director of musical education."[108]

Key summed up the sad situation in an editorial:

> Together the Juilliard Musical Foundation and its Executive Secretary present a pathetic picture of gross ignorance of their duties and a contemptuous disregard for public opinion. They stand convicted, at the close of five years of activity, of moral failure adequately to perform their task. . . . The accomplishments of the Juilliard Graduate School to date are virtually nothing, yet the cost has mounted into the hundreds of thousands of dollars. . . . If the situation were not so tragic it would be humorous, for never was a project more utterly bungled than this one—designed by a great-hearted citizen to perform a vast public good.[109]

But the primary victims of Noble's administration were the fewer than 150 students. Urgently in need of money for lessons, they dared not publicly criticize the all-powerful administrator. Bradley cited a tragic case resulting in one student's apparent suicide: The anomaly of having $1,000 worth of lessons but no money to help support his desperately poor mother and two siblings was too much for the boy.[110]

Criticism and examination of the Foundation came from yet a third source and on a third level. Another person had remembered the Juilliard will and reminded the trustees that they were supposed to have chosen two additional members rather than one. And there was more public criticism over the Foundation's failure to apply its funds to greater advantage.

Public and private criticism of Noble led the JMF once again to regroup. The Foundation's board scoured "the country seeking for the one man preordained to lavish upon America the boons of the Juilliard beneficence, through the office of his enlightened judgement," as one account sarcastically put it.[111] In May 1927 the new nine-member board selected its own John Erskine to head a three-man committee—Allen Wardwell, Paul Warburg, and John Perry (one each from the IMA, Juilliard, and the public)—to direct the work of the Foundation. In an ironic twist the announcement said that Noble's "term expires this summer."[112] After seven years, Eugene Noble would finally be replaced.

In July 1927 Noble tried vainly to contradict this reality by calling a press conference the day before his replacement would be announced. He refused to affirm or deny that pianist Ernest Hutcheson would be named executive head. Consistent to the end, Noble was evasive and blamed the criticism on "personal jealousy and disappointments." The *New York Times* paraphrased him as saying, "That many requests for financial aid by applicants were so ridiculous and unjustified that they could not be considered. For these reasons, Dr. Noble declared the Foundation had been called 'niggardly' and 'stingy' in its attitude toward many aspirants."[113]

The next day John Erskine officially announced that Ernest Hutcheson would succeed Noble. The statement declared that "a thorough reorganization of the Foundation took place last winter following repeated expressions of dissatisfaction by musicians, members of the Foundation's Advisory Committee and others who felt that the Foundation was falling short of the expectations of the late Augustus D. Juilliard," the *New York Times* reported.[114] Erskine declined to discuss Noble publicly beyond saying that he would continue to occupy the position of secretary.

But the public relations damage had been done. In seven years of highhanded treatment of musicians, students, and the press, Noble seriously hurt the reputation of the name Juilliard at its delicate newborn state. Comparing the size and history of the JGS and the IMA, observers ridiculed the Foundation, which, unable to found a good school, had bought a school—one it might destroy.

Even though Damrosch was the obvious and logical choice, he was passed over as president of the new combined Juilliard School of Music. Noble, supported by Frederick Juilliard, would not countenance Damrosch's assuming that position. The new board had trouble, however, finding a president: Two nominees turned it down. Possibly they were straw men nominated by Erskine, who perhaps knew they would not accept. One was William Allen Neilson, longtime president of Smith College, who felt he could not leave Smith. The same reasons deterred the second candidate, the musical Thomas Stockham Baker, president of Carnegie Technological Institute.[115]

Pressure increased to name a president of the new school. Noble still wanted the job. The board delayed making a final decision by asking Erskine to head the executive committee of three to run the school for 1927 and 1928. Finally, in March of 1928, the trustees selected their president. By choosing John Erskine they had not scoured the country, and as he had previously done when he accepted the directorship of the board, Erskine immediately asked for a leave of absence.

Meanwhile, Noble's influence waned. He continued to live at 49 East 52nd Street, an ever-present irritant to Erskine. In 1930, nine months after the death of his wife, Noble, sixty-five, married Therese K. Lownes, a wealthy, widowed, philanthropist from Providence. He finally retired from the JMF board in 1937, due, he claimed, to poor health. In truth, he was forced off the board because his benefactor Frederick

Juilliard had died that year. Noble moved to Reno, Nevada, and died in 1948 at age eighty-three. His replacement Erskine was meanwhile receiving letters of congratulations. He prized one the most:

> My dear Professor Erskine:
>
> I must tell you how glad I was to hear from Paul Warburg that you had consented to accept the presidency of the Juilliard School. As you can imagine, I had followed with eager interest all the developments that led to the adoption of the Institute of Musical Art, and was kept informed of the progress made in the often difficult negotiations.
>
> Even though I knew nothing about your eminent qualifications for the office you have now accepted, your [book] "Adam and Eve" would prove to me how deep is your insight into human nature. James Loeb

"This was the man who founded the Loeb Classical Library," Erskine wrote, clearly impressed. "The Hellenic studies [which Erskine had used to research his novels with mythological characters] had been a basis for our friendship. He happened to be a benefactor of the Institute of Musical Art and a partner in the banking firm of Kuhn, Loeb and Company. He was also a scholar."[116]

However much IMA students might wish otherwise, Erskine and the Juilliard Graduate School were the reality. The students and the IMA itself were able to deny that reality until 1931, when their physical plant was invaded by Juilliard's building plans. Their magazine *The Baton* ignored Juilliard, Hutcheson, and Erskine until construction began. Such was the resistance to the merger, partly expressed by the weight of inertia, that the IMA continued to grant degrees, in its own name and with its own Greek seal, for the next twenty years.

In his published history of the IMA in 1936 Damrosch took his leave:

> The school now enters upon a new era as a part of the great Juilliard School of Music which is backed by an endowment which should make it possible to carry out any and every plan leading to better and higher music education. I therefore resign the leadership which was my sole care, thought and objective for thirty years into the hands of able men who will, I hope and believe, carry on this work in such a way as to make this school as truly national institution by virtue of its service to the needs of the genius of music which lives in America.[117]

It was said of the IMA that "no American cultural institution of the period was so completely the creation of one individual."[118] If that is true, then it is equally true that inasmuch as its better part was created by one individual and was not the product of a self-interested board and administrative mismanagement, the Juilliard School of Music was the child of Frank Damrosch.

4

The Juilliard School of Music:

ERNEST HUTCHESON
& JOHN ERSKINE

THE CHANGES WROUGHT by the merger of the Juilliard Graduate School and the Institute of Musical Art were urged by the JGS and resisted by the IMA. Two men were given authority over Damrosch. Ernest Hutcheson (1871–1951) was dean and John Erskine (1879–1951) was president, while Damrosch was given the title of dean of the IMA. Hutcheson, a member of the JGS faculty, had brought his student, the best-selling author Erskine, to the attention of the JMF board. Erskine's charm and erudition impressed them and sped his rise to the positions of chair of the Juilliard Musical Foundation and president of the Juilliard School of Music.

Noble's successor, pianist Ernest Hutcheson, was born in Melbourne, Australia, the son of a blacksmith.[1] A child prodigy, he had absolute pitch and had studied with Max Vogrich. He began concertizing at age five and at fourteen went to study with Carl Reinecke and Salomon Jadassohn at the Leipzig Conservatory; he was graduated at nineteen in 1890. The next year he moved to Weimar to study piano with Bernhard Stavenhagen in order to absorb the Liszt tradition. There he met the Baroness Irmgart Senfft von Pilsach, an exceptionally talented pianist who came from a musical family. Her family opposed their marriage, so on his twenty-eighth birthday the couple eloped to London.

Having chosen which pianist of the pair to promote, the Hutchesons moved to Berlin, where he studied and taught piano. "He won renown not only as a pianist, composer, and conductor, but also as a man of exceptional general culture and learning."[2] Among the couple's associates were Paderewski, Busoni, and Harold Randolph, the director of the Peabody Conservatory. Hutcheson taught from 1900 to 1912 at Peabody, a school he thought the IMA resembled. His 1912 concert tour of Europe was critically acclaimed, and the couple returned to Germany, staying until the outbreak of war two years later. They had two sons, Arnold and Harold. In 1915 Hutcheson created a sensation in New York with his performance on a single program of three concertos: Liszt's E flat, Tchaikowsky's b-flat minor, and MacDowell's d minor.

Hutcheson helped reorganize the music school at Lake Chautauqua, New York, which flourished under his administration (1911–44). He insisted students at the six-week summer school agree to practice four hours daily as well as attend lectures, recitals, and opera performances. He also continued the tradition of virtuoso performers who composed. He wrote a symphony, a symphonic tone poem, a piano concerto, a two-piano concerto (played by Stokowski in 1926), and a violin concerto.

Ernest Hutcheson and John Erskine, ca. 1928, inside the Vanderbilt building.
(Anna Crouse)

Later in his life he wrote several books: *A Musical Guide to the Richard Wagner* Ring of the Nibelung, *A Guide to* Elektra, *Elements of Piano Technique*, and his successful magnum opus, *The Literature of the Piano.*[3] At the age of seventy-five Hutcheson undertook the study of Greek.

By 1932 Hutcheson had more than a thousand pupils. He recorded their progress in his famous loose-leaf notebooks, with a separate page for each student. From these records he could determine exactly how much general and specific progress the pupil had made. Not all students necessarily understood. "Mrs. Hutcheson says that a new pupil once came to her in considerable distress, complaining that while she played for Mr. Hutcheson, he did nothing but sit at his desk and write. 'Ah,' replied Mrs. Hutcheson, 'but if you could have seen what he was writing!'"[4] Erskine, who felt Hutcheson was "from some points of view as good a teacher as I ever met in any subject," described Hutcheson's teaching:

> The pupil sat at one piano, Mr. Hutcheson beside him at another, but the second piano was not used in order to tell the pupil what he should try to express. Mr. Hutcheson would not touch his piano until his pupil had played the piece to the end. He would then suggest that what the pupil had been trying to say could be made clearer by a different approach. With a surprising clearness he would suggest the different approach, still without specific illustration at the keyboard. The object of the discussions was to arouse the pupil's imagination and to stimulate self-criticism. When the pupil began to understand what he himself wanted to say in the performance of a given piece, Mr. Hutcheson would often remark that the purpose now began to be clear, but it could be achieved by much simpler methods.
>
> At this point he would permit himself to illustrate on the keyboard. At the very end of the lesson his most characteristic comment might be something like this:
>
> "I would not play that passage the way you do, but I think your way of playing it is right for you, and I advise you not to change the interpretation."
>
> The chances would be that your curiosity was at once aroused to hear how he would play the passage, and if you asked him to do so he would demonstrate the contrast and explain the two interpretations, always managing somehow to rouse your appreciation not only of your own interpretation but of his.[5]

Hutcheson, like Damrosch, inspired devotion in others. He made fast friends, and they worked selflessly for him. Erskine wrote of his former piano teacher: "He was even more remarkable for his character than for his accomplishments. I once heard his wife, Irmgart, say that she never knew any human being who had so strong an ethical sense. This praise, however high, did Ernest less than full justice."[6] Students, including George Gershwin, called him "Mr. Hutchie." (Hutcheson invited Gershwin to Chautauqua in July 1925 so that he could compose in tranquillity.) The friendship between Hutcheson and Erskine had begun when Erskine came to lecture at Chautauqua several years before he began studying there in 1924. Another friend was Oscar Wagner (1893–1970), a former student (with, of course, an entry in the book) and sought-after accompanist who became Hutcheson's administrative assistant. Wagner looked after the details that would otherwise have interfered with Hutcheson's life as a concert pianist. He remained at the School until 1946. Irmgart Hutcheson, described by Erskine's daughter as "really a powerhouse," was an exceptionally good administrator and had an office at the School.[7] The three administrators and Irmgart were almost inseparable friends. Erskine lived in the penthouse of the building at 11 West 81st Street and the Hutchesons lived on the second floor; Oscar Wagner's apartment was just around the corner. The Hutchesons kept an open house on Sundays at tea time for friends and pupils and also held frequent musicales for students.

The preponderance of foreign-born artists working in the United States (and at both the JGS and the IMA) had presented a quandary to the chauvinistic JMF board. Adhering to the prevalent anti-Semitism, some on the board would have vetoed the choice of a Jewish musician to head the School, and that bias eliminated many artists. Hutcheson, although neither American-born nor a citizen, was the closest Protestant virtuoso who could be found; he was an Episcopalian. He filled the bill, especially by bringing for the first time a sense of artistic purpose to the JGS administration. It had not been easy, however, for Erskine to persuade Hutcheson to accept the post of dean. The Hutchesons felt that his temperament was as a teacher and an artist rather than as an executive. (Noble discouraged the board from offering Hutcheson the position.) Erskine wrote that he was chosen "not as an administrator, but as a moral force badly needed to improve the School's spirit."[8] He might also have said "image" after the damage done by Noble to the Juilliard reputation.

The obvious choice for dean was Irmgart Hutcheson, who combined musical skills with administrative ability, but she was overlooked. In a pamphlet issued by Juilliard and called *Why Study Abroad?* she pleaded for an end of cultural subservience to Europe. The subheadings of an article she published in *Musical America* spelled out her argument: "Urges cessation of undignified and untrue insistence on American inferiority—student who goes to Europe at a disadvantage today—tables have turned."[9]

Hutcheson took over Frank Damrosch's position as dean of the IMA in 1933 and Erskine's as president of the School in 1937. The primary reason the tactful Hutcheson hesitated to accept the dean's job was that he did not want to be put in a position of possibly disagreeing with his old friend Damrosch. Damrosch recalled that when Hutcheson became dean of the JGS and Damrosch dean of the IMA, "A lot of people grinned and said, 'Watch the dog fight.' Well, sometimes dogs don't fight. In this particular instance, I had such a high regard for Ernest Hutcheson as a man and a musician, that I could not find any cause for fighting, and we have not fought up to date."[10] One divisive issue concerned providing pensions for both teaching staffs. It was finally agreed that faculties at both the IMA and JGS should be treated equally on this point.

Fundamentally uninterested in administration, Hutcheson still found himself inheriting more and more responsibility. His duties as dean and his professional life kept him extremely busy. "One sees him in the lift with music under arm and a pupil in pursuit, bound for a rehearsal or a lesson," a student wrote.[11] He attended all auditions for JGS fellowships and listened to the regular examinations of fellowship-holders. In addition, he attended all the School's concerts and recitals.

Hutcheson's repute as a pianist was aided by the technology of radio. The first network broadcast of a symphony orchestra was in 1926, and the first sponsored one came in 1929. Between 1920 and 1929 the number of families with radio receivers grew from 60,000 to 10,250,000. Hutcheson was on the ground floor of that phenomenon. Rather than travel to perform, he merely crossed 52nd Street to a large studio on the twenty-second floor of the Columbia Broadcasting System at Madison Avenue. On Sunday evenings at 9:30 Hutcheson performed live for a half hour with station WABC's orchestra and its conductor Howard Barlow. Each broadcast had a one-hour rehearsal. Thanks to his extraordinary repertoire of twenty-five concerti, he was able to play one or two movements of a concerto for fifty consecutive broadcasts.

Of radio performance, he said, "Broadcasting interests me especially because of its extraordinary demand on the imagination. The unseen audience is a good instance of what I mean. The artist knows that he is playing to a vast audience comprising millions of persons. Well and good, but if he fails to realize that these millions are all listening in small groups of two or three or half a dozen people in small rooms he misses the point altogether."[12] Speaking philosophically of the art of music, Hutcheson remarked:

It seems strange to me that young pianists should ask if it was worth while for them to study. They probably want to know if I can guarantee them professional success—which no man can do. Art is always worth while. The joy of work, of development, irrespective of success, is keen. The study of music is a great pursuit, full of beauty and alive with intellectual as well as technical interest. It brings you into intimate contact with life and offers unusual personal freedom. As an art, there is none greater; as a study, none more fascinating.[13]

John Erskine, unlike Hutcheson, was not a professional musician. Like Solomon Loeb and Augustus Juilliard, Erskine's father was in the textile business, although a lesser figure—he owned a silk factory. He also sang in Leopold Damrosch's Oratorio Society in the 1880s. The second of five children, John Erskine began study of the piano under Carl Walter and later, as a Columbia University undergraduate, with Edward MacDowell, his primary musical influence. MacDowell encouraged Erskine somewhat, saying that he had no special talent at music but enough skill to make a good craftsman. (Erskine would later transform that defect into a virtue by extolling the value of the craftsman.) Erskine was also haunted by the knowledge of MacDowell's nervous disease, an awareness that might have discouraged him from music. In addition, his Scottish father discouraged him by arguing a familiar parental refrain: A man should pursue a more substantial occupation. When silk sashes went out of fashion, the elder Erskine lost all his money. Erskine was graduated Phi Beta Kappa from Columbia's English department in 1900 with literary prizes.

The next year he received his master's degree and in 1903 a Ph.D. That year he began teaching at Amherst. Columbia's president, Butler, hired him in 1909 to teach English, and he remained until 1927. His students included Mark Van Doren, Mortimer Adler, Alfred Knopf, and Clifton Fadiman. His popularity was such that students, who called him "Roaring Jack" Erskine, cut other classes to slip into his lectures, thus filling the largest hall on campus. He was known at Columbia as "a literary precisionist and a fanatic on syntax."[14]

Erskine held seven university degrees, the Cross of the Legion of Honor, and the Distinguished Service Medal. He was appointed by General John J. Pershing to organize and direct what was then the largest university in the world—the American University in Beaune, France—for two years after War I. His demonstrated executive ability influenced the JMF to hire him.

In 1919 Erskine returned to Columbia and worked on what was to become the central achievement of his academic career, the design of a "great books" program in higher education. The influence on other universities—notably the University of Chicago, Harvard, and Yale—contributed to the establishment of a canon of great books now the subject of debate. He stressed approaching works of art on their own terms, unencumbered by scholarship and criticism. Those who delved in the great books, Erskine said, would "free [them]selves from the prison of egotism" and take part "in the complete citizenship of mankind."[15] This agenda furthered the generalist in him as he viewed with alarm the increasing specialization of the twentieth century. Throughout the 1920s Erskine publicly urged that the university open its doors to all members of American society.

Erskine had given up the piano for twenty-six years, returning to it only in 1924 at the age of forty-five. After six months of practicing arpeggios, finger work, and Czerny studies, he recalled, "I went to my friend Ernest Hutcheson and told him I wanted to study again, expecting him to laugh at me. He did not, however, but took my proposition seriously. He began to straighten my technique and I became a willing pupil."[16] His experience playing the Schumann concerto before an audience liberated him as a writer: It gave him the courage to write his first novel.

The Private Life of Helen of Troy became the best-selling American novel of 1926. Erskine's readers numbered in the millions, and the book was translated into sixteen languages.[17] The success of this and subsequent novels relied on their humanizing and dramatizing of history and upon Erskine's ability to relate Greek mythology to middle-class Americans' lives. He translated classical plots into modern language, using a racy tone that combined sex, topical interest, and iconoclasm.[18] Relying on his strong suit as a raconteur, he wrote *Helen* entirely in dialogue, with no descriptive prose. Marketed to an audience "that wanted to combine culture and 'fun,'" it was an overnight success that thrust the forty-six-year-old academic into the limelight.[19] An adoring profile in the newly founded *New Yorker* noted, "At present [1927] the emancipated Dr. Erskine is sitting on top of the world, slightly dizzy with fame, royalties, and liberalism."[20] Erskine's philosophy as president of the JSM paralleled his great books idea: Music should be accessible and comprehensible to a broad audience. He was committed to its popularization and spoke and wrote on behalf of the amateur, adding radio appearances to his busy lecture schedule during the 1930s.

In an essay entitled "The Juilliard Policy in Operation Throughout the Country" Erskine outlined his national vision. "The policy of the Juilliard School of Music is, of course, to train first-rate talent for performance, but quite as much to lay the foundation for audiences everywhere in the country, and for musical careers which will decentralize the art of music."[21] He set up Juilliard Centers around the country to promote teamwork among musicians who operated in various communities. The Centers were initially established in Atlanta, Georgia, Nashville, Tennessee, and Harrisburg, Pennsylvania, and at Cornell College in Iowa, the State College of Agriculture in New Mexico, and the Toledo Museum of Art. The general supervisor was Oscar Wagner.

Erskine attempted to answer the pressing question, "Is there a career in music?" in a lengthy essay. Published as a pamphlet by the JMF and distributed free to libraries and schools, it was also written up in the musical press. To answer that question, he divided musical careers into two types: those like Franz Liszt's (that is, the careers of those who tour as virtuosos) and those like Bach's, whom Erskine lauded as a craftsman. Ever the generalist, he criticized the life of a touring artist, "racing from city to city over the face of the globe," and argued that too many musicians congregate in large cities, where, once a musician is ensconced, "it is at present almost impossible to blast him out of it."[22] He took composers to task because "they insist on rivaling the debris of former times." They would write symphonies, operas, and in other old forms while "absolutely refus[ing] to furnish music for the occasions in our life when the public demands it, or on such a scale as would be commensurate with our resources." Besides, too many pieces were being written: "What is to be gained by composing so much?"[23] He concluded with the manic, and unrealistic, idea that each state in the union establish an opera house, pay for it with taxes, and support local composers. Unlike Hutcheson, Erskine did not assert that music is a worthwhile pursuit in and of itself.

Many Juilliard teachers—not to mention the students to whom the essay was addressed—could not agree with the implied suggestion to lower their standards and ambitions. Their idea of a professional musician was profoundly at odds with that of their president. Indeed, Erskine's generalist attitude was not shared by his peer Josef Hofmann, director of the Curtis Institute. When Erskine invited him to join him on the board that distributed Carnegie Corporation grants for civic or communal music, Hofmann refused, saying that the business of a music school was to train performing artists rather than worry about the needs of the general public. "Our points of view were diametrically opposed," Erskine wrote.[24]

Erskine possessed a quick wit, erudition, and charm. He used up-to-date phrases such as "swell" and "whale" (as in "a whale of an orchestra"). He also poked fun of himself: "Everyone tells me I should exercise, so I always walk downstairs!" He suffered violent mood swings, however, and contemplated suicide before resigning from the presidency of the combined schools. Like the board who hired him, he was both a

Republican and a Protestant. He harbored an unrealized ambition to be made U.S. ambassador to France. In one of his four autobiographies he complains that "we still indulge in race and color prejudice," yet he never discussed prejudices against women.[25] On the contrary, he was foolish enough to immortalize his misogyny in 1936 in *The Influence of Women—and Its Cure.*[26] In that vitriolic diatribe against women having any say in society, Erskine wrote that he agreed with Hitler: Women should be confined to cooking and raising children.

It is perhaps not surprising that Erskine had more personal difficulties with women than any other president of Juilliard. He was the only one to divorce. Erskine married Pauline Ives in 1910 but carried on a lengthy affair beginning in the year of his success, 1926, with the writer Adelene Pychon. In France he encouraged an infatuation by the wife of a former student, Anaïs Nin, who documented her feelings about Erskine and his novels in her diary.[27] He met another writer, Helen Worden, in 1931 and was openly involved with her during his tenure at Juilliard. After obtaining a divorce from Pauline in 1945, he married Worden. Erskine's son Graham was an architect. His daughter Anna married the playwright Russel Crouse, who worked with Howard Lindsay. Their daughter, Lindsay Crouse, became an actress who married and divorced the playwright David Mamet. Hutcheson hired his son, Harold, and Erskine hired his sister, Rhoda, to teach literature at Juilliard.[28]

George Martin has summarized the relationship between Erskine and Damrosch: "The two were men of quite different character, and Erskine, who made every effort to be tactful, unfortunately was the sort of man whom Frank instinctively disliked. Erskine's love of literature and music was genuine and he soon proved himself a competent administrator, but he was also pretentious, self-advertising and very naïve in his belief that the attention paid to him was owing to personal achievements rather than to the money he controlled."[29] The number of concert engagements that the amateur now received because of his position as head of the JMF was a source of envy to students; the pianists at the School could play better than their president.

Concert reviews were often muted, as might be expected of one whose power derived from control of so much money earmarked for music. When he played the MacDowell concerto, for example, reviewers complimented him on his choice of piece. Of Erskine's first professional appearance in New York, playing with the Musical Art Quartet Brahms's Piano Quintet in f minor, Opus 34, one reviewer wrote: "Mr. Erskine is a careful and fairly adroit pianist and he quite did his share in the wholly admirable performance of Brahms's early and Schumannesque orgy of romanticism."[30] Not all critics were so circumspect. The *New York World* wrote of the same performance:

> For the first time in its career, a number played by the Musical Art Quartet assumed an amateur cast . . . and the decline of standard was due entirely to the presence of Prof. John Erskine at the keyboard instrument. Among musicians Prof. Erskine is admired as a great novelist, and among novelists he is held in awe as a great pianist. . . . With enough fame and power to divide among several men, Prof. Erskine apparently suffers from a form of narcissism, which compels him to exhibit himself in public as a performer upon the instrument of Hofmann and Gieseking. . . . He gave every sign of enjoying himself hugely, but the delight was not shared by his auditors. Like mallets the thudding, unpracticed fingers beat upon the keys, producing tones so harsh and unmusical that one looked twice at the program to make sure the instrument was a Steinway. Worse still, his sense of time was at variance with that of the other players so that with the beginning of many a measure he gave an impression of just arriving breathless in the nick of time, occasionally he missed the train, dropping parcels of notes on the way.[31]

Negative reviews apparently did little to damage Erskine's serenity or deter him from accepting the many offers to perform. Students at both schools cringed over their president embarrassing the School in this manner. IMA students were already uneasy about a new president and were reminded of his peers at similar institutions: Josef Hofmann, a pianist; the composers Howard Hanson of the Eastman School or George W. Chadwick of the New England Conservatory; or the pianist and violinist Clara and David Mannes, Damrosch's sister and brother-in-law, of the Mannes School of Music. The students viewed Erskine as an outsider to the art of music.

In private, one composer spoke out against the JMF. Carl Ruggles, with his usual dismissal of anything not avant-garde, complained bitterly about the distribution of the Juilliard money and the people controlling it: "Juilliard, leaving his millions to music and they spend it all teaching good-for-nothing fiddlers and pianists. Nothing for the composer. That fathead of a John Erskine sitting at the head of it, and Ernest Hutcheson, emasculated moron."[32]

The Musical Art Quartet occupied the reverse pole from Erskine, who, although he could not play well, was indisputably charming. The quartet (Sascha Jacobsen, Paul Bernard, Louis Kaufman, and Marie Roemaet-Rosanoff), a successor to the Kneisel Quartette and a predecessor to the Juilliard String Quartet, had its own problems, but they were not musical. One of their patrons, Paul Warburg, summed up the situation:

[They] are, in my opinion, the outstanding American quartet at this time. While, as players, they are admirable, they are very trying as individuals. They are lacking in human qualities and particularly in grace, which has made it impossible for them to endear themselves to a larger circle of people who would be willing to back them financially. They are most unbusinesslike and whoever has tried to manage their affairs has been disappointed, because they have not given the cooperation in that regard which intelligent people should be able to give.[33]

In 1937 the quartet began playing on four Stradivari instruments Felix Warburg bought for their use. The School had funded them at the rate of $20,000 a year from 1926 through 1930. By 1947 the quartet had disbanded.

∾

The prosperity of the 1920s only appeared permanent. Before the stock market crash in 1929, only 2.3 percent of American families had incomes of more than $10,000 a year; fully 71 percent had incomes of less than $2,500. Overproduction and underconsumption had become rife in America by 1929. During the course of the stock market crash of October and November, $30 billion in paper values vanished into thin air, an amount larger than the national debt.

Young people and women were among those worst hit by the ensuing depression. In early 1933 one out of every four Americans in the labor force was jobless, and a disproportionate number of these were student-age. What few jobs there were required experience, and employers were more willing to give jobs to married men than to single men or to women. The caliber of positions open to married women also declined. Few school systems employed them, and often companies refused to hire the wives of their male workers. By 1933 an estimated 1,500 colleges and schools had gone bankrupt and closed. Music students, already marginal in society, had even more hurdles to face during the 1930s.

For Erskine, however, money problems meant not being able to live within his means as one in the top 2.3 percent income bracket. His teachers' salaries never approached Erskine's own income of $20,000 a year. Although he also earned $5,000 per short story, he gave up his apartment to move to a cheaper place on Park Avenue. At the same time, using Augustus Juilliard's money, he embarked on a $6 million building plan for the JGS and the IMA. In 1927 the JMF began purchasing buildings around the Institute.[34]

"The problem of amalgamating the two schools was formidable,"

Erskine wrote. He was tired of commuting the three traffic-ridden miles between East 52nd and West 122nd Streets and no doubt even more tired of dealing with Eugene Noble, who still lived at the Vanderbilt building. To suit his convenience Erskine persuaded the trustees that "a new building should be put up directly north of the Institute, and the Institute building should be remodeled to fit into the total plan." He foresaw problems: "Dr. Frank Damrosch was glad to see his school developed by Mr. Juilliard's money, but he would have liked to spend the money himself without suggestions or supervision. . . . even though the arrangement gave him immediately increased funds for the work of the Institute, and for himself a much larger salary and a guaranteed pension."[35] Erskine mistook the importance of money to the Damrosches, who, unlike him, were never interested in accumulating it for themselves. In addition, Loeb had guaranteed Damrosch's pension.

Because Damrosch opposed the idea, Hutcheson was also against moving the JGS uptown. "It took about two years for the Graduate School, the Institute and the architects to get together on the plans," Erskine wrote. "By the time we began to build, the two schools had argued with each other so much that they began to be as close as many a human family, intimate but on edge, imperfectly reserving their opinion about each other."[36] Some of the IMA's anger can be imagined at hearing the JGS's wasteful proposal to tear down both the IMA's Loeb-funded buildings, one only six years old and the other twenty. Money appeared to be no object to the JMF, which did not have a buyer for the 52nd Street building (and would not for more than a decade).

During the negotiations Damrosch occasionally prevailed. He strenuously protested alteration to the IMA building, and as more land was purchased Erskine agreed not to demolish the IMA's original building. The annex, however, was destroyed. The 1910 building was left wounded, shorn of its lovely mansard-roofed fourth floor, but standing and autonomous. Not razing the original IMA meant building both to the north and behind to the east on the lot purchased in 1910. After the annex was torn down in 1931, the IMA building remaining was stretched past its physical limit to accommodate the large enrollment in a space now occupied with construction. One student quipped that the only space left for teaching was the elevator. In addition to severing the top floor and mansard roof of the original Barber and Eidlitz building, "certain architectural flourishes incompatible with current simplicity of line [were] discreetly shorn from the older edifice."[37] Neither Damrosch's nor Loeb's consternation is recorded, but can be imagined.

The building was designed by architects Shreve, Lamb and Harmon, the same firm simultaneously constructing the Empire State Building that also opened in 1931. Like the School's building on East 52nd Street, the Empire State Building stayed empty until World War II. The new JGS dwarfed the Institute and covered six times the IMA's footprint on the site. The IMA, however, always had many more students than the JGS. The IMA and the JGS were separated by swinging glass doors and considered by students separate entities—with separate addresses. (In the matter of the address, the IMA won out—later the Juilliard School of Music took the address 120 rather than the JGS's 130 Claremont.) The Institute adroitly manipulated this thin physical separation to maintain its autonomy.

A few months after the new building's completion, in March 1932, John D. Rockefeller gave $350,000 to improve the land in the park between Riverside Church and International House (to which buildings Rockefeller had already donated the major portion of the cost), which included the area directly facing 120 and 130 Claremont. Trees were planted, walks and hedges installed, a wall built from International House to the corner of the IMA and then sloping to Riverside Drive. The two acres were landscaped under the supervision of Olmsted Brothers.

Spectacular ceremonies marked the opening of the 130 Claremont building on November 7, 1931. The next day the Juilliard Graduate School moved from the East 52nd Street mansion into its large new annex adjoining the IMA. Leopold Stokowski, on the recommendation of Olga Samaroff, his former wife, conducted the student orchestra in a concert of Handel, Bach, Rubin Goldmark's "Negro Rhapsody," and a first performance of Prokofiev's Sinfonietta in A major, Opus 5/48.[38] "We paid him $3,000 for conducting one performance but he deserved every bit of it," Erskine wrote. "He worked hard with our Juilliard boys and girls. The night of the concert, just before he raised his baton, I heard him say, 'I want to tell you something. You're going to play the most beautiful concert that has ever been played.' They did."[39] Sergei Rachmaninoff gave a piano recital for invited guests (not students) on November 12, and, on November 20 and 21, *Jack and the Beanstalk* by Louis Gruenberg on Erskine's libretto was produced. Among the notables who attended were Mrs. Curtis Bok and Efrem Zimbalist from the Curtis Institute.

The Baton, the Institute's monthly magazine, described the new building as completely modern and adorned with elegant draperies and furnishings. The interior decorator was Elsie Sloan Farley, even if Irmgart Hutcheson and Olga Samaroff, as well as Erskine and Hutcheson and many other faculty when it came to their own studios, wielded great influence over the decorations. Each studio eventually had a brass doorplate—removed in 1969—naming faculty members and the years she or he had taught there. The traffic design was complicated: One could easily become lost among the numerous stairways and pastel green hallways.

The Juilliard foyer was decorated with rose-tan and white marble with gray, black, and dark red patches. The lobby led directly into the thousand-seat auditorium, in which two stairways covered in snakewood diverged from the entrance. Felix Goettlicher—described as "something of a landmark now . . . who moves solemnly about the stage before and after each performance"—worked as both orchestral librarian and stage manager.[40] On the stage level were eight dressing rooms, rivaling in elegance those at the Metropolitan Opera. Sixty non-union players occupied the orchestra pit. Below this were corridors leading to the orchestra room and two large dressing rooms for the chorus. A beautiful lounge was approached by stairs from the auditorium. It had checkered, walnut-paneled walls, a black carpet with an oval band, and bright, lacquer-red and blue-green suede coverings on chairs and divans. The most unusual feature of the auditorium was a wine-red and gold press room off the foyer, where critics could write their reviews—apparently Erskine's idea. Two Remington typewriters were provided.

The constantly busy elevator, operated by Joe Byrne, rose six stories. Once being taken to the top floor and climbing a stairway, one could see on the roof a cupola and a loggia with long, arched windows. On

Concert hall interior at 130 Claremont Avenue, ca. 1932.
(Samuel H. Gottscho, photo from The Juilliard School Archives)

the sixth floor were both a radio broadcasting room and a recording room, where discs were to be made so students could be trained for radio performances. The broadcasting room had still not been used for this purpose when in 1937 Hutcheson announced that there would be no radio broadcasts from the School (chapter 5). Other schools capitalized on the new technology. The Curtis Institute had already given ten radio broadcasts in 1928–29, and in 1931 NBC radio featured a weekly series of broadcasts by the Eastman School Orchestra. The New England Conservatory Orchestra began broadcasting locally in 1931, moved to NBC in 1938, and added CBS in 1939. Juilliard broadcast performances, belatedly and sporadically, in 1940 and 1947.

Most of the twenty-three teaching studios were on the fourth and fifth floors. The voice and violin studios had mirrors. For its new quarters the JGS had bought 125 Steinway pianos, mostly uprights. Alexander Siloti's studio had two grand pianos. Marcella Sembrich's studio had a "background of peach walls, a divan and chairs in apricot strié satin, and a pale green rug. The piano and Madame's small sloping footstool are placed directly in front of the mirror, presumably so that she will have the pupil before her when she herself plays the accompaniment." Ernest Hutcheson's study had a tall clerk's desk, where he wrote of his pupils' progress in his famous book. Also on the fifth floor, the library occupied two large rooms with long walnut reading tables "and a cork floor [to] insure the utmost in silence." Gwendolyn Mackillop was librarian for several decades.[41]

The new building, which stretched all the way east to Broadway but with one hundred feet to its north remaining unbuilt, had thirty-one practice rooms rather than the intended sixty, whereas the IMA building had twenty practice rooms on its second floor. The JGS had use of nine classrooms, the IMA twenty. Rubin Goldmark's Juilliard classroom contained an easel blackboard beside the desk and rows of mahogany chairs with arm desks. Elaborate methods of soundproofing were applied to the entire building.

Precursing the general plan of the Lincoln Center Juilliard building, the teaching studios were on the fifth floor and the School's three administrators' offices on the second. Erskine had not only had a beautiful office but also a fourth-floor studio decorated with crimson velvet draperies and turquoise suede chairs. Hutcheson's corner office and Oscar Wagner's office were on either side of Erskine's. "I never closed my door," he wrote. "I wanted the faculty and students to feel that I was always on hand ready to discuss any problems."[42] Given his speaking and travel schedule, he was of course rarely in the office.

Walking through the swinging doors landed one back in the Institute building. On the right was the spacious and pleasant Schirmer's music shop. Directly below it, on the Broadway street level, was the cafeteria, with its yellow walls and flowered drapery. As at both the Lincoln Center Juilliard cafeterias, one end was partitioned for the faculty, with "a sub-section within this room for those who must, alas, confer even at meals," a student observed in 1931.[43] The JGS cafeteria operated at a loss during the depression. When even low prices were a hardship, books of luncheon coupons were given gratis to approximately thirty-six students.

On the IMA's first floor were staff offices, including that of Helen Frank, Damrosch's secretary since 1905. There were also separate lounges for men and women. George Wedge and Frank Damrosch had their offices on the second floor; Damrosch's was number 232. "We refrained from intruding upon Dr. Damrosch in his new private study a few doors away. We are told, however, that this is a sanctum in restful blue and gold, of special dignity and individualism," the student writer for *The Baton* recorded reverently.[44]

Obtaining faculty for the JGS was not always easy, as the situation in organ illustrates. The building on 52nd Street did not have an instrument. The 122nd Street building was outfitted with a new organ, and the Institute, where Gaston Dethier was in charge of instruction until his retirement in 1945, had several organ practice rooms as well as an excellent organ in its own concert hall. While the Institute was being enlarged, the practice organs had to be moved to the Jewish Theological Seminary for more than a year. (The Seminary would not charge for this favor, but the Institute's board presented a $5,000 gift.) After the installation of the Casavant organ at the new JGS building, Erskine invited the French organist George Bonnet to head the organ department, but he died suddenly, a few weeks after having played for Hutcheson. Erskine then engaged David McK. Williams, but illness prevented him from taking up his duties. The organ department at Juilliard remained empty, as did the Curtis Institute's in the 1930s. Erskine may have professed to emphasize church music, but he refused to consider hiring the IMA's Dethier.

The conservative composition faculty presented Erskine with a diplomatic problem. He was no modernist; he even tried to talk Anaïs Nin out of her interest in James Joyce. "Having taught English composition for most of my life," he complained, "I was somewhat perplexed to learn . . . that musical composition in that institution and many other music schools was taught by the repetition of set exercises rather than by the composition of anything that by the pupils or their teachers could be considered musical creation."[45] That description applied to the teaching of George Wedge, Rubin Goldmark, and others. To his frustration, Erskine was unable to change the situation.

A solution had presented itself with the arrival in the United States in 1933 of Arnold Schoenberg. After being forced out of his Berlin job by the Nazis, Schoenberg had accepted a teaching position at the Malkin Conservatory in Boston in 1933–34. In October 1933 Hutcheson asked Schoenberg to deliver a lecture at Juilliard, for which Schoenberg asked $500.[46] Gertrud Schoenberg remembered that her husband made a mistake based almost entirely on his misunderstanding of the name of the School: "Juilliard School, for us, was a small school. . . . When you said school, you know, you thought it was a little school with little people, little directors, etcetera, etcetera. They wanted him to make a speech there, and he, right away, declined, and of course, nobody told him about this refusal would be very serious for him."[47] During the summer of 1934, Schoenberg recuperated from an illness in Chautauqua, where he became friendly with Hutcheson. Between 1933 and 1935 Hutcheson sent twelve letters to Schoenberg, and Schoenberg had written eight to Hutcheson.[48]

In October 1934 Hutcheson telegrammed Schoenberg with an offer to teach at Juilliard. Schoenberg at first demurred, asking for time although interested in the "worthy number of talented pupils at your very high estimated institution."[49] Schoenberg wrote to Hutcheson in German:

> First and foremost I want to tell you that your offer gives me very great pleasure indeed, for it shows me that I need not feel superfluous in America; and it confirms what I had already realized in Chautauqua: that we should be able to get on very well together both personally and artistically. This is something that I always value very much; and is the main reason why I have taken so long to reply.
>
> But unfortunately there are too many strong arguments against it, and I cannot take the risk of thrusting these qualms aside.
>
> Above all it is, I am afraid, quite certain that I shall have to spend at least this winter in a milder climate and that I shall not be able to stand up to the New York climate before spring (which I hope will be mild!) at the earliest.[50]

Schoenberg suggested postponing the question until 1935. In February of that year, the *New York Times* prematurely reported that he would join the Juilliard faculty in the fall.[51] By then, however, he had a full-time position at the University of Southern California. In March, Schoenberg wrote to Hutcheson with a list of courses he would teach, including composition, instrumentation, counterpoint, theory of harmony, and analysis, each twice-weekly for a minimum of sixteen hours. He also suggested a master class, such as he had taught at the Berlin Academy.[52] Schoenberg wanted a schedule from September to the middle of December and from April to the middle of June, thereby avoiding the winter weather so bad for his health.

After three months of indecision (and a June 4 letter from Hutcheson prodding him) Schoenberg had to refuse Juilliard's terms.

> I tell you frankly that I would have been prepared to risk my health if even one of the two other qualms had been disposed of. Above all the question of the scope of activity. However little worldly sense I may otherwise have, I do know that I should have had to make a success of it if my appointment at your School were to become a permanent one. Considering the work allotted me and the improbability of my getting the best, most gifted student material, this seemed practically out of the question. Let me pass in silence over the fact that the salary could not be adequate to my needs, to say nothing of my wishes, and that I was offered no certainty of any future improvement.[53]

In August 1934 Schoenberg had turned down Rudolf Ganz's offer to teach at the Chicago Musical College for $4,000; he calculated he could not manage for under $6,000. As with the case of Boulanger, the School lost an opportunity to hire a leading composition teacher.

When Rubin Goldmark died in 1936, Frederick Jacobi (1891–1952) and Bernard Wagenaar (1894–1971) were hired at the JGS. Jacobi had studied at New York City's Ethical Culture School with Rubin Goldmark and with Rafael Joseffy, Damrosch's piano teacher. He had also been an assistant conductor at the Met. Jacobi's wife, Irene, was known for her playing of contemporary piano music. The anti-modernist Wagenaar had been a member of the violin section of the Philharmonic from 1921 to 1925. He had been a composition teacher at the JGS since 1927, when he became an American citizen. Wagenaar's uncle was a well-known Dutch composer and director of the Royal Conservatory of Music at The Hague.

Social relations among students were always problematic. In 1932 a student dance was organized: "At the outset of the party there was an anxious half-hour during which those whose acquaintance had been limited to the terrible experience of sharing a phrase or so in sight-singing class, stood around in classic groups. This difficulty was easily surmounted by the slipper dance, an inspired idea whereby the girls pitch one slipper each into the corner, and the fellows rush the pile to secure a partner, Cinderella style."[54] Two years later, IMA students organized themselves into a student club. One hundred and fifty met in the recital hall and unanimously elected Irwin Freundlich president. Their short-lived journal, *Dynamics* (1934–35), was a "forum for self-expression on the part of the student body" edited by flutist George Lisitzky. In it Freundlich, who had a bachelor's degree from Columbia, summed up the dismal social situation: "We come to classes; practice diligently; keep well within our own little cliques (if we are fortunate enough to have friends at school); perhaps attend a Student Recital when a friend performs and then—what else? Particularly at the Institute it is quite possible for a talented student to spend several years at school without coming into real contact with his equally talented fellow students."[55]

An anonymous student noticed the difference between the atmosphere of the IMA of old and the one of 1934:

> Something has happened in the Institute. We remember our first visits years ago—the tip-toe feeling the ghost-like silence of the halls gave us—the reverential awe with which we contemplated the serious study of our Art—the hesitant steps across the lobby with its forbidden outer entrance, its dim "reception room" filled with imposing sculptures. Our instructors were Olympic figures, dispensing their learning from on high. The entire atmosphere was severely classical, musically and esthetically, a beautiful environment but one formal, aristocratic and slightly frigid.
>
> Slowly things have changed. The amalgamation with the Juilliard brought in new and brighter tints—greens, black, silver, red—and a few dissonant chords. Subtle influences have been at work, relaxing the formality of study, bringing more intimate relations between students and teacher, simplifying the discipline and creating a more congenial atmosphere.[56]

An example of the severity under Damrosch is seen in an episode involving both a student and her teacher. After Martha Halbwachs, a pianist, transferred to the Curtis Institute in 1927, Damrosch dismissed her teacher, Zofia Naimska. Naimska brought the matter to the board because she was let go for ethical reasons; Damrosch felt she had been disloyal to the school. Damrosch denied Halbwachs a certificate, even though she received a passing grade, after she had studied with Naimska for six years. The board sided completely with Damrosch, who wrote to Halbwachs, "Your sudden decision does not relieve you of the stigma of disloyalty and ingratitude and I confess that I am disappointed in finding you capable of such conduct."[57]

The April 1934 issue of *Dynamics* coincided with Anti-War Week, when students across the United States demonstrated their desire to prevent another war. *Dynamics* reprinted an anti-Nazi article on music, first published by the *New Masses*. Students also wanted an employment bureau at the School, but Erskine opposed it and the issue dragged on through the issues of the newspaper. In May 1935 the more activist students wrote to Erskine, asking to hold meetings of their National Student League chapter in the School and also meetings of the Juilliard Chapter Affiliated with the American League against War and Fascism, a chapter with 120 members, one-seventh of the School's population. The conservative Erskine was unsympathetic and asked why, if they were opposed to war and fascism, were they not opposed to communism? He did not want the School used for propaganda, and he changed the subject: "I wonder how long it will be before the young peace lovers in our country will devote their energies and their great influence to doing away with some of the causes of war instead of wasting time in emotional and somewhat histrionic demonstrations."[58] The students asked him to reconsider but received no reply. Erskine had the last word; he discontinued *Dynamics*, which had acquired a reputation as having "dangerous radicals" associated with it.

Only months after moving into its expensive new building, the free-spending Juilliard board recognized a need to retrench. In June 1932 Erskine sent a letter to faculty members to inform them that their salaries would be lowered before opportunities for the students would be curtailed. The faculty voted to accept a 10 percent reduction in salaries for those receiving $25 or more per hour and 5 percent for those receiving between $10 and $25 per hour.[59] For example, in 1932 Bernard Wagenaar's contract for classroom teaching was cut to $1,350, and in 1933 Rosina Lhevinne's income was decreased from $4,900 to $4,410. James Friskin received $15 an hour. By way of comparison, in 1932 the New England Conservatory cut faculty salaries 10 percent and another 25 percent in 1934.

Olga Samaroff Stokowski described a piano faculty that got along famously. "It is said there are climates in which bad weather is conspicuous by its absence. The piano department of the Juilliard Graduate School has such a climate." For her, the qualities that bound the artists together were idealism, sincerity, and generosity. "Finally, I have found in this group a sense of justice that has enabled us to sit around the examination table twice a year for twelve years without a single deadlock or disagreeable experience, in spite of many differences of opinion and heated arguments that often kept us for hours after our examination affairs for the day should have been concluded."[60]

Samaroff had not only studied with Ernest Hutcheson in Europe but also had learned the French technique. She was "an American pianist who exhibited a fusion of French, German, and Russian piano styles and techniques."[61] She spoke French and German fluently and was adequate in Italian and Russian. She knew the benefits of proper manners and behavior and gave dinners for students to meet luminaries. Known in the School as "Madame," Samaroff during the depression began asking students to live with her at 1170 Fifth Avenue, the building where the Hutchesons lived. "Then I had a wonderful time worrying over tonsils and teeth, posture and clothes, diet and exercise, going to bed early, language and table manners."[62] She gave musicales at her home and at those of her society friends, and with Irmgart Hutcheson founded the Schubert Memorial Competition in 1928, a major venue for performers' careers.

When she began teaching, Samaroff had made several rules for herself. "One was, never to correct a detail without mentioning the fundamental issue underlying the mistake. No one can teach or learn emotion. Understanding of music is the only thing that can be given by one person to another, but a deep artistic understanding is the secure foundation upon which the real artist builds his dream castles fashioned of evanescent tone, imagination and emotion."[63] Another rule was not to play for students, fearing they would only learn through imitation.

The Juilliard Graduate School faculty in 1936. *Seated, left to right:* Madeleine Marshall, Alexander Siloti, Florence Page Kimball, Anna Schoen-René, Dean Ernest Hutcheson, Olga Samaroff Stokowski, Rosina Lhevinne, Albert Spalding, and Edith Braun. *Standing, first row:* Paul Reimers, Louis Persinger, James Friskin, Josef Lhevinne, Edouard Dethier, Harold Hutcheson, Horatio Connell, René Vallant, Peter Riccio, and Frederick Kiesler; *second row:* Carl Friedberg, Francis Rogers, Felix Salmond, Oscar Wagner, Frederick Jacobi, Hans Letz, and Georges Barrère; *third row:* Albert Stoessel, Bernard Wagenaar, Arthur Mahoney, Alfredo Valenti, and Alberto Bimboni.
(Photo from The Juilliard School Archives)

Samaroff realized that being an artist is a question of who a person is, and she occupied herself with her students' human development.

Samaroff, who also taught at the Curtis Institute, compared the two schools and their repute. Curtis, she thought, had an advantage over Juilliard in that it accepted music students from all countries, whereas the JGS only accepted American citizens. Samaroff relied on Noble's claim that this was a stipulation of the Juilliard will.

> Students of outstanding talent have naturally flocked to these en-
> dowed schools and competed for fellowships in the autumn entrance
> exams. This was hard on the private teacher and much bitter feeling
> was engendered. For several years teachers who would have thought
> nothing of sending their pupils abroad to study with some European
> master, resented having them go to a teacher of the same type in a
> New York or Philadelphia school. Criticism of the endowed schools
> was a favorite pastime in certain quarters of the musical profession. It
> was natural.[64]

Applicants had to produce the consent and recommendation of their most recent teacher, which was Juilliard's method of counteracting any impression that the School desired to take pupils away from other teachers.

One of Samaroff's colleagues was Carl Friedberg, who had studied piano at the Frankfurt Conservatory with Ivan Knorr and Clara Schumann and given his American debut in 1914.[65] A vegetarian, he was particularly good at advising students on how to control nerves in performance; he was a physician, a healer. Samaroff described both Friedberg and James Friskin as walking encyclopedias of the piano literature, able to recall forgotten opus numbers and distinguish the differences among various editions of the same piece, right down to the last sharp, flat, or thirty-second rest. Friedberg suggested that pupils improvise cadenzas to Mozart concerti. Among his students were Percy Grainger, Ethel Leginska, Elly Ney, Maro Ajemian, Jane Carlson, Arthur Ferrante and Louis Teicher, William Masselos, and Malcolm Frager. Sergius Kagen, a Russian student of Friedberg's who later joined the faculty, described his teacher's playing:

> It was utterly extraordinary in one particular detail: the instrument
> seemed to speak. The rhythm, inflexion and articulation of every
> phrase were so remarkably natural, free of any effort and so utterly
> unselfconscious that his playing seemed somehow to create an illusion
> of transcending the limitations of a percussion instrument. . . . I have
> never before or since heard any pianist match completely the extraor-
> dinary ability that Carl Friedberg possessed to shape a musical phrase
> into something so naturally rhythmical, effortless, unostentatious, and

therefore so eloquent, that the playing reminded one more of human speech, with its inexhaustible variety of inflexion, than of any musical instrument, or even of singing.[66]

Kagen recalled Friedberg's catholic musical tastes, his knowledge of general culture, his generosity by giving free lessons to those who could not afford to pay, and his lesson that "unless one learns to hear the piece of music mentally it is of little use to try to execute it with one's fingers."[67]

Many of the JGS faculty had known each other in Europe. For example, Hutcheson and the Russian Alexander Siloti (1863–1945) had been under the same concert management in Russia. An essentially shy man, Siloti, who had studied with Tchaikowsky and Liszt and was a first cousin of Sergei Rachmaninoff, glided in conversation from one European language to another. He spoke Russian with the Lhevinnes and German with the rest of the piano faculty. According to Siloti, Liszt appeared to him in a dream and scolded him for neglecting his art, telling him to return to the stage. At the age of sixty-eight Siloti played in public after having not been heard since 1921. Invariably before a concert Siloti would inform friends with complete sincerity that Liszt had told him the night before that the concert would be a success.[68] The tall, gaunt Siloti, who was often humming a tune, taught at Juilliard from 1925 to 1942.

The senior member of the piano faculty, Siloti attached more importance than did the other piano faculty to the age of an applicant: never too young to please him. When a contestant was impossible, his laconic notes at entrance examinations consisted of two words: "Soll heiraten" (she should marry). The other faculty suggested that he open a matrimonial agency for rejected applicants. He once made the Juilliard Orchestra laugh during a concert when, after having gone offstage but still in their full view, the double-jointed pianist, pleased at having played well, scratched his ear with his right leg.[69]

Siloti said that Josef Lhevinne (1874–1944) could "smell talent." Lhevinne seldom made a mistake in this regard, no matter how unpromising the student appeared to the others. He had studied at the Moscow Conservatory, taught there from 1902 to 1906, and was known for his rendering of works of the Romantic school, particularly in concertos of Chopin and Tchaikowsky.[70] He taught at Juilliard for twenty years, until his death, where, unusually, his wife Rosina co-taught with him, an arrangement that worked nicely. Rosina Lhevinne said, "One of our principles was always to insist that the student find the long line of the melody and analyze what part of it is the peak, or high point. Josef always had a saying about this: that to have two peaks in the same phrase was like having two heads on one torso. We agreed that each phrase must have one peak—but as to where that peak was, we often felt quite differently."[71] Josef Lhevinne "was insistent in a gentle way. He often ran out of words altogether, and sat at the piano to demonstrate, giving marvelous illustrations that some students felt were worth a thousand pedagogical words."[72] When the School moved from 52nd Street to the new building at 122nd in 1931, the two selected Room 412, which remained the "Lhevinne studio" until 1969.

Rosina Lhevinne (1880–1976) felt it best to play second fiddle to her husband. She had won the gold medal at the Moscow Conservatory in 1898, and in 1919 she and her husband came to the United States and opened a studio. She and Samaroff, the only women on the piano faculty, often joined in defending a student against the other faculty when continuation of a fellowship was concerned. They also would plead for students who had not worked as hard as they should have or had difficult life circumstances to overcome. The men grumbled but usually gave in. The legendary Lhevinne taught at Juilliard until her death at the age of ninety-six, and her pupils included Van Cliburn, Misha Dichter, John Browning, Brooks Smith, Olegna Fuschi, Joseph Raieff, and Garrick Ohlsson.

Anna Schoen-René campaigned successfully in 1936 to prevent students from being debarred from a fellowship if they were faulty in theoretical subjects. At faculty meetings she frequently complained of the loss to the School of great voices because the students were unable to meet the theory requirements. Hutcheson would patiently explain that at a conservatory, as opposed to a private voice studio, the administration must be committed to the overall musicianship of students. Conservative in her musical tastes, Schoen-René pressed to get an oratorio preformed every year and won that battle, with a few excerpts being performed.

On the violin faculty was Paul Kochanski, a Pole who had worked with Karol Szymanowski. He had an inexhaustible humor, wit, and sense of fun but projected impeccable dignity in all public performances. He was a darling of society and had an equal passion for roulades and roulette; the proceeds of his recitals were sacrificed to the gambling tables at Monte Carlo. Kochanski was slim, elegant, and progressive; he taught modern repertoire for the violin. Like Lhevinne, he had an uncanny ability to recognize talent (or the lack of it) in young students. Like Samaroff, he judged students less by their technical equipment than by deeper spiritual hints, indications of their inner life and of the direction in which they were likely to develop. Kochanski died in 1934 at the age of forty-five. His funeral, like Kneisel's, was held at the School. Albert

Spalding (1888–1953) took Kochanski's students. Spalding, related to the wealthy sporting goods family, gave the U.S. premieres of concertos by Dohnányi, Elgar, and Barber and also wrote music himself.[73]

Louis Persinger (1887–1966), like Spalding, was American-born. He replaced Leopold Auer in 1930 and taught at Juilliard until his death thirty-six years later. From Colorado, Persinger had traveled to study violin at the Leipzig Conservatory. He had been, for a year each, concertmaster of the Berlin Philharmonic and of the San Francisco Symphony. He had his own string quartet and directed San Francisco's Chamber Music Society from 1916 to 1928. His pupils included Yehudi Menuhin, Ruggiero Ricci, and Isaac Stern. Not stiff or authoritative, Persinger was beloved for his gentleness, patience, and subtle humor. He was also admired for his musicianship, which included playing the piano and as well as the violin in public.[74]

One of Kochanski's students was Nicolai Berezowsky (1900–1953), a multitalented Russian who, after becoming an American citizen in 1928, had won Juilliard fellowships in both violin and composition. Berezowsky was already a member of the New York Philharmonic violin section, but, having survived the turmoil of the Russian Revolution and a Polish prison, he wanted to continue study on a more secure footing. He studied composition at the 52nd Street building with Rubin Goldmark at 8:00 A.M., the only time his schedule would permit. Goldmark, Philharmonic conductor Willem Mengelberg, and Kochanski all agreed that Berezowsky should devote himself to composition, an impossibility because he played to support his father back in Russia. Nevertheless, he wrote concertos that were played and conducted by some of the best musicians of the day: Flesch played the Violin Concerto, Primrose his Viola Concerto, and Piatigorsky his *Concerto lirico*. As a chamber musician he had a brilliant career in the Coolidge String Quartet, but Berezowsky committed suicide at fifty-three.

∽

On Damrosch's trip to Europe during the summer of 1931 he saw his old friend Loeb for the last time. On his doctor's advice, Damrosch spent the next summer in Bermuda. In 1929 he had suffered a slight stroke, losing the use of his right eye. The 1932 trip gave him the energy to carry on at the IMA for one more year.

That same year, Paul Warburg, Loeb's trusted brother-in-law and IMA board member died. In January 1933 Hitler came to power, but Loeb's Bavarian property would be saved from confiscation because he and his stepsons by marriage were American citizens. In February came three irreparable losses: His wife Tony died on January 28 and one of her two sons, Ernest Hambuechen, died soon after. Then Loeb's half-sister Theresa died on February 26. Saddened and without the support of his wife, Loeb died on May 27, 1933, at the age of sixty-five.

Damrosch grieved over Loeb's death and completely reevaluated his position with the IMA. At the combined commencement exercises of the JGS and the IMA six days after Loeb's death, the orchestra played the slow movement from Brahms's First Symphony as a memorial. Loeb's portrait, now in the library, graced the stage. Damrosch stunned every-one—especially and perhaps deliberately Erskine—by announcing that he himself would retire. He had been at the IMA for twenty-eight years. Already in ill health, Damrosch doubtless felt he could not continue without the support of his co-founder, James Loeb. "When [Damrosch] spoke for the last time to his students he did not suffer alone; a phrase, tender and regretful, was breathed from one to another among faculty and graduates; it was said that the soul of the Institute was departing."[75]

Ernest Hutcheson, dean of the Graduate School, assumed Damrosch's duties as well. John Erskine proposed that Damrosch write a history of the IMA, and he spent the next three years working on that project. When the two-volume manuscript, well over a thousand pages, was finished and ready to send to the printers at Scribner's, Walter Damrosch appeared at his brother's doorstep with a magnum of champagne. One volume was published in 1936, but a longer appendix detailing classes, concerts, faculty, and students remains in typescript.[76] Irving Kolodin remembered Damrosch:

> The incipient Paderewski or Kreisler who came to [the IMA] with the mental reservation that classes in ear-training, sight-singing or theory could be evaded or passively endured soon found that all his talent for playing Liszt or Pagannini would not excuse other deficiencies. Habitual evasion of the scholastic requirements would quickly bring a summons to the office of Dr. Damrosch, and the invariable injunction that he was not interested in adding to the world's burden of pianists or violinists or vocalists—that he was concerned only with producing musicians. If the student could not absorb the implications of such an admonishment, he was apt to find that he had been unceremoniously dropped from the school, advised to take his "talent" elsewhere. . . . The love of an art which had motivated the life's work of the director could not fail to affect any susceptible youth with a similar devotion. . . . The prospect of playing a Mozart sonata or a Kreutzer etude for the white-bearded, seemingly severe Dr. Damrosch, was one of the more formidable experiences of the year's routine, but his attitude was invariably more genial and kindly than the ill-poised youth had reason to expect (a circumstance that can be factually attested, since the writer was once one such).[77]

Late in 1935 Erskine sustained skull and hand fractures from an automobile collision. In February 1937, just over a year after the accident, he suffered a stroke that paralyzed his right side, but, except for the use of his right hand, he recovered. Thinking of the stroke as a nervous breakdown due to exhaustion from overwork, in December 1936 Erskine announced that he would resign from Juilliard. He had hoped to teach at Columbia again but received an unwelcome letter from President Butler designating him instead as emeritus professor. More than once he tried to return to Juilliard, but he was not satisfied with its financial offers. It was perhaps logical that he would go to Hollywood; his second wife thought he might succeed Will Hays as the overseer of movie morals. Erskine resigned his administrative duties but kept his position on the JMF board, controlling the Foundation's money until his death in 1951, a few months after the death of Ernest Hutcheson.

The year 1937 saw the loss of many of the important figures associated with the two schools. John Erskine, who survived the year, had resigned as president. Frederick Juilliard died that year. Without his support Noble finally left the JMF. William J. Henderson, IMA faculty member and critic, shot himself at the age of eighty-one in June, and Felix Warburg, a board member and brother-in-law of James Loeb, died in October. Finally, at the age of seventy-eight, Frank Damrosch died on October 22, 1937, Leopold Damrosch's 105th birthday. Frank Damrosch, Jr., an Episcopalian minister, officiated at the funeral in the filled IMA hall. The Musical Art Quartet played the Andante of Mozart's Quartet in C major. The ten-minute service ended with the Adagio from Haydn's Quartet in C major, after which the carillon of the newly completed Riverside Church across the street sounded Chopin's Funeral March. An era had come to a close.

5

Opera & Orchestra:

ALBERT STOESSEL

WHEN IN OCTOBER 1933 Ernest Hutcheson was introduced at the Institute of Musical Art as the new dean, he restated his original plan for the Juilliard Graduate School: Music would be taught not as a cultural subject, a business, or a means of self-expression, but as an art. He expected that ideal to apply in all the departments of the School. Hutcheson's stewardship (1927–45) is marked by remarkable steadiness, a genuine feat considering that he administered the School during the depression and World War II.

That period marks less a story of Ernest Hutcheson than one of the man who exerted the primary artistic influence in the School: conductor Albert Stoessel. Born in St. Louis in 1894, Stoessel studied violin. After he had completed the eighth grade, his family took him out of school to pursue music. He went to the Berlin Hochschule in 1910, along with four other American musicians, including composer Frederick Jacobi. A protégé of Walter Damrosch, Stoessel began teaching at the IMA in the late 1910s and became chair of the music department at New York University in 1923. The renowned NYU musicologist Martin Bernstein later said that he "owed more to Albert Stoessel than to any one person for his musical training and education."[1]

One of Hutcheson's first actions in 1927 was to organize a string orchestra and ask Albert Stoessel to direct it. Because the JGS did not offer winds or brass, a string orchestra was the only kind it was possible to form at the School. Hutcheson knew of Stoessel's abilities from their association at Chautauqua and installed himself as Stoessel's associate conductor. As one writer described Stoessel, "His admirable traits of patience, politeness, and polish were always in evidence as part of his charming personality; and his smooth efficiency and keen musicianship kept his rehearsals with his students on the same high plane as those with professional groups."[2]

In 1930 Stoessel had to choose between New York University and Juilliard, and he picked Juilliard because New York University would not give him a sabbatical leave. That year he began a conducting class at the JGS, where his influence extended widely. Erskine recalled that in planning and designing the concert hall of 130 Claremont Avenue, "We guided ourselves by his knowledge and experience."[3]

The JGS produced operas but lacked a hall in which to perform them. The first opera, *Hansel and Gretel*, was performed in December 1929 at the rented Heckscher Theatre on Fifth Avenue and 104th Street. The next year Stoessel conducted *Julius Caesar* at the American Woman's Association Club at 361 West 57th Street, and thereafter operas were given in the auditorium at 130 Claremont. The proceeds from *Julius Caesar*, possibly the first performance in New York of the two-hundred-

Albert Stoessel and the 1927 orchestra.
(Empire Flashlight Co., photo from The Juilliard School Archives)

year-old Handel opera, went to aid the city's three thousand unemployed musicians. William J. Henderson of the faculty reviewed it.

The production of 1931, *Jack and the Beanstalk* by Louis Gruenberg and John Erskine, was a "fairy tale opera for the childlike." A tenor and baritone were originally both required to sing the role of the cow, one the front of the animal and the other the back. The giant cow, made of inflated rubber, garnered most of the considerable publicity.

The opera's story is supposed to demonstrate "that courage, ability to face facts, to recognize worth and opportunity even when they are not decked out with fortune's garlands; to look false appearances in the face and pierce bluff and braggadocio with the sword of wit and self-reliance are the things that bring the rewards of earth and heaven."[4] Characteristically, Erskine published an explanation of his purposes, although Olin Downes took exception to these "sweeping statements." After a successful production at the opening ceremonies for the School's new building, *Jack and the Beanstalk* had a two-week Christmas run on Broadway. By then only a baritone sang the cow, who also spoke, as did other characters.[5]

Opera students studied roles in English as well as the original language, and roles were later double-cast to give more singers performance opportunities. Alternating orchestras were first used (for a production of *Così fan Tutte*) in 1940.

After *Jack*, investment in new operas continued. In April 1932 the School performed *The False Harlequin* by Malipiero, an American premiere, and *The Secret of Suzanne* by Wolf-Ferrari. Handel's *Xerxes* followed, and in February 1933 the first New York performance of Monteverdi's *Incoronazione di Poppea*. Cimarosa's *The Secret Marriage* was presented in Washington, D.C., and Worcester, a work that had not been heard in New York for a century. *Helen Retires* (1934) by George Antheil and John Erskine drew criticism over its rumored $40,000 cost, a figure Erskine denied, saying obliquely the cost was the same amount as ever. Although the libretto was based on an original story, its title was bound to capture the attention accruing from Erskine's best-selling *Private Life of Helen of Troy*.

In December 1934 Stoessel conducted the New York premiere of Richard Strauss's *Ariadne auf Naxos*. *The New Yorker*'s critic did not like the singing translation of the work, nor did he care for the performer's diction. Risë Stevens won acclaim for her performance of the title role in Gluck's *Orfeo ed Euridice* (1935). Marvel Biddle (also in *Ariadne*) sang Euridice. The *Orpheus*, too, was done in English, but this time *The New Yorker* critic approved of the translation. Next came *Maria Malibran* with a score by Robert Russell Bennett and a libretto by Robert A. Simon—

not coincidentally the same *New Yorker* critic. Once again the School co-opted its critics by hiring them.

This adventurous opera program became formalized in 1935 as an opera school conducted in connection with the JGS and open to Juilliard fellowship-holders and graduates. Students and graduates of the Department of Singing at the IMA could enter the Opera School for a $150 annual tuition once they passed the audition. The curriculum included general operatic repertoire (individual and class instruction); acting (mise-en-scène); stage technique; English diction; dancing; and the "Art of Make-Up."

The Merry Wives of Windsor by Otto Niccolai was performed in Henry Krehbiel's translation in April 1936. Stoessel conducted, and Alfredo Valenti directed the work. *The Frantic Physician,* a Molière-Gounod comedy, was given its first American performance, and Stoessel and Simon collaborated as composer and librettist of *Garrick* in 1937. The three-act *Poisoned Kiss* by Vaughan Williams and librettist Evelyn Sharp, staged in April 1937, was another American premiere. *The Sleeping Beauty* by Beryl Rubinstein, with Erskine as librettist, received its world premiere in New York in January 1938 and was also performed at Severance Hall in Cleveland. Rubinstein, head of the Cleveland Institute and a well-known concert pianist, had never composed an opera. Erskine, unable to resist dialogue, caused Sleeping Beauty to talk in her sleep—about an affair with a gamekeeper.

During the financially strapped 1930s differences of opinion about what Augustus Juilliard really meant by his will returned to haunt the JMF. In March 1933 William Mathews Sullivan, an attorney for several opera singers, suggested in the newspapers that Juilliard's will and its stipulations regarding the Metropolitan Opera be given a court test. He questioned Augustus Juilliard's intention that the Foundation should take over the IMA and mentioned that the empty 49 East 52nd Street building was still producing no income. He also questioned Juilliard faculty's expensive salaries and whether foreign instructors should be employed there in such numbers. Finally, Sullivan asked why the public should be requested to contribute funds to the Met's $300,000 drive when the Opera was entitled to money under the Juilliard will.[6]

Erskine tried to get Sullivan to retract the statements that implied that the Foundation had neglected its charge to help the Met. It was an unwinnable battle that Erskine should have avoided; instead, he became more deeply involved. With extremely bad timing, and perhaps more sensitive to his treatment by newspaper critics than he acknowledged, Erskine wrote to the *Times* the day after Sullivan's letter. His response implied that the JMF would contribute enough to the Met to "see the opera through" its crisis. That day soprano Lucrezia Bori and Cornelius Bliss appeared in Erskine's box at the Opera. Erskine recalled that they had asked, "What had I meant by implying that the Juilliard would aid the Opera? Didn't I know that this would kill the Met's drive for $300,000?"[7] The two had cause for dismay, because some donors had requested the return of their pledges when they read Erskine's letter. Bori then announced from the Met's stage that the impression given by Erskine's statement was not only "unfortunate but erroneous."[8] Chagrined, he submitted his resignation to the Juilliard board on March 27, 1933, saying the Met episode had nullified a good deal of his work and made his position untenable.[9] He was to wield that threat again, because the board did not accept the resignation.

Erskine interpreted Juilliard's will as he saw fit: "Mr. Juilliard wished the Foundation to assist in the production of operas which otherwise might not get a hearing at the Met—operas of historic interest to students and operas written by American composers." The JMF's gift to the Opera of $50,000 in 1933 and $40,000 in 1934 therefore came with stipulations of Erskine's making. Further understandings also had to be met for the $150,000 gift in 1935. A letter by JMF board member George Davison outlined these: "Our suggestion . . . is that the Metropolitan should sponsor a season supplemental to each regular season. Such seasons should be at very reasonable prices, not over $3.00 for the best seats. [The current price was $7.] While not confined to Americans, the opportunity so far as artistic productions would permit should be given to young Americans to win their spurs."[10]

The supplementary season—the Metropolitan Popular Season—would be conducted by a new corporation whose title would have the word *Metropolitan* in it and whose board would consist equally of representation from the Opera and the JMF. The letter further stipulated that Erskine, Hutcheson, and John Perry should be added to the directorate of the Opera Association. Felix Warburg was added later. Although the *New York Times* raised the question of favoritism toward Juilliard graduates, these proposals were generally well received in the musical and other press.[11] Perhaps emboldened by the board's refusal to accept his resignation two years earlier, Erskine again threatened to resign "if the money were handed over to the Metropolitan without such conditions as would insure Mr. Juilliard's intention, I should not care to be connected with either the Foundation or the School."[12]

Furthermore, the JMF hand-picked Gatti-Casazza's successor as director. Herbert Witherspoon, a sixty-two-year-old American bass singer and former roommate of Allen Wardwell's at Yale, had already been hired by the JGS. When installed by the JMF at the Met in March 1935,

Witherspoon was inundated with seven hundred letters, five hundred telegraphs, and reporters everywhere. Erskine and the JMF had lobbied, negotiated, and outright paid for real influence at the Met to further their ends for the students' benefit. With the appointment of Witherspoon, one of their own, they finally achieved the influence they wanted.

Fate, however, had other plans. After having been in Gatti-Casazza's office only two weeks, Witherspoon died there of a heart attack. The Canadian-born tenor Edward Johnson, rather than Hutcheson or Erskine, whose names had been widely bandied about as possible successors, succeeded Witherspoon in May 1935. Johnson announced that the Met must reduce its large staff of singers despite the Juilliard money. Nine new singers had been chosen, including Julius Huehn, who was Jack in *Jack and the Beanstalk*. Other Juilliard students taken on were bass Dudley Marwick, soprano Josephine Antoine, and Charles Kullman. Plans to produce JGS faculty member Vittorio Giannini's *Lucedia*, in which the composer's sister Dusolina, a student of Sembrich, was to have the title role, were canceled.

Critic Olin Downes noted that the 1935 season was "the most old-fashioned and ultra-conservative that the famous American Metropolitan Opera company—now Association—has offered the public in over a quarter of a century, and probably for much longer." No new operas were scheduled in fourteen weeks, and there were no American works. It was harder to change the leopard's spots than the JMF thought. Despite the hoopla of change, Edward Johnson gave the audience more Verdi, Puccini, and Wagner. He did, however, follow the JMF's recommendation and put a cap of $1,000 per performance on the principal artists' salaries. Economic conditions worldwide permitted that reduction to stay in force. (Unlike the Juilliard faculty, the Met's stars had not been willing to lower their salaries for the good of the institution.) Downes commented wryly about Johnson, "It is the old story of the radical, out of power, who become a conservative upon contact with responsibility."[13]

The Metropolitan Popular Season was broadcast over NBC. Operas were performed in English, for example, Smetana's *Bartered Bride* and Gluck's *Orfeo ed Euridice*, but the supplementary season survived for only two years. Opera in English was discarded by 1937. The JMF's influence over the Met had dissipated. In 1938 Hutcheson told Erskine that control of the Met had passed to Edward Ziegler, who had "shown antagonism to the spring [supplementary] season from first to last. . . . If now the Met wishes to repudiate the ideas that we have successfully advocated, the Foundation's obligation of further support becomes at least debatable. The spring season could only be dropped or suspended equitably by mutual consent."[14] And so it was dropped.

His experience in opera at Juilliard had informed Erskine's views on the Met's programming. The popular novelist turned to writing librettos once again for *Helen Retires* in March 1934. George Antheil, a twenty-nine-year-old American then living in Europe, had written to ask whether Erskine would like to do an opera about Helen of Troy. Erskine jumped at the opportunity but produced a three-hundred-page libretto of fancy poetry. Antheil cut the text, rewrote his music, put in new stage directions, and tried to insert action into Erskine's characteristic wordiness. In so doing, the opera "simply accumulated too much music. . . . During the rehearsals Erskine came in and insisted upon pruning away a lot of orchestration because it obscured his words. . . . Just before *Helen Retires* was officially performed, I knew that the thing I had most worried about was true—the opera lacked action. People stood around on the stage like a load of bricks and yapped, yapped, yapped. No dialogue on earth could be *that* funny, especially when sung instead of spoken."[15] *Helen Retires* was a "gigantic flop." Antheil blamed the libretto, perhaps rightly, but Erskine loudly proclaimed the music to be at fault. Critics, too, preferred to blame the young composer rather than the powerful Erskine. *Helen Retires* was not published by the Juilliard Musical Foundation as *Jack* had been.

The sudden shift to standard opera repertoire in 1937, the year Erskine resigned, clearly indicates that the president had had considerable influence in the selection of the operas. At opera department faculty meetings Stoessel proposed conservative operas, whereas others, such as his colleague Frederick Kiesler, offered modern works. Hutcheson was conservative in his tastes and not a person to impose his will on others. After a diet of innovative works, Stoessel reverted to Mozart and Puccini as soon as he had the opportunity. Starting in February 1938, he did excerpts from *Aïda*, *Faust*, and *Carmen*. By April he had capitulated entirely to standard repertoire, with *The Abduction from the Seraglio*, *Marriage of Figaro*, and *La Bohème* (in Italian but in modern dress).

These operas were reviewed but did not receive the press attention the new operas had garnered. Nevertheless, some of the productions received wonderful notices. Virgil Thomson, for example, wrote of *The Magic Flute* in December 1940: "Much has been said about the stupidity and the useless complexity of *The Magic Flute*'s libretto. It certainly never made much sense to this reviewer. Last night's performance at the Juilliard School made it seem as simple as a Sunday school pageant."[16]

Not content to sing only the operas of Stoessel's now quite conservative choosing, enterprising students calling themselves as the Juilliard Institute Opera Players decided to produce operas. In October 1940 they obtained Brander Matthews Hall of Columbia University, where they produced Vittorio Giannini's *Blennerhasset* and Arthur Benjamin's *The Devil Take Her*. They also did *Cox and Box* and, in April 1940, *The Poet's Dilemma* (with music by Jacobi student Dai-Keong Lee and libretto by Daniel K. Freudenthal) and *Golden Wedding* (with music by Auguste Maurage and libretto by Arnold Crabbe).

Opera School stage designer Frederick Kiesler was assisted by students in stage design at the School of Architecture of Columbia University. Alfredo Valenti, the stage director, was Stoessel's co-worker in all of the operas at Juilliard and at Chautauqua and Worcester. Kiesler wrote:

> I [will] let the cat out of the bag and to tell you a backstage secret. Out of the twenty-three [of thirty-one operas produced in a decade] designed and built opera productions, we have bought entirely new materials for only eight. The rest was the result of our technique of cutting old material apart and resetting it, repainting it, and filling in gaps from our storage of platforms, steps and curtains. And so standing backstage during a performance, here and there still can be seen on the back side of flats and drops familiar painting, vestiges of past operas—silent witnesses to the magic of performances gone by.[17]

When *Iphigenia in Tauris* was given in English in 1942, Virgil Thomson opened his review with "the Juilliard School used to give modern operas. They did but they don't any more, as the ditty hath it." He went on to pronounce Gluck "a second-class composer."[18]

As if to prove Thomson wrong, eight months later Stoessel staged *The Mother* by the twenty-seven-year-old Joseph Wood, who had won the Juilliard American Opera competition. Its world premiere was given, along with *Solomon and Belkis* by Randall Thompson, in December 1942 in connection with twentieth anniversary of the League of Composers. Thompson's opera, based on Kipling's *Just So Stories*, was whimsical, whereas Wood's was about a child's death. The age of the composer did not prevent the *New York Times* from castigating the music, calling it student work and very callow.[19]

The opera in 1943 was Gluck's *Orfeo ed Euridice* in Stoessel's translation. The production consisted entirely of women because of the loss of the School's men to war. *The Abduction from the Seraglio* in April 1944 was conducted by the eminent Austrian conductor Erich Kleiber, who had given the first performance of *Wozzeck*.

The success of the opera program is seen in the following statistics: Of the 218 singers who appeared in name roles conducted by Stoessel at Juilliard from 1929 to 1943, twenty went directly to the Metropolitan Opera to sing in name roles. Seven others became members of the New York City Opera.

Between 1920 and 1930, fifty-five second-level orchestras—regional symphonies—had been founded in the United States, and they accepted small numbers of women. The depression, paradoxically, caused the formation of more than 120 additional regional orchestras, thirty-six of which were supported by the Works Progress Administration. During the 1930s there were twenty all-female orchestras. The depletion of males from professional orchestras meant that during the 1942–43 season all but three of the leading nineteen U.S. symphonies included women, but in small numbers—140 in 1943 and 150 in 1947. The all-women's symphonies did not survive into the postwar period.

Stoessel had inaugurated Juilliard fellowships for orchestral conducting in 1930. The course of study included a three-hour class with Stoessel (one hour with pianos and two hours with a volunteer orchestra) and an hour class in each of baton technique (Edgar Schenkman), orchestration (Stoessel originally, then Wagenaar), score reading (George Volkel), counterpoint, fugue, and composition (one course each year, with Bernard Wagenaar or Frederick Jacobi), German (Edith Braun), and violin lessons if the student was not a violinist. Robert Simon taught an optional class in radio techniques. If the conducting students were instrumentalists, they played in the symphony and opera orchestras.

> Stoessel's method of teaching conducting was primarily one of precept and example. When a student was called upon in class to conduct a portion of a prepared composition, he would be given an opportunity to show how he would conduct the music, until Mr. Stoessel felt that something should be done in a different manner. Thereupon, Stoessel would demonstrate the way in which he would do it, which was usually a clear, surefire method. Stoessel had little patience with a student who tried to insist on his own manner of conducting, with the remark, "But this is the way *I* feel it." To a remark such as that, Stoessel might reply: "Just because you happen to feel it that way is no reason why you should make an audience listen to it that way." It was always clear whose opinion should rule. Those few who dared to "stand up" to Stoessel were quickly removed from the class.[20]

Stoessel hated to relinquish the podium to anyone, not even a student, and almost never gave conducting students a chance in the operas despite the fact that opera is excellent training whereby young conductors rehearse the orchestra or chorus or coach the singers. "Stoessel's

Opera and Orchestra

131

own ambitions as a conductor probably led him to do most of the conducting at Juilliard," his biographer surmises.[21]

His system worked, however. Nearly half of the sixty-four fellowship-holders subsequently became conductors of symphony orchestras, opera or musical comedy productions, or other groups. Stoessel's conducting students included Dean Dixon, Frederik Prausnitz, Jerome Rappaport, Harvey Shapiro, Elie Siegmeister, Robert Ward, Bernard Herrmann, and Jerome Moross. Dixon, a New Yorker, had at seventeen organized his high school orchestra. Later he attracted the attention of Eleanor Roosevelt and became the first black to conduct the New York Philharmonic. Dixon founded the American Symphony Orchestra and had a considerable career conducting in Europe.

On the other side of the glass doors from the JGS, the conductor of the IMA Orchestra, Willem Willeke, selected concerto soloists from lists of prepared students submitted by faculty. There were no competitions. Unlike the orchestras at the Curtis Institute and the Eastman School, the JGS Orchestra did not use teachers as first-chair players.

Stoessel's Juilliard Orchestra of forty players played in public for the first time in 1928. The first program consisted of Bloch's Concerto Grosso (with Jerome Rappaport), Bach's d-minor concerto (with Adele Marcus), and Holst's *St. Paul's Suite.* The third concert, in May, was reviewed. The *New York Times* remarked, "There was something of the thrill of discovery in a first showing at the crowded Town Hall last evening of actual results of the late A. D. Juilliard's posthumous investment of millions in America's musical future."[22] The reviewer noted that all the 'cellists were women. Orchestra concerts were given at the Engineering Auditorium, at 25 West 39th Street, and at Town Hall. By the second season the renamed Juilliard String Orchestra had made a reputation for itself, and more than two thousand attended a concert in Town Hall in November 1929 while hundreds were turned away. Favorable comments appeared both in the New York press and the music journals. Ignoring the second clause in Augustus Juilliard's will—to present concerts free to the public—the School charged admission for its first orchestral concerts.

Ironically, the press did not attend as often when the School built its own hall at 130 Claremont and did not charge for concerts. Music critics did not review the Juilliard concerts unless something unusual was being presented. It was the *New York Time*'s policy, for example, not to review free concerts, considered amateur by definition. Some concerts in the new building were given for an invited audience. When critics did review the concerts, they were more apt to view them as "student performances" than when the Juilliard Orchestra had appeared for a paying audience at Town Hall. As a matter of practice, critics did not give the names of student performers in reviews. "Stoessel undoubtedly felt very keenly this change in his relationship with the press and public and sometimes felt that his work at Juilliard did not receive the recognition which it deserved."[23]

Owing to the presence of one conductor rather than a series of conductors each with his own repertoire, orchestral concerts could be organized into themes. The 1933–34 concert year, for example, was devoted to six concerts on the literature of the concerto, which involved faculty soloists. At the end of a four-day Bach festival in early May 1934, the Juilliard Orchestra and the Oratorio Society of New York presented what they believed was the first uncut performance of the *St. Matthew Passion* in the city. Every seat was reserved for the free concert. During 1935 and 1936 the orchestra performed all the Beethoven symphonies on a six-concert series.

Hutcheson participated creatively in these concerts. His Fantasie for Two Pianos and Orchestra was played by Vivian Rivkin and Irving Owen, with Frederick Dvonch conducting. In January 1936 Stoessel conducted his own Concerto Grosso for Strings and Piano, with Hutcheson as soloist. Other composers also participated. Mrs. H. H. A. Beach was present at a performance of her "Christ in the Universe" for chorus and four solo voices, which Stoessel conducted. In December 1945 the School celebrated Hindemith's fiftieth birthday with three concerts, one of which featured Hindemith conducting his "Die junge Magd."

The Juilliard Orchestra was formed from the top talent of the School; the Juilliard Training Orchestra, conducted by Edgar Schenkman, was a second orchestra. Because of Hutcheson and Stoessel's connection with Chautauqua, half of its orchestra and a third of the soloists were Juilliard students or graduates. Stoessel frequently placed them in his orchestras in Chautauqua, at Worcester, or with the Metropolitan Opera's orchestra. The students could gain extra experience—and regular union scale.

The Juilliard Orchestra leased Carnegie Hall in February 1943 for its only concert in memory of Augustus Juilliard, a benefit for the United Hospital Fund that garnered $656.65. Four soloists appeared: Muriel Kerr, playing the Beethoven Piano Concerto no. 4; Felix Salmond as solo 'cellist in Bloch's *Schelomo;* Josephine Antoine, who sang two Mozart arias; and Carroll Glenn as soloist in the Sibelius Violin Concerto. Because of the war, more than half the orchestra was female.

At a March 1940 orchestra department (brass and woodwinds) meeting the faculty discussed the material to use for a sight-reading test for postgraduate students. It was decided that each teacher write a sight-reading selection for his instrument. The tradition of applied faculty composing was still strong. At the next meeting, the new examples for clarinet, trumpet, trombone, horn and tuba, and oboe were adopted.

Starting in the fall of 1941, all courses were reorganized. The idea was to provide a minimum of required classes, with electives to be greatly enlarged in number. The class in music history was reduced into a one-year survey course that was required of all students in addition to one-year, specialized elective courses from which students could choose. A new subject, the staging of operetta and pageants, was available to all graduate students. Theory 32 was changed from fugue to the study and writing of inventions and other small contrapuntal forms. Fugue-writing was to be taken up in the fourth year.

The string department had thought that instrumental students were required to work too much on theory; the faculty recommended that this course be simplified, thus allowing students more time for practice. Under pressure like this, combined with that emanating from Schoen-René in the voice department, the theory faculty were forced to cave in on the requirements. Instead of students having to pass Theory 32— three years—to get into the JGS, now they only had to pass Theory 21— one and a half years. Beginning in 1934–35, the entrance test in theory was spelled out in the catalog: "1. The harmonization of a melody. 2. A figured bass. 3. A modulation. 4. Two exercises in counterpoint of different species." Singers and string players were not required to take the test in counterpoint.

A state requirement for a Juilliard degree was a course in health and physical education. "Health Education" consisted of a two-point course entitled "Hygiene" and devoted to a study of such topics as communicable disease, food and nutrition, and mental health. The work in physical education consisted of various activities classes in sports and games, which were conducted in swimming pools and gymnasiums in the immediate vicinity. Ernest J. Stewart was in charge of the program.

The number of U.S. high school graduates had soared from the 597,000 who received diplomas in 1928 to 1,221,000 in 1940, which was out of keeping with the low population growth of the 1930s. By 1940 slightly more than 50 percent of seventeen-year-olds had received a diploma. The number of bachelor's degrees conferred mounted from 122,000 in 1930 to 186,000 in 1940. Enrollment at the JGS from 1933 to 1943 averaged 170; at the IMA, it was nearly 1,000. Male–female ratios were being kept again. In May 1945 there were 955 students at the IMA, of whom only 215 were men.

A pervasive snobbism harbored by JGS students had set in toward the IMA. There were stories of JGS students not wanting to share a locker with IMA students. To this day, JGS graduates will proclaim the inferiority of the IMA, whose students were considered a "lesser breed." They even refuse to identify the IMA as a part of Juilliard. Mark Schubart, who became dean of the two schools when they combined, later observed how wrong that attitude was: "The proof was in the pudding, in that the level of talent and success was not lowered [by the merger]."[24]

Degree programs were instituted at the IMA in 1934. By 1938, 136 students were registered in degree courses, and 65 were in the public school music department. They could take courses toward the degree in the new Summer School. It was a bachelor of science degree rather than the bachelor of arts because the New York Department of Education classified music as a science. All the academic work of college level was given in the building. The B.S. with a major in music education was first given at the Institute in 1935; the degree with a major in an instrument was meant to help those seeking positions in colleges and conservatories. The M.S. degree was required in order to teach at most colleges throughout the country.

In 1940 and 1941 the School began its short-lived experiment in radio broadcasting. The IMA broadcast on WNYC on Wednesday afternoons at 4, and the Juilliard Summer School broadcast fifteen afternoon recital hours from the School's auditorium. The artists, including Katherine Bacon, Charles Hackett, Sascha Gorodnitzki, Louis Persinger, and Naoum Benditzky, appeared in solo recitals and in ensembles such as the Bos-Gardner-Krane Trio. The children of the Preparatory Department of the IMA were also heard in eighteen broadcasts between July 9 and August 13, 1940. Somehow, however, Juilliard was slow to capitalize on the value of radio (chapter 6).

Ignoring the silence in Juilliard's will on the subject of American citizenship, the JGS continued to perpetuate nativism and anti-immigrant feelings. The 1935–36 catalog added two new aspects to admission requirements: First, "Each applicant must submit a birth certificate. If a certificate is not available, a statement of the date of birth, attested by a Notary Public, will be acceptable." Second, "Two years must elapse before an unsuccessful applicant may be re-examined, unless the board of examiners at the time of examination requests that the applicant be heard again the following year."[25]

Finally, at a faculty meeting in May 1941, Hutcheson brought up the question of whether to open JGS fellowships to all the Americas. Doing so, he argued, would follow the State Department's policy of cultivating friendly relationships with the South American republics and would aid in a cultural exchange between the United States and the other countries of the Western Hemisphere. The board had unanimously approved the idea, provided there were no restrictions in Juilliard's will, which no one checked. According to Frances Schuman, Australian students had been allowed into Juilliard because Hutcheson was Australian (he bowed to pressure and finally became an American citizen in 1936).[26] Unlike the JGS, however, the IMA had always opened its doors to students from all countries. Now, the JGS executive committee unanimously and heartily approved the idea to admit students from the Western Hemisphere. In October 1941 two Latin American students were admitted.

Changes among the faculty were inevitable. In May 1941 Helen Augustin of piano faculty and Madeleine Walther of the voice department retired. Samuel Gardner and Karl Kraeuter of the violin department also left. Katherine Bacon was added to the piano faculty the next season, as was violinist Mischa Mischakoff. In April 1942 Paul Reimers died and left his estate to the JSM for unrestricted purposes; part of the money was used to purchase the complete music library of the Friends of Music. Anna Schoen-René and Alexander Siloti both retired in 1942; Schoen-René's work was taken over by Queena Mario. In 1944 both Josef Lhevinne and Georges Barrère died.

On May 12, 1943, an audience of five hundred distinguished members and guests gathered at the American Academy of Arts and Letters for the annual ceremony honoring outstanding Americans in art, literature, and music. On the program was Robert Nathan's ballad poem *Dunkirk*, which had been set to music by Walter Damrosch. Albert Stoessel conducted the string orchestra, with Hugh Thompson as soloist and Damrosch himself at the piano. "The performance proceeded smoothly until at the fermata on the word *death*, half way through the 12th stanza . . . Stoessel gave the cut-off with the baton, and then slumped to the floor of the podium, where he lay gasping and groaning in agony. The musicians continued, thinking that the conductor had lost his footing, but after playing a few measures they realized that he lay completely motionless. They stopped abruptly. Before his wife reached his side, Stoessel had died."[27]

Stoessel's sudden death at the age of forty-nine made the front page of the *New York Times* and "brought to a close one of the most brilliant careers in the history of American music."[28] The School reeled from the loss. Once again a man in whom the JMF had invested heavily had died prematurely.

∾

After the demise of *The Baton* in 1932 and its successor, *Dynamics*, in 1936, the IMA had no student publications until *Harmonics* began in January 1939. *Harmonics* was a student, alumni, and faculty effort edited by Victor Wolfram. An editorial revealed the usual apathy among conservatory students: "The lack of interest of the average Institute student in school affairs has been nothing short of colossal," and "it is difficult to understand why we have waited so long to organize for ourselves the many extra-curricular activities found at other colleges. Institute students have always complained about their lack of opportunity for social relaxation."[29] Complete apathy had greeted a poll of student likes and dislikes. The Student Club was still active, however, and offered programs one or two evenings a month, with musical events, discussions, and "just plain fun." Students exchanged information by leaving notes in the cloakroom, although one did propose having mailboxes. They danced with faculty and staff at an annual Christmas party in 1939. In February 1941 a literary club, its membership open to anyone interested, held a second meeting and discussed Ernest Hemingway's best-selling *For Whom the Bell Tolls*.

Although racism was still rampant in many areas of American society, the problem was less severe in music generally and in classical music in particular. Musicians tend to notice first what instrument one plays, then how well, and only then the color of one's skin. Life circumstances and racism may have prevented a student from achieving enough to be accepted to a conservatory but, once in, the only consideration was proficiency in music. Mercer Ellington was a William Vacchiano trumpet student at Juilliard from 1938 to 1940, and Anne Wiggins Brown, who sang Bess in the original 1935 Broadway production of *Porgy and Bess*, was an IMA student (1928–34) of Lucia Dunham and an opera student of Stoessel. She was the first African American singer to win the Margaret McGill scholarship.[30] She remembered being very happy at the School, although she had been discriminated against in a song contest in her native Baltimore.[31] The 1936 graduating class of seventy-one included four African Americans, one of whom was conductor Dean Dixon. A decade later, the student newspaper published an unsigned article in support of Marian Anderson singing at the Lincoln Memorial.

The Placement Bureau that Erskine had opposed was established October 1935, the culminating work of a former student club. In three years it received 2,500 unsolicited requests for teachers and performers. During 1938, employment was given to 489 graduates and students for private teaching, performances, and school and college positions.

George Wedge woke the Alumni Association from its long quiescence. The ubiquitous Dorothy Crowthers (former editor of *The Baton*) was in charge of the Association, whose new platform included assisting American composers, especially IMA alumni composers, by performing their works at alumni concerts.

The "Inquiring Reporter" for the *IMA News* (student Irene E. Sherrock), after interviewing various students in 1942 about their future plans, came to the following conclusions:

> The general consensus shows that most of the singers want careers in opera or radio and would prefer not to teach. The students studying orchestra instruments—brasses and woodwinds—would like a job with a good dance band or symphony for a while and later turn to teaching. Some are more interested in the arranging and scoring side of that work. Most of the pianists would teach. The string instrument players would like to belong to a good quartet or symphony orchestra. Most of these students would change to something different [that is, another career] if it offered a much better living. The Public School Music people only ask for a self-sustaining job so long as they can be good missionaries in the wilderness of music education.[32]

IMA catalogs covering the mid-1930s through the mid-1940s provide nearly uniform estimated expenses for the school year: for room and board for thirty-two weeks, a minimum of $400 and an average of $550; for lunches, carfare, recreation, and incidentals, a minimum of $200 and an average of $350; and for books, a minimum of $15 and an average of $25. "A student cannot expect to earn his living expenses while studying, as the course of study makes such a plan impractical. Most unskilled student work is paid at a low rate and at the present time opportunities in most types of work are few compared to the number of students in search of them," the catalog warned.

Tuition varied; that for singing, at $350, was the most expensive, and the preparatory course (for children) was the least at $150. B.S. degree courses cost $475 a year for singing; $425 for piano, organ, and strings; $375 for other orchestral instruments; $400 for a theory major; and $330 for a public school music major. According to the catalog, "A student in the diploma or degree course must maintain an average in ALL subjects consistent with the standards of the School. A general average of 'B' to 'C' is required. A student who falls below this average or who fails to pass a subject repeated will be asked to withdraw from the course." The grades were: A, excellent; B, good; C, fair; D, poor; F, failure: H, credit for attendance, if examination is not taken." All grades, with the students' names, were posted publicly in the School.

A graduate and faculty picnic supper was held on the North Terrace in May 1942 as a prelude to commencement exercises. Clarinet teacher Arthur Christmann assembled a band of twenty-five. Students played games of quoits, archery, pistol shooting, and darts: "No casualties were reported." The cafeteria furnished a ham dinner, and the evening's highlight occurred when Elsie, the somewhat moth-eaten Opera School cow from *Jack and the Beanstalk*, appeared and cavorted around the terrace.

❧

Faculty at Juilliard were touched by the events in Europe as early as 1938, when Olga Samaroff, in order to publish her book *The Magic World of Music*, was required to prove to her Berlin publishers that she was Aryan and not Jewish.

Male students were seriously affected by the world situation. "We have never had much difficulty with the attitude of students in the JGS," Oscar Wagner reported to the JGS faculty meeting in October 1940, after the draft had been instituted. "An amazing majority of them have always attended to their work admirably. But what we notice is that our children who left us in May have returned to us grown up. It is as if they felt 'I've no idea how long this is going to last; I've got to make every minute count this time.'" Concerning the inevitable conscription, Wagner asked the faculty "to remember that no matter how sincerely you feel on the subject, it does no one any good, and may do real harm if you let any young man feel it is a pity that his work may have to be interrupted just at this time in his development. To begin with, it has not yet been interrupted, and next, it will only take the heart out of him if he suspects you feel it. We are trustees of the art of music and we all understand that these things of the spirit must be kept alive for the years when there is again peace."[33] Wagner suggested that when a man who had been granted a fellowship for next year was subsequently drafted, the fellowship should be held until the student was able to return to school. The faculty of the JGS and the IMA both endorsed the idea wholeheartedly. By May 1942 enrollment was 26 percent lower than the previous year.

The first Juilliard casualty of World War II was IMA trumpet student Alexander Nadelson. A Vacchiano student, he was stationed on the USS *Arizona* in Pearl Harbor. The next day, "Those [students] who were in the Recital Hall Monday morning, December 8, and heard President Roosevelt ask Congress for a declaration of war against the Japanese Empire [would] not soon forget that solemn hour."[34] Ultimately, six hundred men from Juilliard served in the U.S. Army, Navy, Marine Corps, their affiliated air forces, and in the Merchant Marine. By March 1945 five had been killed.

Ernest Hutcheson provided "A Message to Our Boys in Service" for the *IMA News:*

Do not fear that your musical career will be endangered by your service. Provided that you suffer no serious physical injury, which God forbid, you will come back with a depth of background and a richness of experience that will give profounder values to your music and to your entire life. Many of you, I know, will have the opportunity to make effective use of your talents in the entertainment rooms and bands of your camps. Some that I know of are getting in quite a lot of practice and are even feeding classical music to the army![35]

Responding to much discussion about making courses and music study more "practical," in January 1943 Hutcheson reported that new courses pertinent to the war effort were being added to the IMA's curriculum for the second semester. The courses were radio communications, basic German, "Analysis of Propaganda and Its Relation to World Affairs," mimeographing and duplicating, and a mathematics refresher.

By 1943 the students had organized themselves for war activities. A group of women known as the Triple V Club wrote letters to men in the services. "VVV," which also gave its name to a short-lived student newspaper, the *VVV News*, stood for vigilance, valor, and victory. Dorothy Crowthers organized the club and edited its newspaper, which the government censored although it was meant for IMA and JGS servicemen. She reported of one club activity:

> We have designed and made an Honor Roll that is eighty inches wide by thirty-four inches high. At each end, with a background of furled flags, a golden eagle is poised for flight. Under the heading, Honor Roll—in the service of our country—your names appear. Each is on a separate card with a red star for Army, blue star for Navy, green star for Air Force and double stars for those overseas—the second star being silver. The entire honor roll is in the framed, glassed-covered enclosure newly built in the main hallway leading from the Dean's office to Room 115.[36]

The War Stamp Club promoted an afternoon concert through the purchase of 25 cent war stamps and collected $400, due in part to promotional work by Rosina Lhevinne. The students also organized a plasma campaign—donations to be made after examinations. Graduates Risë Stevens and Eleanor Steber made war bond recordings for distribution among servicemen. "Students too have had unprecedented problems and in addition are contributing their effort to war work in camps, canteens, USO activities, as blood donors and nurses' aides, carrying on multitudinous correspondence with boys in service and at the same time pursuing their studies with unremitting diligence and vigor," Ernest Hutcheson told the faculty in 1944.[37]

On May 8, 1945, the Germans surrendered: It was V-E Day. On that same day, Ernest Hutcheson told the faculty that he would retire as president; clearly, he had waited until the war was over. He had joined the IMA faculty during World War I and was to continue teaching at the School until his death in 1951. His tenure rivaled that of the older faculty, and his artistic personality and teaching left a lasting imprint.

From the Institute's beginning until Hutcheson's retirement, 3,468 students were graduated from the IMA. The first year after the war, 1945–46, saw the largest enrollment in the history of the two schools: 1,517 students. Students complained in cartoons and essays of waiting in long lines—said to be worse than the army's—to register and to see Dean Wedge. Hundreds who had left for war had returned to continue their education; for others, the GI bill helped guarantee their schooling. A new era would begin, and a new era needed a new leader.

Opera
and
Orchestra

6

New
Blood:

WILLIAM SCHUMAN

THE YEAR 1945 was one of momentous events. In April, Franklin D. Roosevelt died; in May, Mussolini was killed and Hitler also perished. Thanks in part to the atom bomb in August, World War II ended. In the musical world, both Bartók and Webern died.

The expected recession did not materialize in America. Instead, a postwar boom began. By 1951 incomes grew: One-third of the population earned between $3,000 and $5,000 a year, and one family in seven had an income between $5,000 and $10,000. Life expectancies had also steadily increased, from forty-nine years in 1900 to sixty-eight in 1950. The number of symphony orchestras was likewise growing. Whereas in 1900 only a handful had existed in the United States, by 1951 there were 659 "symphonic groups," including 32 professional, 343 community, 231 college, and other amateur groups.

Albert Stoessel's death shocked Juilliard, making both John Erskine and Ernest Hutcheson contemplate the need to find Hutcheson's successor. More interested in teaching, Hutcheson had never truly wanted to be an administrator. As president, he seemed aloof and out of touch with students. Since the death of his wife Irmgart in 1940, he had relied more heavily on Oscar Wagner to run the School. In addition, his health was not good.

Erskine and the board—Hutcheson, Edward Johnson, Henry S. Drinker, John M. Perry, Parker McCollester, Allen Wardwell, James P. Warburg, and Franklin B. Benkard—took into consideration three criteria for a new president:

1. His standing among other musicians as artist and man.
2. His ability as educator and administrator.
3. His sympathy with the aims of the School to date and the probability of his taking us further, let alone holding on to what we have.[1]

Several board members considered Bruno Walter, but Walter was old and interested in returning to the Viennese world where he had lived before the war. The job of president would not go to a member of his generation.

William Howard Schuman was born in New York in 1910. His father changed their spelling of the name from Schuhmann to Schuman. The family were German Jews, one of only two Jewish families in Englewood, New Jersey, and they had their own prejudices. "Their idea was that if you married out of the religion, that was better than marrying a Jew of East European extraction."[2] Schuman admitted that prejudice against other-than-German Jews took him a long time to overcome.

His father was in the printing business and reasonably successful; he had risen from being a bookkeeper to vice president of the firm of Oberly and Newell. The father was a steady sort, but Schuman's mother had an unspecified disease and was ill for a long time. William, named after William Howard Taft for patriotic reasons, had a sister, Audrey, and a younger brother, Robert. Robert was retarded due to a birth defect and died in his thirties. Family influences included a strong sense of ethics and an enthusiastic Americanism.

A musical career for young William was far from inevitable. In school he was more interested in theater and in baseball than in music. He played violin, double-bass, and banjo, although he never became proficient at any instrument. He also sang and formed a jazz band. One reason for his lack of proficiency was that he slowly developed a mysterious atrophy in his hands; the muscles between thumb and index finger did not operate. Schuman has said, "It never occurred to me to compose at the piano for the very practical reason that I can't play it."[3] He had to give up conducting the Sarah Lawrence chorus because of the condition.

As a teenager, he collaborated with his closest friend, Eddie Marks, Jr., son of music publisher Edward B. Marks. Marks wrote the lyrics and

Schuman the music for about 150 Tin Pan Alley songs. Another close friend, Richard Rodgers, was to become renowned in the genre. Frank Loesser and Schuman turned out some forty (unsuccessful) songs. Schuman realized, however, that he did not have sufficient technique to be able to continue in this vein.

Rodgers and Loesser's half-brother Arthur had both attended the IMA, and it must have occurred to Schuman to apply there. He and his future wife both observed Arthur's "dark shadow" on Frank, whom he treated with "withering snobbishness" because he was in popular music. Later Arthur, Schuman said, was unkind to him about his First Symphony and was "cruelly imperious to me. I never liked him for that." If Schuman associated Arthur with the IMA, he may have formed an animus toward it for making Frank feel "intellectually and creatively inferior" to Arthur.[4]

After graduating from high school in February 1928, Schuman enrolled at the New York University School of Commerce. But an experience shortly before his twentieth birthday altered that course. His sister gave him an extra ticket to the New York Philharmonic for April 4, 1930. The program consisted of Robert Schumann's Symphony No. 3 (the Rhenish), Smetana's *The Moldau*, and the first performance of *Summer Evening* by Kodály. Often retelling this story, Schuman did not relate the rest of the concert program. As a commemorative tribute to Cosima Wagner, whose funeral took place that very day, the conductor Toscanini replaced Mendelssohn's *Midsummer Night's Dream Music* with the funeral music from *Die Götterdämmerung*, a piece Schuman later claimed he would not accept $500 to endure. His biographer describes a purely musical epiphany:

> For him the concert held a private meaning. He felt as if his head would split with the surge of impressions, as if his heart would snap with sheer excitement. Particularly exciting was the way all the fiddlers bowed together and the force with which they could attack a chord. He was intrigued by the tunes that changed as they recurred and the measures in which the drummer had nothing to play. There seemed to be more inventive ability displayed at this one concert by the New York Philharmonic than by all the jazz bands on Broadway. The evening meant discovery. It was poignant, pregnant of things to come, baffling.[5]

According to Schuman, the next day (a Saturday) he walked out of his business class at NYU, returned—always practical—to collect the balance of his tuition, and kept on walking. He called to quit his job at the Paramount Advertising Agency. On his way uptown he spotted the

Malkin Conservatory at 77th Street and West End Avenue. He asked the receptionist what he should study to become a composer. "Harmony," she replied, and he enrolled in harmony lessons. His father, knowing that age twenty was late to start a serious musical career, supported this about-face. "Bill, you don't have to be a business man if you don't want to," Schuman related, "but if you go into music, you're up against genius. If you're not at the top, it's no good."[6] That was the melodramatic story that Schuman, the former ad man, promulgated.

The Malkin Conservatory's harmony teacher was Max Persin, a student of Anton Arensky. Lessons at Schuman's home lasted four and five hours. Schuman also studied counterpoint with Charles Haubiel. He worked at it daily, supported by his prosperous family that would weather the Great Depression unscathed.

In 1931 Schuman enrolled at Teachers College at Columbia University. He then enrolled in the Supervisor's Orchestra in the Special Studies Department of the IMA in 1932. During the spring of 1934 he studied piano with Abby Starkey and violin with Conrad Held at the IMA through Teachers College, and during 1934 and 1935 he just studied piano with Starkey. In addition, he attended the newly created Juilliard Summer School in 1932, 1933, and 1936. He was never a regular student at either the IMA or the JGS.

In 1935 Schuman earned a bachelor of science degree in music education at Columbia in the program that had affiliated with the IMA only a few years earlier. During one semester he studied John Dewey's *Art as Experience*.[7] The best-known educator in America and abroad and also the most influential thinker of his time, Dewey (1859–1952) presented a pragmatic philosophy—"instrumentalism" or "experimentalism"—that stressed learning by doing; he also advocated workshop and laboratory courses to foster creativity. American secondary schools—and Schuman—became increasingly influenced by Dewey's concepts, which opposed dogmatic and authoritarian teaching methods and rote learning.[8]

Schuman's experience at Teachers College, however, was primarily negative. By stressing methodology over substance—how to teach over what to teach—the school taught him how not to instruct his students. Schuman particularly disliked the connections drawn, literally, between the arts. One professor advocated teaching children by having them listen to a piece and then draw what they heard. Schuman was outraged and, in what was to become a typical pattern of outspokenness, said so in a public forum. Nevertheless, he continued at Teachers College and earned an M.A. in 1937.

Upon graduation with his bachelor's degree only five years after the life-changing concert, Schuman decided he could teach at the university level. Sarah Lawrence had no openings in its music department, still in time Schuman managed to convince the college's president that he, Schuman, was the right person to administer a Rockefeller Foundation grant intended to explore the arts at the school. He succeeded by championing some of Dewey's premises.

When Schuman married Frances Prince in 1936, he told her, "I started late. Very late. I have to make up for lost time."[9] He set to work immediately. That July, while still pursuing his master's at Teachers College, he re-enrolled for three courses in the Juilliard Summer School: composition with Roy Harris, who had just joined the faculty; harmony with Bernard Wagenaar; and orchestration with Adolf Schmid. In the fall, he continued to study at Harris's Princeton home because Harris did not teach in the Regular Division at the School.[10] Schuman later criticized his teachers, saying later that the courses he took at Juilliard, although he did not specify the Summer School, were "highly rigid and conventional."[11] Once president, he would institute Literature and Materials (L&M), a theory program, in part as a reaction against his Summer School training.

Schuman's first important performance was his First Symphony, the piece Arthur Loesser had not liked, at a Composers' Forum Laboratory concert in the fall of 1936, during his first several months' of study with Harris. The First Quartet was on the same program. Neither piece was received well, and, lacking confidence in his work, Schuman withdrew both.

His next performance was to have been the result of a competition held by the politically liberal Musicians' Committee of the North American Committee to Aid Spanish Democracy. The judges included two of his teachers, Roy Harris and Bernard Wagenaar, in addition to Roger Sessions and Aaron Copland. Schuman's Second Symphony won the competition. Only Sessions had not voted for the piece. Schuman wrote to him and was invited to Princeton, where the two hit it off. Sessions changed his mind and said Schuman should continue working on the symphony, but the composer withdrew that work as well.

In any case, the competition had failed to raise enough money for the proposed performance, publication, or recording. Its most practical effect was to bring Schuman's music to the attention of Aaron Copland. Schuman's Second Symphony was performed in June 1938, with Edgar Schenkman conducting the WPA's Greenwich Village Orchestra. It was the first real success Schuman experienced as a composer. Copland described it as "the musical find of the year . . . it seems to me that Schuman is a composer who is going places."[12] CBS radio also played the work under Howard Barlow. Copland then recommended it to Serge Koussevitzky, who played it with the Boston Symphony Orchestra in February 1939. Boston reviewers declared it ugly, however. Schuman later remarked, referring to the experience of hearing a quartet laughing at his music during a rehearsal, that composers must develop a thick skin if they are going to be public figures. Schuman thickened his skin in Boston.

Schuman wrote his *American Festival Overture* for Koussevitzky. "Fine! Now you must begin to hate Roy Harris," Koussevitzky advised after its premiere in 1939.[13] The comment hit the psychological mark; much of Schuman's subsequent behavior involved a disloyalty toward father figures and a conscious erasure of his not-glorious-enough past.

When World War II came, Schuman could not enlist because of his marriage and his neurological condition. During the war years he blossomed as a composer. Starting in 1941, his career rocketed in a way that few American composers have experienced. The list of his musical triumphs was dizzying. Koussevitzky conducted Symphony No. 3, and the New York Music Critics' Circle awarded it as best orchestral work of the season. Carl Engel, president of G. Schirmer publishers, asked that his firm have first option on everything Schuman wrote and even furnished him with a monthly stipend. Arthur Rodzinski and the Cleveland Orchestra performed the Fourth Symphony, and Philadelphia and New York performances under Eugene Ormandy followed. In January 1943 a Town Hall program was entirely devoted to Schuman's music. Another symphony (No. 5, for strings) was composed for Koussevitzky and the Boston Symphony Orchestra. Performed numerous times, the work secured his position in the music world. Schuman's *A Free Song* won the first Pulitzer Prize given in music in 1943, and he also won two Guggenheim Fellowships, the Koussevitzky Foundation Award, and the composition award from the National Institute of Arts and Letters. In 1945 Antony Tudor asked for a ballet score, which resulted in the dark, male-dominated *Undertow*. Alfred Wallenstein conducted the concert version with the Los Angeles Philharmonic in April 1945, and Fritz Reiner and the Pittsburgh Symphony gave a concert version of Schuman's theater piece *Side Show*.

Carl Engel died suddenly in May 1944, and G. Schirmer searched for a new director of publications. Koussevitzky recommended Schuman, who accepted immediately. Schirmer held the position open until June 1945 so Schuman could fulfill his contract at Sarah Lawrence. Three days after he began full-time work at Schirmer's, however, a better offer came his way. He already harbored negative feelings about the firm. "I knew that I had made a terrible mistake," he recalled, "because I dis-

William Schuman, 1962.
*(Impact Photos, Inc., photo from The
Juilliard School Archives)*

liked Mr. [Gustav] Schirmer—everybody disliked Mr. Schirmer, he was
a very vulger and horrible man and was not always completely honest
in his business dealings as I had occasion to know, and I suddenly realized that I couldn't not be in the business, I couldn't divorce the publications job from the others, and it just seemed wrong to me and I felt
trapped."[14] Although Gustav Schirmer released him from his contract
in October 1945, only five months later, Schuman was loath to give up
the job's power over other composers' compositions. He continued there
until 1952. As a peculiar reward for Sessions's having voted against his
symphony, Schuman arranged for Schirmer to publish Sessions's Symphony No. 2.

Schuman had read Erskine's books. At a fund-raiser Schuman defended modern music against the conservative Erskine, who in his typical manner had said, "Modern music has two problems. The first is, it's
not heard; the second is, it's heard." Copland, who was present, warned
Schuman not to antagonize people in such public disagreements. But
Erskine, according to Schuman, was impressed with his defense of
modernism: "Now I want you to know Schuman, that I wasn't always
an old fuddy-duddy and I loved the way you came at me tonight." He
asked Schuman to lunch at the all-male Century Club.

Erskine had served for a short time as one of the directors of
G. Schirmer and had come to know Schuman through that venue as
well. James Paul Warburg (1896–1969)—James Loeb's nephew and Paul
Warburg's son—also knew Schuman. His daughter, Kay (b. 1924), one

of Warburg's three daughters with Kay Swift, was Schuman's student at Sarah Lawrence.

When it came to being president of Juilliard, Erskine considered Schuman "a dynamic person, . . . not a rash one, but certainly he is full of new ideas. He had my confidence and the support of Ernest Hutcheson, who still in my opinion and I believe in Bill's, is the strongest teacher in the School."[15] Erskine may have been wrong on one count. Despite Hutcheson's support, Schuman dismissed his accomplishments: "Hutcheson was always the gentleman. I am sure that he would have quite happily slit my throat, but at any rate he hadn't been president long enough [eight years] to have made any difference. He was a very weak president, sort of an interim one."[16]

When Warburg, a New Dealer, tried to persuade Schuman to stand as a candidate for president, he protested loudly that the board would not want him, a stance that would protect him from potential rejection. He had no experience as an administrator, the second qualification for the job. And there was reason to believe he did not fit the board's third criterion either—that of sympathy with the School's aims. According to Schuman, James Paul Warburg invited him to tell the Juilliard board what he had been broadcasting as being wrong with the School.[17] "Now look," Schuman bullied them, "there will be a revolution if I come, and you don't want revolution. And another thing, let me ask you a question. If you want me to come, if the answer to this question is yes, I'll never come. My question is, does the faculty have tenure? They said, 'Why do you ask?' I said, 'Because if the faculty has tenure I can't do anything.' So they said, 'No, it doesn't.'"[18] It was obvious that Schuman intended to fire many faculty. Equally obvious was his fundamental lack of knowledge about how conservatories functioned. No independent conservatory, in the past or present, has a universitylike system of tenure. Neither do conservatories have professorship hierarchies or mandatory retirements. All faculty at Juilliard continue to be hired on one-year contracts.

Impressed with Schuman's recent credentials in music and with his youth and vigor, the board decided in July 1945 to hire him. According to the thirty-five-year-old Schuman, it was the first time conservative Erskine and liberal Warburg agreed on anything. Also according to Schuman, the ninety-year-old John Perry, Augustus Juilliard's lawyer, expressed their reservations in dramatic terms: "It's either the greatest thing that has ever happened to the Juilliard School or the most colossal error of [our] collective lives." A writer from *Time* magazine compared Schuman's situation with the magazine world: "It is like a *New Republic* editor taking over *The Saturday Evening Post*."[19]

Although Roy Harris had asked Schuman to persuade the Steinway family to put his own name up for president of Juilliard, Schuman had already been picked. He was placed in an awkward position with regard to his former teacher. He rose quickly over Harris, however, and did not look back; he rarely credited Harris for what he had learned from him and did nothing to promote Harris's music. When a major critic, Alfred Frankenstein, wrote that Schuman's music "has much more rhythmic fire, variety, and vivacity than Harris," he must have felt the break to be complete.[20]

His biographer wrote in 1954 of Schuman's personality, "Schuman is relatively free of introspection and of psychic conflict. . . . he seems *too* well-adjusted to be an artist at all." A Democrat, his politics were best described as middle of the road. He was "given to sharp changes of personality. . . . Sometimes the impetuousness [led] him into a high enthusiasm which swiftly develop[ed] into a lost enthusiasm, leaving those whom he involved in it dazed and forgotten on the sidelines."[21] A few years later, Juilliard would feel the force of that personality trait.

Once at Juilliard, Schuman ruthlessly set about demolishing two of the remains of his past. He dissolved the forty-year-old, venerable Institute of Musical Art and killed off the successful Juilliard Summer School. His justification of the dissolution of the IMA was not quite persuasive in the face of "enormous opposition":

> I felt it was ridiculous to have both the IMA and the JGS. I felt that there was a big snob business. At the Graduate School they just taught piano, violin, 'cello, voice, and perhaps a couple of harp students, and flute, but none of the other orchestral instruments which were apparently considered beneath contempt, and the IMA just about anybody could go to, but only [get a] scholarship in the upper school. . . . Well, the board was with me, but there was enormous opposition on the faculty of the Graduate School [and no doubt by the IMA as well], but we put it through at great cost, it was very difficult to do. I pointed out that in a few years nobody would even remember that there were two institutions, and nobody ever thinks of it anymore.[22]

Thus the achievements of Damrosch, Loeb, Erskine, and Hutcheson were suddenly swept into the dustbin of history. On the positive side, the legacy of Eugene Noble also vanished: the stricture that only Americans and only performers of certain instruments may apply to the School. Henceforth, the entire school was known only by its formal name, the Juilliard School of Music, and the words *Institute of Musical Art* disappeared from musicians' vocabularies.

Schuman wanted no trace of his musical past to intrude upon the present. He eliminated the possibility that others would meet the most important influence of their musical lives, as Harris had been for him:

> There had been a Juilliard Summer School which really existed be-cause George Wedge had it and they made money on that, as distin-guished from losing money in the others, and I pointed out to my di-rectors that we should close it because people [like Schuman himself] would come and say they went to Juilliard when they actually went to the Summer School, and it was hurting the reputation of the School because anybody could go, so we eventually closed down the Summer School, which was unpopular—a lot of the people wanted to keep the Summer School going.[23]

In the summer of 1948, for example, the Summer School had 1,431 stu-dents. After twenty successful years it was dissolved in 1952, along with its public concert series. Nonetheless, Schuman and the board hoped "that it would be allowed to lapse quietly, for Juilliard spokesmen [in 1954] were reluctant to discuss the matter."[24]

The Music Education Program at Juilliard, which was affiliated with Schuman's alma mater, Teachers College, was also eliminated in 1949. It did not matter that the program had been Frank Damrosch's pet project and vision. Schuman likely never met Frank Damrosch; if he had, he could not have tolerated such a father figure. Because he had a de-gree in music education the Music Education Program had to disappear, part of Schuman's effort to reinvent himself as a president worthy of running a renowned performance school. The reason for this may have been insecurities about his inability to play an instrument, his lack of a doctorate, or his master's degree in the field that he denigrated.

"The [School] never did any new music," Schuman recalled. "They did more new music the first year that I was there than in the entire previous forty years or whatever it was in one season." His sense of the School's history was inaccurate: A considerable number of contempo-rary pieces and operas had been performed before his presidency (chap-ter 5). Schuman also claimed not to want his own music played:

> [Wilfred] Pelletier was the conductor and I remember he pro-grammed my *American Festival Overture* and I was so furious I just showed my attitude by not going to the concert. And in subsequent years I told my colleagues, I said, "Howard Hanson did some wonder-ful things at the Eastman School—that was one of the first great mu-sic schools in the country to be serious about education—but he turned it into a personal vehicle for his own compositions, and I will never do that at Juilliard." I never did, and I am happy to say that nei-ther has Peter Mennin.[25]

Schuman's music, however, was taught in a course on fugue, as catalogs testify, and both his *New England Triptych* and Symphony for Strings (but none of Roy Harris's works) were played five times when the orchestra toured six European countries in 1958.

Although the buildings underwent few physical changes, the wrecking ball hit the two schools in other ways. It started at the top. The board appeared to give Schuman a free hand to fire administration and faculty. He recalled that in 1946 he "had to dismiss Dean Wagner—Oscar Wagner who had been the dean there, but I thought he was an absolute incompetent."[26] Wagner's competence, however, had never been previously questioned in almost twenty years of service to the JGS. George Wedge took over.

As Wedge and Wagner's replacement, Schuman wanted Mark Schubart (b. 1918), a *New York Times* music editor. The men had met through editing Max Rudolf's *The Grammar of Conducting*.[27] Olin Downes, Schubart's superior at the *Times*, had instituted a policy that *Times* critics should have nothing to do with the musical world, financially or professionally. Schubart chose to give up newspaper work to accept the position at Juilliard in 1946. That was not too difficult, because Juilliard paid significantly more than he had earned at the newspaper. Schubart's loyalty to Schuman was more important than his qualifications. When he began, he has admitted, he was a "greenhorn" who did not know what a transcript or an academic credit was.[28] He nonetheless became a highly successful administrator.

In 1948 Schuman appointed as registrar Judson Ehrbar, a former student, faculty member, and administrative assistant. There was no separate admissions director, so Erhbar's power grew when he took on those responsibilities. For three decades Ehrbar's power was out of all proportion to his job title; almost every Juilliard student had a horror story about dealing with him.

The Summer School director and IMA dean, who had served even longer than Wagner, met a fate similar to Wagner's. "Mr. George Wedge was there, and after all it was his program that I was throwing out, the Wedge System, not because it was any worse than any other, it was just another system." Schuman was reacting negatively to Wedge's prominence in the world of music theory: Wedge's textbooks were widely used. Schuman wanted to replace Wedge's system with his own—as soon as he came up with one—and finally got rid of Wedge in 1948. Then "the time came when I knew I had to replace [Edgar] Schenkman, which was another one of those terribly difficult things. I couldn't say, 'Look, Edgar, you are fine man and you are a solid conductor, but you don't have any flair, we need a better technician.'"[29] The memory of Schenkman conducting Schuman's earliest successful work did not inspire enough loyalty to keep him. Indeed, disloyalty toward those who had helped him became Schuman's trademark.

Schuman's attitude toward age limits for faculty reflected his experience at Sarah Lawrence, although there never had been mandatory retirement at Juilliard such as at Sarah Lawrence. The thirty-five-year-old Schuman informed longtime piano faculty member Carl Friedberg, seventy-three, in January 1946 that "for the best interests of long-term over-all planning" his services were no longer needed. He offered that Friedberg could teach in the soon-to-be extinguished Summer School and in the Extension Division but must relinquish his positions at the IMA and the JGS. Friedberg's biographer relates, "Severance from his teaching positions left him, for the moment, stunned. In the best of health and at the peak of his mental powers, he was regarded by many as one of the greatest teachers in the world. To be counted as old, and therefore no longer useful, came to him as a severe shock."[30]

Friedberg's influential old friends rallied and in May 1946 sent a letter of support to Schuman that bore the signatures of Bruno Walter, Fritz Kreisler, Walter Damrosch, Vladimir Horowitz, Ralph Kirkpatrick, Myra Hess, Adrian Boult, Adolph Busch, Daniel Gregory Mason, and Walter W. Naumberg. The group expressed "regret and astonishment that Professor Carl Friedberg will not be with the Juilliard School for the coming year." It continued:

> We feel and we are sure wide circles will agree with us—that Professor Friedberg is one of the outstanding musicians of our time. He is not only a great performer, but also an eminent teacher and one of the most inspiring musical personalities of whom we have only a very few in the world today. . . .
>
> We fail to understand that any musical institution that has the great fortune to call Professor Friedberg a member of its faculty would voluntarily dispense with his services. We are told that the Juilliard does not want to renew his contract because of his age. May we point out in this connection that there is no age limit in art.[31]

The letter urged Schuman to reconsider, but he was unpersuaded. He never replied and delayed answering similar letters from Friedberg's former students.

Schuman likely did not know or care about the episode in the then-distant past when Friedberg had voluntarily left the IMA during World War I to protect Frank Damrosch and the IMA from accusations of domination by Germans. Nor did Schuman care that, before he was born, James Loeb had recommended Friedberg to Damrosch. The

Flesch-Piatagorsky-Friedberg trio may have seemed remote to so young and brash a president, who much later reinterpreted events to portray himself as the champion of older faculty: "I think that the administration should be permitted to allow people to remain."[32]

Friedberg's students all left the School to stay with him. Juilliard's loss was the country's gain. For the next decade Friedberg was much sought after to conduct master classes and give solo recitals throughout the United States. Two of his many distinguished students were later faculty members, Jane Carlson and William Masselos.

Although Schuman ignored the appeals of famous musicians defending Carl Friedberg, he quietly reversed his policy. Another example in the piano department illustrates his actions. Olga Samaroff was considered the greatest piano teacher at Juilliard, whereas Schuman and Schubart considered Rosina Lhevinne as merely one of the "others." Lhevinne was used as a test case to see whether retaining someone of her age (sixty-seven) would work. Typically self-serving, Schuman later congratulated himself for his prescience about Lhevinne's teaching successes.[33]

Every corner of the School—including opera, violin, and classroom teachers—was affected by Schuman's heavy-handed firing of faculty. A few of these people, randomly chosen, provide examples. Henry Fusner, on the theory and organ faculty, was told that "the School cannot make the same use in the future of the kind of specialized approach which has characterized our work in the Theory courses in the past."[34] In 1947 voice teacher Richardson Irwin was let go, as was William Jonson, the conductor of the opera chorus. Others simply quit. Muriel Kerr, a piano faculty member, wrote in March 1950, "As I still find myself in disagreement with the School on issues which I regard as of great importance, I ask you to accept my resignation as final."[35]

The discarded faculty were not replaced by the very best who could be found. Hutcheson wrote to Schuman, reminding him that Arnold Schoenberg had retired and once again raised the possibility of hiring Schoenberg. The tiny pension he received in California was a scandalous matter to other musicians. Schuman replied, evasively in the passive voice, in June 1946: "Mr. Schoenberg's retirement has been known to me for some time and the possibility of inviting him to the School has been discussed but for a variety of reasons no action has been taken."[36] He did not argue that Schoenberg's age would be a factor against him, although Schoenberg was almost exactly Friedberg's age. Despite Hutcheson's urging, Schuman never offered Schoenberg a job.[37]

Some firings blew up in Schuman's face when a faculty member would not go quietly. Only four months after assuming the office of president, for example, Schuman gave violinist Albert Spalding notice of termination at the end of the school year. Spalding replied:

> You have not chosen to give any explanation of your decision in this abrupt communication beyond a brief mention of a new organizational plan which required adjustments in your teaching program. And this, may I add, is the first and only contact which I have been privileged to have with the new President of an institution with which I have been associated for the past twelve years. May I, therefore, suggest that you accept my resignation as of today. . . . In closing let me add a word of the personal pleasure I have had in the twelve years I have been associated with the Juilliard School. The relationship with the former President, the Dean, the entire Faculty, and the students has been one of cordial and intimate team work rarely to be found elsewhere.[38]

Schuman was forced to write back to ask Spalding to teach the second semester, but he refused and left Schuman to deal with students irate over the firing of their teacher.

A similar episode occurred with Frederick Jacobi, of the composition faculty. Schuman made it plain to him that the two differed philosophically concerning the efficacy of Schuman's theory system, Literature and Materials. Again he used the passive voice, this time in a memo for his personal records: "The point was made to Mr. Jacobi that the L&M program was being evaluated on a nationwide basis and that while it had many friends, it had a number of enemies intent on discrediting it in any manner possible. It was therefore essential that every teacher taking part in the L&M program have unquestioned conviction as to its basic validity."[39] There is little evidence that anyone outside the School had any active interest in seeing L&M fail, however. Asked to leave at the end of the school year of 1950, Jacobi resigned as of the end of the first semester from the school where he had taught for almost fifteen years. Schuman need not have pushed Jacobi out the door: The composer kept secret his terminal illness and died two years later.[40]

The inevitable effect of this "new broom" was a drastic lowering of morale among the faculty, which, in turn, affected the students. In April 1947 a self-appointed student research committee submitted a thirty-one-page "Report on Administration-Faculty-Student Relations at the Juilliard School of Music." Its abstract begins: "The lack of interaction between groups and individuals at the Juilliard School of Music has caused an absence of a favorable administration-faculty-student relationship."[41] It continued, "The introduction of the academic department aroused serious antagonism from members of the music faculty. This

was carried on to the extreme of ostracizing the academic teachers socially within the school for almost two years." The students blamed the
School's European background for much of this, along with the separation of the IMA and JGS, which promoted "great clannishness and
desire for separations into cliques. These artificial divisions and subdi-
visions internally, caused a complete lack of cohesiveness between the
elements in the school." They also complained that the faculty criticized
the student council as being too leftist and immature; that the school
newspaper, *Stretto*, was unsatisfactory; and that there was no advisory
system to help them select courses for graduation.[42] They proposed a
student government, reactivating social interests, organizing advisory
aid, subdividing the student body into smaller, socially workable units,
and revising the student constitution. The administration instituted
none of the suggestions. Concerned with maintaining his own power,
Schuman never allowed either faculty or student councils. He snuffed
out attempts to unionize. Only in 1955 did the School's catalog begin
to list faculty biographies.

In a 1946–47 report, faculty in the Teacher Training Department also
made their views known, calling the department "something of a mess
administratively" and noting that students did not possess the keyboard
skills to teach.[43] As a professional school, the faculty observed, Juilliard
did not have as much opportunity to provide for social graces as does a
college or university. The department had made special efforts to develop students' social poise by holding informal teas at faculty and students' homes, reminiscent of the IMA's Auxiliary Society and Olga
Samaroff's and Irmgart Hutcheson's events.

Among the academic courses was the two-year "Contemporary Civi-
lizations." The 1949–50 catalog describes the second year as "a study
of the contemporary social relationships in the cultures of Bali, India,
Russia, England, South Africa, Palestine, United States and Argentina.
The common problems of family life, religion, health, music and art,
economic welfare and social organization will be examined."[44] It was
multiculturalism before its time. In addition, outside lecturers presented.
Alfred Kinsey, eager to include more artists in his survey, spoke on "Sex
and Marriage Relations" in April 1948.

≈

One night in 1948, Schuman heard singer Maggie Teyte's concert at
City Center and was impressed with the conductor accompanying her.
Given to impulsive decisions, he asked the Frenchman, Jean Morel, to
conduct a festival of French music at the School. "And before the first
concert of the festival I offered him the [permanent] job, and he said,

'Don't offer me the job before the concert.' I said, 'I don't know if the concert will be successful or unsuccessful, but the rehearsals were successful, and this is a school, and that's more important.'"[45] Morel turned out to be a "wonderful teacher" whose conducting students during his tenure at Juilliard (1949–73) included James Levine, Dennis Russell Davies, Jorge Mester, and Leonard Slatkin.

Morel (1903–75) became as important a figure as Albert Stoessel had been. Born in Abbeville, France, in 1903, he had studied at the École Normale de Musique, where he received his license in 1922. He studied piano with Isidor Philip, had played tympani at the Opéra-Comique, and become "the most celebrated percussion-instruments performer in France."[46] From 1921 to 1936 he was on the faculty of the American Conservatory at Fontainebleau, along with Nadia Boulanger. He left France in 1938 and sailed, jobless, to the United States, where he became head of the orchestra department at Brooklyn College from 1940 to 1943. Morel combined virtuosity and scholarship, speaking Greek and Latin as well as French, Spanish, and English. At City Center Opera he popularized *Pelléas et Mélisande.* He was particularly admired for his keen sense of rhythm, his ear, and his sight-reading skills. During nearly a quarter of a century at Juilliard he also listened to entrance examinations, a responsibility that increased his influence.

This influence extended to composers in the School, such as Philip Glass, who wrote, "Morel did not have a remarkable international career, but he impressed those who had the good luck to work with him by the clarity of his musical thinking and the high standards he brought to the performance of orchestral music of all periods. His influence extended well beyond his conducting students, to the young players in his orchestra at Juilliard. My first lessons in orchestration really were from Morel who, as a young man, I spent many hours following his morning orchestra rehearsals with a score."[47]

Others Schuman brought to the School included violinist Ivan Galamian, "because we needed a real technician"; pianist Beveridge Webster; and 'cellist Leonard Rose.[48] The story of one composer's hiring was often retold. When Vincent Persichetti interviewed for a job teaching composition and L&M, he and Schuman hit it off. After returning home to Philadelphia, Persichetti realized he had neglected to mention his recently acquired doctorate in music. He sent a note to Schuman and received a humorous reply: "Congratulations on receiving your doctorate. I promise I won't hold it against you." At that moment Persichetti, who was to head the composition department for forty years, realized that this was the man for whom he wanted to work. It never occurred to anyone retelling the story—such as Milton Babbitt at Juilliard's memorial for Persichetti in 1987—that Schuman, who did not have a doctorate himself, may have meant it literally.

By 1949 enough foreign students were applying that the catalog included the first of what would be many instructions and requirements: Students must be over fifteen and "must be able to speak and understand English sufficiently well to pursue satisfactorily the required course of study."

Another major project Schuman helped institute was the Juilliard String Quartet, the brainchild of its founder Robert Mann. Earlier American quartets in the twentieth century had cultivated an elegant image in the European tradition. Indeed, most of the members of the Kneisel, Flonzaley, Kolisch, and later the Budapest, Kroll, Busch, and Coolidge quartets were European. The Kneisel Quartette had formed the nucleus of the IMA's string department for twenty years, and the Warburgs had supported the Musical Art Quartet. During the 1940s, however, the School had no quartet formally associated with it.

Before he was fired, Edgar Schenkman had recommended Robert Mann to Schuman. Mann already had two players. Arthur Winograd was a 'cellist trained at Curtis and had served with Mann in the army; the violinist Robert Koff later became Mann's brother-in-law. To obtain a violist, the School raided the Boston Symphony for Raphael Hillyer; Schuman had to negotiate with his patron Koussevitzky to obtain Hillyer's release.

"I'll never forget it if I live to be a thousand," Schuman described the quartet's first concert at the School. "It was greater than anything I'd ever dreamed of; because here were four men absolutely on fire with what they were doing . . . just on *fire* with it."[49] The School gave the players a small teaching assignment, and they guaranteed the School a percentage of the returns from their engagements for the next three years. (Juilliard obtained the engagements.) The one stipulation was that the name "Juilliard String Quartet" remain constant no matter who the players were. The name "Juilliard" was therefore permanently associated with the excellence of these performers.

The Juilliard Quartet's Town Hall debut took place in December 1947. They played Berg's Lyric Suite, Haydn's G-major quartet, and Beethoven's Opus 130. In 1948 they learned the six Bartók and the four Schoenberg quartets and performed the Bartók at Tanglewood.

In 1951 the quartet gave the entire Beethoven cycle. "The only discussions I ever had with Bobby," Schuman recalled in 1974, "were about their appearance, because they looked like *pigs*. . . . they looked absolutely disreputable."[50] Their looks aside, the Juilliard String Quartet has made an indelible impact on chamber music in the United States and abroad. They have premiered many new works. Their coaching of student groups at the School has produced some of the best quartets of the younger generation, including the Tokyo, Emerson, American, LaSalle, St. Lawrence, Colorado, and Mendelssohn quartets. Joel Smirnoff, the second violinist who replaced Mann after fifty years, has observed:

> It has always seemed to me that it is uniquely in the quartet coaching situation that students in the school get to bridge the sometimes seemingly unbridgeable gap between music analysis and execution. In other words, the two sets of tools (analysis and instrumental technique) find their proper relationship in looking at a work in a group with a coach who encourages it to happen, so that the interpretation and execution of a work is based upon a better and better understanding of how it is constructed. This is the unique function of the quartet in the school for the string player.[51]

Juilliard String Quartet, ca. 1948. Original members were Robert Mann and Robert Koff, violins; Arthur Winograd, 'cello; and Raphael Hillyer, viola. Subsequent members were Joel Smirnoff, first violin; Isidore Cohen, Earl Carlyss, Joel Smirnoff, and Ronald Copes, second violin; Samuel Rhodes, viola; and Claus Adam and Joel Krosnick, 'cellos.
(Eileen Darby, photo from The Juilliary School Archives)

Schuman's most far-reaching curricular change was a total revision of the theory and history programs: Literature and Materials of Music. After the program was instituted there were no longer separate courses, such as three years of ear training, three years of theory, music history, piano sight reading, and contemporary music. All were subsumed under the rubric of the four-year L&M, whose curriculum Schuman and Norman Lloyd (1910–80) spent four days in Atlantic City working around the clock to devise. Ultimately, both Lloyd and Richard Franko Goldman had more to do with instituting L&M than did Schuman. Virgil Thomson observed about L&M before it was inaugurated:

> Revising the curriculum is a major American sport. Everybody enjoys it. Students and faculties alike find it invigorating. For presidents of educational institutions it is the *sine qua non* of tenure. It is the perfect mechanism for getting rid of one's predecessor's aides-de-camp and putting in one's own. And it is proof both to students and to the intellectual world that the job is no sinecure but a full-time occupation. It offers to all the comforting conviction of progress. And it is intrinsically good for educational institutions, for without it they do go to seed.
>
> [The L&M] procedure is similar to the famous "case system" of the Harvard Law School, where the principles of law are arrived at through the study of many court cases rather than learned in advance and applied to the interpretation of court cases.[52]

The L&M Program was initiated in the 1947–48 school year, and in April 1948 Schuman published an article in *Musical Quarterly* to laud its accomplishments.[53] First he criticized traditional approaches to teaching harmony, species counterpoint, dictation, and sight singing. He stated that "no effective antidote to routine theory instruction has been developed on a large scale," and "it is my opinion that instruction in conventional theory has failed to educate." He questioned the usefulness of dictation: "Is it not plain that the ability to record a melody, or in the case of advanced students, even a figured chorale from aural dictation is but a tool and in itself does not necessarily imply ability beyond the specific skill called into play?" The answer was not plain: Many musicians find dictation essential to developing their ears. He also complained "that conventional theory education shows a consistent lack of concern with the entire work of art." That was quite true.

Schuman's solutions involved drastic changes in the curriculum. First the school year was lengthened from thirty to thirty-five weeks. Then the B.S. undergraduate course was lengthened to five years in order for students to finish L&M as well as the necessary academic work. (The new academic courses were acoustics, sociology, social psychology, the history of education, English literature, American literature, and American history.) L&M was concentrated in the first twenty weeks of school and met four times a week for an hour and a half. Major lessons were given during the first and last fifteen weeks of the year. That left a five-week period in the middle of the year with no lessons when "the work in the Literature and Materials courses" would be "brought to a point of focus and completion for the year."[54]

The first two years of L&M were "to give the student an awareness of the dynamic nature of the materials of music," Schuman stated vaguely. After faculty and student meetings it was agreed not to attempt a uniform plan "on how the students would be introduced to the great variety of music materials." Each teacher taught in his or her own way, which meant that some used music from programs given at the School and others relied on programs given by an orchestra outside the School. One proceeded in reverse chronological order and another in conventional chronological order. There were no required textbooks, for which Schuman instinctively held a distaste. Ultimately, he wanted to make the student "understand that he must assume the responsibility for his own education."[55]

Four out of five students who responded to an anonymous questionnaire were positive about the new curriculum after one semester. In his *Musical Quarterly* article Schuman did not attempt to describe the third and fourth years of L&M, which had not yet occurred. The fifth year would be "given by a historian whose particular job it is to synthesize the work of the first four years." Finally, Schuman asserted that "the point of view to which we hold is not a system, but a way of musical life."[56]

The faculty assembled for the L&M curriculum originally consisted of William Bergsma, Judson Ehrbar, Irwin Freundlich, Vittorio Giannini, Roger Goeb, Richard Franko Goldman, Frederick Hart, Julius Herford, Robert Hufstader, Frederick Jacobi, Sergius Kagen, Norman Lloyd, Peter Mennin, Vincent Persichetti, Robert Tangeman, Bernard Wagenaar, and Robert Ward. Goldman served as the director of education and supervised the program. The group is remarkable for their similarities to the president—nearly his age, heterosexual, and male despite the fact that women had dominated the ear-training faculty for a long time before (and have since).

These composer-teachers were given great freedom in how to teach L&M. The natural consequence was that students may or may not have received adequate music history, ear training, or harmony; whether they did so depended on their L&M instructor. The program never reached the five-year mark: Among many subsequent changes, the curriculum was switched back to the four-year plan. A 1955 accreditation report discussed the matter:

The program in L&M is an excellent example [of a real desire never to be satisfied with what has been or is being done]. Here Juilliard has broken with tradition and has aimed at presenting the material in a fresh manner, hopefully more effectively related to the work in applied music. In the world of music education the program is highly controversial. It has its staunch supporters and its strong critics. Some feel that the program is too different, some feel it is not really different at all—only confusing; some feel it is just right.[57]

The concern Schuman had expressed to Jacobi about criticism of L&M is evident in the statement. It was Schuman himself rather than L&M, however, who seemed to prompt criticism. The report praised L&M and the School but added, "The Committee would also like to call attention to a tendency encountered in some of the literature published by the Juilliard School of defending its program by a thinly veiled disapproval of the work being done elsewhere. This seems contrary to the dignity one expects and it fails to recognize that many of our fine artists and composers have been developed by other procedures than those presently employed at Juilliard."[58] The reference was likely to passages from Schuman and Goldman's book *The Juilliard Report on Teaching the Literature and Materials of Music:*

Offerings in music in many liberal-arts colleges still gravitate towards one or the other of two unfortunate extremes: the general course of music appreciation or "Introduction to Music," and the theory courses. In the instance of the general course, many enlightened young college music enthusiasts are discouraged by being given a music-history course in which they are subjected to constant quizzing on dates and factual data, or an "analysis" course in which they are obliged to memorize what are purported to be rigid forms as the key to listening to music. In the standard theory course, the young student who loves music is likely to be discouraged by the routine of writing abstract harmony exercises whose musical application he fails to glean.[59]

The reactions to L&M were mixed and can be gleaned from the reviews of the 1953 book. The reviewer for *Musical America* said that students found the lack of rules disturbing: "He [the student] receives a severe shock when he runs head-on into the Juilliard demand that he explore, correlate and manipulate the raw materials of music on his own initiative and responsibility."[60] Critics often felt strongly that the success of the program rested principally on the abilities of individual teachers.[61] The success, or lack of it, of the L&M Program has been studied and questioned for decades. Fifty years later, the School still offered the program, and its final evaluation may yet rest on the results of individual teaching. One sign of success is the fact that more than one hundred colleges used its Hardy and Fish anthologies, which did not go out of print until 1995 and had never undergone revision.[62]

In 1945 new professional courses were added to the curriculum—"Music in Industry" and "Radio Technique." The catalog explained that "the rapid development of industrial music in war plants had opened a new field for the trained musician." The new courses included "The Organization of an Industrial Broadcasting Studio," "Programming for Industry and Radio," "Radio Choral Ensemble," "Script Writing and Production," and "Radio Diction and General Broadcast Technique." There were also courses in commercial music for string instruments, practical arranging and orchestration, radio choral ensemble, and conducting for radio. The radio and theater music courses included "Orchestral Playing for Radio," "Radio Choral Ensemble," an orientation course called "Introduction of Broadcasting Techniques," and "Radio Diction and Microphone Technique for Singers," "Production Techniques in Radio and Television," "Basic Acting—Stage—Radio—Television," "Composition of Lyrics and Libretti," and "Practical Arranging and Orchestration." By 1952, however, the radio courses, which had shrunk in number every year, evaporated entirely from the curriculum due to the spectacular inroads television had made upon the business of radio.

The 1947 catalog announced that "The Juilliard School of Music has been approved by the Veterans Administration to accept veterans for study under the so-called 'G.I. Bill of Rights.'" High school students and returning GIs planning to enter the JSM could accelerate their course by attending the Summer School, while it lasted. The 1949 and subsequent catalogs opened with a statement: "It is not enough that the musician be content with technical proficiency alone. He must be equipped to contribute, through his profession, to the development of music as a constructive force in contemporary life—William Schuman."

Schuman began another project in 1954, the *Juilliard Review*, but "always thought that was sort of a flop. It seemed to me to be a rather lugubrious magazine and excessively intellectual in capital letters, and I made the mistake of putting Dick Goldman in charge of that. . . . But the problem was that it was a magazine that couldn't be understood by the Juilliard faculty, which could be as much of a comment about the faculty as about the magazine, but it really didn't carry out my hope for it, so I was always rather disappointed in it."[63] The *Juilliard Review* lasted from January 1954 to spring of 1962 and contained serious articles about the music of Stravinsky, Persichetti, Mennin, Bergsma, Bartók, and other contemporary composers, complete with music examples. Schuman's successor discontinued it.

To mark its fiftieth birthday in 1955, the School commissioned thirty-three American composers and two choreographers, whose works were performed on five concerts and in two dance productions. Among them were Schuman's Concerto for Violin and Orchestra and a José Limón choreography of his Symphony for Strings. Other composers commissioned included Roger Sessions, Peter Mennin, William Bergsma, Paul Creston, Mark Schubart, Norman Dello Joio, and Walter Piston.

Also in 1955, the *Juilliard Review* published "The Economic Situation of the Performer."[64] Using figures from the American Federation of Musicians, the author provided a listing of average salaries resulting from full-time jobs in music.

Field of Employment	Number of Full-Time Jobs	Average Annual Wage
Moving Pictures	303	$8,677.80
Radio	1,354	$7,200.00
Television	440	$4,000.00
Musicals and legitimate theater	1,584	$2,000.00 apiece
Symphony	2,671	$1,980.00*
Opera and ballet	967	$1,000.00**
Traveling dance bands	5,000 est.	$6,000.00 apiece

* 400 average $5,000 apiece, the rest make well under $2,000.
** 300 receive much more than the average.

If students were concerned about their economic prospects in music this listing should have given them pause. They might (although Juilliard salaries have never been public) have compared their teachers' salaries as examples of pay for musicians. In 1961, for example, Leonard Rose's contract called for 360 hours of teaching and an annual salary of $5,000 (approximately $14 an hour). Dorothy DeLay taught 28 hours a week and Galamian 26½; Galamian received $20 per hour for the first twenty students and $15 per hour for any above that number. DeLay's rate was $8 an hour. DeLay had attended the IMA in 1937–38 and the JGS from 1938 to 1942, where she studied with Hans Letz but did not receive a degree.

An influential book on the economic dilemma of performing noted in 1966 that productivity cannot be increased in the field at anything like the general rate, therefore costs inevitably mount. "In general, we shall see that performer incomes have been rising at a rate faster than that of the price level, but still have not kept up with incomes elsewhere in the economy, and that salary payments have constituted a declining portion of over-all costs of performance in recent years."[65]

Despite composition concerts and much lip service devoted to composition students' efforts in the first years of Schuman's presidency, the situation had been allowed to deteriorate by 1957. Composers were required to take "Composers' Forum" two hours a week, as well as a year of "Methods of Teaching L&M." The number of orchestral readings of composers' pieces had dwindled to a total of three during 1955 and 1956. The reason given was "insufficient time" to do student works. The "general inexperience and indifferent attitude [of the players] made adequate performances virtually impossible" the composers complained. Attendance at the readings, which Frederik Prausnitz conducted, varied from day to day. It was "not uncommon to find a whole woodwind or brass section missing."[66] The readings were scheduled in the spring, therefore students proposed a May deadline for submission of scores and an October week for the first orchestra to read them. For the next three decades the lack of attention given to composers, despite the fact that a composer ran the School, was to remain a sore point.

In 1948 a thirteen-year-old boy accompanied his mother from Texas to New York to attend the Juilliard Summer School. Rildia Bee Cliburn and her son Van studied with Ernest Hutcheson during the summer. The young Van had wanted to switch to Olga Samaroff, who had offered him a scholarship on the strength of his reputation. Samaroff died on May 17, 1948, however, and "after that he refused even to consider another teacher and returned to Texas to enter high school."[67] The path to Juilliard picked up again in 1951 when Cliburn and his mother returned to the soon-to-be-defunct Summer School, where he studied with Carl Friedberg, recently fired from the Regular Division. She had planned to study again with Hutcheson, who had died that February. Van wanted to study in the Regular Division with Rosina Lhevinne but got an assistant instead. "[I] was standing by the school elevator one day," Lhevinne remembered, "when a tall, shockheaded young man with a long, buoyant stride bore down upon [me]. 'Honey,' he said with a smile, 'I'm here to study with you.'"[68] Van Cliburn spent the next two summers in Chautauqua and graduated from Juilliard in 1954, winning the Frank Damrosch Scholarship that entitled him to one year of postgraduate study. Mark Schubart succeeded in obtaining manager Arthur Judd to represent him.

Already well known in musical circles for having won the Leventritt Competition in 1954, Cliburn had to be coaxed by Lhevinne into entering the first Tchaikowsky Competition in Moscow in 1958. Her arguments included: "Point 1: You will have to work with great intensity, and this will be good for you, regardless of the contest. Point 2: You will have to learn a great deal of new material. Point 3: You will meet the elite of the young pianists from other parts of the world. Point 4: Last, but not least—I believe you will win."[69]

Lhevinne gave up her Sundays—normally reserved for rest from teaching six days a week—in order to coach Cliburn. They both went on a diet of Knox gelatin, which seemed to give them energy. In training, he was practicing more than six hours a day, seeing no one but her, and learning an enormous amount of repertoire. Lhevinne knew how Russians liked to hear their music played, and she and Josef Lhevinne had known Rachmaninoff personally. Cliburn played his Third Concerto and won first place. Daniel Pollack, another Lhevinne student, won ninth place. Joyce Flissler, a student of Edouard Dethier from 1946 to 1952, who had won the Naumberg Competition, played the Berg

Rosina Lhevinne and Van Cliburn, ca. 1953.
(Graphic House, Inc., photo from The Juilliard School Archives)

Concerto with the Juilliard Orchestra, and given a Town Hall debut, won the highest rank by an American in the violin competition—seventh place.

National attention on Juilliard grew because of the flurry of articles written about Cliburn. A peculiar confluence of cold war politics and music produced the publicity. An American had won over the Russians on their home turf, a political revenge for the success of the Soviet Sputnik. Schuman telegrammed Cliburn, "The day your triumph was announced the atmosphere at Juilliard was unmistakably akin to that of a college campus following victory in the big game of the year."[70] "Nothing like this had ever happened before in American history," wrote Cliburn's first biographer. "A musician—an artist—was a national hero."[71] Circle Line boat tours pointed out the building near Grant's Tomb as Van Cliburn's school. He received unheard of attention for a pianist, including a ticker-tape parade in Manhattan. A household word, he lent Juilliard even more publicity and fame.

Lhevinne's reputation was capped when another student, John Browning, won the next Leventritt. Later, her student Misha Dichter won second place in Moscow. It was fortunate that Schuman had not retired Lhevinne because of her age. At seventy-seven, she was at the peak of her career. Described as combining the autocracy of Catherine the Great with the informality of a taxicab driver, Lhevinne taught at Juilliard until her death at ninety-six.

The American concept of winner-take-all was played out with a vengeance on Flissler, who was completely overshadowed and ignored upon returning from her victory in Moscow. Referring to not being invited to a luncheon for Moscow winners, she told Abram Chasins, "Oh, that's all right. I admire Van, and he certainly deserved the reception. As for me, there hasn't been any sign of recognition since I returned, and this [lunch] was just one more little pill along with the others."[72] Not one American engagement, not one inquiry to her managers resulted from her accomplishment in Moscow.

~

Under Schuman the School indulged in a passion for festivals. The original French Festival was conducted by Morel, and then there were subsequent festivals of British music and Italian music in addition to the American music for the golden jubilee and the Bloch and Copland festivals (one for Copland's sixtieth and another for his seventieth birthday). The orchestra also performed by invitation at special events. It played during the opening week at Philharmonic Hall in September 1962, and the next month, at the eighteenth anniversary of the United

Nations, the orchestra played on a concert in Washington, D.C., that John F. and Jacqueline Kennedy attended.[73]

One of the great events in the history of the Juilliard Orchestra was its fifty-three-day tour to six countries during the summer of 1958. The orchestra was invited to participate in the International Festival of Youth Orchestras as part of the 1958 Brussels Worlds Fair, which dance director Martha Hill's husband helped administer. Accompanying it was Felix Goetlicher, the venerable orchestral librarian. Rather than have the orchestra travel abroad for only one concert, Schuman approached the U.S. government to support a tour through its International Cultural Exchange Service. Even the government's gift of $60,000 did not cover the costs. Juilliard had underwritten the tour with $20,000, and ASCAP had given $3,000. Schuman, however, wrote to Douglas Moore at ASCAP requesting additional funds. The tour began in England and then traveled to Belgium, Germany, Denmark, Austria, and Italy. Nearly fifty thousand people attended the twenty-five concerts, and reviews were splendid. One example is from *La Cité* in Paris: "Here is an ensemble of real first rank, as brilliant as the most famous ones. With the Juilliard Orchestra, one has the impression of an adult orchestra—a world reputation perfectly justified."[74] A German newspaper admitted defeat: "Let us speak frankly: What German, what European Hochschule, could put together such a highly qualified orchestra? None."[75]

There was, however, some negative fallout from the tour. Envy of the School surfaced on the part of those supporting other orchestras in the competition for federal dollars. E. William Doty, president of the National Association of Schools of Music (NASM), supposedly cited a confidential Middle States Association report. In it, the ninety-member Juilliard Orchestra was said to have had only fifty actual students; therefore, it was not seen as appropriate that a government agency send it to the Worlds Fair as representing the United States. Schuman became incensed, and after about a year Doty apologized—somewhat. Yet even though the orchestra had already returned from abroad and any debate was over, Schuman was not willing to let the issue lie. One-sidedly, he insisted on viewing the report as a grave injustice done to Juilliard, demanded an apology, and then resigned from the NASM in 1959.

That act provoked trouble from the otherwise moribund-on-the-subject NASM. Only after Schuman's resignation did they investigate how the Juilliard Orchestra had been constituted on the tour. It appeared that Juilliard had brought in ringers and former students to supplement the orchestra. The NASM contacted some of these students, wanting to know when they graduated from, or if they even had attended,

Juilliard. The situation was dicey, and Schuman became further enraged. Without explicitly denying the charges, he spread the "facts of this disgraceful situation" to other schools, including the New England Conservatory and Oberlin.[76] Juilliard remained exiled from the NASM for the next thirty years.

∾

John D. Rockefeller 3rd liked to conduct business over meals. Upon being asked to lunch by Rockefeller in 1961, Schuman appeared with a list of candidates for the newly vacated job of president of the as-yet-unbuilt Lincoln Center. Board member Charles Spofford had recommended Schuman for the job although W. McNeil Lowry, head of humanities at the multi-million-dollar Ford Foundation and therefore in a position to voice his true feelings without fear of repercussion, had told Rockefeller that he and the musical community would oppose that idea.

Schuman recalled the lunch: "Then Rockefeller surprised me. He said, 'The board of directors want me to sound you out and see if you would be interested in coming here. I would personally be delighted.' I told him I was greatly flattered, and Rockefeller, ever charming, said, 'Didn't I do that well?'" Impulsive as ever, Schuman telephoned his wife immediately and told her he would call Rockefeller right back and suggest a meeting with the Lincoln Center board. He decided instantly that

Students and faculty in the cafeteria, 1957.
(Impact Photos, Inc., photo from The Juilliard School Archives)

he wanted the job. Four friends with whom he later discussed the of-fer—James P. Warburg (chair of Juilliard's board), Leonard Bernstein, Mark Schubart, and Goddard Lieberson—all advised against accepting it. "But I said, 'I'm not going to take your advice.'"[77]

Lowry voiced a common attitude toward Schuman as president of Lincoln Center: "[Schuman]'s a 'flâneur,' and any composer who would rather be a tame castrate for Rockefeller and the board than to be among the boys, as composers still, [has] a problem, but it didn't bother Bill Schuman. . . . But he was always, always using whatever role he had for his own aggrandizement."[78] Others, asking for and receiving anonymity from the press, wryly commented that one did not see Stravinsky accepting such an administrative position. (They seem not to have noticed that Schuman's compositional career had by then dwindled.) Even his old friend Frank Loesser mildly disapproved of the concept of Lincoln Center: "New York *is* a center, a world's fair, and a den of thieves, and a house of miracles."[79]

To the great surprise of everyone at Juilliard, a statement was issued announcing that Schuman had been elected president of Lincoln Center, effective January 1, 1962, the middle of a school year. He had tired of Juilliard, and his enthusiasms were now directed toward what seemed like a career boost. As his biographer had predicted, he left colleagues at Juilliard "dazed and forgotten on the sidelines."[80] The Juilliard job looked like it would become increasingly one of having to raise funds—not the case when he became president—and, as Frances Schuman said later, he disliked fund-raising.[81]

Schuman sent a signed letter to each member of the faculty and staff at Juilliard, explaining himself to those who felt abandoned. "After a great deal of soul-searching," Schuman wrote not quite truthfully, "I have accepted the presidency of Lincoln Center. . . . Only so exciting a prospect could have induced me to request my colleagues on the Juilliard Board to accept my resignation as president of the School after sixteen years of the most gratifying association with them."[82]

Schuman had a grandiose idea that the Manhattan and Mannes schools should merge and take over the 122nd Street building Juilliard was vacating. Janet Schenck, still president of Manhattan School, wrote a congratulatory note to him in November 1961 and politely made clear that neither she nor the Mannes School were interested in such a merger. The William Schuman era at Juilliard was over at the beginning of 1962. For better or worse, he had committed the School to yet another move, major changes in its size and offerings, and a considerable financial burden. Someone else, however, would inherit the problem of implementing these profound changes—and of paying for them.

7

Lincoln Center:

INCREASED STATUS

TWICE IN THE HISTORY of the School a fortuitous meeting occurred between a man who had a great idea and an enlightened patron who had money. The first time was when Frank Damrosch met James Loeb on a ferry to New York in 1903. Lightening struck once again in 1955, when Charles M. Spofford and John D. Rockefeller 3rd met in the Pocono Mountains.

Originally from St. Louis, Spofford (1902–91) was graduated from Yale and Harvard. In 1930 he joined the law firm of Davis, Polk, Wardwell, Sunderland and Kiendl, Allen Wardwell's firm, and became a partner in 1940. Wardwell had been on the Juilliard Musical Foundation's board and formed one-third of the triumvirate who ran the School one year. A member of the Metropolitan Opera board, Spofford had met with Mayor Fiorello H. LaGuardia in the 1930s, who had suggested "a music center, a place where music of all kinds will be performed, and maybe the New York Philharmonic will join in—something like that!"[1] Spofford never forgot the idea even though his approach to the New York Philharmonic had been rebuffed with the comment that it was a waste of time because it would be so expensive. Robert Moses, the powerful New York City parks commissioner, also torpedoed his idea, arguing that opera was a dying art form fit only for social climbers.

Meanwhile, the JMF board added Henry Drye, Jr., to replace John Erskine, who had died in 1951. General counsel and a director of Union Carbide Corporation, Drye also served on the board of the Met, where he was chair of the new house committee. Charles Spofford and David Keiser joined the JMF board in 1953. By 1956 the board stood at nine members: Spofford, Keiser, and Drye, Franklin B. Benkard, Henry S. Drinker, Edward Johnson, William Schuman, James P. Warburg, and Allen Wardwell. Despite its original mandate, the JMF had devolved to providing money solely for the JSM, which had its own board of directors. The two boards, however, frequently shared members, and members of both boards were duty-bound to look after the best interests of the School.

A decade after his failed attempts to establish a music center in New York, Spofford approached another mayor, the music lover William O'Dwyer, who suggested putting the new Metropolitan Opera in a corner of Central Park. Robert Moses again killed the notion—this time saying about a proposed meeting: "If [Spofford] wants to put it in Central Park, tell him to save his carfare."[2]

Moses, a graduate of Yale and Oxford with a degree in philosophy, made a greater mark on New York City's physical surroundings than any other man. He was described as having an "edifice complex" because of the many buildings, bridges, tunnels, parks, power projects, even beaches for which he was responsible. Spofford's third approach met with more sympathy from Moses, who could see a way to accomplish such a task through use of the Title I provision of the 1949 Federal Housing Act for Slum Clearance. That provision allowed a city to condemn slum property and sell it at a loss to private developers, the federal government making good two-thirds of the loss and the city one-third. Moses offered the Met a variety of sites, including a slum area at Columbus Circle, Washington Square, and a barn on Third Avenue. All were considered and regretfully refused.

While in a cab with his friend Robert Blum, head of the Brooklyn Institute of Arts and Letters, Moses passed a slum area in the West Sixties called Lincoln Square (named in the nineteenth century when other public squares were named Washington and Madison). Moses said to Blum, "Someday we've got to do something about that slum." By early 1955 Moses had offered Lincoln Square to the Metropolitan Opera with the proviso that it raise $1.5 million within six weeks. When the thirty members of the Met's board visited the site, they viewed one of the most congested areas in the city. It was a roach-infested, thirteen-block area that contained 5,400 families, most of them Puerto Rican, and 600 small businesses. From 62nd to 66th Streets between Columbus and Amsterdam were 1,647 families who lived in 188 tenements.[3] The neighborhood would soon be immortalized by Stephen Sondheim and Leonard Bernstein in *West Side Story* (1957).

The Twelfth Regiment Armory, located on 62nd and Columbus, lent its medieval looks to backgrounds of Hollywood movies. Joseph P. Kennedy owned a twelve-story building opposite the Armory that housed units of the Department of Justice, including the Immigration and Naturalization Service. The buildings occupied the area that the New York State Theater building now occupies. Moses paid for the Kennedy building separately and paid considerably more than for the other buildings. In the New Deal days, the Works Progress Administration had its city headquarters in a loft in the heart of Lincoln Square.

An unencouraging precedent for the proposed complex was the fabulous Century Theater built just a block east on Central Park West in a past massive effort to rejuvenate the area. An attempt to create a national theater, the Century Theater failed despite its ornate horseshoe and Florenz Ziegfeld's musicals. Nevertheless, the Lincoln Square area became home to writers, artists, musicians, and actors. Aaron Copland had lived since 1936 at the Empire Hotel and rented an unheated, fourth-floor walk-up loft at 115 West 63rd Street for $25 a month. There were Spanish-speaking businesses in the building, and a strong smell of chocolate came from Flavors by F. W. Kaye and Company.

At 1947 Broadway (at 66th Street), the eventual Juilliard site, was the six-story Lincoln Arcade Building into whose dark, echoing environment George Bellows had moved his art supplies in 1906. Between 1906 and 1910 he shared the $40 rent for Number 616 with a succession of roommates, including Eugene O'Neill. Studio Number 606 was a portrait class—Edward Hopper was a student—set up by Robert Henri in 1909. Marcel Duchamp also lived and worked in the Arcade from 1915 to 1916. At the corner of the Arcade at 65th was an establishment devoted to "Sportswear, Corsets and Gloves." In 1959 all thirty-three tenants of the Lincoln Arcade, including an artist, a sculptor, and a ballet dancer who protested in court, were evicted.

The Met's architectural consultant, Wallace K. Harrison, had been involved with the planning of Rockefeller Center (the original drawings for which contained an opera house) and was chief architect for the United Nations. The most powerful architect in the country, Harrison now suggested to the New York Philharmonic, which had once asked him to draw plans for another site, that the Met and the Philharmonic work on a combined concept for their new homes. The Opera wanted to move in part because of the still-unsolved set storage problem that Augustus Juilliard had begun to consider before his death, and the Philharmonic was spurred to action by having received a three-year eviction notice from Carnegie Hall, which was to be razed.

Arthur Houghton, president of the New York Philharmonic and cousin of Alice Tully, the granddaughter of the founder of Corning Glass and once a dramatic soprano, set up a meeting with Moses and Spofford on Randall's Island. Out of this came a joint exploratory committee between the Met and the Philharmonic. Both decided in April 1955 to build new houses at Lincoln Square, and within a few months discussions began with Juilliard to join them. John Drye, David Keiser, or Charles Spofford, all privy to the new idea, first raised the issue with the Juilliard board that spring.

Like his father Cornelius, Anthony Bliss was a member of the Met's board. In the opera's files he found a plan from the 1920s for a new opera house, concert hall, theater, and school (chapter 3). Bliss determined to fulfill his father's dreams. He was, however, opposed to the inclusion of either Juilliard or City Center (the New York State Opera and New York City Ballet). In both cases he was eventually overruled.

At the first meeting of the exploratory committee, Bliss told the members that he had heard that Rockefeller had finished a major philanthropic endeavor and was looking for another important civic project. Charles Spofford leaped at the opportunity to sound out Rockefeller that weekend, September 8 and 9, 1955. The men were both members of a Council on Foreign Relations study group that was to meet in the Poconos to discuss Russia. "John and I sat out on a bench," Spofford recalled, "and I told him about the thing, and what I thought it might mean for the cultural life of the city and the country. I told him I thought it was a really big project."[4] The conversation was later described as Spofford's "epochal chat with Mr. Rockefeller."[5]

Rockefeller (1906–78) was the eldest of five brothers born to John D. Rockefeller, Jr., the only son of John D. Rockefeller. Rockefeller Junior was a music lover who had been taught violin as a child and who married, in 1951, Martha Baird Allen, a concert pianist. One of his sons, Nelson, became governor of New York. Nelson's brother, John D. Rockefeller 3rd, was interested in foreign relations. Unlike his father and stepmother, he had no personal interest in the arts; he was not an operagoer, a symphony fan, or a balletomane. He did, however, wish to compete with his younger brothers' successful philanthropic efforts and to succeed at something they had not tried to accomplish.

In June 1956 Rockefeller was made president of Lincoln Center, Inc., a project he realized might be one of the biggest challenges of his life.

He also knew how to pick busy men to get something accomplished. "It's a strange thing," he said, "but in all the many things I've seen happen, there are always only a half dozen people who truly make it happen—no matter how big the thing is, it's often the same few people who make it happen."[6] Rockefeller recruited Devereux C. Josephs and Robert Blum to serve as liaisons to Moses. The group had twelve members, including Spofford, Harrison, Blum, Josephs, Bliss, and Keiser.

David Keiser had to leave the JGS in 1930 before graduating in piano (he studied with Carl Friedberg) "because of affluence," as William Schuman wittily remarked. He took over his father's Cuban American Sugar Company and became president of the New York Philharmonic and president of the Juilliard board. A quiet man, Keiser had considerable influence in Lincoln Center's musical discussions—he had spoken with people such as Copland—about what kind of place the arts complex should be.

Rockefeller, Bliss, and Harrison toured fourteen cities in eight European countries in April 1956 to talk with experts in the performing arts and visit schools. Although Rockefeller was impressed with actor and director Michel Saint-Denis in Strasbourg, no European city provided a model of what the exploratory committee wanted to accomplish for New York. A complex of comparable size and scope had never been assembled elsewhere.

The timing for such an ambitious civic plan was propitious. In 1957 the United States had more than eighty opera companies, close to a thousand symphony orchestras, and approximately five thousand community theaters. "Every fourth phonograph record sold was of classical music, and, unbelievable though it seemed, paid admissions to concerts exceeded those of baseball games by more than $5 million every year."[7] The Lincoln Center committee's fund-raising principle was not to strap constituent arts organizations with a mortgage in addition to their almost certain future deficits. Boldly, the group wanted to pay for the $75 million proposed cost in full, without loans. Such a plan was unheard of, but the 1950s were a prosperous decade. Civic pride also played a role. The planning committee's 1957 report called the proposed arts center "an unparalleled cultural opportunity that will almost certainly make New York City the musical capital of the world now and for many years to come."[8]

"There was still another reason for creating a center," architectural critic Brendan Gill later wrote, "rightly or wrongly, institutions having little in common except that they bear the label 'cultural' gain public attention and sympathy by clustering protectively together, like sheep in a fold cowering before the approach of wolves."[9] Yet not all agreed.

W. McNeil Lowry was opposed to the idea of Lincoln Center and later criticized all its boards as "absolutely moronic, destructive, indifferent and stupid! I mean, how many people can waste money better than bankers or real estate people? Nobody. No artist. They talk about the improvident artist, who is not realistic about getting things done or can't administer anything. Hell! They're hardnosed, firm managers—the artist himself, I'm not talking about the managing directors—compared to these characters. It was wasteful, materialistic, as though you could measure culture by buildings."[10] The argument was to recur during the next four decades.

In those pre-National Endowment for the Arts days, subsidy for the arts came entirely from private contributions. Unlike the rest of the civilized world, where government support and public sponsorship are the rule, in the America of the 1950s, as in the nineteenth century and now, government was suspect. On the one hand, among legislators there was strong opposition to spending tax money on such "frills" as the arts. Conservative trustees of arts institutions on the other hand strongly resisted any form of governmental subsidy; they feared political intervention in artistic matters. Peter Mennin, for example, warned in 1965 of the diluted standard that might result from well-meaning attempts such as the proposed NEA to make the arts more "available" to greater numbers of people. "With the passage of time, you will come to grips with all of these pressures," he told students. "In part, your resistance to these debilitating influences will depend on the judgment and background that will have been stimulated and generated by Juilliard, and in part by the quality of your own artistic moral fiber."[11]

As early as June 1955, discussions began concerning the possible participation of Juilliard at Lincoln Center. Rockefeller was pressing to include a school and asked Spofford whether Juilliard might be interested. The Center's board had concluded in February 1956 that Lincoln Center should include education "if the appropriate instrument can be found."[12] Three possibilities were pursued: Juilliard, Columbia (which was uninterested in providing professional training), and New York University.[13] The Manhattan School and Mannes College of Music were not considered. Juilliard had a enviable worldwide reputation and prestige, although Van Cliburn had yet to win the Moscow competition. One factor against Juilliard, however, was its large Preparatory School, seen as not professional enough. Lincoln Center insisted that nothing approaching music education become a constituent. The focus was to be professional rather than on training music teachers.

Newspapers reported that Juilliard was being seriously considered, along with a separate school for dramatic training.[14] The School was reluctant to talk to the press about relocating until its board could see how to dispose of the 122nd Street buildings. It seemed possible that Columbia would acquire the Morningside Heights plant for a proposed arts center.

By July 1956 the inclusion of Juilliard seemed less certain. Upon reflection, the board was reluctant to accept Lincoln Center's notion of a school. "The battle was not Juilliard versus another school," Mark Schubart later said, "the battle was between the Juilliard notion of a music school and this other sort of abstract idea of an advanced meeting place [such as the Institute for Advanced Study in Princeton]."[15] Lincoln Center wanted a workshop approach to bridge the gap between formal training and performance. It also wanted the school to be restricted to "advanced study" only, as in the original Noble plan for the JGS. In addition, drama would have to be added to dance and music.

The Juilliard board was hesitant to give up their sizable Preparatory School and reduce the number of students enrolled. In addition, the JMF money was strictly limited to music training and could not be applied to a drama program. Negotiations were at an impasse, and therefore Lincoln Center considered—and dropped—the idea of forming a new school.[16] Newspapers reported that the JSM had been mentioned but that several factors made its inclusion seem doubtful: Juilliard already had its own plant and appeared unwilling to train far fewer students.[17]

Schuman and Schubart felt that Juilliard had "no choice but to move," however; they saw it as a life-or-death situation for the School.[18] In December 1956 the president urged the board to expand to include drama and to endorse the idea of concentration on advanced training of persons with exceptional talent—in other words, to cut the student body to approximately two hundred.[19] Enrollment for 1956–57 was 645 students, 336 of whom received scholarships. Juilliard had lobbied for four hundred but compromised at two hundred because Lincoln Center had wanted even fewer students than that. That would mean a drastic reduction of the student body, which would seriously affect the orchestras and chorus as well as opera productions.

After deliberation, on February 1, 1957, the JSM board accepted a December 17 invitation from Lincoln Center. The *New York Times* reported that "no name has been decided for the new school, although the word 'Juilliard' will appear in the title."[20] The School, to open in 1960, would occupy a $5.5 million building on the southeast corner of Amsterdam Avenue and 65th Street. "There will be a dormitory," Gideon Waldrop wrote.[21] Site drawings in 1958 placed that facility across 65th Street, running as a thin slice of the block. The JMF would not have to raise the money for the building; Lincoln Center would pay for it. The board had agreed to all three of Lincoln Center's demands: The School would only train advanced students, drama would be added, and the Preparatory School would be discontinued. In agreeing to move to Lincoln Center, Juilliard was also ceding some of its autonomy.

Bliss and Rudolf Bing, the artistic director of the Metropolitan Opera, were not enthusiastic about having Juilliard appear equal in status to their organization. "At that particular time," Bliss recalled, "the professionals [the artistic heads of the two constituents, the Met and Philharmonic] were not very high on Juilliard, and they felt we would be bringing it into the center and making it the pre-eminent school in America, a school that was not up to the quality of the other constituents."[22] Bliss felt this attitude was "very, very strong" (it was he who had suggested that Lincoln Center form its own school). Rockefeller, however, wanted Juilliard, Bliss reckoned, for two reasons: "One was that Juilliard had money. Two, he felt more comfortable with [a] school, and the word school, and felt uncomfortable with the words opera and Philharmonic. Those were the two principal reasons. He could visualize and almost feel what a school means, whereas he had no clue as to how an opera functions, or the Philharmonic."[23]

Lincoln Center hired six major architects, all fierce individualists: Eero Saarinen (the Vivian Beaumont Theater), Wallace Harrison (the Met), Philip Johnson (the New York State Theater), Gordon Bunshaft (the Library of the Performing Arts), Max Abramovitz (the Philharmonic), and Pietro Belluschi (Juilliard). Belluschi's first architectural drawing, which called for an Italianate, fifteen-story building, was vetoed by the other five architects, who wanted a height restriction. The Juilliard architect found he needed more space. General Otto Nelson, in charge of Lincoln Center construction, devised a plan to get more land and in the spring of 1958 persuaded Washington officials to condemn as slums the half-block area north of the original site, the Lincoln Arcade. The land was considered desirable—and therefore more expensive—because it contained more Broadway frontage than the rest of Lincoln Center. For six weeks Johnson and Saarinen, architects of two theaters, devised ways to put *their* buildings on the new site, "[but] Juilliard . . . needed the larger site far more than either of the other two buildings needed it."[24] On October 1, 1958, Spofford, acting for Lincoln Center, bought the property at auction for $850,000. Hampering the six architects' visions was Robert Moses's unexplained insistence that the southwest corner of the site be a park (later named Damrosch Park after the Damrosch family). The architects could not move the park around the site drawings.

Belluschi had been recommended in 1958 by Harrison. The Roman-born Belluschi was dean of architecture at the Massachusetts Institute of Technology and had designed a small concert hall for the University of California at Berkeley as well as numerous college buildings elsewhere. "More than any of the others on the Lincoln Center architectural team, he seemed to focus on human considerations in architectural design," Edgar Young recalled.[25] One of Belluschi's first suggestions concerned a common exterior material. He recommended a Roman travertine from the same quarries near Tivoli that had provided the marble to build ancient Rome. The Italian government, as a gesture of goodwill, had agreed to donate the funds to purchase the travertine and gave half a million dollars for that purpose. Years later it was discovered that travertine was less durable in New York's climate than in central Italy, and some of the cladding on the Met had to be replaced. Perhaps not coincidentally, the only foreign countries to respond to Lincoln Center's appeals for aid were those the United States had fought in World War II. The governments of Italy and Germany donated money, and private contributions came from Austria and Japan. The acoustician chosen for The Juilliard School was Heinrich Keilholz, a German.

Twelve thousand people attended the ground-breaking ceremony for Lincoln Center on May 14, 1959. Half a million watched the event on local New York television as Juilliard students sang the Hallelujah chorus from Handel's *Messiah*. The first building to be completed was Philharmonic Hall in September 1962, even though the save Carnegie Hall movement under Isaac Stern was gaining momentum. Lincoln Center's public relations firm had advised total silence on that subject.

In September 1960 the Lincoln Center board began a search for a new president. Spofford recommended Gen. Maxwell D. Taylor, retired U.S. Army chief of staff. The men had worked together during the formative days of NATO, and Taylor was also known at West Point as an educator. He became president of Lincoln Center January 1, 1961, and found the political, artistic, and architectural situation a challenge: "Nothing in the Pentagon was ever so complicated!"[26]

As distant as Taylor's appointment might have seemed from Juilliard affairs up on 122nd Street, it was to have a far-reaching impact on the School. Only four months after Taylor had assumed duties at Lincoln Center, John F. Kennedy called Rockefeller to ask him to release Taylor immediately; he was needed in Washington to help with the aftermath of the failed Bay of Pigs invasion. Taylor's two-month leave dragged on, and Lincoln Center had to find another president. He resigned in late June, and in September William Schuman was elected as his successor, effective January 1, 1962 (chapter 5).

Rockefeller was particularly concerned that Schuman carry the full responsibility for the financial planning for the future, although that was not Schuman's understanding. By necessity, when Schuman changed jobs it meant a switch in allegiance from Juilliard to Lincoln Center. The aims of each would not always be consonant, and Schuman was now obligated to look after Lincoln Center's—not Juilliard's—interests. He also tried to lure two of Juilliard's top administrators to accompany him to Lincoln Center. The recently hired Gideon Waldrop preferred to stay at Juilliard, however, and Mark Schubart said he would leave only after he served a year as interim president.

Although Juilliard was one of the first three (of the original nine) constituents at Lincoln Center, its building was the last to be completed. There were several reasons for the twelve-year delay, and the School had no control over any of them.

The first had to do with money, and it echoes the lawsuit brought by Frederick Juilliard and his cousins against the JMF in the early 1920s. Forty-two years earlier John D. Rockefeller had created a trust for his granddaughter, Muriel McCormick Hubbard. If she died without issue, which she did in 1959, the remainder of the money would be distributed to charities chosen by the trust. John D. Rockefeller 3rd was on the trust committee and designated the funds to support Juilliard, but Mrs. McCormick's four adopted children sued. The case dragged on for five years and was not settled until 1965. Lincoln Center then received $9 million.[27] In 1951 J. P. Morgan's granddaughter had also died. After six years of litigation and two sensational trials, the $200,000 inheritance was awarded to Sol Rosenblatt, who turned it over to Juilliard in 1957.

A second reason for the frustrating delay was because of the sheer complexity of the new structure, "one of the most complicated buildings ever made."[28] Both functional needs and engineering necessities led to the complexity. Soundproofed practice rooms and teaching studios were required; large studios with high ceilings were needed for opera, dance, and drama coaching; and provision for three pipe organs was necessary, as were performance halls and shops for scenery and costumes. All of that was in addition to classrooms, a library, and still other rooms. In 1959 Lincoln Center's Chamber Music Hall (later named Alice Tully Hall) had been shifted on the drawings from the Philharmonic building to Juilliard. Spaces at Juilliard for a large public restaurant, for commercial stores and banks, and for Lincoln Center offices were also considered. Belluschi was to fit all of that into a building that would relate to the rest of Lincoln Center in mass and height (approximately five stories).

In June 1959 Belluschi estimated that $18.5 million would be necessary to build Juilliard, although the budget only granted $10 million—

$6.5 million for the School, $1 million for the Chamber Music Hall, and $2.5 million to be borrowed for student housing. The estimate in May 1960 was $131 million for Lincoln Center as a whole.[29] The directors realized that the only significant economic saving would be to eliminate either dance or drama but found those alternatives unacceptable. Although the prospect of McCormick's $9 million encouraged them, both the dormitory and several stories were eliminated. By losing the dormitory, Juilliard had lost one of its main incentives to join Lincoln Center.

In spite of these eliminations, engineering costs had increased the price of a new Juilliard to $23 million by April 1960. By eliminating a service road between 65th and 66th Streets and by placing the theater and the Chamber Music Hall side by side rather than one above the other, Belluschi was able to cut the figure to $18 million. The capital budget for Lincoln Center was revised upward from $75 million to $102 million. W. McNeil Lowry, acting on behalf of the Ford Foundation, which eventually gave $30 million to Lincoln Center (more than the Rockefellers), thought that everyone, including John D. Rockefeller 3rd, knew the $75 million figure was "a joke."[30]

The third cause for delay had to do with the possibility of a site enlargement to include more of the west end of Juilliard's block. The LaGuardia High School for Performing Arts, representing a planned merger of the High School of Music and Art and the High School of Performing Arts, was part of the original idea for the 65th Street block. The proposed school and Juilliard each wanted space on that block. The dispute was solved in May 1969 when the city allocated yet another block—between 64th and 65th and Amsterdam and West End Avenue— for the new high school.

The High School of Commerce occupied the west end of the 65th Street block at 155 West 65th. The price for the School's land would be $1.2 million. That sum was offered, but the city rejected it. Six months of stalemate resulted in Lincoln Center agreeing in May 1963 (with money donated by Rockefeller) to buy the site without a protection of a maximum price. The city accepted the offer but could not deliver the property until a new High School of Commerce (with its then three thousand students) could be opened, supposedly in 1965. There would be two more years of delay, therefore, before Juilliard construction could begin.

In the meantime, the architects could revise their drawings, taking into account the proposed new space. Now the site encompassed 350 feet along 65th Street and 200 feet along Broadway—half a million square feet and eight million cubic feet. The new plans brought down the height of the building from eight stories to five while increasing the cubic footage in such places as the theater (an increase from six hundred to a thousand seats), the Chamber Music Hall (for better reverberation), and the orchestra rehearsal hall (greater ceiling height), all enlargements Keilholz desired. It also meant an increase in the projected cost well beyond the March 1964 budget of $17.2 million. Eliminating the Dance or Drama Departments was again considered and rejected. Instead, Lincoln Center increased the budget by $4 million.

When 1965 finally arrived, the board of education delayed the closing of the High School of Commerce because of a citywide shortage of high school classrooms. Parents of students there objected to the razing of 155th West 65th because the West Side School had not yet been built. In February 1965, 250 High School of Commerce students picketed Lincoln Center to protest the plan. The high school was housed in two buildings, and the older building, next to the Juilliard site, was vacated to allow demolition and excavation to begin in April 1965. The second high school building, to be used as an annex for three years following 1965, was still in use in the 1980s (chapter 11).

A fourth cause for delay concerned increases in material costs, although Lincoln Center could not sustain a claim for damages. Anticipated savings in the subcontract for steel had been based on a major error of the engineers who had calculated the required quantity. They had estimated that 3,800 tons would be required, whereas the actual number was 6,800. In addition, Keilholz needed heavy concrete to create thick walls and floors for sound isolation. Practice rooms were to be located above the theaters. Therefore, ceiling beams were to be huge girders to bridge the wide theater spaces (so as not to create unwanted columns) and bear the increased weight of the heavy concrete above. A sixty-foot I-beam, one of the biggest interior beams in the city, was placed over the theater in order to eliminate a two-foot-wide column in a traffic area between the scene shop and the stage. All of this increased cost. Reluctantly, Lincoln Center increased Juilliard's budget to $24,340,000. Each increase meant that Rockefeller and the many Lincoln Center fund-raisers were put in the embarrassing position of revisiting donors who had been told that their gifts were one-time-only contributions. Although Juilliard reapplied within a few years, the Ford Foundation's $30 million had come with the demand that none of Lincoln Center's constituents apply again for ten years.

Finally, delay was caused by a strike of hoisting engineers that began during the summer of 1966 and was settled in November. In March 1967 a floor gave way during pouring of concrete, and seven construction workers were injured.[31] Later, a special drill was required to bore through thirty-four feet of rock to create the elevator shaft at Juilliard.

The facility's opening had to be shifted to 1969. In 1962 it was arranged that the Manhattan School of Music would buy Juilliard's Claremont Avenue buildings for $4 million, a price predicated on a move to Lincoln Center in 1966. The arrangement became more of a bargain for Manhattan as time elapsed.

Friction between Lincoln Center and Juilliard was inevitable. A principal cause concerned funding. One of the primary goals of Juilliard's move was to provide sufficient scholarship aid so that none of the few students who were accepted would be unable to attend because of financial need.[32] Much-sought-after scholarship money led to a bitter dispute:

> Again, the issue was over money, specifically the relationship between a grant [awarded in November 1958] of $.5 million to Lincoln Center from the Carnegie Corporation (designated for Juilliard scholarships) and Lincoln Center's commitment of $2.5 million to support the Juilliard drama training program. Peter Mennin, president of Juilliard, with strong support from his trustees, took the position that the Carnegie grant was separate from, and in addition to, Lincoln Center's obligation. Schuman's position was, on the other hand, that the Carnegie grant should be credited to this obligation. Several attempts at negotiation and amicable settlement failed. In November 1965 the board approved Schuman's position, with the further proviso that accumulated interest earned on the Carnegie grant should also remain with Lincoln Center. The Juilliard reaction was strong and bitter, and this issue remained a festering sore in the Juilliard relationship.[33]

It took four years to settle the question with the Carnegie Corporation. The grant was eventually credited to the Drama Division, but the interest would belong to Juilliard rather than to Lincoln Center. Peter Mennin never forgave William Schuman for appropriating the money, and his relationship to the newly created Drama Division became ambivalent at best (chapter 9). The relationship between Juilliard and Lincoln Center deteriorated further.

A second cause of serious friction had to do with Juilliard's use of Tully Hall. One of Juilliard's performance halls had been eliminated during the fiscal belt-tightening. The chair of Juilliard's board and the chair of Lincoln Center disagreed over Juilliard's access to Tully Hall and asked Edgar Young to arbitrate. After he had searched through much old paperwork he wrote a memorandum: Juilliard had indeed been promised free access to the hall several times a week. Lincoln Center was not happy to lose the case, which meant a loss in income from potential rentals of Tully Hall on Tuesday and Friday evenings. The case was critical for Juilliard; without Tully Hall there was no other venue where orchestras could perform. The theater would have been overtaxed. Years later the Juilliard Orchestra also played in Fisher Hall at Lincoln Center.

A third cause of friction between Juilliard and Lincoln Center dealt with the requirements in theater technology desired by the acoustician and by the lighting designer, Jean Rosenthal. Keilholz wanted a movable ceiling for the theater in order to vary reverberation time and serve both spoken drama and music. The ceiling's cost rose from $208,000 to $590,000, but Belluschi and Keilholz considered it essential. Rosenthal had specified the most advanced theater technology. Lincoln Center proposed that adequate lighting could be achieved with fewer electric winches and less lighting equipment. The executive committee directed a cut of $220,000 and left it to Juilliard to decide on its distribution. The millwork and interior wood surfaces also came in at $565,000 over budget. Furnishings such as carpeting and audio equipment cost $1,308,000, a sum exceeding the budgeted amount by $288,000. Yet another new budget for the building was authorized in February 1967. The estimated cost now stood at $27.5 million.

Cost-cutting meant, for example, that the Juilliard Theater lobby, which was to have wood paneling, was left with the concrete exposed (as it still is). The final cost of Lincoln Center was $185 million, well over twice that of the original proposals. The total cost of Juilliard, including furnishings, was just under $30 million.

Architectural Record described the finished building as "an almost infinite variety of spaces fitted together with a sorcerer's skill in an arrangement as intricate as a Chinese puzzle."[34] The article stressed that the performance halls were column-free but had to carry heavy loads from rooms above. Sixty-five different sets of preliminary drawings and three hundred on-the-job sketches were made during the twelve years of the building's planning (1957–69). Because Juilliard was the final part of Lincoln Center, its designers learned from the other buildings' mistakes. The man originally hired as orchestra manager, Philip Hart, was "more responsible for the interior configuration of the new building than any other person," said Waldrop. "The result is a thoroughly unique building for an equally unique School" boasted the *Juilliard School Bulletin*.[35]

The glory of the building is the award-winning Juilliard Theater, which seats 960 to 1,026. Public hints that for a donation of $3 million the theater (and for $1 million the 278-seat drama workshop) could have a name drew no takers. The most complicated of all the performance spaces, the theater was the last to be finished. Sixty percent of the ceiling adjusts to three positions within a seven-foot range to change the angle and reflection of sound. The 1,900–ton ceiling designed by Olaf

Lincoln Center Juilliard building in 1969.

Peter Mennin and
John D. Rockefeller
3rd in the Juilliard
Theater, 1969.

Soöt has a fail-safe system to protect the audience. A wood interior was considered important for both aesthetic and acoustical reasons. The proscenium can be varied from forty-five to fifty-eight feet in width, and its height from twenty-one to twenty-eight feet, depending in part on the location of the ceiling. An orchestra pit accommodates ninety-five players and through two lifts is capable of reaching stage level, thereby giving the stage more depth. The stage area is just as large as that of the New York State Theater—nine thousand square feet (6,600 for performance)—and Juilliard's building is 50 percent larger. It is also three times the cubic feet of the 120 Claremont Avenue building.

Sound transmission in the building was a critical issue. All outside windows were triple-glazed to keep out noise. Architects found it necessary to place the library directly above a two-story orchestra rehearsal room, and it is possible to recognize the piece being rehearsed while studying in the library. The IRT subway stop at 66th Street and Broadway was just twenty feet from the northeast corner of Tully Hall, so a special envelope was made for the hall in that corner. Although Keilholz did not design Tully Hall for use by large orchestras, each of Juilliard's three orchestras have used the hall about once a month. An additional fourteen feet of stage depth can be acquired by removing the first three rows.

Alice Tully took great interest in her hall. The distinctive purple carpeting that was replaced in the mid-1990s, for example, had been her choice. In order to retain more control over her life, she never married, although she had a male companion. Tully wanted anonymity; she knew that many, seeing her name on the wall, would ask for help. When Rockefeller asked whether the hall should be named for her, she asked the name of the acoustician. Learning that it was Heinrich Keilholz, she agreed. She supported him in arguments with the architect, such as over the amount of space between rows.[36]

Paul Hall, the recital hall, seats 277 and was named after its benefactor, Col. C. Michael Paul, a violinist who had given $1 million toward the facility.[37] Paul Hall, paneled in cherry wood, was dedicated November 30, 1970, and contains a forty-four-rank Holtkamp organ.

The most drastic problem with sound transmission occurred in the eighty-four practice rooms. Georganne Mennin recalled:

> [George] Szell was helpful with the acoustics too. He and Peter discussed it a great deal. . . . One summer evening when the school was near completion, we were walking through the school, just the two of us. Peter went into one of the practice rooms to try out the piano. I went down the hall to get a drink of water and suddenly I realized I could hear him playing. When I told him the rooms weren't exactly soundproof he was terribly upset and called Ed Young, [who] came

over. Peter demonstrated the flaw and he and Ed called Keilholz [in Germany] that night. The whole thing finally got straightened out by the opening. I think they found out something weird, like the work-men had put garbage in the air conditioning ducts. In any case, since the carpeting was already down and the pianos moved in, it was time-consuming and costly to remedy the situation, but it got done.[38]

All teaching and performance areas at Juilliard have walls and floors that float free of the structure to minimize sound transmission. The rehearsal floors were especially constructed to achieve a resilience that would help lessen fatigue and injury on the part of dancers, actors, and musicians. A fiberglass pad separated structural concrete from a second-ary concrete slab on which a wooden floor was suspended by steel-coil springs. The final surface was either wood or battleship linoleum. The air-conditioning system was designed to provide optimum humidity and move air at low velocity. A conventional system would dry singers' throats and harm students who might be perspiring after strenuous physical activity.

The completed building had fifteen large, two-story studios for re-hearsals, thirty-five private teaching studios, twenty-seven classrooms, eighty-four practice rooms, three organ studios, and more than two hundred pianos. In addition to playback facilities in every classroom and a large listening library, headed for three decades by Sandra Czajkowski, there was also a system for making tape-recordings from various loca-tions in the building.

The acoustics laboratory was originally intended for students to make their own recordings from either Paul Hall, the theater, or Alice Tully Hall.[39] The staff commandeered the recording facilities, however, and proceeded to charge students for the service and pocket the proceeds. Recording of student performances in Tully Hall must be done by Lin-coln Center's union technicians, and the costs of doing so are high. At the old building, students could practice every day of the week. In the new building, practicing was and still is not possible on Sundays because of the expenses—approximately $5,000 per Sunday in the 1980s—in-volved in keeping the building open. Juilliard's operating budget at Lin-coln Center was several times that of the Claremont Avenue buildings, a fact Peter Mennin never tired of trumpeting.

Four sculptures were given to the Juilliard building. Alice Tully do-nated a bronze cast of Bourdelle's "Beethoven à la Colonne" (1901) for the foyer of Tully Hall. Louise Nevelson's "Nightsphere-Light, 1969," forty-eight feet long and eight feet high, was not designed for the space, although it covers most of the wall of the theater lobby. Rockefeller donated Masayuki Nagare's black-granite, untitled work that had commanded the landing of the main staircase facing the 65th Street entrance before being moved to the theater lobby. In 1970 the American-Israel Cultural Foundation donated Yaacov Agam's rotating "Three × Three Interplay," which stood outside on the terrace at the southeast corner of the building over the Tully Hall entrance. Absent for several years during the 1990s while an outside escalator to the new lobby was being installed, it was returned to a spot near its original location.

Harold Schonberg of the *New York Times* described the building as "the Taj Mahal of conservatories, opulent, beautiful, domineering—and big." (Perhaps he forgot that the Taj Mahal is a tomb.) Among Lincoln Center buildings, Juilliard was second in size only to the Met. Trustee John W. Drye, Jr., said it "crowd[ed] a University into a shoe box." "If I wanted to be reserved," Peter Mennin remarked, "I'd say it's all merely fantastic." And Leonard Bernstein added, "I have always believed that the inclusion of The Juilliard School in the Lincoln Center complex was the ultimate reason for the existence of the Center."[40] One journalist called it "the most handsome and complex conservatory plant ever built," and another author called the move to Lincoln Center "the greatest single event in [Juilliard's] history."[41] Schonberg wrote, "For with its move to Lincoln Center, the Juilliard School has become the most impressive conservatory in the entire world, with facilities at its disposal that no other conservatory can begin to approach."[42]

Some visible architectural blunders lingered for more than two decades. The most conspicuous was the entrance to the building, once planned as a grand double staircase facing Broadway. Belluschi placed the entrances to the School, the theater, and Alice Tully Hall at street level below a surrounding unused balcony and bridge. "The great length and width of the bridge turned that segment of Sixty-fifth Street into a forbidding cellar," an architecture critic wrote, "artificially lit by day as well as by night. Its perennial gloom was deepened by the walls of the structures on both sides of the street, which were largely windowless and therefore inimical to passersby." The situation with Tully Hall was not much better. "What had the look of being a secondary entrance to Alice Tully Hall—a set of low doors tucked obscurely beneath an overhanging flight of stairs on Broadway—is, in fact, the main entrance. The flight of stairs had the appearance of a grand ceremonial approach to a building that, once one had mounted the stairs, turned out, to one's astonishment, not to exist: all that one had reached was a narrow balcony along the southern face of Tully Hall, which led to the bridge spanning Sixty-fifth Street." So inconspicuous was the entrance to the School that strangers would frequently try first the Broadway doors (Alice Tully Hall), then the stairs (to no avail), then the 65th Street door (chained closed), and finally the 66th Street entrance to find their way into Juilliard. "An unprepossessing entrance on Sixty-sixth Street served as the main entrance, and as a result the school appeared to have deliberately turned its back upon Lincoln Center in order to face the near-cipher of an ordinary Manhattan side street."[43]

Peter Mennin expressed the School's ambivalence about the move in an address to the last class to graduate from the "old building" in May 1969:

> This involves more than a physical move from one location to another. For the faculty, students and administration, it means transferring one's habits, likes and dislikes, memories and associations, from one location to another. It is never easy, and rarely is one totally enthusiastic. Such moves also mean certain unavoidable heartaches. . . . Neither bricks and mortar and location improve the institution or make it permanent. This is done by the quality of work that goes on between faculty and students and by the School's unfaltering adherence to the highest artistic values and ideals.[44]

By the time the Juilliard building was finally ready for students William Schuman no longer had anything to do with either Juilliard or Lincoln Center. He had provided Lincoln Center with vision, fighting for a film society, the Chamber Music Society, the Music Theater of Lincoln Center, and two expensive summer festivals (1967 and 1968) that brought performers and companies from around the world. He also began a Haydn-Mozart series, which evolved into Mostly Mozart, and brought the able Mark Schubart from Juilliard to direct Lincoln Center's student program. Schubart was the only Schuman appointee to survive him at Lincoln Center.

Schuman was convinced that Lincoln Center's potential for leadership in the arts rested on these activities, which amounted—so it appeared to some of the nine constituents—to a competition with their own programming and vision. As Edgar Young wrote of the situation, Schuman wanted Lincoln Center "to have its own place in the sun in the artistic firmament."[45] That raised a basic philosophical issue concerning Lincoln Center's leadership. Some of the board (Rockefeller, Spofford, Josephs, and Young) felt that Lincoln Center should resist the role of a constituent and remain as coordinator. They had practical concerns as well: How much more money were these programs going to cost?

Schuman's bull-in-a-china shop style never abated. As he had often done, he made inflammatory remarks in public, this time on the subject of deficits in the arts. At a 1966 Princeton conference on the economic problems of the performing arts, Schuman said, "Nonprofit institutions in the performing arts compromise their reason for being in direct proportion to the programs and policies which are adopted for fiscal reasons extrinsic to artistic purpose. . . . all of us in the performing arts sw[i]m in the same sea: the sea of deficit. This sea is obviously a red sea, and only a p-r-o-f-i-t can part it. Now, as deep as that red sea is, I think it should be deeper. Basic to our problem is not that our deficits are too large, but that they are too small."[46] He meant in part that the size of the budgets did not permit him to do the artistic job properly. Schuman's own salary was estimated in the press as between $75,000 and $100,000.

Rockefeller read the address and wrote Schuman, "This kind of deficit philosophy can be the downfall of Lincoln Center or any other artistic institution unless as much attention is given to sound financial planning and effective fund-raising as to the creation and development of programs."[47] That same month, Spofford suffered a stroke. The remainder of the executive committee recognized the feeling among the constituents (especially the Met, Philharmonic, and Juilliard) that Lincoln Center was competing with them in programming as well as fund-raising. The board and Schuman agreed to Rockefeller's summary statement: "In the last analysis the constituents' success will determine the success of Lincoln Center . . . [and they] must always be given highest priority."[48]

Nevertheless, Schuman, who disliked fund-raising and had done none of it while at Juilliard, continued to make expensive plans for a chamber music program. He wanted a schedule of 120 concerts the first year, which would cost more than half a million dollars—a sum he felt Alice Tully would underwrite. Rockefeller was again concerned and acknowledged that some constituents felt mistrust, fear, competition, and even bitterness toward Lincoln Center (chapter 9). David Keiser had a private talk with Schuman and stressed that Lincoln Center should not itself be presenting artistic programs. In saying that, he challenged Schuman's vision of his role as an impresario.

When Spofford's health improved enough for him to resume chairmanship of the executive committee in February 1968, he focused attention on the deficit and financial crisis. Schuman wrote to Rockefeller hinting that he provide leadership "in helping us raise operating funds."[49] Rockefeller wrote back, politely: "no."

Schuman then left for Europe to assemble the next year's festival. But world events were overtaking him. In April, Martin Luther King, Jr., was assassinated, and two months later Robert F. Kennedy met his death. The outburst of anger and sadness over King's death led to riots, which perhaps led foundations to prefer giving for urban problems rather than to the arts. For his part, Lincoln Center's chief fund-raiser, Hoyt Ammidon, blamed "racial tensions" for difficulties in fund-raising. Based on Ammidon's comments, Rockefeller notified Schuman that he felt the Lincoln Center budget for 1968–69 must be reduced by a minimum of $1 million.

Faced with radical reductions of his dreams for programming for Lincoln Center, Schuman suffered a mild heart attack in April. That postponed but did not prevent action on the budget cuts. During his summer-long absence, John Mazzola acted as chief executive officer of Lincoln Center. The earlier authorization for Schuman's Festival '69 was rescinded. When he returned in September, he tried to salvage the film and chamber music programs. By October he had organized seventy-eight concerts of chamber music for 1969–70, a number even Alice Tully thought might be too ambitious, and other constituents also voiced reservations. Undeterred, Schuman pressed for public announcement of the series, but Rockefeller intervened and personally stopped the announcement. When the Chamber Music Society of Lincoln Center was inaugurated on September 11, 1969, it subsequently gave sixteen concerts rather than seventy-two or 120 and continued to give sixteen well into the 1980s. Now the Society gives about forty concerts a season in Tully Hall and fifty to sixty elsewhere.

Pressed by Rockefeller, Schuman resigned the presidency of Lincoln Center in December with the statement that "I have, of necessity, become less involved with the artistic and cultural phases, and more and more with the administrative activities, particularly those dealing with the financial problems of the Center."[50] He had been fired but was allowed to save face publicly by stating that the reason he left was to have more time to compose. Schuman's desire to shock by giving radical-sounding public pronouncements—a trait he considered to have carried him far—finally capsized him. Rockefeller, for one, would not put up with it.

For more than two decades after his departure from Juilliard in 1962 Schuman had no influence whatsoever over policies at the School. After 1968 he had no influence at Lincoln Center. In 1970 his Lincoln Center brainchild, the Music Theater operation, was liquidated. Schuman had never realized his dream of instituting a modern dance company at Lincoln Center. A year after his departure, Rockefeller felt confident enough in the administration of Lincoln Center that he could resign from the committee. Schuman tried to pursue a career as a lecturer but failed despite his considerable talent for public speaking. The next decade of leadership at Lincoln Center, however, was colorless in comparison and lacked Schuman's grand visions.

Christopher Rouse has compared Schuman's music and personality: "The urgency of Schuman's music is matched only by the vitality of Schuman himself. With his unflagging energy, boundless enthusiasm, his keen eye and ear for the world's foibles and strengths, his penetrating wit, and withal, his deep compassion, it is inconceivable that he can ever cease originating ideas or rest on his achievements."[51] At Lincoln Center he had overreached himself and fallen. Decades later he would rise again.

On Sunday afternoon, October 26, 1969, a concert marked both the formal opening of Juilliard and the completion of Lincoln Center. Leopold Stokowski conducted the Preludes to acts 1 and 3 of *Lohengrin.* Stokowski had appeared on the opening concert thirty-eight years earlier, when Juilliard inaugurated its previous new quarters on Claremont Avenue. After remarks from Nelson Rockefeller and Peter Mennin, the concert continued with Itzhak Perlman playing the first movement of Paganini's First Violin Concerto. Then Shirley Verrett sang the Alleluia from Mozart's *Exultate, Jubilate* and other arias. The orchestra performed Ravel's *Danse Generale* from *Daphnis et Chloe Suite* under Jean Morel, and Van Cliburn closed with Liszt's First Piano Concerto in E flat. The concert was broadcast on CBS (the network long associated with the School) to an estimated audience of 8.8 million. The *Times* took issue with the programming: "It does not stand for anything, except for an emphasis on personality and virtuosity. And while those are two elements of music making, the dignity of the occasion would have benefited from something deeper, stronger, more noble and beautiful."[52] Glenn Gould agreed, calling the program "a worthy contender for the title of 'All-time Awful Inaugural.'"[53] It was far removed from Schuman's long-expressed desire to open Juilliard with a program of commissioned works.

Leonard Bernstein, narrator of the event, took the opportunity to say of William Schuman that he "lent an originality and grandeur of concept to the whole project that it easily could have lacked without him."[54] Guests included First Lady Pat Nixon and Julie and David Eisenhower. John D. Rockefeller 3rd spoke: "And so the setting is complete—dedicated to art, to public service and to the training of the young. Now it is the time of the artist and his audience, for only they can make this Center a living testament to the quality of life."[55] The Juilliard String Quartet also performed on the series of concerts dedicating the move. They played a program of Mozart's C-major quartet, Beethoven's Opus 131 in c-sharp minor, and a commissioned work, Stefan Wolpe's String Quartet. The architects had learned from Philharmonic Hall's mistakes; acoustics in Tully Hall were universally praised.

Raining on the parade of the October 26 opening was William

Schuman's four-column rebuttal in the *New York Times* that day: "William Schuman Protests a 'Completely False History.'"[56] Unable to resist the limelight even when no longer associated with either Juilliard or Lincoln Center, he blasted an article by Martin Mayer, published a month earlier, that had given Mennin's perspective on the School's history with Lincoln Center.[57] That article had raised many of Juilliard's sore points with Lincoln Center. Mayer quoted Drye as having told Rockefeller that "every institution at Lincoln Center is broke, except Juilliard. And Juilliard *will* be when it gets there." He also cited the expense of keeping up the "castle" of Lincoln Center; the complete lack of financial support for the Dance Department (chapter 8); and, the sorest point, the seized Carnegie grant. The article was filled with Menninesque gloom: "The fact is that without major new public contributions to its operating expenses in the new building, Juilliard cannot possibly survive." Schuman's ill-timed rebuttal, which claimed that Mayer's article "grossly distort[ed] the facts," did not address all of those points.

Mayer's reply filled four columns on the same page. In it he described Schuman's position variously as "out of focus" and "remarkably untroubled about the subsequent falsity" of a stated assumption of his report to the board. "Like much else that happened during Mr. Schuman's late incumbency at Lincoln Center," he concluded, had "presented a problem for others to solve."[58]

Juilliard had barely survived the move to Lincoln Center. In addition to the financial upheaval, a certain psychological distress also was noticed. Mark Schubart compared the reactions to the new building with those of the distant past: "[The faculty] talked about the 'new building' and the 'old building' and everyone hated the new building, because it was too big. 'Oh, it's not like the old building. It's not homey anymore and it's lost all its charm, and this is a great big factory!' They talk about it exactly the same way that the Institite of Musical Art talked about the building that was built in 1931. It's true!"[59]

8

Dancers' Training:

MARTHA HILL

"THE DANCE IS ONE of the irrepressible propensities of the human species. Homo Sapiens has always claimed it as a birthright and has hugged it to his bosom, so to speak, from the pre-dawn of his history to the present perilous and perhaps crepuscular moment. Ancient cultures gave the dance an exalted position, often allied to, if not indistinguishable from, their religion; at the very core of the spirituality and civilization."[1] So spoke José Limón, perhaps the greatest male dancer of his generation, shortly before his death in 1972. His was the first modern dance company to survive its creator. The incorporation of dance departments into American conservatories was first achieved by the modern dancer Jan Veen (Hans Wiener) in 1944 at the Boston Conservatory of Music.

The Juilliard Dance Department was founded in 1951, coinciding with the twenty-fifth anniversary of the merging of the JGS with the IMA, when William Schuman and Norman Lloyd invited the choreographers with whom Lloyd had worked to come to Juilliard. He and his wife Ruth had served as musical directors of the Bennington School of the Dance and the Humphrey-Weidman Company from 1936 to

1938. Lloyd had also written for the dance, including *Panorama* (Martha Graham), *Dance of Work and Play* (Hanya Holm), and *Inquest* and *Lament for Ignacio Sánchez Mejías* (Doris Humphrey). Schuman had written *Undertow* (1945) for Antony Tudor and *Night Journey* (1947) and *Judith* (1950), both for Martha Graham.

Also in 1951, the New York State Department of Education advised the School that it was no longer necessary to require physical training. Physical education classes, which were held off-campus, were dropped from the curriculum. Dance would give physical training to only a small portion of Juilliard students.

Janet Soares, a dance faculty member from 1963 to 1986, wrote of the department founder Martha Hill (1900–95) as "one of those unsung people in the arts who is dedicated to making things happen for others."[2] Hill was always elegantly dressed, her silver hair twisted in her signature asymmetrical knot and held with a grey velvet ribbon. Vida Ginsberg remembers her as "an inconceivable and improbable combination of a Geisha and a Grant Wood with an aura of glamour."[3]

A no-nonsense, unpretentious woman from the Midwest, Hill was sure of her mission. Soares wrote that her "ability to side-step the unnecessary has always been her strong point. She is a woman guided by her own terms. Extraordinary self-reliance and good sense have marked her success at creating a secure terrain upon which others can dance and create." Soares also called Hill "a stoic mentor and powerful authority

Martha Hill.
(Jane Rady, photo from The Juilliard School)

figure, right about everything."[4] A former Bennington student thought of Hill as "a crusader for American dance, with a vision as big as Whitman's or Martin Luther King's."[5]

Hill, a live-wire character and nonstop talker, is remembered as a fine teacher who expressed "a kind of universal love and acceptance for every student which created an atmosphere conducive to growth." She possessed the ability that makes teachers great—the ability to detect talent and cultivate excellent dancing through excellent teaching. One student relayed Hill's iconoclastic concepts: "Don't be 'pretty'; don't use music 'bigger' than your work; don't be literal, tell a story or ride on a cliché."[6]

Hill had been raised in East Palestine, Ohio, the eldest child of four. Her strict father was a mining engineer who insisted that the East was not a place for a decent woman, so she gave up early dreams of studying ballet in New York. Instead, she studied dance during two summers at Perry-Mansfield in Colorado in the early 1920s and taught physical education at Kansas State Teachers College. She also studied ballet with Edna McRae, who taught in Chicago. By 1926 she did come to New York, however, to study Dalcroze eurhythmics at the IMA. That experience marked a pivotal change in Hill's life. In New York, she attended a Martha Graham concert. "As a ballet person, before I saw Martha, I didn't even know Isadora [Duncan] existed. It was instant conversion!" Hill had studied modern music and now found a parallel in dance. "I realized it was possible to communicate contemporary and serious ideas in movement."[7]

She spent two years teaching at the University of Oregon, saved her money, and returned to New York to join Graham's studio and the company in 1929. "I remember Martha admonishing my port-de-bras as looking too balletic. I had to work very hard to fight the lightness my ballet training had taught me," she recalled.[8] Because she thought the Lincoln School, where she taught, would frown upon her being a professional dancer, Hill listed herself with the Graham Company as Martha Todd (her mother's maiden name). Graham recommended Hill to head the dance department at the Cornish School in Seattle. Wanting to preserve her foothold in New York, she declined.

Hill began to teach dance in the physical education department at New York University in the summer of 1930, having acquired a degree from Teacher's College at Columbia. Finances forced a decision between NYU or remaining in the Graham Company, and she had to choose NYU. In 1932 Martha Graham gave a performance at Bennington College, and in 1934 Hill and Mary Jo Shelly founded and codirected the Bennington (summer) School of Dance. Hill continued at NYU and commuted to Bennington—more than seven hundred train trips on the Green Mountain Flyer—and worked three days a week as choreographer for all Bennington's theatrical productions.[9]

Gradually, Hill's administrative responsibilities and talents increased. She became a producer, a role few others in dance were either equipped or interested to perform. She was a behind-the-scenes person. "I like to say my major is people. That's my talent—I am good about understanding and reconciling different points of view. . . . I'm sort of a catalyst—pushing things ahead. That's always been my role."[10] She also arranged for an impressive array of faculty to teach at Bennington, at first careful to schedule rivals so that they not meet. Hill produced Bennington's classics: Martha Graham's *Panorama* (1935) and *American Document* (1938), Doris Humphrey's *New Dance* (1935) and *Passacaglia and Fugue in C Minor* (1938), and Hanya Holm's *Trend* (1937), *Dance Sonata*, and *Dance of Work and Play* (both 1938). There was very little money for these productions, but the summer school was always in the black.

Hill moved to the West Coast when the Bennington group was transplanted to Mills College in the summer of 1939. There, she identified Merce Cunningham as a dancer to watch and recommended him to Graham. In 1951, the year she set up the dance program at Juilliard, Hill married Thurston ("Lefty") Davies, former president of Colorado College, who helped administer the 1958 Brussels World's Fair. After he died in 1961, Hill continued to work: "What else was there to do?"[11]

June Dunbar, who assisted Hill and took over administrative duties at Juilliard during her absences, has explained the novelty of what Hill was trying to accomplish by expecting dance students to move from Fokine to Sokolow and back again: "Martha Hill had established something that was violently new, in that she did bring dancers from various philosophical camps together to teach at a conservatory in tandem. Dance was enormously divided in those years. People who were Graham oriented had disdain for any other technique, and vice versa. . . . Certainly one of the most innovative things Martha Hill did was to create a position for Antony Tudor to head up the ballet department."[12]

Muriel Topaz, a dancer who entered the program in its first year and was later a faculty member and director from 1985 to 1992, has remarked:

> At the time when Martha Hill and William Schuman conceived of and started this program, there was no program in the United States that was anything like it for several reasons. One of them is that there was no conservatory model of training in dance like that of Juilliard that Martha Hill shepherded through. The second thing is that it was unheard of at that time for dancers to study both ballet and modern

dance, not to mention several styles of modern dance. That was a complete innovation on Hill's part. Her insistence on integrating various styles of dance has affected dance training all over the world and particularly here in the United States. Now there isn't any self-respecting dancer who doesn't study both classical and modern dance techniques. It was entirely Martha Hill's vision which caused that.[13]

At Juilliard, Hill gathered some of the finest dancers and choreographers in America. The outstanding faculty included Martha Graham, probably America's greatest dancer; Antony Tudor, the British-born ballet choreographer who changed the course of American contemporary ballet; José Limón; Louis Horst, founder and editor of *Dance Observer* and innovative dance composition teacher; Ann Hutchinson, the ranking specialist in dance notation; and Margaret Craske, then considered the greatest ballet teacher in America. With the addition of Doris Humphrey and Anna Sokolow, the department could claim the brightest names in dance. Hill transferred her years of experience with rivals at Bennington to Juilliard; clannishness in the dance world began to disappear.

A March 20, 1951, Juilliard announcement listed the new department's faculty as Agnes de Mille, Martha Graham, Martha Hill, Doris Humphrey, José Limón, and Antony Tudor. The following statement was appended to faculty contracts: "It is understood between us that your professional commitments may necessitate your missing certain classes. A proportionate reduction in your salary will be made for classes you can not teach personally."[14] The Juilliard faculty had still not won their long-standing battle for annual contracts rather than hourly pay. Hill, an administrator, was hired at a salary of $7,000.

Hill agreed with those in Labanotation who argued that an art form without an archive is not taken seriously. She hired Labanotation faculty and required students to study the system for three years of her original five-year program. Shortly after the opening of the Dance Department, choreography was copyrighted for the first time. The *New York Herald-Tribune* reported, "Dances of 'Kiss Me Kate' Get Same Legal Protection as Given to Author, Musician."[15] The issue was advanced by Hanya Holm, the choreographer of *Kiss Me Kate*, who microfilmed a version of her work that had been notated in Rudolf Laban's system and registered it in Washington.

As *Musical America* described the "vital experiment in dance education" at Juilliard, "Students will learn to approach dance as a basically unified art with myriad forms of expression, rather than as a narrow cult or aesthetic dogma, rigidly denying truth in any but an approved form. Complementary studies will give them a sound education in music and in the humanities, very often sadly neglected in the training of dancers."[16]

Faculty member Louis Horst (1884–1964) was Graham's pianist, former lover, and lifelong ally. He taught in Room 607 (the orchestra rehearsal room) on the sixth floor on one afternoon a week. Cantankerous and short-tempered, a large man with white hair and blue eyes, Horst was "probably the most loved character in modern dance." "You're young," he would encourage students. "You can do anything. Use your imagination. If you can move your leg in one direction, you can move it in others." His assistant explained, "He taught that craft is discipline with the outward observable form at one with the inner content."[17]

Paul Taylor, a potential student, took the audition during the fall of 1952. He had not known what to wear on his feet. Taylor has described the audition in his typical ironic, farcical style:

> After the judges had seen enough of my socks and asked me to remove them, they asked for jetés, turns à la seconde, and pas de chats. Not wanting to seem ignorant, I showed them some other stuff that I hoped would look French enough. Tudor either was being rude or was simply unable to hide his snickers. Later I was asked why I wanted to be a dancer. I'd overheard some of the other auditioner's answers—mostly about inspiration and other cosmic-sounding claptrap, during which I'd noticed Miss Craske yawn six and a half times. All the fancy words were making me feel lowbrow and tongue-tied. I stood there in front of the panel and couldn't say why I wanted to dance.
>
> "Come now, dear, you must have a reason," says Miss Craske.
>
> I tell her I don't know, and she nods in an understanding way, urging me on. "Dear," she calls me again. I like her, so I tell her that it's just because I like to move.
>
> She says, "That is a very good reason, dear." (For many years she kept reminding me of this with a smile.)
>
> I've never found out if it was my steps, my motivation, or what, but after a short huddle with the other judges Miss Hill turns toward me, happy as if she'd won the scholarship herself, and blares, "Paul, you've *got* it!"[18]

In 1955 Agnes de Mille outlined the situation inherent in teaching dance to college-age students:

> I can say with conviction that [the Juilliard dance faculty] is the most remarkable group of dance teachers ever to be assembled by a single organization and has no counterpart in the music world. These are the pioneers and leading creators in our field—people of unparalleled achievement. If the Juilliard School has a fault, it is one it shares in common with all colleges, namely the age of the student group for a professional career. Dancers have to start training seriously by twelve. By the time they are of college age, they usually graduate into profes-

sional work or if they wish further education, they find themselves, as a rule, unprepared to matriculate. I have never found any dance training in an American college on the professional level. If, however, Juilliard aims to train choreographers, teachers, directors, and provide auxiliary discipline for actors and singers, it is well equipped to do a brilliant job.[19]

Hill pointed out to the administration that other ballet schools—the royal schools of dance in England, Denmark, and Sweden and the Bolshoi and Kirov—enroll students at age nine and take them into the companies at eighteen.

At the end of the Dance Department's first year, Martha Graham and her troupe presented six sold-out benefit performances to raise money for scholarships. Graham had not danced in New York for the two previous years due to an injury. She repeated Schuman's *Judith* and gave the New York premiere of *The Triumph of St. Joan*, with music by Norman Dello Joio. Other works included *Herodiade, Errand into the Maze* (both with sets by Isamu Noguchi), and *Canticle for Innocent Comedians*. Paul Taylor described seeing *Canticle for Innocent Comedians* as one of four highlights of his year.

> Except for her dancers, no one was allowed inside the Juilliard concert hall, but who was to know if anyone was watching through the slit of the lobby doors? Anita [Dencks], some others, and I stacked our faces like a totem pole with eyes glued at the crack. *Canticle* was one of the few dances Martha wasn't in, and was about the sun, moon, stars, water, fire—a nature lover's dance. Martha loved nature but preferred artifice (I loved nature and hated Art). At the beginning her dancers were standing inside what looked to be a large circular nest, their arms draped along its upper edge. The set was designed by Frederick Kiesler to be sound bouncers for Juilliard music concerts. When the sections of the nest were slid apart by the dancers, it was if the planet earth were unfolding to show all its wonders. . . . The whole dance was the loveliest, most impressive, most magical thing I'd ever seen.[20]

After Graham's death in April 1991, former student Diane Gray, now the director of the Martha Graham School and associate artistic director of the Graham Company, was asked about her:

> As always, I immediately respond that she was, above everything, the most extraordinary teacher. Martha Graham's dance classes were ever so simple and clear. She sought the truth of the movement rather than the design. . . . Martha taught me the dignity of being a dancer, the joy and anguish of commitment. She taught me to listen to myself and never to compromise my standards. How to share space with a musi-

cal score, how to design costumes out of scraps, how to use steely colored side lights to make the body look like sculpture. She taught me how to work with fabric; how silk catches the air, how to dress my hair and apply theatrical makeup; how to enter a room—and the best way to shake a gentleman's hand.[21]

By 1953 Juilliard's own dancers were ready to be seen in a public performance of Tudor's *Exercise Piece* and Humphrey's *Desert Gods*. Humphrey revived her landmark *With My Red Fires* in May 1954 at Juilliard, the score by IMA alumnus Wallingford Riegger. The dance concerts were being regularly reviewed by John Martin in the *New York Times*. The fiftieth anniversary festival in 1955, the first time that the School publicly dated itself from the founding of the IMA, included six pieces commissioned from American composers. Those by Dello Joio, William Schuman, and Stanley Wolfe were choreographed by José Limón, and works by Otto Luening, Vivian Fine, and Hunter Johnson were done by Humphrey. Reviews were excellent, although the performances had to be postponed because of a fire that damaged stage equipment.

Doris Humphrey, who had known Hill since the Bennington days, was appointed to teach both choreography and repertory. She and Hill formed the Juilliard Dance Theatre to smooth the transition between student and professional life. The Dance Theatre began in 1954 and lasted until Humphrey's death in 1958. During that season, it performed at the 92d Street YMCA. Humphrey's "works for Juilliard were subsidized with money for production, orchestra, and all the rest—a situation 'unheard of in the modern dance.' After all those years, after all the work and the sacrifice and the frustration—could it be that now, as she was nearing sixty, there was a chance to work without constant terror of financial disaster?"[22] Among the works Humphrey created for the Juilliard Dance Theatre are *Dawn in New York* (1956), *Descent into the Dream* (1957), and *Brandenburg Concerto No. 4* (1959, unfinished at her death and completed by Ruth Currier). Humphrey was also artistic director of José Limón's company, which continued in her footsteps at Juilliard and provided a professional model, a teaching pool, a creative example, and a source of jobs for graduates.

Auditions for the Juilliard Dance Theatre were competitive, and dancers chosen could enroll as regular students of the Dance Department, but that was not a prerequisite. In 1956 there were nineteen members: six enrolled as regular Juilliard students, three former students, and ten not affiliated. All were under twenty-five. Each program was rehearsed for seven months, and no one was paid. Students could take dance technique classes at Juilliard free of charge (something Hill must have finessed), rehearse two hours a day, take weekly choreography classes with Humphrey, and attend frequent, lengthy after-rehearsal discussions with her.

When Humphrey died in 1958, she was replaced at Juilliard by maverick choreographer Anna Sokolow, who continued teaching at the School until 1993. Whereas Humphrey, Limón, and Graham were each connected with a training system that they had created, Sokolow did not teach a technique. "Sometimes cantankerous, sometimes angelic" and possessing a "demonic intensity," she "would often bypass the better-trained dancers and focus instead on the raw talent." Somewhat analogous to the Stanislavsky technique of method acting, Sokolow's compositional approach was "method dancing." She looked for truthful movement; insincerity was anathema to her. "Motion comes from emotion," she would say. She sought "not simply the appearance of anger, but its essence."[23] Martha Hill remarked about Sokolow, "Her intensity as a director keeps people excited about working for her. The others drop out. It is a self-selective process. Some students don't want to see life that [dark] way. She will take one of the dancers by the shirt and

Doris Humphrey's *Descent into the Dream*, January 1957.
(W. H. Stephan, photo from The Juilliard School Archives)

say, 'Do you like what we're doing?' God help them if they are luke-warm about it. Anna will say, 'Out! Get Out!'"[24]

Dancers who worked with Sokolow over the years included Libby Nye, Ray Cook, Cliff Keuter, Daniel Lewis, Martha Clarke, Paula Kelly, Michael Uthoff, Dennis Nahat, Linda Kent, Carla Maxwell, Lynne Wimmer, and Gary Masters. Some of her most important work was created for Juilliard students, whom she treated no differently from dancers in professional companies. In 1968 Robert Sabin of *Dance Magazine* wrote, "If it had produced nothing but the nine works of Anna Sokolow between 1955 and 1967, the Juilliard Dance Department would have amply justified itself. For Miss Sokolow, who is at home in Webern and Berio as well as Cimarosa, has added a whole new dimension to the modern theatre."[25] In 1964 Anna Sokolow and Edgar Varèse collabo-rated on a new piece for instruments, electronic music, and dance, but the next year Varèse died and Sokolow fell back on *Density 21.5*, *Octandre*, and *Poème Électronique*. One of her greatest successes was cho-reographed to Varèse's *Déserts* (1967).

The new president, composer Peter Mennin, had distinct ideas about music: "Either Juilliard or Lincoln Center productions should not be jazz versions or gimmicked versions of existing masterpieces."[26] The prohibition against jazz at Juilliard was complete. New England Con-servatory, however, under its president Gunther Schuller, during the 1960s inaugurated a "third stream" department devoted to jazz. In ad-dition, during the 1950s and 1960s, when electronic music was in its heyday at places such as the Columbia-Princeton Electronic Music Center, Juilliard staunchly refused to incorporate an electronic music studio. That affected dance, whose concerts were accompanied by the school orchestra. Some professional dance companies still use recorded music. The ever-changing entity known as modern dance often works with modern music, frequently commissioned by the choreographer. "It is not an exaggeration," Schuman wrote, "to claim that the great patron of twentieth-century music has been the art of dance."[27]

During the early years of the Dance Department, works were cho-reographed to music by contemporary composers, including Paul Hindemith, Frank Martin, Stanley Wolfe, Hunter Johnson, Vivian Fine, Goffredo Petrassi, Zoltan Kodály, Ernest Bloch, David Diamond, Gunther Schuller, Benjamin Britten, and Teo Macero. Of the three departments at Juilliard—dance, drama, and music—it is the Dance Department that has consistently created new works. Perhaps paradoxi-cally, the department that expected the most rigorous physical discipline and technique from its students was also the one that fostered the most creativity in its art.

Antony Tudor (1908–87), born in Britain as William Cook, had been Margaret Craske's student and later helped get her appointed to the Metropolitan Opera Ballet and School, founded in 1909, where he taught. In 1961 Tudor directed the newly named, twenty-seven-member Juilliard Dance Ensemble in Philadelphia in a performance of *Sleeping Beauty* with the Philadelphia Orchestra under Ormandy.

Renowned as a teacher, Tudor would always start from the beginning. "What is this movement?" he would ask. "What does it say? Why are you doing it?" He analyzed motivation—where did an impulse come from and why—and worked within the frame of ballet rather than modern dance, "even though he found dancers of a sensibility closer to his own among the barefoot variety."[28] A thorough pedagogue, he could describe stylistic differences among the Ballets Russes, the Royal Ballet, and New York City Ballet. Juilliard students could learn how a ballerina from each company would dance *The Sleeping Beauty*.

Tudor could also be extraordinarily cruel: He battled with Craske in class and rehearsal and called his loyal pianist a "chinless wonder." In addition, he made sexual innuendoes (and then blushed) during class.[29] His methods resembled sensitivity training, using psychological ploys to teach. Tudor could be extremely sensitive to others' fragile egos. Graham recalled one incident: "In the cafeteria, he summoned a girl to our table and said, 'You don't love yourself enough. . . . I see it in how badly you put your lipstick on.'"[30]

In 1954 there were fifty-nine students in dance, and they paid $585 in tuition. Each had a weekly schedule that occupied almost every waking hour from Monday through Saturday. It included Music Department concerts, which dancers were expected to attend, along with the Wednesday one o'clock concerts required of all L&M students. Attendance was required for every class in both departments. In 1960 the weekly curriculum for diploma course students included ballet at least four times a week; modern dance (either Graham or Limón technique) at least four; composition once a week; notation twice a week; L&M; stagecraft once a week for first-year students; and "Anatomy for Dancers," which could be an elective. Students in the B.S. degree program took all of these in addition to two academic courses weekly. In the early 1960s a dance films club showed movies.

Male-female ratios were resurrected at the School, this time for dance. By 1963 the total number of graduates was "Girls, 52, men, 7." Thirty-seven of these earned B.S. degrees, and twenty-two gained diplomas. In 1972 the department had sixty-five students, twenty-one of whom were men. Men are a sought-after commodity in every dance school; there are always too few. They get to dance solo roles more frequently than women and, realizing their value from scarcity, can indulge in prima donna–like behavior. Hill's memos state the immediate need succinctly: "More men."

Gender distribution and professional opportunities in the field of modern dance were initially weighted toward women. Martha Graham's first troupe, for example, was an all-women ensemble. During the late 1970s and into the 1980s, however, Juilliard acquired a reputation for having a group of strong male dancers. Although the division actively sought males, cultural developments ultimately had more influence over enrollment than recruitment. One factor was the influence of Russian émigrés such as Mikhail Baryshnikov on the way many in the United States perceived male dancers. Some dance administrators also contend that films that featured Patrick Swayze and John Travolta, *Dirty Dancing* and *Saturday Night Fever*, demonstrated that it was acceptable for men to dance. It was considered good at Juilliard if entering dance classes included eight or nine men in groups of thirty to forty-five.

Muriel Topaz has commented on the issue of age and dancing:

> The problem about Juilliard and ballet dancers is that by the time most of them are of college age, they're already in companies. It's a much younger "sport" than modern dance. It's an irrefutable fact of life in classical dance. It used to be not uncommon for fourteen-to-fifteen-year-olds to join companies. Now [in 1995] I think there's more of a feeling in many [ballet] companies that they should at least graduate from high school. That was not the case even one generation back. Sixteen is a more desirable age now; what the kids sometimes do is accelerate by studying during the summers, finish their high school at sixteen, and then go into companies. Some companies still take them earlier.
>
> The men have it a little easier. They can be a little bit older; they might be eighteen rather than sixteen. At Juilliard we had trouble hanging on to them; they would be recruited right out of school into companies. Occasionally this would also happen with the women, but rarely and not so early as with the men.
>
> An unfortunate note is that now in the era of AIDS the male dance population is decimated, so there are a lot of jobs out there. It's not my impression that many dancers at Juilliard have AIDS. They're young for AIDS to manifest itself. I think the Music Division is more affected simply because they're older. As director of the Dance Division I wouldn't necessarily know; that kind of information would be hidden from me by the student.[31]

The initial idea at Juilliard was for students to achieve a broad primary education in dance techniques and gain a greater understanding of music in relation to dance. Limón could not conceive of a good dancer not being a good musician. Graham, too, considered the common bond of music at Juilliard to be the reason that Dance Department members located themselves there. Horst wished to awaken musicians to the dance and give their compositions added vigor and vitality. Schuman wanted student composers to work directly with choreographers, hoping they would gain a heightened awareness of music in relation to dance. Hill began dance in the Preparatory Department so the dancers would study music. She wanted "musicianly" dancers.

Students were not the only ones affected by two different techniques under one roof. Tudor, for example, had been influenced by Graham. The interaction between Tudor and Limón also produced changes in the choreographic thinking of each. Agnes de Mille has described Graham's reactions as she began to observe the value of ballet training:

> This was the first time [Graham] had been brought into working proximity with ballet artists of great caliber. She taught in the room next to Antony Tudor and Margaret Craske, among the finest ballet instructors in the world. She saw and understood with her extraordinary perception the true value of the classic technique. Probably it was at this point that she began to add the turnout and port de bras of the classic school to her curriculum and her regular vocabulary of gesture. Having found balletic training for the foot unmatched in producing jumpers, Martha began to permit the inclusion of ballet preparations. She remained, however, somewhat dubious and reluctant, until her technique was at length recognized as part of our culture. She in turn could accept without fear of contamination ballet jumps, ballet turns, ballet port de bras. The result is a much wider technique for the average dancer and a general strengthening of the body.[32]

Juilliard rules stated that students could not wear studio clothes in the halls or cafeteria, where Schuman was apt to eat. He also insisted that the faculty dress properly. Younger teachers who appeared in the halls without neckties did so only once if Schuman saw them. From 1949 on there was no smoking in the Concert Hall, stage or pit. New York's drinking age of eighteen meant that the dancers could have a beer party in the cafeteria, however.

Alumni of the early years of the Dance Department include Paul Taylor, Bruce Marks, Martha Clarke, Richard Englund, Myron Nadel, Jaime Rogers, Carolyn Brown, Michael Uthoff, and Mercedes Ellington (granddaughter of Duke Ellington). By 1968 thirteen out of sixteen in Limón's company, and many in Graham's, were Juilliard people. (For years Hill housed the Limón Company at Juilliard.) Seven members of the Alvin Ailey Company in 1971 were former Juilliard students.

As part of an outreach program into the New York public schools beginning in the 1963–64 year, the Juilliard Dance Department toured. For three years, the Lincoln Center Student Program had sponsored performances in public schools by Juilliard musicians. Now students presented dance and encountered audiences that tested their performance abilities. Two ensembles were formed, ballet and modern, and performed at the regular Friday concert series before going on the road for ten days. The first tour, in 1964, presented the ballets *A Choreographer Comments* and *Little Improvisations* by Tudor, a pas de deux from *Swan Lake*, and Kevin Carlisle's *Part-Time Invention*. The modern repertory included *Sometimes* by Paul Draper, an excerpt from Humphrey's *Ruins and Visions*, Limón's *Concerto in D Minor*, and *Session for Six* by Sokolow.

Some of the schools visited had varnished floors, which are disastrous for dancers. The ballet mistress would sprinkle rosin over the slippery areas, dust with kitchen cleanser, and then splash the floor with water (the surface would occasionally began to foam). Another problem concerned the puritanical attitude of school principals. One, for example, rushed backstage before a performance and demanded to know of anything erotic; if found, he wanted it cut or he would stop the show. Afraid the students might giggle upon seeing dancers in tights, the schools provided a narrator to explain that these were the working clothes for a dancer. The students did not giggle.

One of the most difficult aspects of performing spoofs of ballet in schools—such as the "Pas de Chat" in Tudor's *A Choreographer Comments*—was that young audiences did not know traditions well enough to catch the humor of a take-off. On the one hand, dancers performed in silence when they were accustomed to hearing explosive laughter. On the other, Limón's *Concerto in D Minor* was not meant to be funny— perhaps it was the deep pliés that initially set off giggles. Sokolow's *Session for Six* incorporated popular dances, and students enjoyed spotting the twist, the Lindy, and others.

On the whole, students liked the dance and the dancers. At one all-female school, a student found the male dancers "better than the Beatles."[33] The Dance Department performed for almost twenty thousand school children, and every school wanted dance back the next year. Not only did the dancers return in 1966, with Humphrey's *Ritmo Jondo* and Tudor's *Little Improvisations* as well as Sokolow's *Session for Six*, but the event was also covered by Clive Barnes for the *New York Times*.[34]

A serious issue for Juilliard's administration concerned terrorism founded upon extreme prejudice. Mennin received a bomb threat in 1971, for example, because the School had given residence to "that degenerate group known as Paul Taylor Company." The writer added that "we abhore warped minds such as his, and the perverts within his company."[35] Although dance companies typically have some members who are homosexual, the fact seldom bothers the heterosexual women and men who dance and work with them but appears to perturb some observers.

During the 1960s the Dance Department continued its success, defined by almost any terms in which one wanted to measure it: good reviews in prominent places; success after graduation for students (75 percent of whom struggled to stay in the field, a statistic likely not paralleled in music); an all-star faculty, some of whom remained until the ends of their lives; and sold-out audience approval. In one critical area, however, it suffered the problem of other schools and companies: no endowment. Lack of financial clout, even in the face of unquestioned artistic and educational success, placed the department in a highly vulnerable position regarding its move to Lincoln Center and threatened its very existence. The powers that be in both the Lincoln Center and Juilliard administrations were neither dancers nor choreographers. Music was important to them, but the Dance Department seemed expendable.

Events sixty blocks south were destined to have a profound effect on the department. When capitulating to the demands of Lincoln Center (chapter 7), William Schuman—in his December 7, 1956, report adopted by both the Juilliard and the Lincoln Center boards—had sold out the Dance Department. Since the summer of 1955 Juilliard's position regarding dance and drama remained fixed, the report stated. "As a school of music, Juilliard has no obligation to embrace either the field of drama or that of dance. If separate facilities for a comprehensive education in the field of dance were established at the Center, and Juilliard were part of the Center, there would then be no reason for Juilliard to continue its present Department of Dance."[36]

Schuman later harbored ultimately unfulfilled desires of establishing a separate modern dance troupe as a constituent of Lincoln Center. If he genuinely wanted to continue dance at Juilliard, he was unable to persuade the board. It is also possible, however, that in his intense desire for the Music Department to move to Lincoln Center he was willing to sacrifice his own Dance Department. The almost entirely female department was betrayed by the entirely male Juilliard and Lincoln Center boards.

During the late 1950s, therefore, the fortunes of other companies that might become Lincoln Center constituents had a direct bearing on the future of Juilliard's Dance Department. Balanchine's and Lincoln Kirstein's New York City Ballet, operating at City Center, was invited to join Lincoln Center. Kirstein had been close to the Rockefeller family since the early 1940s. The older constituents of Lincoln Center, the Metropolitan Opera and the New York Philharmonic, wanted only one member in each performing art to have constituent status. That created a problem when in late 1956 Lucia Chase and Oliver Smith of the American Ballet Theater asked that Lincoln Center include the ABT.

By January 1957 the exclusivity policy had been modified so that an exploratory committee on the dance was formed, with dance critics John Martin (who had abandoned his crusade for modern dance after becoming a Balanchine convert around 1949) and Walter Terry (who liked the glamour of ballet) as consultants. The committee finally recommended the New York City Ballet after their idea of merging the two companies met with considerable resistance on both sides. But the board deferred a vote to include the City Ballet. Chase was willing to cooperate in a plan in which both companies would be at Lincoln Center, each with a guarantee of artistic independence, but Kirstein was opposed and the situation remained in stalemate.

By fall of 1958 Kirstein had resolved to keep his ballet company under the sponsorship of City Center. Morton Baum, an influential member of City Center's board, now wanted the entire City Center to become part of Lincoln Center rather than just the New York City Ballet. City Center was the country's oldest cultural center and the world's largest single producing unit, including six companies. Its move to Lincoln Center would mean bringing the New York City Opera, and the Met objected. Because New York City itself was involved as the owner of the proposed State Theater, the matter became even more complicated. An important issue was ticket prices, which by City Center policy were to be kept low. By May 1959, the groundbreaking for Lincoln Center's Philharmonic Hall, the participation of City Center, and the question of a dance constituent were still unresolved. In 1963 the Ford Foundation under W. McNeil Lowry gave the New York City Ballet a grant of $2 million for a ten-year period. That financial backing gave Kirstein and Balanchine additional clout at Lincoln Center to the detriment of Juilliard's Dance Department. Ballet had an elitist, aesthetic caché that modern dance never attained.

"One of the results of this autonomy," *Dance Magazine* reported, "has been that New York City Ballet need answer to no one if it chooses— as it apparently has chosen—to eliminate appearances of all other dance companies from the State Theater. One must now ask oneself: Is it also trying to eliminate other ballet schools from Lincoln Center as well? It certainly looks that way." Deborah Jowitt, writing for the *Village Voice*, noted that "a sum of $3 million has been given to establish a Drama

Department at Juilliard . . . just when the Dance Department is beginning to look like something, there is no space and no money for it. . . . What a selfish monster Lincoln Center is—to destroy all that it cannot swallow."[37]

The 1960s at Juilliard were a time of constant upheaval because of the move to Lincoln Center and the precarious future of the Dance Department. In 1965 Lincoln Center decided for reasons of expense and space to place Balanchine's School of American Ballet in Juilliard's building, then projected to open in 1967. In March 1968, Dean Gideon Waldrop wrote an ominous memo to dance students: "We would be less than honest if we did not indicate to you that there is a clear possibility that dance training at Juilliard may not be continued beyond the school year 1968–69."[38]

Events that led to this distressing situation were outlined in various dance magazines. One argument was literally over turf—space for the School of American Ballet and Juilliard studios at the Lincoln Center building. The other issue was, of course, money. In the "old building" the Dance Department functioned with a $20,000 annual deficit for a $100,000 budget. That would be a financial drain on the School at Lincoln Center. "Ironically, the prestige and success of the Juilliard approach to dance education lulled interested people into a false sense of security over what would amount to a virtual annihilation of the former Juilliard Dance Department. . . . Even if the Dance Department came into untold riches, it may only be allowed to possess a limited modern dance department," wrote Robert Sabin.[39]

The financial history of dance is bleaker than that of other performing arts. At the start of the 1966 season the Metropolitan Opera came to terms with its musicians and established an unprecedented minimum salary rate that would reach $13,500 a year by 1968–69. Other orchestras, including the Philadelphia Orchestra, then went on strike. Yet dance had nothing like the financial stability of those other performing arts organizations. Choreographers in many dance groups were also directors and managers, so unionization was unlikely. Salaries as high as those of the orchestra members were completely unattainable and, for the most part, still remain so.

The influential dance critic Clive Barnes and the directors of Lincoln Center each had ideas about how dance should be treated at Lincoln Center. Barnes blithely suggested that the American Dance Theatre be absorbed into Lincoln Center.[40] He also thought that Balanchine's School of American Ballet should become even bigger and more important and that the Martha Graham School should be made a part of Juilliard. The editor of *Dance Scope* responded:

It is disturbing to consider the future of a Juilliard that purveys nothing but Balanchineballet and Graham technique. As presently constituted, for all its deficiencies, Juilliard does offer both Graham and
Limón techniques, as well as the non-Balanchine ballet of Tudor and
Craske. . . . The spectacle of Juilliard succumbing to the Lincoln Center formula would be tragic beyond the fate of any individual who
might be left out. Lincoln Center's performing companies can come
and go with the popular style, but Juilliard's value exists only in the future tense. Its job is to train professional dancers and choreographers
for all of America, not to groom a stableful of entries for the Lincoln
Center sweepstakes. . . . Dance is fortunate at this moment because in
its field there are no precedents. Apart from Lincoln Center there are
no large institutions, no theatres, no year-round companies, no
inflexible salary scales, no management-labor grievances, nothing at
all, in fact, except enormous talent and a need for recognition.[41]

Nevertheless, by the summer of 1968 the power of Balanchine and
Kirstein directly affected Juilliard. "Flushed with satisfaction at what may
be known as the massacre of the Juilliard Dance Department," one journalist reported bitterly, "the culture barons who rule the big spread at
Lincoln Center have decided to finish the job of eliminating any resi-
dent competition for Mr. Balanchine."[42] The author bemoaned the
decision to eliminate the Metropolitan Opera Ballet School, directed
since 1950 by Tudor. In what might have been a campaign orchestrated
by the formidable Martha Hill, letters poured in both to *New York Magazine* and to Peter Mennin in support of continuing the Dance Department at Juilliard.[43] In October 1968 the *San Francisco Chronicle* reported
on "the squeeze-out at the Juilliard." The author called the Dance
Department "the country's most important dance school independent
of a performing company" and a "very important small guy" compared
with the might of Lincoln Center's constituents.[44]

After a decade of planning by Hill, Limón, Tudor, and the rest of the
faculty, Juilliard had planned for and gotten six dance studios at Lincoln Center's slowly rising ten-floor edifice (five below ground, five
above). Suddenly, four of the six studios were to be occupied instead by
the School of American Ballet. "School of Ballet to Join Juilliard" the
New York Times announced in November 1965: "The classic training,
now under the direction of such teachers as Margaret Craske and Antony
Tudor, will either be absorbed by the School of American Ballet or be
replaced."[45] "If the Juilliard Dance Department was to continue at all,
it would be sharply restricted to modern dance," the *Chronicle* reported,
"a reduction not acceptable to the Juilliard dance staff."[46] For Topaz, "It
was Peter Mennin's idea that Balanchine was going to be the ballet de-

partment of Juilliard, if not the whole Juilliard Dance Department. That did not happen and the reason may have been that Balanchine was not interested in joining an academic institution; he wanted his own school."[47]

Mennin's reason for the switch in studio space was his usual complaint: the increased operating costs of moving Lincoln Center, variously given as between three and seven times more than the Claremont Avenue buildings. From the perspective of the Dance Department's proponents, however, the villain was Lincoln Kirstein, longtime opponent of modern dance and "accused by many of trying to control all dance in Lincoln Center."[48] They pointed to the closing of the sixty-year-old Metropolitan Opera Ballet School, which had one hundred students and excellent faculty that in addition to Tudor included Margaret Craske and Alfredo Corvino. Rudolf Bing, capitulating to Kirstein's interests, was also held accountable.

The anticipated demise of the Juilliard Dance Department and the Metropolitan Ballet School created a monopoly for the Russian-based ballet style favored by Balanchine, the "cultural baron of the dance world."[49] Tudor and Craske had come from the English school of ballet teaching based on the Cecchetti method; Balanchine, however, came from the Petipa-based Russian school. There was no reconciling the two approaches or the two groups.

A strong commitment from the top would have made a considerable difference. Mennin, however, "wasn't really supportive of the Dance Department."[50] Unlike Schuman, what interested him was ballet rather than modern dance. The other main problem was the lack of an endowment for dance. Mennin told the irate dance faculty that an effort would be made to find foundation support, but that did not allay their fears; they felt their department was doomed. Students such as Risa Steinberg became involved in the fight and passed out handbills in front of the State Theater, thereby infuriating its staff.

Both Schuman and Mennin had obviously acquiesced in giving dance control to Balanchine and Kirstein, who were backed by the Ford Foundation money. Hardly giving a ringing endorsement to dance, Mennin said, "We are doing our damnedest to raise the money before we move downtown. The dance department has its space [the two studios, 320 and 321] provided. While the dance department was uptown in the old building it required less, was without comparable problems. It was under an umbrella. Downtown, it would become more of a separate department and has to be more self-sufficient."[51] Mennin thus seemed to cut dance loose, dumping the financial problems into their laps.

The confusion over which company would be Lincoln Center's dance constituent ultimately helped Juilliard's Dance Department. Cooler heads prevailed at Lincoln Center, which had originally wanted Juilliard precisely because of its Dance Department (later renamed the Dance Division). Martha Hill's struggles against the considerable forces arrayed against her department were Herculean. It was just barely saved, although Balanchine got his four studios in the Juilliard building and the Dance Department continued to operate at a deficit. The School of American Ballet became a Lincoln Center constituent in 1987, a time when it was loudly complaining that it needed more space. The SAB remained on Juilliard's premises from 1968 until 1991, when another facility was built at Lincoln Center to accommodate it (chapter 11). For twenty-two years, rigid artistic if not a physical separation obtained between the SAB and the Juilliard Dance Department. "There was no influence from Balanchine on the Juilliard Dance Department, absolutely not. The two programs were quite separate," Muriel Topaz stressed.[52]

The fact that dance had survived the move to Lincoln Center did not mean that it was out of the fire. At least four events conspired to place it in jeopardy again. First, a Carnegie Corporation grant had made the operation of the Dance Department possible in 1972, but the corporation refused Juilliard's grant proposal for future support. Second, the department did not receive good reviews in *Dance Magazine* in 1971 for its Lincoln Center debut, and it had mixed reviews elsewhere. James Conlon had conducted Limón's *Unsung* and *Revel*, Graham's *Diversion of Angels*, and Sokolow's *Scenes from the Music of Charles Ives*. Third, the bomb threat based on the purported immorality of the Dance Department may have had an influence on a musician president. And, finally, Antony Tudor "resigned." A more plausible scenario, considering Mennin's agenda for ballet, is that Mennin pushed him out.

Reviews and threats could be ignored, but Tudor's departure was particularly unfortunate. It gave Mennin the excuse he needed to close down the ballet major at the school, a step toward his dream for the School of American Ballet to become part of Juilliard. He wrote to Martha Hill in January 1971, informing her of the termination of the major in ballet.[53] Mennin had not consulted Hill, who had every reason to object strongly. She knew of the tears that would greet such an announcement and responded that Mennin himself should meet with the students to explain the new policy. He, however, demanded that Hill, as an administrator, carry out the policies of the president and refused to meet with students about the issue. Because of Mennin, it is no longer possible to major in ballet at Juilliard. Now students study both ballet and modern dance but major in neither.

In May 1972 Mennin actively planned to rid himself of Hill. He considered as possible new directors Muriel Topaz, Deborah Jowitt, Joseph Gifford, and Janet Soares but underestimated the woman who had founded the department. Martha Hill survived the attempted purge; in fact, she survived Mennin. She formally retired in 1985, became professor emerita, and remained active in Dance Department affairs into her mid-nineties. She died in 1995.

As of February 1972, the department had trained more than a thousand dancers, including 107 from 36 foreign countries. Japan with fourteen, Israel with eighteen, and the Netherlands with eight topped the list. That year two of its glowing faculty were celebrated. First, the Dance Ensemble presented a four-day concert series dedicated to the memory of Doris Humphrey, who had died in 1958. Reconstructed works of hers presented were *The Shakers* (1931), *Day on Earth* (1947), *Lament for Ignacio Sánchez Mejías* (1946), and *Passacaglia and Fugue in C Minor* (1938). José Limón directed. A generation after the founding of the department the faculty included Alfredo Corvino, Martha Graham, Martha Hill, Kazuko Hirabayashi, Daniel Lewis, Billie Mahoney, Helen McGehee, Genia Melikova, Doris Rudko, Elizabeth Sawyer, Jennifer Scanlon, Janet Mansfield Soares, Anna Sokolow, Stanley Sussman, Lulu E. Sweigard, Ethel Winter, and Hector Zaraspe. Margaret Black, Tudor's assistant, later became an enormously popular teacher.

Limón died on December 2, 1972, after twenty years of teaching in the Dance Department, where students had adored him. His *Missa Brevis* (1958, to Kodály), given its premiere by Juilliard, is considered one of his masterpieces, "one of, if not the most enduring hymns to human courage and fortitude that came out of World War II."[54] On December 14 the School presented a program in the theater in his honor. Violin faculty member Joseph Fuchs performed the Bach *Chaconne*, which Limón had choreographed in 1942. Humphrey's *Day on Earth*, to Copland's Piano Sonata, was also done.

In July 1986 the twenty-four-member Juilliard Dance Ensemble under Muriel Topaz traveled with Martha Hill to Hong Kong and Taiwan to participate in the International Festival of Dance Academies. Faculty Daniel Lewis and Alfredo Corvino taught packed studios. The ensemble performed to music by William Schuman, *New England Triptych*, choreography by Michael Uthoff, commissioned to honor Schuman's seventy-fifth birthday. They also performed *Haiku* (Martha Clark–George Crumb), *The Traitor* (José Limón–Gunther Schuller), *The Envelope* (David Parsons–Rossini), and Paul Taylor's *Aurole* (Handel).

By the late 1980s, the board thought the dance performances not professional enough, however. Over the objections of the faculty and students, Director Muriel Topaz, the modern proponent, was replaced in 1992. Her successor, Benjamin Harkarvy, was known in the ballet world. Curricular changes involved reducing the four-year music course—so important to the original dance faculty—to a two-year course. Academic courses were added to broaden the dancers' education; they could now pursue B.F.A. rather than the older B.S. degrees. Martha Hill's legacy is still strong: The equivalence of ballet and modern dance is sacred writ to today's Dance Division.

9

Dramatic Progress:

JOHN HOUSEMAN

WHEN JOHN D. ROCKEFELLER 3RD and his committee created Lincoln Center, they decided that the performing arts complex should have an educational arm, which Juilliard, with its Music and Dance Departments, seemed to fill. Drama, however, was missing, so Lincoln Center wanted a drama school added as a condition of the move to Lincoln Center. The Rockefellers sent playwright Robert Chapman to Europe for a year to study the training there and report on it. As was true in 1904 when Damrosch went to Europe to survey the field, so it was in the mid-1950s. Americans felt it necessary to imitate a European model of training. In 1956 Rockefeller himself, along with Anthony Bliss and Wallace Harrison, traveled to Europe to examine the architecture of new theaters and concert halls.

Chapman's report had centered on one outstanding figure, Michel Saint-Denis (1897–1971), then general director of the Centre Dramatique de l'Est in Strasbourg. Saint-Denis had organized, along with Tyrone Guthrie and John Gielgud, the London Theatre Studio, a school for professional actors and stage technicians. His former pupils included Alec Guinness, Laurence Olivier, and Peter Ustinov. Saint-Denis had also written about theater. He and two others had organized the enormously influential Old Vic School, and he and his wife Suria founded the bilingual Canadian National Theatre School in Montreal. With Peter Hall and Peter Brook, Saint-Denis ran Britain's Royal Shakespeare Theatre at Stratford-upon-Avon. The puckish, pipe-smoking, bespectacled sixty-two-year-old Frenchman spoke English fluently. On Chapman's recommendation, the visiting Americans introduced themselves to Saint-Denis. They were highly impressed.

The Rockefeller Foundation invited Saint-Denis to spend May 1958 and January through June 1959 in the United States to make suggestions for a drama school that would meet American professional needs. His detailed report filled with recommendations became known at Juilliard as "the Saint-Denis Bible."[1] At the time, the approach to acting in the United States was based loosely on the realism of Stanislavsky, or the American "Method," which Saint-Denis found "a bit too abstract, too intellectual."[2] "A complete divorce seemed to exist between style and realism. . . . I saw extremely good work in the universities on the technical side—direction and design were often quite sophisticated," but the acting, he found, was on an amateur level.[3]

Cultural conditions in the United States presented Saint-Denis with "problems far more complex than those I had had to face in Europe." These included "the widespread conventional ideas about prestige and the necessity for financial success. There was, too, a very uneven diffusion of real culture and theatrical practice around the country [and this] lack of a unified culture could not help but hinder the development of the young actor/artists. . . . The new Drama Division of the Juilliard School could only develop originality in acting if it could train its own actors from the very beginning."[4]

In January 1958 Schuman appointed Saint-Denis as chief consultant to the projected Drama Division. "You are the Pope," he would say. As pope, Saint-Denis had jurisdiction over several areas. He collaborated on the theater designs with the new building's architect, Pietro Belluschi; he also recommended taking twenty to twenty-five students each year. Once accepted, they would remain with their classes—to be called "groups" and given roman numerals at Saint-Denis's recommendation— for the four-year course. In effect, each group would become a small company. In addition, he wanted a two-year advanced course for young professionals and recommended a group of forty students, all older than twenty-three, in directing, design, and play-writing. The total number of acting students in the four-year program would be about eighty-five.

Michel and Suria Saint-Denis spoke frequently with Robert Whitehead, the Broadway producer appointed director of the Lincoln Center Repertory Theater, which had become Lincoln Center's constituent for drama in February 1960. Together they devised a plan to link the Juilliard Drama Division with the Repertory Theater's company, both jointly responsible for all aesthetic decisions relating to the training program.

Influenced by his co-producing director Elia Kazan, Whitehead, who had independent means from Canadian banking and brewing interests, changed his mind and by March 1961 advocated that Lincoln Center's School of Drama should not be under Juilliard's control but entirely under the control of the Lincoln Center Repertory Theater.[5] Schuman replied by stressing autonomy for Juilliard and stating that Whitehead's proposal was "not acceptable."[6] Lincoln Center's executive committee agreed with Schuman and in 1961 voted $2.5 million for Juilliard's Drama Division and $.5 million for a separate repertory theater. By July 1962 Saint-Denis had withdrawn from the project because of disagreements with Kazan.

By October 1964 Saint-Denis had resisted Mennin's blandishments and signed a three-year contract with the Royal Shakespeare Company. He was leaving because he could not wait three more years for the new building to be completed in order to start the program; the salary offered him was too low; and he wanted to help Stratford, which had been attacked for its supposedly pessimistic and immoral new repertoire. One of the costs of the Lincoln Center construction delays was the loss of years of Saint-Denis's vital guidance and instruction. He was also convinced that the Drama Division should be headed by an American; he would be available as a consultant. He recommended Harold Clurman in March 1963 and later Alan Schneider for the position. Sanford Meisner was also considered, but Saint-Denis vetoed the idea and remarked, "We will never leave the level of theatrical vulgarity."[7]

Peter Mennin needed to find someone to head the new division. The Juilliard building at Lincoln Center was finally rising and due for students in 1968. Rockefeller still wanted Saint-Denis. Mennin needed to please Rockefeller, but bringing Saint-Denis back into the Juilliard fold required great persistence. In May 1965 Mennin traveled to England to see him. "[Mennin] seemed to be a very determined person and took a great personal interest in getting the Drama Division started," Saint-Denis wrote of him.[8] Mennin asked him to direct the program, but Saint-Denis was still convinced that it should be run by an American. He suggested that John Houseman, then living in Paris, should co-direct the program, although Houseman later assumed that Lincoln Kirstein and W. McNeil Lowry had recommended him.

Houseman (1902–88), a producer and director, was born Jacques

Haussman in Bucharest, Romania. He had run the Negro Theater Project in Harlem, part of the WPA-sponsored Federal Theatre Project, and produced a Haitian adaptation of *Macbeth* in 1936. Orson Welles directed the show, which toured successfully. The next year Houseman and Welles founded the Mercury Theatre, one of whose acclaimed productions was a modern-dress version of *Julius Caesar.* Houseman subsequently headed the American Shakespeare Festival, founded six theater companies, produced eighteen major Hollywood movies, and in 1973 won an Academy Award for his role as Professor Kingsfield in *The Paper Chase.* He also wrote five books, four of which constituted his autobiography.[9]

In the spring of 1965, the sixty-three-year-old Houseman considered Mennin's offer to co-direct the Drama Division. He had serious doubts:

> Juilliard represented a position of prestige and security. At the same time it could be regarded as an acceptance of defeat and a final surrender of the illusion, so dear to every man and woman in show business, that the Big Break is just around the corner. It also represented a sharp drop in income—from over one hundred thousand dollars down to twenty-five thousand dollars a year . . . [meaning] a drastic change in our life-style.
>
> My decision to accept the Juilliard offer was motivated, finally, by none of these things. It was made in direct response to the challenge offered by this unexpected opportunity to attempt something quite new and different. Faced with the question of whether I was capable of creating and directing the country's most advanced and effective theatre conservatory, it became absolutely necessary for me to prove that I could.[10]

Another consideration concerned the cultural timing. Houseman had observed the recent creation of several dozen regional repertory theaters whose demands on artists differed from those of either Broadway or the mass media. The variety of regional offerings required actors who could work in a wide range of styles and periods, and Houseman was eager to create an actor-training program to meet those needs. Competition abounded, however; both Columbia and New York University began theater training in the fall of 1967. Major foundations supported various theatrical organizations. During the previous year the Rockefeller Fund had given New York University a $750,000 grant for its stage school; the Ford Foundation gave the Association of Producing Artists–Phoenix Repertory Company $900,000; and the Rockefellers gave $77,900 to the Minnesota Theater Company and $390,000 to the drama school at Yale University.

Attempting to start from scratch and with no physical plant for drama,

Juilliard also lacked precise financial guidance. W. McNeil Lowry of the Ford Foundation recalled:

> [Mennin] woefully misjudged the resources that were necessary [for drama]. . . . Mennin really shortchanged Juilliard, without meaning to, because all he could see that was radically different from Morningside Heights to the Lincoln Center campus was a drama training program. He didn't know how to budget that, so he asked for, I'm afraid it was as little as $457,000, something like that, for the drama training program. I quickly settled for it because it was modest, but also because I really still didn't think that Juilliard was the right place to do it.[11]

Delays in the construction of what would be the Vivian Beaumont Theater meant deferring the Repertory Theater's opening until 1965, although artists' contracts were based on a 1963 opening. The acting company of thirty-five, which planned to present four or five plays, had to find temporary quarters. Lincoln Center had no room for a temporary theater, so the Repertory Theater found space at New York University. The company produced Arthur Miller's *After the Fall* in January 1964, and audiences liked it. The enterprise was already in the red, however. Next came Eugene O'Neill's *Marco Millions*, but subscriptions declined drastically in the second year. Thomas Middleton's *The Changeling*, a critical failure, was withdrawn that year and replaced with Miller's *Incident at Vichy*.

By late 1964 the Repertory Theater's board was growing discontented with Whitehead and Kazan. Most worries centered around money although the two had stayed within the projected deficit. Robert L. Hoguet, Jr., had become the Repertory Theater's president in August 1964. Perhaps inappropriately, he secretly sought out William Schuman, now at Lincoln Center, to find a new director to replace Whitehead. Already not on good terms with Whitehead, Schuman made a drastic error by offering to sound out Herman Krawitz, the assistant manager of the Metropolitan Opera who specialized in business, for Whitehead's drama job. Hoguet, "anticipating discretion and secrecy in the development of his personnel search, had not yet given Whitehead or Kazan any intimation of an impending change in their status. Neither Anthony Bliss, the Opera President, nor Rudolf Bing, the General Manager had been advised. Schuman talked to Krawitz."[12]

The ensuing uproar made the front page of the *New York Times*. Bing, furious that Schuman had suggested raiding the administration of one constituent for the benefit of another, accused Lincoln Center of "apparently deteriorating into a free-for-all jungle" and threatened to resign.[13] He might have remembered, however, that Schuman had already raided the Juilliard administration for Lincoln Center. According to Bing, Schuman had offered Krawitz undisputed control of the Repertory Theater after Bliss had told Hoguet how important Krawitz was to the Met. The "violent controversy in the public arena shook the foundation of federation of the new center," Lincoln Center's historian wrote.[14]

Whitehead considered himself ousted and told the *New York Times* that "any further working arrangement with Mr. Schuman as president of Lincoln Center is doomed."[15] Arthur Miller weighed in: "For myself, I agreed to give my plays to the repertory company so long as Mr. Whitehead was there. I don't see how that will be possible if the administration is such as to make the fruition of the repertory ideal impossible. [And] it seems to be a tragic misuse of [Schuman's] power to explode this situation just when the company of actors is demonstrating that the idea behind the theater is alive."[16]

Schuman could not be reached by the many reporters who tried to interview him during the three weeks that the controversy raged in the papers. The artists associated with Whitehead, correctly reading the writing on the wall concerning his future at Lincoln Center, threatened to walk out as a group if Whitehead were not reinstated. The *New York Post*'s headline ran "Storm over Lincoln Center": "The doors and corridors shudder with the exits of the mighty. Robert Whitehead, Arthur Miller, Elia Kazan, Maureen Stapleton, [and] Joseph Verner Reed."[17] Hal Holbrook spoke on behalf of the troupe, and Stapleton resigned from the title role of *The Madwoman of Chaillot* in protest. Reed, executive producer of the American Shakespeare Festival in Stratford, resigned from Lincoln Center over the treatment of Whitehead. *Newsweek*, devoting a page to the story, hyperbolically declared that "everything that has been undermining Lincoln Center has now been revealed in a single, dismaying, incredibly ludicrous 'happening' whose audience is the entire city and, beyond that, the nation and the civilized world."[18]

When Schuman finally did talk to the press a month later—that is, to former IMA student Irving Kolodin for the *Newark Star-Ledger*—he did not exactly apologize: "The first thing I did when I became president of Juilliard was to fire the press department. I felt that we ought to be known by our accomplishments [rather] than through press releases." But of late he had been "not only naive but poor about press and public relations."[19]

At this point, Bing of the Met was bitter toward Schuman, and Whitehead in drama had even more cause to be upset.[20] Lincoln Kirstein, director of the New York City Ballet, had declared of Lincoln Center, "They hate us here. William Schuman wants us to go back [to the City

Center] and we are going back."[21] "There is no denying that [Schuman] has made a lot of his constituent colleagues at Lincoln Center good and mad at him," one journalist wrote. Yet another relayed that "cultural observers have recently said that Mr. Schuman is seeking to assume a greater degree of artistic control over the Lincoln Center constituents, which are autonomous, and that this is being resented."[22] Despite the catastrophe, which badly tarnished Lincoln Center's image and left the Repertory Theater with no professional leadership, the board of Lincoln Center accepted Schuman's defense of his public silence as "an effort to avoid reducing the dispute to the personal" and expressed complete confidence in him.[23] The episode, in late 1964, may have contributed to Schuman's dismissal four years later, however (chapter 7).

These highly publicized disputes renewed examination of the entire idea of an arts complex in New York. Herbert Kupferberg, critic at the *New York Herald-Tribune*, noted that Lincoln Center was a success as slum clearance and wrote, "Is it a *cultural* success? . . . The Krawitz affair, like so many recent occurrences, underlined the question of whether Lincoln Center is in the business of culture or in culture as a business." Kupferberg noted the proposal was "attributed to Mr. Schuman, of opening the Center's own Repertory building with a production of *Caesar and Cleopatra* with Rex Harrison—sure-fire at the box-office, but totally unrelated to the repertory theater for which the edifice was supposedly built. It was this suggestion that led playwright Arthur Miller to denounce the Lincoln Center's policies as those of a 'booking agent.'" He went on to decry the "habitual pomposity and pretentiousness of the Center's announcements and declarations":

> It has never really come to grips with the challenge of enriching, rather than merely ornamenting, New York's cultural life. Constructing buildings is an American specialty, and Lincoln Center is doing a magnificent job of erecting splendid edifices. But it may be doubted that enough thought has given to the question of what is to be put into those buildings. . . . Most disturbing of all are the initial moves of the Center's administration itself toward providing cultural events for its halls. . . . But in the arts, at least, there are other criteria for success than the size and opulence of the audience and the grandeur and modernity of the building. . . . [Lincoln Center] can fulfill a proper function by encouraging adventurousness, imagination, originality and daring, . . . Lincoln Center has broken ground for buildings, but none for the arts.[24]

Juilliard had hitched its star to Lincoln Center. To some degree its failure or success would be Juilliard's own although frustratingly outside of its direct control. Even some of its most illustrious faculty disagreed with how the money was being spent. Roger Sessions, Elliott Carter, and Luciano Berio were quoted as saying that they "appreciate what Juilliard is doing, [but] agree that if there had to be a choice they would have preferred to see less money going into construction of the new building and more into grants and scholarships. They point out with some sadness that too many American students still must go to Europe for their initial recognition and development."[25]

Houseman had been linked to the Repertory Theater problems. It was reported that Lincoln Center officials had offered the job of artistic director to Tyrone Guthrie, Michael Langham, John Houseman, and Oliver Rea.[26] All declined. Houseman, reviewing the recent history and calculating these risks, went ahead with his plans to join Juilliard. He met with both Saint-Denises in Paris in 1965 and laid out the Drama Division's curriculum during several eight-hour meetings. Saint-Denis was already suffering from strokes that would incapacitate him.

Houseman spent the fall of 1966 at the old Juilliard building, meeting with Peter Mennin and Gideon Waldrop and going over budgets and academic requirements necessary for the Drama Division to have accredited university status. Saint-Denis, however, opposed the awarding of a B.F.A. degree; he felt that acting students must make a total commitment to the theater and not be able to fall back upon teaching. He also wanted to accept actors who were older than twenty-three. The Vietnam War partly settled that issue: Draft exemptions were granted only to students at educational institutions that awarded degrees, and

John Houseman.
(The Acting Company)

so the Drama Division gave degrees. Houseman accepted students as young as seventeen.

Houseman's full employment started on January 1, 1967, and he moved into one of the old IMA rooms on the ground floor. "Our equipment," he recalled, "consisted of two desks, one table, one filing cabinet (all ancient), two telephones, busts of Beethoven and Brahms, and a huge, exploded sofa purloined from upstairs."[27] He also traveled around the United States, Canada, and Sweden to observe theatrical training and attend theater conferences. At the time, as after the Drama Division opened, Houseman accepted invitations to undertake other major directing and administrative responsibilities. He addressed the Juilliard music and dance students at the 1967 Convocation.

> Now, as we proceed with our preparations in the Faculty Room, under the questioning eyes of Frank Damrosch, James Loeb, Felix Salmond, Ludwig van Beethoven and Johann Sebastian Bach, you have, whether you like it or not, assumed responsibility for us—just as we have assumed the obligation and accepted the challenge of meeting, in the field of drama, the high standards set by you of the Juilliard School of Music over the years. . . . [A]fter more than half a century of commercial exploitation, the American theater, for all its occasional flashes of inspiration and energy, has neither professional tradition nor cultural status. . . . [C]ompared to your professional world and to the theaters of most civilized countries, it remains hopelessly fragmented, disoriented and perplexed . . . with none of those clear, exacting but reassuring professional standards that prevail in the world of music.[28]

Dealings with Peter Mennin, who used "social occasions to impart the latest unfavorable and doleful news," were always depressing.[29] During a lunch in February 1967 at the Lotos Club, for example, he informed Houseman that the new building could not be ready in time for the school to open in 1968. That left two choices: postponement or opening at or near the old building. Mennin advocated postponement, but Houseman was adamant about getting started: "It was not Mennin's habit to make definite or positive decisions, but I was allowed to continue preparing for a September 1968 opening."[30] At a subsequent lunch, Mennin told him something not congruent with the facts of how the money was spent at Lincoln Center.

> Peter Mennin informed me, with grim satisfaction, that the enormous losses incurred by William Schuman's International Season at Lincoln Center had been defrayed out of funds previously set aside for the first two years of the Drama Division, which was consequently in serious

jeopardy—and might never open! I had learned to discount such jeremiads, secure in the knowledge (imparted to me by my friend Lincoln Kirstein) that, no matter what happened, the Rockefellers were morally and publicly committed, for a time at least, to support the school. And gradually I came to understand and to discount Mennin's emotional, doom-laden moods, which were partly subjective and partly related to the operating tactics of this shrewd, complicated, jealous and devious man—known to some as "the Sinuous Sicilian."[31]

Houseman prepared a red and black brochure to advertise the Drama Division and answer the question, "What kind of an artist do we hope to train at the Juilliard School and what sort of theatre are we training him for?" His goals were ambitious: "We are trying to form an actor equipped with all possible means of dramatic production, capable of meeting the demands of today's and tomorrow's ever-changing theatre— an actor who is capable of participating in those changes and who is, himself, inventive enough to contribute to them. For, in the final analysis, whatever experiments may be attempted through fresh forms of writing, on new stages, using the latest technical devices, everything ultimately depends on the human being—the actor."[32]

After the brochure had been printed and sent out to several thousand individuals and institutions in January 1968, Mennin again convened a gloomy lunch with Houseman. "Did I really feel, he asked, that we should launch the Drama Division in the fall? Would it not be wiser to postpone our opening until after the move to Lincoln Center? He listened to my indignant reaction and to my proffered resignation if such a postponement occurred."[33]

Asked to document his threat in writing, Houseman did so, knowing that Rockefeller would see the letter. Indeed, Mennin backed off. Houseman wrote:

> I have stuck my neck out in academic and theatrical circles where my reputation is important to me besides being one of the principal assets of Juilliard's projected Drama Division. I can go no further in this direction. In the circumstances I have neither the heart nor the gall to continue my belated attempts to hire a staff or recruit a student body for what well may be a nonexistent enterprise. . . . I prefer not to think of my own [situation] under the waves of contempt and ridicule that would greet the postponement or abandonment of the Juilliard School's Drama Division at this time.[34]

Houseman might have heard Mennin's frequently expressed course of last resort: "Because it's so much trouble, we just won't move to Lincoln Center." Composer Mennin was willing to abandon both the dance and drama programs, especially because the Drama Division had been foisted upon him by the Lincoln Center board.

In August 1968 the Rockefeller Foundation paid for a retreat—a two-week residence in Connecticut—for the new faculty of the Drama Division and both Saint-Denises. Four young Canadian actors agreed to act as guinea pigs so the faculty could demonstrate their teaching techniques. Houseman kept a diary that outlined the events of the retreat and of that year.[35] Those present at the retreat included the newly arrived Saint-Denises; Edith Skinner, Elizabeth Smith, and Margaret Freed for speech; and Anna Sokolow, Barbara Goodman, and Judith Leibowitz for movement. Others attending were Stephen Aaron, Peggy Loft-Freed, Marian Seldes, René Auberjonois, William Hickey, Solomon Yakim, and Brian Bedford.[36] The Drama Division faculty, unlike that of the Music Division, has always been predominately American. So absorbed were the potential faculty at the retreat that they barely noticed the violence attending the Democratic National Convention in Chicago. Two months into the first year of the Drama Division, Richard Nixon was elected president.

Saint-Denis's ill health affected his opening speech: "Very rattled," Houseman recorded, "[he] made a disastrous start, referring to notes he couldn't follow and unable to recall the simplest dates and facts. To make matters worse, his hearing aid was bust."[37] The future faculty was alarmed, especially those such as Michael Kahn who had not met Saint-Denis previously. With the help of his wife Suria, however, Saint-Denis recovered enough to outline the areas of teaching into "the discovery phase," "improvisation," "nondramatic reading," and "speech delivery." He called for a kind of training that prepared actors to do everything: sing, mime, and even dance. The group also studied Alexander Technique—a course conservatories offer to help performing musicians achieve body and mind awareness, alignment, and relaxation—with Judith Leibowitz, and Hovey Burgess demonstrated circus acrobatic techniques. Houseman reasoned that juggling demands coordination, releases inhibitions, and builds self-confidence. The retreat demonstrated to Houseman, however, that Saint-Denis was "incapable of sustained effort; we will have to use him for guidance, advice, criticism and occasional star appearances."[38]

Jack Landau was to be the principal acting teacher and Houseman's cohort during the extensive audition process for the members of Group I (the first year's students) because Saint-Denis was too ill to travel to America. Tragedy intervened, however, when Landau was murdered by a stranger. His replacement, Michael Kahn, was selected after countless interviews.

Born in New York in 1940 and educated at the High School of Performing Arts and Columbia University, the twenty-eight-year-old Kahn had already directed off-Broadway premieres of *The Funny House of the Negro*, *America Hurrah*, *The Merchant of Venice*, and *Measure for Measure* for the American Shakespeare Festival. He also directed *The Rimers of Eldritch* and Edward Albee's *The Death of Bessie Smith* and had taught acting at the Circle-in-the-Square Workshop at Brooklyn College. Both Landau and Kahn were "young, intelligent, mercurial, Jewish and basically unstable," according to Houseman, who noted that the majority of the original faculty was Jewish.[39]

Houseman and Kahn immediately learned what separated their auditions from those of colleagues in the Music and Dance Departments: "Young musicians seeking to enter Juilliard do not consider applying unless they can demonstrate a high level of technical accomplishment. The same is true of dancers. For younger actors no such test is possible. Since the essence of acting is the portrayal of mature human emotions, the selection of young acting students is inevitably intuitive and subjective, an appraisal of potential quality rather than performance."[40]

Of the five hundred applications the Drama Department received from all over the United States, only thirty-six would be accepted. Determined to set a higher value on originality and temperament than on looks, Houseman and Kahn spent fifteen minutes with each candidate. The applicant would perform a classical work in verse and a contemporary one. Kahn asked some to perform exercises that would provide insight into their imaginations: "You are going through a revolving door on your way to an important appointment and it gets stuck"; "Sing 'Happy Birthday' in three different situations: to your baby, to your lover, to your dying mother"; and "As you are crossing the stage you are suddenly confronted by a huge puddle of thick black mud. React to it."[41] Lively students leaped or waded into the mud, whereas the more timid skirted it. The School's consulting psychologist, James Koutrelakos, found the drama students to be almost uniformly extroverts, unlike the dance and music students, who were often introverts and sought him out less frequently.

Although the brochure stated that applicants would be judged entirely on the basis of merit, financial considerations played a large role in the selection of sixteen of the thirty-six. In order to offset the top eighteen—who had been selected on merit but were indigent—Houseman and Kahn had to accept others who could afford to pay. Half of the original class was male, half female, and three of the males were African American. Because there are more roles for men than women in classical plays, the frequent study of *The House of Bernalda Alba* and *The Trojan Women* for their women's roles became a standing joke. Whenever a female student left the Drama Division, Houseman would quickly point out that it was for romantic reasons. He never wrote of romantic attachments for the men.

In Houseman's opinion, Group I was "the most variegated, brilliant and troublesome class that ever attended the Drama Division of the Juilliard School."[42] Its members included Tony (Nicholas) Azito, Ronald Baker, Cathy Culnane, Woudjie (Phyllis) Dwyer, Stephen Henderson, Gerald Gutierrez, Benjamin Hendrickson, Cynthia Herman, Cindia Huppeler, Patti LuPone, James Moody, Anna Maria McNaughton, Kathleen Quinn, Mary Lou Rosato, Jared Sakren, David Schramm, Norman Snow, and Sam Tsoutsouvas.[43] Kevin Kline and David Ogden Stiers were admitted to Group I in 1970 as advanced students.

Commenting on Group II auditions, Houseman observed, "Applications slightly below last year (due to Mennin's insistence on an audition fee) but still over five hundred, I have no fears about girls; what we need are ten to fifteen strong, heterosexual boys!"[44] He considered it a crisis when Tony Azito had himself photographed for his ID card in drag and full makeup. The faculty's attitude toward Group II was "that of parent toward a second child." Of the first child, Group I, Houseman wrote, "For four long years we alternately loved and loathed them, spoiled and persecuted them and gave them a consistently disproportionate share of our concern and affection."[45]

If music students were Juilliard's natural children and dance students their adopted brothers and sisters, drama students occupied the position of step-children. The administration had difficulty handling them and integrating them into the Juilliard family. Drama students continually complained to deaf ears about their overcrowded and exhausting schedule, although they might have compared theirs with the busy schedules that dance students accepted as part of the discipline. In addition to their regular courses and rehearsals they also studied judo, folk dancing, circus acrobatics, and choral singing as well as art appreciation, theater history, costume, makeup and style, and the academic courses required for the B.F.A. degree.

When in 1969 Houseman hired Marian Seldes to direct, she wept: She thought Houseman assumed her acting career to be over. Among the faculty of two dozen assembled to teach Group I's thirty-six students were two members of the voice and speech department: Edith Skinner, a highly regarded speech teacher whose name lent instant prestige to the Drama Division, and Elizabeth Smith, a Scot.[46] She and Kahn were still teaching at the School in 1998. Students in Smith's class were described as "holding their nostrils and humm[ing]; [they] formed a circle and, swinging their arms like elephant trunks, rippled their lips with the fingers and murmured in unison, 'Mamala, mum-mum-mum, remember the money remember the money remember the money.'"[47] Largely because of Smith's presence on the faculty, Juilliard students are distinguished because of their voices. Smith's work has led to actors who have good vocal range, good sound, and the ability to use their voices.

Pierre Lefèvre, one of Saint-Denis's disciples, taught advanced improvisation and masks. Mask work is silent; students are given neutral-appearing face masks of youth, middle age, or old age and required not to speak while they wear them. They must rely entirely on the expressiveness of their bodies. "In one large studio, students dressed in leotards were stretched out on the floor listening to a teacher detail the proper way to breathe," Ralph Martin reported. "In another studio, where a group of students was studying improvisation, the teacher was explaining to them how imagination can liberate their bodies, that their use of masks could encourage expressive movement."[48]

Saint-Denis's training schedule, outlined in the bible, consisted of twelve terms, three terms for each of four years. The first year was called the "Discovery Year"; the second, the "Transformation Year"; the third, the "Interpretation Year"; and the fourth, the "Performing Year."[49] Saint-Denis and Houseman subscribed to the European plan of three semesters per year, as had Frank Damrosch with the IMA. By contrast, the curriculum at the Yale School of Drama directed by Robert Brustein lasted three years.

At a meeting on January 17, 1969, Mennin told Houseman that Juilliard, for reasons of space and money, could have neither a scene-design department nor a directing arm. There was no further discussion of teaching and fostering playwrights. With these three omissions Mennin and the Juilliard board had retreated substantially from their commitment to the artistic aims of Lincoln Center and Michel Saint-Denis.

The Drama Division had opened at Eidlitz's International House in October 1968. In the fall of 1969 the division, along with the rest of the School, moved into spectacular quarters on the fourth floor of Lincoln Center, where they remain. In addition to the Drama Theater, entered on the fourth floor and seating just over two hundred, the division also had six studios, some of which were unused until four years' worth of students had enrolled. Four studios on the north side of the building were classrooms or rehearsal rooms. One, 301, was acoustically good enough to function as a second theater. Two more large studios were located on the south side of the fourth floor. The first play to be rehearsed in the new Drama Theater was Bertolt Brecht's *Caucasian Chalk Circle*, directed by Houseman.

The idea that the fourth year form an acting company dated from 1959, a part of Saint-Denis's original concept that had even included the notion that they would tour.[50] Houseman did not want Group I to disperse upon graduation in 1972. With characteristic boundless energy the determined, and frequently overbearing, Houseman wheeled and dealed to set up Group I as a repertory company in New York. It would be housed next door to Juilliard at the Good Shepherd–Faith Church. All attempts at getting Juilliard's cooperation in the professional presentation of its own students were futile. Houseman tried to persuade Mennin to support the project, but "happy as he had been to share in the kudos that the Drama Division had brought to the institution of which he was president, Dr. Mennin was temperamentally and neurotically opposed to any activity which he himself did not personally and absolutely control."[51] Mennin reasoned that the name "Juilliard" applied to an acting company would confuse donors. The group would be known not as the Juilliard Acting Company but as the Acting Company and was run by Drama Division administrator Margot Harley.

Money was needed to launch the Acting Company, not least to advance the students' fees to join Actor's Equity. Other unions, however, were unhappy with Juilliard. In February 1973, for example, members of the International Alliance of Theatrical Stage Employees local struck and picketed. They had worked for three and a half years at Juilliard without a contract and wanted to negotiate a regular commercial contract. The stagehands had tried to penetrate educational theater all over the country and chose Juilliard—conspicuous at Lincoln Center—for their target. Every day for months all students and staff entering the School had to cross a picket line. The stagehands lost their struggle with Mennin, however. The Juilliard Theater remains the only major hall at Lincoln Center that is not unionized. That same picket line meant potential trouble for the Acting Company next door, which paid its crew union scale. Here the lack of the Juilliard name was an advantage.

The Acting Company's initial production (with the same Juilliard cast) of *The School for Scandal* received raves. Even Clive Barnes found the company's production "in many respects a better performance than that being currently given by Britain's National Theater."[52] The other productions in the repertory were Thomas Middleton's *Women Beware Women*, Brendan Behan's *The Hostage*, and John dos Passos and Paul Shyre's *U.S.A.*

In the spring of 1972 Houseman received an unusual invitation: to perform in a film about an elite school, an awe-inspiring teacher, and talented students: *The Paper Chase*. James Mason, Edward G. Robinson, Melvyn Douglas, John Gielgud, and Paul Scofield had all turned down the part of the law professor, and, in something approaching desperation, the director, James Bridges, sought Houseman. For his debut performance at the age of seventy-one Houseman won a Best Supporting Actor Academy Award.

Those whose opinions mattered most, however, were not in Hollywood but at Juilliard. After a private showing of the film for the Drama Division, the students showed no reaction. Impatiently, Houseman, in his characteristic manner of addressing them, asked,

> "Well, you sons of bitches—how was it?"
> They played it cool. They said they had enjoyed the picture and they had liked Timothy Bottoms.
> "What about *me?*" I insisted. "What did you think of *my* performance?"
> "Performance?" they said. "That was no performance. That's the way you behave around here."[53]

The success of the Acting Company's first season had greatly benefited the School and lifted the Drama Division's stock with Lincoln Center's board. Schuman's successor, Amyas Ames, remarked that "the

Group I cast for *School for Scandal.* The cast includes Mary Lou Rosato, Sam Tsoutsouvas, David Ogden Stiers, David Schramm, Patti LuPone, and Kevin Kline.

(Steven Aaron, courtesy of The Acting Company)

great success of the Drama Division and its recent graduates as the best indication that our payments to Juilliard represent one of Lincoln Center's best investments."[54]

By October 1975 the Acting Company had performed eighteen plays before more than half a million people in ninety-two cities in thirteen states. The group, which still included Patti LuPone, Kevin Kline, and Mary Lou Rosato and received funding from the NEA, was also successful with critics. Glenna Syse wrote in the *Chicago Sun-Times*, for example, "This cast can turn into anything, including woods, streams, snakes, bull-frogs, and steamboats," and a feature article in the *New York Times* highlighted their achievements.[55]

Too much success, however, proved dangerous for the Drama Division's founder. As early as March 1971, Mennin had approached Alan Schneider about succeeding Houseman; he was to take over full-time in the 1973–74 year. Schneider asked for a letter of commitment but did not receive one. Mennin finally forced Houseman to leave in early 1976, two months after the laudatory *Times* piece, although Houseman does not describe his departure in those terms in *Final Dress.*

W. McNeil Lowry has said that Mennin "was jealous of him [Houseman]."[56] Mennin's excuse, according to Margot Harley, was that Houseman was often absent from the School. She stressed that Houseman devoted a great deal of time to Juilliard and that his fame did not sit well with Mennin. Houseman was left with the face-saving excuse that many new film commitments precluded him from remaining at Juilliard. But he had been fired.

In February 1976 a new director of the Drama Division was announced: Alan Schneider (1917–84), considered one of the foremost directors of the avant-garde.[57] He had directed the premiere of *Who's Afraid of Virginia Woolf?* and his directorial credits also included *A Delicate Balance* and *The Birthday Party*. His biggest commercial success had been *You Know I Can't Hear You When the Water's Running* (1967). Schneider was Edward Albee's principal director during the 1960s; in addition, he staged Harold Pinter's first U.S. productions and championed the works of Bertolt Brecht, giving the first professional production of *The Caucasian Chalk Circle* in the United States. He also directed all of the American premieres of Samuel Beckett's plays, including *Waiting for Godot*. A theatrical dictionary has described Schneider's directing perspective:

> Ultimately, he approached dramatic works as self-contained expressions of reality. His main concern was to allow the form of the play to evolve of itself. He thereby expanded the traditional American psychological perspective of directing to incorporate a subjective reality,

the private vision of the playwright. In searching for each play's particular tone and style, its texture and basic structure, Schneider avoided imposing his own virtuosity on a play; rather, he sought to serve the playwright. As artist, educator, champion of new plays, and promoter of the avant-garde, Schneider infused vitality into the American stage. His pioneering stagings of Albee, Pinter, Beckett, and others changed the nature of the contemporary theatre.[58]

Schneider described himself as being "the only American theater director who ever went from the avant-garde to the Old Guard without having passed through the Establishment."[59] His Juilliard salary in 1976–77 was $35,000, but even then his contract had a clause invalidating it if the School closed the Drama Division. Schneider also had confidence in his students' abilities. In 1976 he had predicted, "Twenty years from now, there will be a kid from Juilliard and he'll be as good as Marlon [Brando] ever was. He'll change the American theater."[60]

In Schneider, Juilliard gained a forceful, not to say pugnacious, personality. One example of his feistiness had to do with critics, some of whom considered the American Conservatory Theater in San Francisco "perhaps the most extensive actor training program in the U.S., many also think it is the best."[61] Once again indulging in unsolicited advice and kingmaking, as he had glibly done with the Dance Department, Clive Barnes had suggested in print that the San Francisco acting troupe take over the Vivian Beaumont and the Juilliard Drama Division. Schneider's initial riposte was that a San Francisco critic come and take over Barnes's job at the *Post*.[62]

The Drama Division's relationship with the press was complicated. Wriston Locklair, Mennin's press relations aide, outlined the reasons for Schneider in 1976.[63] He also reiterated Houseman's desire not to have the productions reviewed. That same year, the *Daily News* drama critic had told Locklair that it was unable to review school productions because there were too many of them, although the *Daily News* had reviewed *The Rose Tattoo* and *Murder in the Cathedral* at Juilliard the previous year. Barnes, now at the *New York Times*, had explained to Locklair that the *Times* covered almost every opera production at the School because *Times* music critic Harold Schonberg had a staff of five full-time reviewers and three stringers. The newspaper had only two drama critics, however, and they had to cover all Broadway and off-Broadway events. There was no time to get to undergraduate events. The limited, three-performance runs were another problem. The *Village Voice* and *SoHo News* drama desks had pointed out that a show would be over by the time a review could appear, and so a notice would not serve readers.

Locklair had come to the following conclusions: The press viewed drama at Juilliard as an undergraduate program; established classics did not have appeal to the majority of the press, who would be more interested if there were a production of a new play or a seldom-seen one; the limit of three performances was insufficient for coverage, especially for weeklies; and, finally, a show at Juilliard ended its run before a notice could appear in weekend editions.

In part as a result of Houseman's admonitions to be an "incubator," the Drama Division was "out of the mainstream of interest to the school's general public and publicity media," Locklair wrote. Music, however, had been extensively covered. Locklair saw to it that reviewers Andrew Porter and Harriett Johnson lunched informally with Peter Mennin, and he gave them library cards to the Lila Acheson Wallace Library. For years, personal contacts were kept up with *Time*, *Newsweek*, and critics at *Cue*.

History repeated itself. Mennin became as dissatisfied with Schneider as he had been with Houseman. The two constantly fought. Schneider tried to involve Mennin in the Drama Division, but the men would disagree with each other. In March 1979, three years after his arrival, Schneider "resigned" as director. He became professor of drama and head of the Graduate Directing Program at the University of California, San Diego. The *New York Times* reported, "Apparently there was a disagreement between Mr. Schneider and Peter Mennin, President of Juilliard. Asked to amplify his statement, Mr. Schneider said, 'The differences within Juilliard we will leave to the historians.'"[64] Not much of a trail has been left for historians. No documents at the School explain Schneider's departure, but W. McNeil Lowry has recalled one early area of disagreement:

> Peter Mennin never quite trusted personal relations. Mennin didn't like a woman named Margot Harley, who still runs the Acting Company, whom Houseman had brought in there as the administrative director of that Juilliard training center. When Houseman was cleared out, Mennin called Schneider in and said, "Alan, I want you to fire Margot Harley. She's too acerbic, she's too big for her britches. And besides, you don't owe her anything; she's Houseman's appointee." Alan said, "Look, she's worked very well with the students and the faculty. What the hell do I care whether she's Houseman's? She's the Juilliard training center, and that means she's mine and no, I won't fire her."[65]

Firing Schneider strained the friendship between Mennin and Lowry, whose cooperation Mennin needed in gaining extensions for the $36 million Ford Foundation matching grant. Harley, too, was let go the same year as Schneider.[66] Schneider met a cruel fate. Nine days after he delivered the completed copy of the first volume of his autobiography, May 5, 1984, he was struck and killed by a motorcycle in London.

Peter Hall, Michael Langham, and Richard Kirchner were considered as replacements. Forgetting Saint-Denis's advice that the Drama Division be headed by an American, in 1979 Mennin chose Michael Langham (b. 1919), who was British. He had become interested in theater while a prisoner of war from 1940 to 1945. He became artistic director of the Birmingham Repertory Company, the Glasgow Citizen's Theater, and Canada's Stratford Festival and also directed for the Royal Shakespeare Company and the Old Vic. In the United States, he was artistic director at the Guthrie Theatre in Minneapolis from 1971 to 1977. It was Langham's opinion that American students arrived with "the huge disadvantage of the education they've had in English, as though they belonged to a cult of inarticulateness."[67]

In 1988, twenty years after its founding, the Drama Division invited three important leaders of the New York Shakespeare Festival, the largest theatrical institution in the country, to discuss American conservatory training centers. The speakers—Joseph Papp, Stuart Vaughan, and Rosemary Tishler—agreed that the most evident effect of conservatories was to give actors more tools to use for the diversity of plays they might encounter. "When Juilliard started and when Yale spiffed up their conservatory program," Vaughn said, "we began to have some really excellent training. It shows up enormously in the level of acting we find at auditions now. There's been a tremendous improvement, since I've been directing, in the quality of young actors and their skills. I put it squarely at the door of the kind of training Juilliard is able to offer. It is an example to everybody else."[68]

Tishler pointed out that for most jobs—television, naturalistic plays, and movies—a conservatory training is not necessary. Studying with a good acting teacher for a year would make it possible to cope with any role on television, but a conservatory training was still necessary for actors who wanted to perform repertoire of the English and world theater. Vaughan felt that the level of actor training had still not approached the level of musical training, nor did actors know as much about their instrument as do dancers.

In Papp's opinion, the importance of schools was not in the training given but in the performance opportunities that provide actors with experience. Schools he thought good at this were Juilliard, Yale, New York University, and Southern Methodist University. Ultimately, however, demands on actors gradually change because playwrights and directors want different types of skills. Schools must keep abreast of such changes, he felt.

Group XVIII performing *King Lear* (Matt Servitto).
(Jessica Katz, photo from The Juilliard School Archives)

Returning students, such as Gerald Gutierrez in 1988, lamented the fact that even second-year students now had agents. Margot Harley had special cause to dislike agents, because no agent would want an actor to enter the Acting Company she administrated: There was no money in it—for the agent. She would bodily throw agents out of the School, saying, "Agents are the scum of the earth, for the most part."[69]

Langham directed the Drama Division for twelve years until his retirement in 1992, when Michael Kahn, who had previously resigned from Juilliard and was artistic director of the Shakespeare Theatre in Washington, D.C., finally became director. Kahn's "strong personal commitment to multiculturalism has resulted in the most diverse faculty and student body in the School's history," the Drama Division boasted in 1994.[70]

Although the Lila Acheson Wallace American Playwright's Program had been in place since 1979, made possible by $2 million from Wallace, no formal play-writing program was instituted until after 1984, when Tony Kushner, Terrence McNally, and Eric Bogosian were in residence. As Kahn commented, "I wasn't sure that the Playwrights-in-Residence program was the best use of the resources available to us, and it didn't always result in a significant connection between the playwright and the school. I thought it might be more productive to bring in writers who were contemporaries of the acting students, possibly creating working relationships that might go beyond the school."[71] Not until 1993 were playwrights admitted as students. Leah Ryan, Daniel Goldfarb, Robert

Kerr, Kira Obloensky, Julia Jordan, Stephen Belber, and David Auburn were the first group.

The program (co-directed in 1993–94 by John Guare and Terrence McNally) provides six student playwrights with year-long fellowships to develop their skills. By contrast, Yale, with which Juilliard is perpetually in competition, has had a playwrights' program since the 1970s. In 1992 the Drama Division performed an uncensored production of *Millennium Approaches* from *Angels in America* by Kushner, playwright-in-residence. Bogosian directed his new *SubUrbia* in 1992. In 1993 the fourth-year drama students performed Athol Fugard's *Blood Knot* and Caryl Churchill's *Cloud Nine*.

Training only actors for twenty-five years fossilized the Drama Division, which made it harder to integrate play-writing. The Dance Division, by contrast, continually produced new choreographies by faculty and taught all students choreography. Yet the Drama Division had not offered play-writing as a discipline to be studied and was therefore not contributing in the most fundamental sense to the storehouse of its art. The absence of both play-writing and directing (it would be like having no composers or conductors in the Music Division) was a fundamental flaw in the Drama Division that could not be papered over by pointing to movie-star graduates. Schuman, Mennin, and Lincoln Center had both created and crippled the Drama Division.

It took twenty-seven years to establish a directing program at Juilliard. In March 1995 the School announced its first, to be led by JoAnne Akalaitis, Garland Wright, and Michael Kahn. The Andrew W. Mellon Foundation gave the financial support, offering full tuition for three candidates to the two-year, graduate-level course. The Directors' Fund is named after Alan Schneider, which is ironic considering his history at the School. Michael Kahn has found "complete support" from President Joseph Polisi, contrasted with the lack of support that Mennin gave him and the division.[72]

For the first time since Group I had formed a separate acting company, the nineteen members of Group XXIII formed their own company in 1995. To help launch it, they gave a benefit performance of Arthur Miller's *The American Clock*. Their first summer season consisted of *The Taming of the Shrew* and *In the Boom Boom Room* by David Rabe. The productions were directed by Juilliard faculty. In 1998 Group XXVII would enter the Acting Company en masse, the first class to do so since Group I.

Kahn has described Juilliard's approach as a combination of both European and American acting techniques. "It is an approach that synthesizes what was once considered European in terms of vocal training, physical training, text and style with what was peculiarly and brilliantly American—immense physical energy, real intellectual and imaginative daring, willingness to take risks and a fierce commitment to emotional honesty."[73] If there is a criticism of Juilliard actors, it is that they do not have enough soul.

The original dream of the founders of Lincoln Center, for its constituents to work together, is far from fulfilled. The Dance Division and the School of American Ballet have resolutely avoided each other, even while sharing the same building. The cohabitation of the Metropolitan Opera and Juilliard at Lincoln Center has not fulfilled the long-held desire to allow Juilliard singers to attend Met rehearsals. Indeed, at the Met no student ticket prices exist (aside from score desks), either for Juilliard or for any other students. To music students, the prospect of membership in the New York Philharmonic, despite or even because of its location across the street, seems even more remote, although nearly 50 percent of the Philharmonic are Juilliard alumni. The direct benefits supposed to accrue to Juilliard students upon moving the School to Lincoln Center have yet to materialize.

In an attempt to forge some kind of relationship with the Lincoln Center Theater, Kahn invited John Guare to Juilliard to work for six weeks on *Moon over Miami*. Guare has commented about the invitation:

> I work across the street at Lincoln Center Theater and I've always looked up and said "What is it like there? I mean, here's this theater, [t]here's a school for theater students, why aren't they together?" . . . It's been almost a quarter of a century that these two worlds have existed across the street from each other, and they might as well have been on different planets. Since Andrew Bishop has taken over as Artistic Director of Lincoln Center Theater, more positive steps have been made to make the two work together.[74]

The most distressing policy for students—one not uniformly applied since the Drama Division's beginning—has been that of dismissing students after two years in the program. The bitterness and blows to self-esteem that a third of each entering class suffers cannot be denied. For sheer cruelty to students, the policy rivals no other at the School. The eliminations—Houseman called them "liquidations" and "executions"— began at the end of the first year of Group I, when only twenty-one of the original thirty-six of that group remained. At graduation in 1972, only thirteen of Group I received B.F.A. degrees; the remaining seven received diplomas.

Some of Group I were asked to leave because they were taking the drugs common in the late 1960s. Patti LuPone has remarked that a grade of *D* stood for "drugs." Some students were unwilling or unprepared to undergo the extensive effort involved in becoming an actor. Having not had the discipline of the years of training that dancers and musicians undergo, they sometimes have found the curriculum too much work. Houseman tried to justify the purges by saying "the survivors emerged stronger and better for their ordeal."[75] Nevertheless, like Mennin and other administrators, he preferred not to deliver bad news himself; later he unloaded that unpleasant task onto the faculty.

The system of "executions" guaranteed blunders that would eventually embarrass the School. Houseman's abilities sometimes deserted him. "Robin Williams has no talent," he once thundered, and Williams, in Group IV, was cut out of the School after his third year. He appears to hold no animus and has returned to give talks to the students and receive an honorary doctorate.[76]

Another embarrassing case involved a student from Group XII, Eriq La Salle. After becoming a household name on the hit television show *ER*, La Salle vividly described his experience at Juilliard to the *New York Times*: "I wasn't asked back, or I was asked to leave. Or kicked out—however you want to put it. I was truly devastated. That was the first time I really knew what the word devastation meant."[77] To make matters worse, his teachers told the black actor that they did not think he would be able to suppress his inner-city speech patterns, although he subsequently enrolled in New York University's drama school and did just that.

The system was flawed from the beginning; even Patti LuPone was marked for dismissal.[78] Neither did an implied racism disappear. "At Juilliard, [La Salle] was among a group of black students who lobbied the school's administration to hire a black stage director. The black director the school chose was incompetent, says Mr. La Salle, and was subsequently demoted. 'After I was gone,' he added, 'another group of black actors got together and said, "We want a black director." And Juilliard's response was "We tried that, and it didn't work."' Would they have said the same thing if it had been an incompetent white director?"[79]

In a sense, La Salle's problem was the opposite of that faced by black students a dozen years earlier. One of the three Group I students faced accusations by other blacks for attending an elite white school and for concentrating on mid-Atlantic speech rather than using black idiom. He left Juilliard on his own.

By 1982 Juilliard had trained students whom Suria Saint-Denis singled out as its "outstanding actors": Tony Azito, Frances Conroy, Benjamin Hendrickson, William Hurt, Kevin Kline, Patti LuPone, Leigh McCloskey, Kenneth Marshall, Elizabeth McGovern, Mandy

Patinkin, Christopher Reeve, Norman Snow, David Ogden Stiers, and Robin Williams.[80] Since then other students have distinguished themselves, including Val Kilmer, Kelly McGillis, Linda Kozlowski, Christine Baranski, Laura Linney, Jeanne Tripplehorn, Michael Haydn, Michael Stuhlbarg, Mary Lou Rosato, Lisa Banes, Harriet Harris, Randall Mell, Pamela Nyberg, Keith David, Richard Howard, David Schramm, Derek Smith, and Henry Stram.

It has always been a problem for drama students to fit into the School socially. Margot Harley realized that they "did not integrate well." "I would try to budge and help integrate drama students into the life of Juilliard," Gideon Waldrop commented. "Believe me, that is hard to do and it never has happened. I'm not sure it can happen."[81] The lack of understanding went both directions. Peter Mennin "was a little frightened of the actors in a way," Harley remembers. "He didn't understand them."[82] LuPone put it succinctly: "There was great hatred toward the drama division, and for good reason. We were not—polite."[83] They may not have been polite, but they certainly were successful and brought more fame to the School.

10

The
Juilliard
School:

PETER MENNIN

THE SOCIAL AND financial climate for music had changed considerably since the prosperous 1950s. Between 1965 and 1971 more than one hundred U.S. orchestras went out of business. Juilliard's move to Lincoln Center had coincided with a crisis in the arts. It was difficult for music students to get a job, especially in a professional orchestra where "the job structure is much more rigid . . . than it is at IBM."[1] Peter Mennin summed up the problem in 1969:

> Somehow, we are not at a point where the arts are a major portion of our national life. Managements are flooded with enormous talents, but there are too many empty seats in the concert halls. Rubinstein fills them, yes—but that is the exception; a leading soprano of the Met did not sell even a hundred tickets for a lieder recital this season. I would like to think that the onus is on the audiences to make the arts part of their lives—strictly for the purposes of their own enrichment. I mean, we are supposed to have more leisure than ever before. Everybody knows that. But more leisure to do what—watch TV? We have got to do better than that.[2]

By 1962 Juilliard needed someone to replace William Schuman and deal with the move to Lincoln Center. For the remainder of the year, while the board looked for a replacement, Mark Schubart acted as president. Schuman had pressed for his own candidate, composer Hugo Weisgall; second on Schuman's list was William Bergsma. Having conducted fifteen interviews, the board was most impressed with the last person on the list, the thirty-nine-year-old composer Peter Mennin.

Mennin was born May 17, 1923, in Erie, Pennsylvania, to Attilio and Amelia Mennini; his elder brother was Louis Mennini, who became a composer and administrator in his own right. (Unlike Louis, but like Walter Pistone, Mennin removed the final letter from his surname.) Their father had been a restaurateur, and he passionately collected phonograph recordings. Mennin's teacher, Tito Spompani, insisted that the six-year-old learn solfège before he learn an instrument, an approach reminiscent of Frank Damrosch's experiment. He left the Catholic Church as a boy, along with the rest of his family.

As a youngster Mennin had played in an accordion duo with his brother ("the Mennini Brothers"). Like some other twentieth-century composers (William Schuman, Elliott Carter, and Milton Babbitt, for example), he did not play an instrument well enough to perform in public. Everywhere Louis went Peter followed. After graduating from high school, he followed Louis to the Oberlin Conservatory to study with Normand Lockwood from 1940 to 1942. In 1942 both brothers left Oberlin to join the U.S. Army Air Force. Mennin already knew how to fly an airplane but was wounded while on maneuvers in Miami Beach. It was then discovered he was too nearsighted to fly and was honorably discharged the next year. Louis, however, served until the end of the war. After working in a wartime factory, Mennin decided to continue his broken-off studies at either Juilliard or Columbia. His wife Georganne Bairnson, who studied violin at the Eastman School of Music with Jacques Gordon, a Kneisel student, tells the story: "In October 1944 he hopped on a train for New York with his music under his arm. The train stopped in Rochester on the way. It was Sunday, and he got off the train and went to Howard Hanson's house, which none of the Eastman students would ever have dared to do, Dr. Hanson being the formidable head of the Eastman School of Music. Anyway, he did and Hanson was very gracious. They had a meeting and Hanson offered him two orchestration fellowships to pay his tuition if he would stay at Eastman."[3]

For the first time Mennin had beaten his brother to the punch. Louis attended Eastman later—from 1945 to 1948—where he received a bachelor's and master's degree. Both brothers studied with Bernard Rogers and Howard Hanson. Mennin finished his bachelor's and master's in the same year and started to pull ahead of his brother in his career. He won the first Gershwin Memorial Prize in 1945, and in 1948 he won a Guggenheim grant. That award led to his Symphony No. 2 being performed by the New York Philharmonic, with Leonard Bernstein conducting. The same work also won Columbia University's Bearns Prize (won previously by Schuman). In 1946 Mennin was awarded a grant from the American Academy of Arts and Letters for *Folk Overture*. That work was performed in Carnegie Hall in January 1946, with Howard Hanson conducting the Eastman-Rochester Orchestra. Mennin's Third Symphony—his doctoral dissertation at Eastman, completed on his twenty-third birthday—had its premier by the New York Philharmonic in February 1947, with Walter Hendl conducting. He received his doctorate at the age of twenty-four in 1947 before Louis received his master's degree in 1948.

This early recognition and success led to job offers. In 1947 Schuman asked Mennin to teach composition at Juilliard and to join the new L&M faculty. Louis went to the University of Texas to teach for the 1948–49 year and then returned to teach composition at Eastman, receiving his doctorate in 1961.

Mennin still composed while teaching; the Boston Symphony Orchestra played his Fifth Symphony in 1951. In 1956 he won his second Guggenheim as well as a Fulbright and was on a leave of absence from Juilliard when the board decided to move to Lincoln Center (not that a faculty member would have had any influence on that decision). It was

Peter Mennin.
(Conway Studios, courtesy of Georganne Mennin)

a propitious time for Mennin to leave Juilliard. *Life* magazine had singled him out as being among nine "U.S. Composers in a Bright Era"; his photograph was the first and largest of those accompanying the article. William Schuman was upset because he was not included on the illustrious list.[4] Perhaps Mennin's appearance helped him. At six feet two inches, he had a mustache, gray-blue eyes, and looked like a movie star. The press compared him with Errol Flynn, and *Time* magazine described him as "a firm administrator and an impeccable dresser."[5]

When Mennin returned from Europe in 1958, Peabody Conservatory invited him to become its director. He would reorganize the school and guide the growth of the Peabody Art Theater. Also in 1958, he examined the leading music schools in Paris, London, Rome, Milan, Brussels, and Vienna under State Department auspices. During September and October he took part in the first cultural exchange of composers between the United States and the Soviet Union and studied the Moscow and Leningrad conservatories.

After four years at Peabody, Mennin's abilities as an administrator distinguished him to the degree that he was offered the presidencies of the Oberlin Conservatory, the Eastman School of Music, and the Curtis Institute in addition to Juilliard. His acceptance of Juilliard made the front page of the *New York Times*.[6] Mennin had chosen Juilliard because he wanted the challenge of building a new school at Lincoln Center to rival and surpass the great European conservatories, especially those in Moscow and Paris. Georganne Mennin explained:

> Peter's Juilliard was for the deeply committed, highly talented person who needed to spend their student years concentrating on honing their talents to the highest possible point. . . . Peter agreed with the theory that there is no democracy in the arts. Conservatories by their very name are meant to focus on one field. Universities can feed the "whole man." . . . [S]omething must have been right in his type of school, as Juilliard was receiving the lion's share of all the international prizes and was the most sought-after performing arts school on the international scene.[7]

No ceremonies were held on November 1, 1962, when Mennin became Juilliard's president, but the next day a reception was given at the Lotos Club for William Schuman. From 1963 to 1968 the two were rivals in fund-raising, which strained their relationship. The men lived one floor apart (Schuman on the seventh floor, Mennin on the sixth) in the same apartment building on East 78th Street and Park Avenue. Mennin's typical mode of behavior when someone's actions displeased him was to not speak to that person. Schuman eventually fell into the same category as Louis Mennini, with whom Mennin barely communicated as well.[8]

When Mennin became president he drafted a chart, the "Juilliard Master Plan," which clearly showed his interests in using the School to foster the creative arts. Under three columns, one each for Drama, Music, and Dance, were numbered lists of plans for each division. The first row across read: "Drama (in consultation with head): 1. Commission contemporary playwrights. Music: 1. Commission instrumental and operatic works, and orchestra works. Dance (in consultation with head): 1. Commission choreographic music." For the Drama Division, Mennin envisioned "about 50 or 60 members. Enough for two and possibly three productions being prepared at the same time." In the Music Division column, he envisioned three hundred students, two orchestras, eighty to ninety pianists, forty singers, ten conductors, and fifteen to twenty composers; for the Dance Division, sixty to seventy dancers "in various stages of development." He listed faculty for music only, mentioning Aaron Copland as "(head)?" of the composition department.[9]

The dean, Gideon Waldrop, had met Mennin at Eastman, where he too received a doctorate in composition. The Mennins and Waldrop formed a bond in running the school similar to that of the Hutchesons and Wagner. Georganne Mennin, whose charm and friendliness offset her husband's aloofness, was an asset to his career. She gave up the violin to devote herself full-time to rearing their two children and promoting his aims and over the years arranged innumerable social occasions for the benefit of Juilliard. She was unperturbed when at the School's seventy-fifth anniversary celebration a board member publicly praised her by disparaging feminists.

Mennin and Waldrop studiously avoided promoting their own work at Juilliard. They believed, perhaps idealistically, that works of merit would surface and that was preferable to having hired image-builders promote the music. (Schuman had an agent.) Times have changed, and now illustrious composers as well as younger ones hire managers and public relations agents.

Mennin's creative production slowed after he took the job at Juilliard. He had completed six symphonies before the age of thirty, but it took a decade each to complete his next three. He had perfect pitch and a retentive memory similar to Vincent Persichetti's. His works have been described as having integrity of purpose and being compulsively frantic. Mennin's hallmarks include a long, singing line—a good example is the Seventh Symphony—coupled with a driving rhythmic pulse. The *New York Times* described his music as "extremely busy and quite dissonant. But tonalities are nevertheless suggested, and there is a strong, if severe, melodic profile. The orchestra is brilliant. On paper, the scoring looks overthick and overcomplicated, but on the stage it works."[10]

Like Schuman, who would not tolerate faculty committees, Mennin was a benevolent dictator. He, too, was reluctant to delegate authority. According to Jacob Druckman, he was "a kind of Macbeth-like character; he was always worried about insubordination." A Dance Division administrator described him as "a hidden and a driven, compulsive, 'minjy' man" with no "generosity of spirit."[11] Mennin mistrusted others, and they mistrusted him. He had problems with gay faculty (like Tudor) and students and would ask suspiciously, "Does he like girls?" Here, too, he resembled Schuman, who felt uncomfortable around Aaron Copland's gay friends.[12]

Unlike the extroverted Schuman, Peter Mennin, thirteen years younger, was an introvert and always a loner, his wife recalled. As he said, "Being a creator is the loneliest of pursuits and each composer must protect this aloneness." Publicly, Mennin stressed individualism and disparaged committees; he believed in doing things single-handedly. Although "he enjoyed teaching, [he] found that it drained him. Administrative work seemed to be easier for him, because after a day at Lincoln Center he could come home and write all night. . . . But when he taught composition he would get very wound up and a lot of his energies were exerted that he probably would have channeled into his own work."[13] Mennin often told people—in part to avoid personal questions—that those who wanted to learn about him could listen to his music. He would even write out his answers ahead of time for "interviews."

It cannot be said that Mennin was a popular figure at the School, although few students ever came into direct contact with him. He was rarely seen in the halls and never in the three large elevators where everyone bumps into everyone else. Students had only two opportunities to hear him speak during their Juilliard career—convocation and commencement. So removed was Mennin from the students and many faculty that it was possible to spend years at the School and never enter his office or even know where it was. Those who did find their way to the second-floor room behind a wall of glass encountered a secretary who made sure they did not meet with the president.

"Peter never compromised to reach his goals," Georganne Mennin acknowledges, "which doesn't make you the most popular person."[14] He was an elitist, a traditionalist, and quite difficult for many to deal with. A distinct climate of fear existed, and people always felt that they could be replaced. Paranoia resulted. Pianist Beveridge Webster, for example, joked that microphones were secretly installed in the water fountains. The grim atmosphere was reflected in the surroundings. For the first fifteen years at Lincoln Center, no paintings, pictures, or plants decorated the many barren hallways or the tomblike 66th Street lobby. The few bulletin boards were locked and controlled by the administration.

No dormitories existed for students, who either struggled to pay New York City apartment rental prices or found it necessary to move to the outer boroughs. Mennin's hope of buying a hotel across 66th Street was frustrated when mainland China's delegation to the United Nations moved into that space. No thought was given to making students comfortable or to meeting their psychological needs. In the mid-1960s, when two apparently committed suicide (one jumped into the Hudson River), Waldrop urged hiring a psychological counselor. Mennin's response was that needing counseling was a sign of weakness. The dean prevailed, however, and in 1966 Dr. James Koutrelakos joined the staff. Edward Gordon filled the same role after 1972. No statistics were kept on student suicide, although everyone in the School knew when it occurred. When students died, their records were immediately removed.

Mennin instituted profound changes at Juilliard, both in terms of curricula and faculty. His longtime devotion to solfège demanded a major shift in the L&M program. Rather than subsume ear training in L&M, Mennin reinstituted it as a separate course and hired the eminent pedagogue Renée Longy(-Miquelle) in 1963. Two years of solfège would be required of all music students.

For the remainder of her career Longy (1897–1979) was one of Juilliard's most important teachers. Her father, Georges Longy, had been the Boston Symphony Orchestra's oboist and founder of the Longy

Renée Longy.
(Herschel Levit)

School of Music in Cambridge. Renée Longy had taught ear training at New England Conservatory in 1915 and at the Curtis Institute from 1926 to 1941, where her students had included Leonard Bernstein and Vincent Persichetti. She had also written a text on the subject; *Principles of Music Theory* was originally published in 1925 and reprinted through 1975. A pupil of Dalcroze, she also taught "rhythmic gymnastics." After being fired from Curtis, Longy had taught at Peabody from 1943 to 1951 and then taught for twelve years in Miami before coming to Juilliard.

Longy was an especially strong influence on composition and conducting students, for whom her system of learning clefs, rhythm, and pitch was required for four years. She taught in a rigid French manner that included humiliation; both men and women ran from her classroom in tears. Her reputation made others plead at registration to be placed in someone else's ear-training section. Longy considered Nadia Boulanger her principal competition; learning that a student had studied with Boulanger was sufficient to demonstrate that he or she knew nothing whatsoever. She forced those who already had significant performing careers to recognize that they did not even understand what a time signature was.

Madame Longy (as she was always called) was totally dedicated to teaching and, ill during her last years, would be wheeled in her chair by a teaching assistant. Students who survived the harsh classroom treatment became devoted to her and visited her nearby apartment on Saturdays to pursue a fifth, sixth, and seventh year of solfège. For other students, the mention of her name or the sight of her rhythmic notation of numbers, checks, and dashes brings unhappy memories. At her memorial held at Juilliard in 1979 Leonard Bernstein played a piece he had written on her initials, expressed as solfège sylables (re-la-mi).

Mennin's most significant curriculum changes concerned the shift from bachelor and master of science (M.S.) degrees to bachelor of music (B.M.), master of music (M.M.), and bachelor of fine arts (B.F.A.) degrees and the addition of doctor of musical arts (D.M.A.) degree. The new undergraduate degrees, which began with the 1963–64 school year, paralleled the old in all curricular regards, except the requirement of sixty academic credits was cut to thirty. A more radical elimination took place in the master of music curriculum, first conferred in 1972. Academic courses were no longer required. Forty-eight of the seventy master's students preferred the M.M. to the M.S.

The D.M.A. course was inaugurated in the fall of 1967. Extremely competitive, it accepted only about ten students a year and concentrated on composition, piano, voice, and violin. Although these advanced students were required to complete a doctoral document, a lack of emphasis on academics led the School not to send these documents to be microfilmed and housed with theses and dissertations from other conservatories and universities. Mennin hired the eminent musicologist Gustave Reese to head the D.M.A. program. Nevertheless, music history was considered of low importance at Juilliard and never offered as a major. The required undergraduate two-year music history courses, now separated from L&M, were taught by L&M Fellows. Those same teachers were elevated to faculty status by the subsequent administration.

Some faculty and students did write for publication, however. David Schiff, a doctoral candidate, wrote an authoritative book on the music of his teacher, Elliott Carter. Simultaneously, I worked with Roger Sessions on a book about him. Faculty member Joseph Machlis wrote the extremely popular *Enjoyment of Music*, which went into five editions.[15] Applied faculty also wrote valuable texts concerning their instruments; examples are Ivan Galamian's *Principles of Violin Playing and Teaching* and *Contemporary Violin Technique*.[16]

Between 1966 and 1973 fewer than twenty diplomas were awarded annually; postgraduate diplomas were fewer than ten a year. Between sixty and ninety students received B.M. degrees each year, and the numbers for B.S. and M.S. degrees trickled down as earlier students eventually graduated. The most revealing statistics, however, concern the total number of graduates each year during this period, when the School was supposed to limit enrollment to the two hundred students dictated by Lincoln Center. Between 1966 and 1973 almost two hundred graduated each year. The figure in 1973—184—nearly equalled the number of graduates in 1966 (189) before the move to Lincoln Center. Mennin had triumphed in his goal to raise enough money to maintain the size of the student body.

Statistics for 1973 also indicated trends. String majors made up about 25 percent of the student body, and piano accounted for almost a third of all students at the School. The percentage of foreign students had steadily increased since World War II. In 1946 the number totaled only 2.8 percent of the student body; by 1953 it had grown to 10.6 percent; and in 1973 the figure had grown to 20 percent, with the largest proportion coming from Japan.

In 1966, 19 percent of Juilliard's students were not from the United States, the largest percentage of any institution of higher learning in the United States. MIT, a near competitor, had 12.9 percent, and Columbia University enrolled 9.4 percent. As was true for the previous two decades, more than half the international population at Juilliard came from four countries: Canada, Israel, Japan, and China. The percentages of foreign-born students continued to climb throughout the 1970s and 1980s.

One colloquial name for the Juilliard, "Jew-iard," was coined because of the School's large proportion of Jewish students during its first sixty years. Other facetious names were "Jailyard," "the Yard," or "the Factory." Held over from the days of the Juilliard Musical Foundation was the habit, still retained by a few, of saying "the Juilliard." The omnipotence of the School versus the powerlessness felt by students has been captured in a joke: How do you spell Juilliard? Big J, little you. During the twenty-one years under Peter Mennin the School was known to faculty and students (echoing stationery, posters, and concert programs) as "The-Juilliard-School-Peter-Mennin-President." The correct spelling involves three capital letters: The Juilliard School.

Under Mennin, new music faculty and administration were hired and some academic faculty were let go. Mark Schubart went to Lincoln Center, and Norman Lloyd left to become dean of the Oberlin Conservatory and then director of the arts for the Rockefeller Foundation. Gideon Waldrop, who had declined Schuman's invitation to accompany him to Lincoln Center, replaced Frederik Prausnitz as dean. Faculty member Gordon Hardy replaced William Bergsma as associate dean. Stanley Wolfe, a former student and currently a faculty member, administered the lucrative Extension Division, which made a $2.5 million profit for the School in his thirty-three years.

In addition to Longy, Mennin's faculty appointments included Jennie Tourel, Rudolf Firkusny, Ruggiero Ricci, Abbey Simon, Gyorgy Sandor, Syzmon Goldberg, Mieczyslaw Munz, and Ilona Kabos. He brought in conductors Sixten Ehrling, Alfred Wallenstein, and, loyally, Walter Hendl. Interested in fostering conducting talent, Mennin established a conducting program in 1972. The Ford Foundation under W. McNeil Lowry had granted him and the Peabody Institute large sums to start conductors' programs. (Gideon Waldrop had worked for the Ford Foundation and knew Lowry.)

It was on the composition department, understandably, where composer Mennin made his greatest mark. He and Waldrop felt that they had come from the best school in the country as far as composition was concerned—Eastman with its Howard Hanson and Bernard Rogers—and were determined that Juilliard be even better. Mennin spent four years trying to obtain Roger Sessions before his retirement at seventy from Princeton. Sessions replaced Vittorio Giannini, who left to head the new North Carolina School of the Arts. Luciano Berio and Elliott Carter were also hired. Milton Babbitt replaced Berio, and David Diamond took over for Hall Overton when he died in the early 1970s. None of these composers' music sounded like Mennin's own, which spoke well of his tolerance for other musical styles. Generally, the group, including Persichetti, would be called "uptown" unlike the "downtown" style fostered by Philip Glass and Steve Reich, two Juilliard students.

Glass's experience at the School included two years in the Extension Division and four years in the Regular Division (1958–62). He received a diploma in composition in 1960 and an M.S. in 1962. He wrote of the School before the arrival of Mennin and Longy:

> I suppose I had been a good student at Juilliard, though there were certainly more obviously gifted people around than myself. I had two very good teachers there—Vincent Persichetti and William Bergsma—both accomplished and well-known composers. My five years there had been highly productive. I had written a great deal of music (over seventy works), all of which had been performed. . . . The conservatory environment of Juilliard had been an ideal place to learn the practical side of a composer's craft. However, in the end, I felt I lacked the rigorous training which, at that time, seemed more a part of a traditional European music education.[17]

A classmate of Glass, Reich did not graduate from Juilliard. He said of his former teacher:

> Great teachers like Vincent Persichetti or Hall Overton are not necessarily great composers. I don't believe Vincent Persichetti was a great composer. He was a phenomenal teacher because he had enormous musicianship and he could be a complete chameleon. He could listen to you, look at your score, and he became you. He could improvise pieces in your style. He knew what information you needed at this point in your life today. And that's a great teacher. Because, he has more technique than you have and he can see where you're going, not as a reflection of himself, but as an amplification of yourself. There are precious few people like this and when you find teachers like this they become enormously helpful, because they solve specific problems that you have at a certain period of time.[18]

With Persichetti, the only Schuman holdover, as chair, the composition department entered a golden age during the 1970s. Babbitt, Carter, Diamond, Persichetti, and Sessions taught some of the most talented composers of the younger generation, including Ellen Taaffe Zwilich, Tobias Picker, Tod Machover, George Tsontakis, Paul Levi, Larry Alan Smith, Kenneth Frazelle, Larry Bell, Daron Hagen, Joel Hoffman, Richard Danielpour, Eric Ewazen, and Bruce Adolphe.

New music flourished. Luciano Berio founded the Juilliard Ensemble in the fall of 1967 and took them to Europe, where they performed and recorded for Cologne Radio and the BBC in London. The nucleus of the group, later conducted by Dennis Russell Davies, consisted of fourteen players. The formation of the Juilliard Ensemble was also important because some of its members went on to found the new music group Speculum Musicae. Its members graduated and won the Naumberg Chamber Music competition, which helped to launch the group professionally. In the mid-1990s an echo of the Berio group was formed: the New Juilliard Ensemble.

The prestige of the School, however, still lay in the virtuoso superstars whose numbers appeared to increase under Mennin. Juilliard students were winning international competitions, starting in the 1950s with Lhevinne students John Browning, Van Cliburn, and Tong ("Tony") Il Han, who won first place in the Leventritt competition. (A Korean refugee, Han had been "discovered" by the men of the U.S. Fifth Air Force in 1954 and sent to Juilliard, where he studied from 1959 to 1968.) At the Third International Tchaikowsky competition in 1966, soprano Veronica Tyler, a student of Florence Page Kimball, won second place. After singing from *Porgy and Bess,* "She received five minutes of wild applause and the audience had to be asked to be quiet so the competition could continue."[19] At the same competition, Misha Dichter won second place in piano and Stephen Kates second place in 'cello. Also in the 1960s, Kyung-Wha Chung, Pinchas Zukerman, and Itzhak Perlman won the Leventritt competition. In the 1970s Emanuel Ax, Yo-Yo Ma, Barbara Hendricks, Cho-Liang Lin, Mark Peskanov, Nadja Salerno-Sonnenberg, John Aler, Schlomo Mintz, and Yefim Bronfman, among others, made reputations for themselves. The success of these students brought more fame to the School.

One Juilliard voice student became an extraordinary success. "Chauvinistically pro-Juilliard," Leontyne Price felt:

> like a walking advertisement for the school. It was here that I worked with my one and only voice teacher, Florence Page Kimball, and here that I met David Garvey, who is still my accompanist. But there is more. The conductor Jean Morel gave me my first orchestral experience. I took courses in diction, literature, twentieth-century music, and staging. I know I've had the opportunity to become a better artist than I ever would have been. I'm in what one might call the "mature" phase of my career [in 1984], and one of the reasons I'm still active is the wealth of knowledge I inherited here.[20]

Mennin obtained funds from Norman Lloyd's Rockefeller Foundation for the American Opera Center. In his first year as president, the School gave the American premiere of Hindemith's *Long Christmas*

Dinner, with the composer conducting. In 1964 the AOC presented the American premiere of Henze's *Elegy for Young Lovers*, and in 1966 it gave Sessions's *The Trial of Lucullus* and Weisgall's *Purgatory*. As was the case with Albert Stoessel, early death continued to stalk Juilliard's opera directors. Christopher West died at fifty-two in 1968 and was replaced by Tito Capobianco, a thirty-six-year-old Argentinean. That year the Opera Theater gave the American premiere of Richard Rodney Bennett's *The Mines of Sulphur*. In 1970 Harold Farberman's *The Losers* was performed (Houseman directed), and the next year Hall Overton's *Huckleberry Finn*. Virgil Thomson's *Lord Byron* was also premiered. In 1982 the AOC mounted the New York premiere of Sessions's *Montezuma*.

In February 1984 the American Opera Center presented *Lady Macbeth of Mtsensk*, the first of the original score seen in New York in fifty years. Maxim Shostakovich made his U.S. operatic conducting debut with the production. The work played to capacity audiences and enthusiastic reviews. The *New York Daily News* wrote, "In all aspects it is a sensational production. Juilliard has never looked or sounded better," and Harriet Johnson of the *New York Post* called it a "riveting experience" and the production "unforgettable."[21]

⤳

Conservatories are notoriously apolitical, but the emotions surrounding the Vietnam War aroused even Juilliard students and faculty. In 1966 a few students had formed the Juilliard Student Committee to End the War in Vietnam and marched in a Fifth Avenue parade on March 26. Three years later the war had still not ended, and Richard Nixon was president. A national moratorium was proclaimed for October 15, 1969, just days after the School had moved into its new quarters at Lincoln Center. At noon the orchestra appeared outside the building and played the slow movement from the "Eroica" and the Brahms *Requiem*. Dressed in black jeans and shirts, their faces painted white, dance and drama students performed a dance of death. When they arose from the ground, all joined hands and led the crowd singing John Lennon's "Give peace a chance." The group walked to the fountain at Lincoln Center and later marched across town to the United Nations. The administration had always promoted collaboration among the divisions—and was little heeded—but such a demonstration was not what it had intended.

Dismay at the bombing of Cambodia on April 30, 1970, and the killings at Kent State on May 4 led to two events at Juilliard. In the first, several hundred students and faculty lay as dead for an hour around the fountain. The faculty included Jean Morel, Hugh Aitken, John Houseman, Jacob Druckman, Hugo Weisgall, and administrator Margot Harley. Peter Mennin had told them not to participate in the protest. According to W. McNeil Lowry, Weisgall replied, "'Fuck off, I have my own views about this, and you can't tell me' . . . and [Mennin] fired him."[22] Morel died shortly afterward, and Houseman, Druckman, Aitken, and Margot Harley were let go in the next couple of years.

The second event at Juilliard was meant to coincide with a national student strike called for May. At the New England Conservatory, for example, examinations and classes were canceled and the year-end concert was dedicated to the memory of the students shot at Kent State. On May 10 New England students gave a round-the-clock marathon concert for peace. Uptown at Juilliard's old building, the Manhattan School of Music issued a statement, "Why We Strike," which the students, faculty, and administration ratified on May 6. The school struck for a week and used the time to give a memorial concert.

Within Juilliard, pro-strike and anti-strike positions solidified. In the Drama Division, Patti LuPone and Mary Lou Rosato were anti-strike, citing disruption to their training. Others were elected to the Juilliard Student Action Committee: Louise Bernikov, Vida Deming, Puston Waddington (all academic faculty) and Hugh Aitken (L&M); music students William Henry, Dennis Russell Davies, Lee Owen, Ryan Edwards, Fred Raimy, Barney Lehrer, and Nancy Elan; drama students Beverly Ross and Kathleen Quinn; and dancers Peter Sparkling and Margery Farniola. Immediately after the shootings at Kent State, and without waiting for a vote from the students or approval from Mennin, the committee had sent a telegram to Richard Nixon, with copies to Jacob Javits, Charles Goodell, and William Fulbright:

> As human beings, artists, and students at The Juilliard School, we express horror at the brutal murders of four Kent State University students. We know the rising repression of the people of the United States is directly linked to the perpetration of an immoral war in Southeast Asia. We believe that the events of the past weeks in particular demonstrate the administration's blatant violation of the United States Constitution and their deliberate attempt to polarize the people of the United States. Juilliard students express complete solidarity with the national Student Strike.[23]

Obtaining that promised solidarity was problematic. Unlike students at the Manhattan School under George Schick or New England students under Gunther Schuller, Juilliard students had to deal with an outraged Peter Mennin.

Mennin announced that "with an alignment with an outside [political] organization, certain circumstances might very well arise that would make it impossible to continue the operation of the Juilliard School and would necessitate its closing." Although no one really believed him, the move was calculated to hit students where they lived—their devotion to their studies—and frighten them into thinking that political protest might destroy the School. After being debated by students, the issue was voted on during a meeting of the entire school in the new theater. Mennin rigged the balloting by demanding that "all ballots had to be signed, only [the] 745 currently registered students could vote, and administration will only respond if a majority votes—a majority is defined as 75 percent."[24]

Under such circumstances, it would be impossible to obtain approval by Juilliard students on any issue. They had reason to be afraid for their futures if they signed their ballots. Among the six issues defeated were whether each performing group could vote for the program, whether performances could be publicly dedicated to peace or in memory of student deaths, and whether the Student Action Committee could set up machinery for draft counseling and a student strike. The only issue approved was that major lessons would continue as usual and juries take place as scheduled.

Mennin's need to maintain power also extended to board members, who were kept at arm's length from faculty. As one recalled, "You came in and had a very nice lunch and Peter reported and you went home. It was a very controlled thing."[25]

Students were not the only ones who had grievances against authority. The faculty was trying to improve its working conditions. Salaries had not been high since the depression. One faculty member under Mennin referred to the pay as "a joke." During the 1970s, full-time faculty typically made only $12,000 a year. The lack of money for salaries and the attitude that somehow rent could be paid using only the prestige of the name "Juilliard" led to problems obtaining faculty. Many who were sought after would not teach at Juilliard because they earned far more elsewhere.

Even during the prosperous 1950s and 1960s Schuman and Mennin resisted attempts to raise salaries to a level proportionate with other college-level teachers. The Juilliard faculty earned less than half of that of a beginning college instructor. In addition, the large number of hours needed to be considered a full-time faculty member at Juilliard caused college faculty elsewhere to howl with disbelief. Those in the Pre-College Division, for example, who taught all eight class hours on Saturdays, were ineligible for health insurance because they were not considered full-time. Faculty acceptance of extremely low pay provided what the *New York Times* in 1969 called a "massive subsidy" for Juilliard.[26] As Juilliard's sources of income, the *Times* listed first the faculty's subsidy, then private patronage, and finally the JMF. "Professional music teachers are scandalously underpaid," Richard Franko Goldman, the former head of L&M and in 1970 president of the Peabody Institute, said. "They are among the biggest philanthropists in the musical world."[27]

To increase their salaries, faculty accepted guest or adjunct teaching posts outside the School. The rise of other music schools, particularly at the State University of New York at Purchase in the 1970s, worried Mennin, who tried to prevent Juilliard's faculty from teaching elsewhere. He had little leverage but tried to intimidate those who strayed. The effects were ultimately felt by students. The unspoken, underground fact was that some took lessons outside the School. Feeling their training on their major instrument was not adequate, they scraped together the money to study secretly with someone else while still paying tuition and maintaining important connections at Juilliard.

In 1971 and 1972, librarian Bennett Ludden, L&M faculty Hugh Aitken and Jacob Druckman, and others attempted to unionize the Juilliard faculty and brought in the American Association of University Professors to help. Mennin responded negatively. With the exception of the needed librarian those who participated in the unionizing attempt—the same ones involved in the protest against the Vietman War—were not given their one-year contracts for 1972. Ironically, Druckman, never asked to join the composition faculty, won the Pulitzer Prize the year he left. The year L&M faculty Lester Trimble was on the Pulitzer committee he, too, was not asked to return to Juilliard.

Judith Kogan, a harp student of Susann McDonald in 1979 and 1980, has asserted in her book that "Juilliard is the most famous music school in the world." She describes what it is like to attend:

> Juilliard is a training ground where the distinction between student and professional blurs. At times Juilliard seems less a school than a collection of people who happened to do the same thing. The students don't live together and don't work together. Anonymity is easy to come by. In some ways, Juilliard students are like commuters who meet on a train platform at the same time each morning and disperse when the train pulls in at the final stop. . . . Professional motivation is more important than artistic, the glamour of personality more important than the art of music.[28]

As Chautauqua in the 1930s and 1940s had been a kind of Juilliard summer school and orchestra, with Ernest Hutcheson acting as administrator of both, so in the 1970s and 1980s did the Aspen Music Festival function as an extension of Juilliard. Gordon Hardy, dean of students, was made dean of the Aspen Music School in 1963 and remained until 1989. Students who played in the same orchestra in the Lincoln Center building might not speak to each other there, yet in the relaxed social atmosphere of Aspen they might become friends or even marry (soprano Evelyn Lear and baritone Thomas Stewart, who married after meeting at Juilliard, were exceptions that proved the rule). Students in Aspen could study with faculty members, who might then accept them into their studios at Juilliard.

In 1971 Gordon Hardy was faced with one of the many dilemmas of his dual position. Dorothy DeLay, Ivan Galamian's assistant at the summer music retreat Meadowmount, asked Hardy if she could come to Aspen. That meant both a split with Galamian (who gallantly never mentioned the departure to Hardy) and an immediate increase of two orchestras—from three to five—for the Aspen Music Festival. Hardy made sure that all Juilliard students had their teachers' permissions to study at Aspen. DeLay's reputation as a violin teacher rested in part on the success of students such as Itzhak Perlman, Nadja Salerno-Sonnenberg, Robert McDuffie, Schlomo Mintz, Cho-Liang Lin, Mark Kaplan, and many other fine soloists and orchestral players. For decades she has been considered an institution at both Juilliard and the Aspen Music School. She also teaches at Cincinnati College-Conservatory despite the current administration's desire that she teach exclusively at Juilliard.

To Peter Mennin, Aspen seemed to be operating out of Juilliard's Room 222 (Hardy's office) rather than out of its New York office a few blocks down Broadway. Despite the fact that Hardy had been one of the first L&M students, an L&M faculty member, the author of the two L&M anthologies, and a popular dean, by the mid-1970s he had left the School. Students no longer had the generous Hardy, whose eyes would crinkle into slits when he smiled, to turn to. Meanwhile, the imperious Judson Ehrbar, the registrar, sustained a power out of proportion to his title. Not even Hardy had contradicted Ehrbar's edicts. The well-liked Mary Smith, who had replaced Hardy, eventually replaced Ehrbar. Hardy helped choose Mennin as composer-in-residence in Aspen for the summer of 1983, a residency Mennin would not be able to fulfill.

Gideon Waldrop has described the acquisition of one piano faculty member:

> Rosina Lhevinne's mind was active. I played bridge with Rosina. You [normally] pick up your hand and sort it. She didn't have to sort her hand. And after the bidding she knew everything that everybody had anyway—incredible mind. [Nevertheless] we felt that someone [else]

of great stature should be brought in. We researched, and discovered there was a woman in London who American students were flocking to; even Juilliard graduates had withdrawn and gone with her.

Peter went over and met Ilona Kabos. At first she was not interested in living in New York. Finally he convinced her; and she came in 1965. Along with Lhevinne, there was Gorodnitzky, Steuermann, Dorfmann, Marcus, a stellar piano faculty. At first there was a little bit of jealousy. Kabos brought something to the School that I so appreciate; it was somewhat rare. Lhevinne would send her students for a lesson with other teacher/scholars. From the very beginning Rosina Lhevinne and Kabos hit it off; they started exchanging students. You know there were members of the piano faculty who would never allow a student to be heard by another teacher, except at competitions or exams. It helped me when students wanted to change teachers. I met once with the entire piano faculty and called to their attention the arrangement that Kabos and Lhevinne had. I didn't make too much headway; they were still not impressed with that idea. It's a very healthy thing, though—two brilliant minds are better than one brilliant mind.[29]

Robin McCabe described studying with Ilona Kabos:

She was Hungarian, and an excellent teacher, though she was extremely tempestuous. She used to scream at me—lots of Hungarian histrionics—but she was good for me. She liked my playing but felt I needed more chutzpah—needed to come out more. She pushed me quite a bit. . . . We fought like cats and dogs—she wanted to throw me out of her class. For the first two years, it was sheer torture, though I have to admit she really pulled me together—especially the third year I studied with her. No matter how stormy she was, she would always say things for the benefit of the student, not to show off. Sometimes there was the element of her being the queen, but she always tried to extract from me what was there to extract. Through it all, I learned a great deal from her.[30]

Kogan vividly describes the relationship between teachers and students:

Some teachers behave like army generals. They treat their students as soldiers and other classes as enemy camps. They guard their artistic advice as if it were war secrets. The student who dares to defect to another camp risks vindictiveness: his departure is often seen as an ad hominem attack on his teacher.

The teacher and the student work together behind heavy red doors one hour a week. The teacher sits and listens, coaches and demonstrates. What he neither says nor shows the student expects to absorb from his presence. The student spends the rest of the week in the practice room, the voice of his teacher echoing in his memory.

The teacher and the student communicate in music. It is a language more powerful than words. It says nothing, but says everything. It comes straight from the heart and cuts straight to the bone.

The result of all of this is that relationships between the teachers and the students are filled with the tension and gratitude of the most troubled relationships between children and their parents and with the love and hate of the most tempestuous love affairs.[31]

Some of the tension involved in teaching music is part of Terrence McNally's Broadway play *Master Class* (1995), which uses Maria Callas's classes at Juilliard as its focus (the classes, held in 1971 and entitled "The Lyric Tradition," were documented by John Ardoin).[32] Zoe Caldwell originated the role of Callas, and Robert Whitehead produced *Master Class*. The Tony award–winning play's connection to Juilliard went further when former opera student Audra McDonald acknowledged the School in her Best Supporting Actress acceptance speech for teaching her about nervousness. In yet another tie to Juilliard, in June 1996 the Callas role was taken by Patti LuPone.

Ania Dorfmann (1900–1984) taught at Juilliard from 1966 until her death. In 1929 the Russian pianist had been the first female soloist to appear under Toscanini, and she taught many distinguished pianists. Of her, McCabe said:

In many ways, Mme. Dorfmann is an enigma to me—I suspect we get along because my ego is stronger now. She tends to exaggerate when she criticizes, and if you keep that in mind it's fine. She has such an ear, and was a great performer. Now she's teaching instead of playing, and I have a lot of empathy with her. Of course she can't help living vicariously through her pupils' playing, and the result is that she's very demanding and hard to please. But she has helped me a lot with sound. I think about sound, and sound production, in a different way because of her. She's such a tremendous person, and when she is at her best there is no one equal to her. But you have to catch her in the right mood.[33]

Memorable master classes included those by Herbert Von Karajan in November 1976, Georg Solti in April 1980, and Luciano Pavarotti in January 1979, although television cameras at the Pavarotti class provoked a negative reaction against the hype associated with the event. At Mennin's suggestion that, under Pavarotti, the Juilliard Theater would turn into a classroom for a while, the *Times* hooted: "He must have been joking . . . to suggest that it has anything to do with serious teaching would have been misleading in the extreme."[34] Yet the Solti and Bernstein rehearsals with conductors in orchestral rehearsal Room 309 produced genuine musical results and invaluable experience for the conducting students.

The move to Lincoln Center was so expensive that during the late 1960s and early 1970s the School ran deficits for the first time. Drye's prediction that Juilliard, once moved, would be "broke" was coming true. In 1967, however, Mennin made a study of tuition fees at other schools and, possibly foreseeing the expense of Lincoln Center, recommended an across-the-board increase of 20 percent. Yearly tuition for a degree would be $1,550 and for a diploma, $1,375. Despite Mennin's fierce individualism and initial suspicion of the new National Endowment for the Arts, he rapidly converted. Henry Allen Moe, chair of the NEA, was invited to give the 1966 commencement address, as was Roger L. Stevens, Moe's successor, the following year.

The board thought highly of Mennin's fund-raising abilities. Their

Juilliard piano faculty, 1971. *Front row:* Katherine Bacon, Adele Marcus, Rosina Lhevinne, Ania Dorfmann, and Ilona Kabos. *Second row:* Mieczyslaw Munz, Sascha Gorodnitzki, Gideon Waldrop, Jacob Lateiner, Peter Mennin, Joseph Raieff, Irwin Freundlich, and Beveridge Webster.

(© Heinz H. Weissenstein/Whitestone Photo. All rights reserved, photo from The Juilliard School Archives)

suggestions to contact successful drama alumni for contributions, how-ever, were met with dismissals. Mennin thought the sums too small. He was after bigger fish. An application for $7 million intended to wipe out the operating deficit of $1.5 million went to the Ford Foundation in 1971. At the foundation, however, Lowry's terms were much stiffer than those applied to institutions not allied to Lincoln Center. The funds were granted but had to be matched three-to-one by 1975. When in 1980, after several extensions, the goal of $36 million was raised, it rep-resented a major financial turning point for the School.

Juilliard's relationship with the Metropolitan Opera, dicey in the past (chapters 4 and 9), entered a new, ambiguous, and competitive stage. One of Juilliard's primary contributors was Lila Acheson Wallace, wife of the founder of *Reader's Digest*.[35] Wallace's proposed $1 million gift to the Met in 1966 had been turned down by Rudolf Bing, who objected to the idea of a Metropolitan National Company.[36] Mennin, too, had a history with the Met and on three occasions was asked to become its artistic director: before 1971, at the announcement of Goeran Gentele's death in a car crash in July 1972, and in January of 1983.[37] In 1973 Harold Schonberg, the *Times* critic, accused Juilliard of being uncoop-erative with the Met over using the Juilliard Theater for their Minimet project.[38] Wallace's money would follow him if he accepted the prof-fered post of general director of the Metropolitan Opera. A possible reason for Mennin not accepting may have been that he wanted the funds to go to Juilliard. Wallace's personal loyalty to Mennin was such that none of her money went to Juilliard after Mennin died.

Wallace gave, in increments of $1 and $.5 million, a total of $11 mil-lion to Juilliard. A preacher's daughter, she also liked alcoholic bever-ages with lunch. Mennin would return from such meals slightly inebri-ated and hand the dean a check for a million dollars. The spacious Lila Acheson Wallace Library at Juilliard was partly funded by one such gift. It has been headed in succession by Bennet Ludden, Brinton Jackson, and Jane Gottlieb. Mennin did not want turnstiles in the library because he was sure that the scores would not be stolen. He was sadly mistaken, and turnstiles had to be installed.

At any large arts organization, fund-raising during the 1980s and 1990s became a business, an organized effort no longer dependent on four or five major donors such as Lila Wallace or Alice Tully. Juilliard's 1997 endowment of $305 million represented capital and interest, of which the School was allowed to spend only 5 percent of the interest. Nearly 40 percent of income came from tuition; 65 percent of students in 1997 received some kind of scholarship.

Irving Berlin was another benefactor. In 1950 he gave the school a scholarship that would ensure that composers could study in a way he had not been able to. Juilliard and various Jewish charities became Berlin's major philanthropic outlets, and from 1967 until his death in 1989 he donated to the school annually. The Irving Berlin Fellowships total $760,500 and were given in memory of Judy Garland, Bing Crosby, Fanny Brice, Cole Porter, Oscar Hammerstein, Richard Rodgers, George and Ira Gershwin, Duke Ellington, and Fred Astaire. Berlin's daughter, writer Mary Ellin Barrett, is a board member.

Not only did Peter Mennin save Juilliard from financial distress, but he also rescued at least one faculty member facing divorce in the same manner. "Peter Mennin saved my life," declared pianist Olegna Fuschi.[39] In 1969 Lincoln Center forced Juilliard to abandon its Preparatory Department to the Manhattan School. Once again, Mennin was able to reverse Lincoln Center's dictates, however; he reconstituted the Preparatory Department as the Pre-College Division and hired Fuschi to direct it.

As director of the successful Pre-College Division, Fuschi could be extraordinarily personal. She would tell parents concentrating too much attention on an only child to have more children, for example. Pre-College parents are a breed unto themselves. Although a sign is posted at the second-floor elevators that NO PARENTS ALLOWED ABOVE THE SEC-OND FLOOR, parents routinely ignore it and approach faculty on the fifth floor before classes and lessons. The Pre-College Division has four ensembles, including a contemporary orchestra. Roger Nierenberg and Myung-Whun Chung were two of the conductors of the Pre-College Orchestra, which rivaled those of the Regular Division. Fuschi wanted a diploma for Pre-College graduates, Mennin said "Why not?" and in 1979 the first Pre-College commencement was celebrated. "Peter Mennin gave me carte blanche." After she had given Mennin a bottle of wine at the 1983 faculty luncheon after commencement and praised him as a composer, an administrator, and a good friend, he replied, "Thank you for what you've done for Juilliard." The response surprised Gideon Waldrop: "He said that to you! He never said anything that nice to me!"

In some ways, Pre-College Division students did as well as those in the Regular Division. Charles Kim was twelve, for example, when he played Sarasate's *Introduction and Tarantella* with Zubin Mehta as part of a New York Philharmonic Young People's Concert. He later gave up a career in music and pursued a MBA at Harvard University. Another DeLay student, Mi Dori (later, Midori), at age ten performed Paganini's Violin Concerto No. 1 with the Philharmonic.

During the 1970s L&M was still the theory program at Juilliard. "You heard different stories about L&M philosophically if you talked to Peter, or to Vincent Persichetti," Waldrop remembers. "Persichetti and Peter Mennin agreed on one thing: It is better to use the music itself rather than theory books. The philosophy is golden. It takes a Vincent Persichetti, a David Diamond, a Peter Mennin to teach it—it takes almost a genius to handle it. And the best of them was Persichetti."[40]

L&M faculty member Michael White had studied with both Vincent Persichetti and Peter Mennin and found Mennin to be a good private teacher, demanding and knowledgeable, but not as good in the classroom. Because he had worked at various teaching positions elsewhere, White was able to see the influence of L&M throughout the country.[41] During the 1960s at Oberlin College, for example, it was called Theory and Literature (T&L). The University of Washington in Seattle's curriculum in the early 1960s was based on L&M and, like many schools, used *Fundamentals of Sight Singing and Ear Training* by Arnold Fish and Norman Lloyd, by then a standard ear-training text. When Vittorio Giannini founded the North Carolina School of the Arts, he and a subsequent dean, Larry Smith, modeled their theory program on L&M. Because of Gordon Hardy's position at the Aspen Music School and Michael Czajkowski and Jorge Mester's presence on that faculty, Aspen, too, was close to the Juilliard L&M program, which was also used at the Philadelphia Musical Academy.

The L&M philosophy, which has not been uniformly followed at Juilliard itself, has incorporated three ideas: first, to focus on the literature of music rather than exercises from a text; second, to compose (although that has not been adhered to); and, third, to emphasize live music in class. Since the mid-1990s four concerts a semester have been added to L&M. First-year L&M students each lecture once, and one of the three required recitals for a D.M.A. degree must now be a lecture-recital. It is not difficult to encourage students to play in front of each other, but it has sometimes been problematic to persuade some to speak publicly.

Another attempt at Juilliard to influence national music education was aimed at primary and secondary schools. A $308,000 grant from the U.S. Office of Education marked the inception of the Juilliard Repertory Library, a compilation of 230 vocal pieces and 52 instrumental works, begun in 1964 and published in 1970. Originally Giannini headed the project, and then Gordon Hardy and Arnold Fish took it over.

For two and a half years, members of the library project searched for material from every period of music history. To find music that was appropriate, six scholars and musicians—specialists in their respective areas—were appointed as consultants: Gustave Reese for early music,

Noah Greenberg for Renaissance, Claude V. Palisca for Baroque, Paul Henry Lang for classical, Alfred Wallenstein for Romantic, and Norman Dello Joio for contemporary music. Three music educators advised them. What resulted was the anthology known as the Juilliard Repertory Library, which attempts to provide a wider collection of good music from which teachers may choose rather than a curriculum that must be imposed. The effort represented the first collaboration among educators, composers, performers, and music historians to provide an anthology for elementary schools.

By the end of the 1960s, Peter Mennin could boast that "eighty-five percent of all the major contests are won by Juilliard students."[42] In 1983, for example, four of the five recipients of the first Avery Fisher Career Grants were Juilliard-trained. In 1984 four other Juilliard students won Avery Fisher Grants. Juilliard pianists took the three top prizes in the Ninth International Piano Competition held in Chile the same year. All four pianists who won appointments to participate in the Xerox Pianists Program for 1983 were Juilliard students, and the International American Music Competition was won several times by Juilliard students, as was the Naumberg Competition.

"The real solid growth of the name Juilliard, internationally renowned, comes in my opinion from the Mennin years, and I'm delighted to have had a small hand in this," remarked Gideon Waldrop. He also said that if indeed he was a good administrator, it was because he had watched Mark Schubart and copied him. As to the source of Juilliard's reputation, Waldrop observed that it was a matter of "style. Peter Mennin was so opposed to anything that was not in good taste. About advertising Mennin said, 'Word of mouth is the best advertising.' He did not want to see the School advertised along with everybody else."[43] Mennin, an elitist, was perfectly content to let the School remain banished from the NASM.

Because Juilliard had no retirement age, its faculty often taught until the ends of their lives. Seventy-eight-year-old Ivan Galamian died in April 1981 after being part of Juilliard's violin faculty for thirty-five years. His students included Itzhak Perlman, Pinchas Zukerman, Kyung-Wha Chung, James Buswell, Michael Rabin, Glen Dicterow, Earl Carlyss, Jaime Laredo, and Erick Freidman. At a tribute to Galamian, who had no children of his own, Mennin said, "In dedicating his life to the teaching profession, he became a legend in his own time. His greatest joy, which even he could not disguise, was when his students began to receive the musical recognition he felt they deserved. He was like a father with many children with whom he continued to be concerned, long after they were making an artistic life of their own."[44]

The esteem in which his colleagues and students held 'cellist Leonard Rose was evidenced in a memorial at Juilliard in which Isaac Stern, Itzhak Perlman, Lynn Harrell, Yo-Yo Ma, and Eugene Istomin performed. Rose (1918–84) had taught at the School since 1947. Other considerable losses during 1984 were Ania Dorfmann and Edith Skinner, an original speech faculty member in the Drama Division.

The Juilliard Orchestra traveled abroad during the fall of 1983 for the first time since the 1958 orchestra tour and visited thirteen cities in Germany, Austria, and Italy, playing under Jorge Mester. Nadja Salerno-Sonnenberg, Jon Kimura Parker, and Joseph Swensen were the soloists. Before the orchestra's departure, alumni of the 1958 orchestra tour joined it for an after-dress-rehearsal party, and both groups listened to tapes of the 1958 concerts. During the summer of 1982, a chamber orchestra conducted by José Serebrier had given seventeen concerts in eleven countries in South America. During the 1990s, the orchestra and chamber symphonies traveled abroad for tours of Japan and elsewhere.

∿

A loner, Peter Mennin relished power to such a degree that he kept his terminal pancreatic cancer a secret, foregoing the companionship, sympathy, and solicitude of friends such as Vincent Persichetti and others at Juilliard. He did not even tell his widowed mother that doctors had given him only a 2 percent chance of survival. The sealed letters of explanation he wrote to her and others were not to be opened until after his death.

Students, faculty, and the administration were therefore completely unprepared and considerably shocked to learn from the newspapers of Peter Mennin's death on June 17, 1983, at the age of sixty. The *New York Times* published a lengthy obituary, and *Time* magazine recorded the death in its "Milestones" column.[45] Damrosch, Hutcheson, and Erskine had all retired when they thought the time was right, and Schuman used the presidency of Juilliard as a stepping stone to a more glamorous and powerful job. Only Mennin died in office, "with his boots on." Within hours of his death, recorded performances of his works were broadcast on classical music stations in New York and across the country. Georganne Mennin received over a thousand letters of condolence.

That summer Mennin was to have been a composer-in-residence in Aspen. Now those concerts would become memorials. The Music Festival published a profile in Mennin's own words:

> I can't stand labels. Think of the composers whose music forms the basis of our standard symphonic repertoire. Some of them, in their

day, were conservatives. Others, in their time, were considered wild radicals. If you label things, you are fooled by emphasizing external technical matters rather than content and meaning. Music history is full of the errors of premature labeling.

I am concerned with having an unassailable technique.

It is the total artistic statement that is of paramount importance, not the working process; it is what the music truly is, not what it is not or would like to be, that is of genuine value. With the passage of time, all that really counts is the final musical result. To the committed composer, all other matters are peripheral.[46]

Mennin had presided over many sad memorials for faculty, and now it was his turn to be memorialized. Gideon Waldrop, Peter S. Paine (chair of the board), Vincent Persichetti, Martha Hill, and Michael Langham all spoke at the service in the Juilliard Theater on October 25, and the Juilliard Orchestra, conducted by Jorge Mester, performed the Adagio Arioso movement from Mennin's Symphony No. 9.

A second blow to the administration came a few months later, in March 1984, when Wriston Locklair, assistant to Mennin and head of press relations since 1970, died of a heart attack while standing on a subway platform. The former critic was invaluable to Waldrop, who had been made acting president of Juilliard for 1983–84. Gideon Waldrop was left alone to administer the School. A pivotal era in Juilliard's history, stamped with an indelible imprint of Peter Mennin's personality, had come to a close.

I I

Juilliard in the Postmodern World:

JOSEPH POLISI

WHEN PETER MENNIN died, Ronald Reagan was president and a prosperity not unlike that of the 1920s reigned. Its most significant financial aspect for Juilliard would concern the New York City real estate market, which skyrocketed in price during the mid- and late-1980s. The job market for performing artists, however, was still difficult.

The search for a new Juilliard president was conducted by a committee of faculty, alumni, and friends of Juilliard assisted by a board committee led by Ralph Leach. The logical candidate for president from the point of view of many faculty was Vincent Persichetti. Like Schuman and Mennin, he had a considerable reputation as a composer. But Persichetti, who had spent almost forty years teaching at Juilliard, was not interested in becoming president. Robert Mann also eliminated himself, but Joseph Fuchs, nearly eighty, wanted the job. Once Persichetti was out of the running, there seemed to be no obvious second choice. The board passed over Gideon Waldrop despite support for him. Well over one hundred people applied, and the committee interviewed about forty of them, sometimes more than once. The interviewing continued until late spring of 1984.

The long list was whittled down to three candidates. The board offered the job to Phyllis Curtin, who had left Boston University for Yale. She turned Juilliard down. Curtin and William Schuman together pushed for their own candidate, described by W. McNeil Lowry: "Schuman used Mrs. John Rockefeller, 3rd, the widow of Johnny, thinking that that would have clout—and it did—and they pushed like hell for [Joseph W.] Polisi, at Schuman's say-so, because Schuman knew he could control Polisi. He also knew that Polisi would have a kind of revisionist treatment of Schuman's role."[1]

Polisi's father, William Polisi, was an internationally known bassoonist who had taught at Juilliard from 1951 until his retirement in 1982. His mother, Pauline Kaye, was a dancer at Radio City Music Hall. William Polisi had attended the Curtis Institute and joined the Cleveland Orchestra and in 1937 the NBC Symphony under Arturo Toscanini. In 1943 he joined the New York Philharmonic, where he was principal bassoonist until 1958. Also a member of the Metropolitan Opera Orchestra, Polisi manufactured the Polisi bassoon and published the Polisi bassoon chart. Although Polisi did not pressure Joseph to become a musician, "It just naturally happened," his son recalled, "since I had a very close association with my father, in that he was my primary teacher and a good friend."[2] Joseph's views of Juilliard were influenced by his father and by friends who had attended, especially Michael Kamen, an oboist and future Hollywood composer.[3]

Polisi, born December 30, 1947, also played bassoon. He had studied music at Flushing High School in New York City, which he described as having "a fantastic music program in the late fifties and early sixties."[4] That background was to influence him as president to reach out to New York City schools.

Polisi's first course of study in college was not music, however. He earned a bachelor's degree in political science from the University of Connecticut (and spent his junior year at the Paris Conservatory, studying bassoon with Maurice Allard) and a master's degree in international relations from Tufts University. At the Fletcher School of Law and Diplomacy at Tufts he learned the philosophy of conflict resolution and that arguing a point is useless unless the argument is carefully thought out and based on facts. Polisi thought seriously of entering the foreign service, but he missed music. Therefore, in 1971 he entered Yale and earned an M.M. and, in 1980, a D.M.A. He married Elizabeth Marlowe, a high school French teacher, and, in the tradition of all Juilliard presidents, the couple had two children. A third was born while Polisi was president.

Polisi's first taste of administration came as Yale's director of alumni affairs from 1976 to 1978. In 1978 he met William Schuman, who had come to Yale for a composers' conference. After he received his doctorate, Polisi was hired as dean of the faculty at the Manhattan School of Music, where he was well regarded by some of the faculty but castigated by others for having fired venerable older faculty. Although he had given Manhattan a longer commitment than the three years he stayed there, Polisi left for what seemed a better offer—to be dean of the Cincinnati College–Conservatory. There he served only one year of a multiple-year contract. Peter S. Paine and the trustees of Juilliard negotiated with the Cincinnati school to obtain Polisi's release.

William Schuman had risen like a phoenix with regard to Juilliard's fortunes. Board members may have asked his advice, but more likely he saw a chance to ingratiate himself back into control of Juilliard now that Peter Mennin was no longer alive. Frances Schuman recalls her husband being a father figure to Polisi during the difficult spring of 1984. William Polisi, nearly the same age as Schuman, had died on February 16 while the Juilliard board was deliberating.

To the great surprise of many at Juilliard, Schuman, after twenty-two years away from the School, was apparently again calling the shots, this time through his young protégé. He began using the title "president emeritus," never previously used in Juilliard publications. Those same publications now referred to Schuman—not quite impartially—as "the dean of American composers."[5] Polisi, with little professional standing of his own as a musician, leaned on Schuman's reputation.

Polisi told the New Haven *Register*, "Though you never know precisely why you were chosen, I think it was because the ideas I was talk-

Joseph Polisi.
(Christian Steiner, photo from The Juilliard School)

ing about related not only to the future of Juilliard but to the future of arts training in the United States and the world." He articulated what would become the theme of his administration: "You can create programs that broaden an individuals' view of life. I think you have to look at the entire human being and I believe that there's a definite relationship between being well educated and being a success in any field."[6] He wanted to instill in students "an entrepreneurial spirit." Polisi addressed freshman: "I urge you to understand that this is the time when you will have the most freedom to explore the world. Do not take a narrow view of life but look out beyond the practice room and delve into the extraordinary beauty of the world." He spoke of creating a "literate artist" and honing "intellectual skills."

With statements like these, Polisi differentiated himself from his predecessor, who would never have identified such goals. Polisi reflected Erskine's generalist attitudes as opposed to Damrosch's or Hutcheson's specializing approach to music. He even cited Erskine's plans to decentralize music. He subscribed to Schuman's version of Juilliard's history: "Under William Schuman, Juilliard became a name which symbolized excellence in musical training." Mennin and Waldrop regarded Juilliard's reputation as having increased under their tenure, although the IMA and Juilliard had significant reputations before the advent of either Schuman or Mennin.

An orchestra concert on October 12, 1984, in Avery Fisher Hall, already scheduled by Mennin, was the first time Juilliard performed in there since 1962. The concert was to include Barber's Violin Concerto played by Robert McDuffie. If any further proof were needed that Schuman was in control, it came with the news that the concerto would now be the Schuman Violin Concerto (still with McDuffie). Polisi's experience as alumni director at Yale was exerting itself; the occasion had been labeled "Reunion Day." Mary Smith was in charge of alumni relations and of the event, which included a dinner for more than seven hundred. Alumni were invited to the concert and a large reception that followed. Schuman was honorary chair, Leontyne Price was chair, and Van Cliburn, Patti LuPone, and Paul Taylor were co-chairs. A glance through the long committee lists revealed that many former faculty had come in from the cold. Gordon Hardy, Hugh Aitken, and Jacob Druckman were among those welcomed back to Juilliard. Juilliard T-shirts were even sold. Peter Mennin would have blanched at the thought.

Reunion Day was repeated the next year, in October 1985, to coincide with the School's eightieth birthday. The event was marked by "Juilliard at Eighty," a two-hour television program of performances that was broadcast on PBS's *Live from Lincoln Center* series. The co-hosts were former students Kelly McGillis and John Rubinstein. Leontyne Price sang from *Antony and Cleopatra*, the Dance Division presented Paul Taylor's *Cloven Kingdom*, the Juilliard String Quartet along with two students performed Brahms, and the Drama Division presented Brecht's *The Resistible Rise of Arturo Ui*. The celebration drew congratulations from Ronald and Nancy Reagan, Mario Cuomo, and Edward I. Koch.

Polisi also organized regional reunions, the first time in decades that alumni had been invited to anything connected with Juilliard. Alumni had felt cut adrift by Schuman and Mennin. Polisi had another motive for the invitations as well: fund-raising.

During the 1985–86 school year, 907 students were enrolled in the Regular Division, 52 percent were male and 48 percent female; there were also 69 Drama Division students and 71 who studied dance. Among the 767 Music Division students, 284 majored in strings (150 in violin) and 206 studied piano. Nine students planned to be choral conductors, six studied to become orchestral conductors, and thirty-three were composers. The Pre-College Division had 312 students, and the Extension Division, to be renamed the Evening Division, 345.

Also during 1985–86, Jerome L. Greene gave Juilliard $1 million for much-needed scholarships—the first major endowed fund to support training in all three divisions. In 1992 Irene Diamond topped that with the largest donation in the history of the School: $10 million for student scholarships and faculty salaries. Diamond's money supported minority student recruitment as well as the Music Advancement Program. In addition, a foundation she financed is the largest private supporter of AIDS research in the United States. An inversion in power had occurred. Mennin had found the money to accomplish his goals, and the board followed him. Polisi had a larger board to work with and found himself implementing its goals.

Like most of his predecessors, Polisi wanted to reform the curriculum, a process he compared to moving a graveyard and concluded:

> It has often been stated that "to the degree that we fail to listen, we fail to learn." If we do not confront the problems of today's world, we may make the mistake of correcting yesterday's ills. We must strive to be visionary, yet practical; to be clearly focused in our goals, yet compassionate in our approach. We must protect that which now exists and view change within the context of continuity of the great traditions for which Juilliard has been known since its inception. We must also function as a community, in a climate of consultation and mutual respect.[7]

Between 1980 and 1997 educational institutions and conservatories saw a 123 percent increase in the numbers of administrators, departments, secretaries, and technical support people.[8] That reflected corporate America's trend of employing more middle managers. The multiplication of administrators may be compared with the enlargement of theater administrative and backstage areas during the 1960s. Designing for the same seating capacity, architects needed to increase technical and support space considerably. As at summer music festivals—Aspen, for example—the number of students at Juilliard remained the same or even decreased (Polisi used the word *downsizing*), whereas the number of administrators jumped. Polisi explained the increase:

> Over the past ten years, not just at Juilliard but around the country, more and more responsibilities have been showing up at the doorstep of institutions in terms of support for students. That's pretty wide-ranging support: psychological services, health services, physical therapy issues, social issues, multi-cultural issues, academic issues, outreach issues, you name it. It's really the changing role of an educational institution that now one looks to an educational institution to provide an enormous number of support services that are no longer tangential to the basic mission of the school.[9]

Despite expressing qualms about what the computer age might mean to music, Polisi brought Juilliard out of the dark ages by computerizing its offices. Under Mennin, Juilliard may have been the only school in the country whose registration and transcripts were not computerized. The library relied on a card catalog until the spring of 1995.

Polisi wanted a clean sweep. He asked for Gideon Waldrop's resignation as dean. Waldrop had other alternatives, however. Both the Manhattan School of Music and the Curtis Institute sought him for president. Deciding in part on the basis of retaining his Riverside Drive penthouse—apartments are a New Yorker's classic reason for major decisions—he chose Manhattan, which he headed for three years. "I'm not saying that the current administration is wrong," he has said. "Juilliard is more like Yale than it used to be. You can say students are better educated. But if you look at what's happening with the big, big talents—at least if you can go by competitions—it doesn't happen anymore. Maybe it's better to have better-educated artists, rather than robots."[10]

According to the 1989–90 catalog, the new academic courses provided undergraduates with "the general humanistic learning they need to fulfill their roles as artists and interpreters of art. It strives to help them conduct their careers and their lives with intelligence and versatility. In the first two years of this curriculum students take a series of seminars in which they read and discuss classics of our civilization bearing on such topics as ethics and human nature, society and politics, art and imagination. The classes are small. Everyone is encouraged to participate in the lively, thought-provoking discussions. Later elective courses are more specialized but are imaginatively interdisciplinary and unique to Juilliard." The program was headed by an academic, James Sloan Allen, who later became dean.[11]

The faculty, who resented being dictated to by a non-musician, succeeded in having violinist Stephen Clapp installed as dean. Clapp, who had taught violin at the School since 1987, had been dean of the Aspen Music Festival and acting dean of the Oberlin Conservatory. He had begun teaching in the Preparatory Department at Juilliard in 1962 while earning his master's degree and had studied with Dorothy DeLay and Ivan Galamian. A respected chamber musician and concertmaster, Clapp possessed the musical skills to satisfy the faculty. He became the only Juilliard dean who had been a student at the School and the only dean to teach an instrument. He viewed his mission as training students to use their talents more effectively to prepare them for the world of the future.[12]

New music flourished at Juilliard. Three members of the composition faculty, Vincent Persichetti, Milton Babbitt, and David Diamond, turned seventy during 1985, and the Juilliard Orchestra scheduled performances of a major work by each composer. The ease and logic by which that occurred contrasted sharply with the difficulty Roger Sessions's students encountered trying to convince Peter Mennin to celebrate his eightieth birthday in 1976 with a piece on an orchestra concert. Mennin had argued that the School could not recognize Sessions in this manner because there would then have to be concerts for other faculty birthdays. None of the students saw that as a problem, and they succeeded in persuading Juilliard to give the New York premiere of Sessions's Sixth Symphony. Under Polisi, the Opera Center performed *The Mighty Casey* and *A Question of Taste* in December 1990 as an eightieth birthday present for Schuman.

Persichetti still held the composition department together. L&M faculty Michael White surveyed his encyclopedic knowledge of repertoire and his teaching:

> Fifteen years after her graduation, one former student remembered a
> class when Vincent was explaining the concept of *hemiola*. In the
> course of convincing the student[s] to "use their ears," he kept run-

Vincent Persichetti

ning back and forth to the piano. (She emphasized the word "running" with the same look of amazement on her face that she must have worn in 1975.) "I wrote down all the works he played: a Brahms Intermezzo, a Courante of Bach, a movement from *La Mer*, a Scarlatti sonata, and another short work of Brahms. My god, he didn't just play a few bars here and there, he did a whole section—talking, singing, and bouncing over to the blackboard all the while!" She paused a moment, thinking back to that afternoon. "All the students in that class looked at their neighbors, mouths open, thinking, 'does this guy know the entire repertoire by heart?'"

. . . Everything he spoke about or played had one purpose: to help the students make essential aural connections to what would otherwise be just intellectual concepts. Anybody could look up the definition of *hemiola* in the *Harvard Dictionary*—but, would they really understand? "You can look at music, talk about music, and read about music until the Second Coming," he'd say, "but if you don't have it in your ears, you'll never *get* it." . . . Vincent believed in the 'time-bomb effect' when it came to teaching and learning. He knew that if you piqued students' curiosities and senses of wonder (as opposed to filling their head with facts), students would be encouraged to seek knowledge on their own. This would not happen immediately, the pressures of conservatory life being what they are, but he knew that it would happen eventually. His humility would not allow him to recall praise received, but generations of teaching assistants could testify to the comments of former students, such as, "Thank you, Mr. Persichetti, for helping me to understand," or "Thank you for teaching me how to listen," or, simply, "Thank you."[13]

Persichetti's reputation was so high, and the demand to enroll in his always-filled classes so great, that students wanting his section of L&M began a line for registration at 5 A.M. His death from cancer in August 1987 cast a pall of gloom over the entire school.

Sessions had retired in 1983 and died in 1985, Elliott Carter had left the School, and Persichetti died. By the mid-1980s only Babbitt and Diamond were left from the golden age of composition at Juilliard. Diamond repeatedly spoke of retiring but did not do so until 1997. The new administration scrambled to rebuild the department. The first replacement was Leon Kirchner, who claimed that before his death Peter Mennin had promised him the job. He lasted only a year. Bernard Rands taught for a short while but could earn a great deal more at Boston University and later Harvard. Stephen Albert taught only three years before he was killed in an automobile accident in 1992. The administration asked major composers in the United States and abroad, but Juilliard's low salaries presented a problem.

Many prominent composers declined. Others, John Corigliano (in 1991), David Del Tredici (in 1994), and Robert Beaser (in 1994), accepted. Alumna Ellen Taaffe Zwilich, the first female composer to receive a doctorate from Juilliard, would not commit herself to weekly lessons but agreed to give occasional master classes. In short order Zwilich and Del Tredici left and were replaced by Samuel Adler and Christopher Rouse. The camaraderie of the previous five-member composition faculty dissolved with these changes. Rather than take a single audition, applicants were even burdened with four separate interviews because the faculty could not get along well enough to be seated in the same room.

One of Polisi's first acts was to fire the entire academic department, many of whom had excellent credentials (Guggenheim Fellowships, for example) and had loyally toiled under Mennin in something approaching total obscurity. Students—especially drama students—had frequently complained about having to take academic courses. The academic faculty had suffered at the very bottom of the faculty heap, were paid even less than the others, and were pressured not to give assignments that would mean work outside of class and interference with practicing. Loyalty to their profession and enduring the Mennin years were repaid by being replaced by higher-paid teachers. The department was renamed the "liberal arts department" and directed to make the curriculum relevant to performers. Liberal arts became based on the Socratic method and on the Great Books.

The second department—after academics—to feel the threat of change was L&M, which Polisi decided had been a shambles during the

1960s when his friends had attended Juilliard. Peter Mennin had brought in Michael White to reorganize L&M and make it coherent, and Polisi (and probably Schuman) was determined to revamp it. For two difficult years the L&M faculty fought to hang onto their jobs. Alumni applicants to head L&M were disqualified by an administration that saw them as part of the Juilliard problem they were determined to fix. After a nationwide search for an L&M chair closed without the administration's choosing a candidate, the dean called Richard Hervig, who had taught composition at the University of Iowa, and persuaded him to take the job. Part of his duties involved firing members of the existing faculty. Forming an almost instant solidarity with his new colleagues, Hervig refused.

In 1992 yet another thrust to renovate L&M took place, with Edward Bilous in charge. In part that meant returning to the original concept of Wednesday one o'clock concerts—performance as part of the L&M curriculum. Another change concerned the addition of the first and only woman to teach L&M in the history of the department—Michelle DiBucci. The third and fourth year were to be turned into one-semester modules on Bach, on nineteenth-century music, and one on each half of the twentieth century.[14]

Erskine's idea of a Juilliard outreach had recurred during the early 1960s. Part of Lincoln Center's goal was to stimulate the community's young people with presentations of classical music. Mark Schubart was in charge of the Lincoln Center student program, which within three months in 1961 had reached eighty schools in the metropolitan area. During 1962 and 1963, thirty Juilliard students visited more than a hundred high schools and performed during assembly periods. By the mid-1970s, Juilliard students had given 350 performances at 150 schools annually.

The Dance Department's contribution, added in 1964—choreographies by faculty especially designed for high school students—was so successful that an alumni dance group was formed to meet the booking demands. Dino Anagnot, a master's student of Abraham Kaplan in choral conducting, directed the Juilliard Madrigal Ensemble in performances for high schools. Their programs used narrative description, demonstration, and performance of Renaissance and traditional American composers. The Drama Division and the American Opera Center became a part of the program in due course.

The idea of art as community service—shades of Eugene Noble—was endowed at Juilliard. A $1 million fund from the Maxwell H. Gluck Foundation was established in 1989 to send students—initially dancers and musicians but after 1992 drama students, too—into hospitals and hospices to entertain people who were sick or dying. The profound experience reminded the young people, often involved in a pursuit of excellence, of their true purpose as performing artists—to communicate with others on a deep emotional level.

The first four years of the Gluck fellowship program brought more than 250 students into fifty-two area facilities and sponsored nearly 1,200 performances. Kevin Orton, a drama student, has said, "The Fellowship has made me realize that there are other things out there—these people are really in need of some relief, some new perspectives on things. It inspires me to give a performance that will provide this and the focus is gratefully no longer on myself."[15]

Little in the history of Juilliard has caused as much faculty and parent hue and cry as the Music Advancement Program (MAP), begun in 1991, designed exclusively for minority (defined as black and Latino) New York City children, and heavily funded by Irene Diamond. The program brought forty minority children to the School for lessons on Saturdays. It took physical space—practice rooms—from the Pre-College Division, which in 1993 was placed under the administrative supervision of the new MAP director, Roberta Ciuffo. Then the administration fired the director of the Pre-College Division, Linda Granitto, in February 1994. In March, 137 parents of Pre-College students and faculty signed letters to the board in support of Granitto. In addition, the parents' letter complained of being treated in an "insulting" manner by Polisi and Allen, of having been "untruthfully" assured months earlier that MAP would not co-opt the Pre-College Division, and of being "frightened" of the president's and the dean's actions. Pointing out that the standards for admission to the Juilliard Pre-College were "among the highest in the world," they wrote, "The primary standard of admission for the Music Advancement Program is that the applicant be black or Hispanic."[16] In their letter, the parents argued that the School was diminishing and cheapening the world-renowned prestige of being a Juilliard graduate. Contributing to the bitterness were the facts that the MAP faculty were being paid more than Pre-College faculty and every student in the MAP program received a scholarship while many parents struggled to pay the $4,000 Pre-College tuition.

Both programs graduated students—Music Advancement Program students received the same Fuschi- and Mennin-devised diploma after two years as Pre-College Division students did after eight years of attending classes and giving recitals. "You're giving them something that they did not earn," Fuschi warned. She had already felt alienated from some of the goals of the new administration. Speaking of what she perceived as a corporate approach, she recalled, "I didn't want to be a part of it anymore." On the first day of class in 1987 Fuschi resigned as director but continues to teach piano at Juilliard. "There's no way to go forward without maintaining a great admiration for the past. [If not,] it's an aberration; it's a mutant," Fuschi, a traditionalist, has commented.[17]

Fuschi had some strong discussions with Polisi. He felt that the Pre-College had to be an open rather than closed environment; she argued that some students attended for twelve years, their most formative time, and compared the division to a cocoon. Polisi said that the School had to get rid of such a cocoon, to which Fuschi countered, "If you don't have a cocoon, the butterfly won't emerge." She was referring to Pre-College Division alumni, including Midori, Gil Shaham, and Melissa Brooks, and the fact that the Regular Division orchestra included numerous people who came from the Pre-College. Fuschi doubted that Juilliard was the place for the Music Advancement Program and quoted others, saying that there was "no place a Brahms intermezzo could be better taught than at Juilliard." When Polisi asked whether she had a problem with MAP racially, Fuschi was shocked. The faculty did not consider themselves racists. Minority students had always entered the School, meeting its high standards, and Juilliard was an eclectic mix. It had not occurred to Fuschi that she "must have a black person in this instrument."

After the March letter the board supported Polisi and Allen, and Allen called a Tuesday meeting with parents. An anonymous letter that contained personal charges against Allen was sent to the board. Events moved rapidly thereafter, and within days Roberta Ciuffo resigned. A few months later James Allen resigned. Granitto was not reinstated, but the Pre-College Division faculty and parents helped select their own composition faculty member Andrew Thomas as director.

As if to illustrate the parents' concerns, in May a *60 Minutes* television segment on the Music Advancement Program aired, and the Pre-College Orchestra, including one or two MAP members, was shown playing.[18] The show featured alumnus Wynton Marsalis and Sean Coleman, a student. The distinction between the Music Advancement Program and the Pre-College Division had been blurred, and Cindy Liou, parent of a Pre-College student, wrote to CBS to complain.[19]

The MAP incident demonstrated a long-standing friction between traditionalists—in this case, parents, faculty, and Pre-College Division students—and progressives—here the board, administration, and the private donors funding MAP. The conflict between elitism and democracy in the United States will not be easily resolved. Parents could take some comfort in a circulated opinion piece by Robert Brustein, however. He observed that major art funding organizations such as the Lila

Wallace–Reader's Digest Fund, the Rockefeller Foundation, the Ford Foundation in the absence of W. McNeil Lowry, and even the Catherine T. MacArthur Foundation tended to treat art as social service. "Whatever its impact on education or its success in minority communities," Brustein wrote, "the new coercive philanthropy is demoralizing many artists and artistic institutions."[20]

A wholly different kind of outreach was achieved in February 1994 when the Juilliard Orchestra performed at Roger Daltrey's fiftieth birthday celebration at Carnegie Hall. The two concerts were billed as "Daltrey Sings Townshend" and offered as a pay-per-view television program, to be aired two days later. The performance was also released on a CD.

The question of racism at Juilliard is a sensitive one. Although some black students have credited their teachers and the school with fostering them as artists, others have felt excluded. Miles Davis, who admitted attending Juilliard so he could hang around New York with Dizzy Gillespie and Charlie Parker, wrote ambivalently of the experience. Davis attended the School from 1944 to 1945 and studied (and continually fought) with William Vacchiano (b. 1917), who still teaches at Juilliard.

> I started really getting pissed off with what they was talking about at Juilliard. It just wasn't happening for me there. . . . I played in the school symphony orchestra. We played about two notes every ninety bars, and that was that. . . . Plus, they were so fucking white-oriented and so racist. Shit, I could learn more in one session at Minton's than it would take me two years to learn at Juilliard. At Juilliard, after it was all over, all I was going to know was a bunch of white styles; nothing new. And I was just getting mad and embarrassed with their prejudice and shit. . . . Before I quit Juilliard, I did take Dizzy's advice to take some piano lessons. I also took some lessons in symphonic trumpet playing that helped me out with my playing. . . . When I say that Juilliard didn't help me, what I mean is it didn't help me as far as helping me understand what I really wanted to play. I figured there wasn't nothing left for me to do at that school.[21]

Although Polisi was pleased with the minority representation in both drama and dance, he was unhappy with the small percentage of blacks in music (fifteen of 730 students). Black students continued to feel that they had to perform even better than white students. In the Drama Division, where professional roles were scarce, actors felt they could not afford to make mistakes. The School's first Martin Luther King, Jr., Day, on January 17, 1989, may have helped black students feel some recognition. All three divisions participated in the event, which has been repeated annually.

A subtle and perhaps more pervasive racism affects the large Asian student population. French hornist Michael Ishii and Emma Moon, a flutist, garnered the nerve to write about the problem for the *Juilliard Journal*: "Racism persists at Juilliard despite people's efforts to free themselves from racist attitudes and behaviors. Thus some minority students feel isolated, intimidated, unsupported and not able to be truly themselves, but rather they feel pressure to assimilate into the mainstream."[22] They gave examples: "People of color are hurt by white supremacist graffiti in stairwells, comments concerning their lack of command of English, and inane racial jokes, such as those referring to 'yellow fever'" (a Juilliard colloquialism for the trend of Western male students becoming romantically involved with Asian women). The article prompted "A Comment" by Polisi on the same page, in which he sought to address the specific solutions offered by the students.

But feelings of isolation and lack of support at Juilliard go beyond race. The judging of the twelve yearly concerto competitions, for example, provided instances of alleged unfairness. Students, exquisitely sensitive to internal politics, wanted judges from outside the School for the final round, and by 1994 that was being done at a cost to the School and under criticism that female judges were underrepresented. One student compiled a statistical study of female representation in four years' worth of competitions (1991–94). In nearly 50 percent of the competitions, not one female musician had been on the adjudicating panel; 87 of the 112 judges were male.[23] The number of women in professional music in proportion to their number as students has improved since 1905 but still has not reached parity.

In 1988 the School sponsored a symposium on the opportunities available to women in classical music, the first formal look at the issue in the history of the School. Eugenia Zukerman assembled a panel of eleven women representing every aspect of the field: composing, conducting, opera singing, musicology, teaching, management, publicity, and recording. "When I was asked to do this," she said, "I thought what I would have loved, when I went to Juilliard, was to hear from a group of women who could tell me what their careers are like, how they got where they are and what the obstacles were."[24]

∼

William Schuman and Peter Mennin thought it undignified to advertise the name of Juilliard, although Joseph Polisi has increasingly brought the School's accomplishments to public attention. He may be reacting to a new reality. During the 1960s and 1970s the classical music industry debated the need for press relations. Only in the mid-1970s did that field grow, and by the 1980s it had taken hold. Even then, people debated whether real art would need PR; traditionalists at Juilliard and elsewhere railed against it.

When Janet Kessin, the School's current communications director, came to Juilliard in 1987, the press release file contained some two dozen clippings representing several hundred performances. The mailing list was skimpy and unorganized, and a fair number of people on it were dead. Yet none of the programs established at Juilliard was created to achieve a PR goal, unlike those at a venue such as Carnegie Hall.[25] Newspaper reviews are more difficult to come by. Some dailies in New York have gone out of business; others, such as the *New York Times*, have cut back severely on music coverage. No longer does the city have seven or eight daily newspapers that always cover commercial concerts.

A connection between buying advertising for films, books, and concerts in the print media and the likelihood of the "product" being reviewed is not supposed to exist but does. Journalists will not discuss the blurring of advertising and editorial; indeed, an editor at the *Daily News* was fired during the 1980s for admitting it. At Juilliard, the Drama Division is the most affected by the situation; like all schools, Juilliard has a limited budget for advertising. Because of the number of pages of movie advertising, films are reviewed and theater coverage is diminished.

Admissions director Mary Gray, says of the School's reputation for excellence, "It does effect a lot of people, from peer groups, especially in Asia, where there's this tremendous word of mouth. The faculty has always been the reason why Juilliard became what it is. Because in New York and at Lincoln Center it has been able to continue with a group of people who have careers as performers as well as teachers."[26] Proposals to move the School to Asia have failed because it would not be possible to relocate the faculty, on whom Juilliard's reputation is based, abroad.

A major shift occurred in 1983, when Korea made visas more available; within a few years one in eight students at Juilliard was Korean. There were more Korean students than Chinese and Japanese students, and they continue to outnumber those from other countries three to one. Asian women far outnumber Asian men, for whom a professional life in music is still not culturally accepted. Of Chinese students, 90 percent return to China to pursue careers. Since 1989 a new wave of students has come from Eastern Europe—Bulgaria, Yugoslavia, and Russia.

By 1995 international students made up 39.8 percent of the student body: 15.4 percent of the Dance Division, 11 percent of drama students, and 47.5 percent of music students. For example, ten of the fourteen flutists in 1995 were international (seven were Asian), as were 61.9 percent of the pianists, 52 percent of the violinists, 50 percent of the 'cellists, and 34.6 percent of the voice majors. Gray has remarked of a typical student:

> If one is asked to generalize, it may be said that there are three major categories of music students (and several minor categories!). First, the Eastern European student, who has tremendous confidence and flair, and often comes from a really difficult situation where musical training has been something that they have achieved at great personal cost and little financial backing. These are kids who approach the process with great intensity to get what they want; they know what they want.
>
> Second are American students brought up through the system. Usually they have tremendous amount of family or community support, a lot more confidence, a more integrated approach. They've been to good schools and many come through performing arts schools, have been in a youth symphony or community system, and have traveled to pre-college programs on weekends.
>
> Third is the Asian student, whose family was single-minded from birth about instrumental education. They tend not to be as well rounded; in some cases, the academics may fall by the wayside. The arts have been chosen as the road to success, and this is what you're going to do and this is what you're going to focus on. It's more the Asian-American student who might consider going to Harvard as an undergraduate and Juilliard as graduate. To those from Asia, Juilliard has been a goal since third grade. It takes a little while to sort out for those kids whether it's their own idea, or whether it's parental pressure.
>
> Dancers are usually very bright, serious kids who have chosen college because they want an education, but are absolutely geared toward performance and are incredibly disciplined through their early ballet training. They are looking for another kind of creative spark, pulled by Juilliard's modern and contemporary program.
>
> In Drama, it is much more difficult to identify a "type." Some are twenty-eight or thirty, but still spend four years in the BFA program. Generally, an incoming class consists of ten or fewer first-time college students. The faculty looks at life experience and sees it as valuable. Juilliard contends that our four-year undergraduate is commensurate with NYU's or Yale's master's degree. It's a hard sell for students who are looking for a master's. Juilliard is committed to a BFA program only. In a graduate program, you are more likely to have students who are not malleable, who are set on how they perform, see their instruments in a particular way, and may not be open to the kind of voice and physical training that this program offers.[27]

Ten years earlier, in 1985, enrollment was 906 (544 undergraduate and 362 graduate students). In 1993 the president and dean announced a reduction of the piano department from 150 to 100 pianists, but by 1995 there were 134 pianists and a total School enrollment of 768.

Of those who applied to Juilliard during the mid-1980s, 19 percent of were admitted in 1984, 22 percent in 1985, and 16 percent in 1986. The most competitive departments were the Drama Division and flute, voice, and orchestral conducting. By 1995 only about 10 percent of those who applied in music were admitted, a percentage that varied by instrument. Between 40 and 50 percent of those who applied in double bass were accepted, but only 5 percent of the flutists. Drama is even more selective. Of a thousand applicants, only twenty—2 percent—are admitted. In the Dance Division, nearly 12 percent of applicants are accepted—25 of 200 applicants in 1995. In 1996 fifty-six thousand college students rated Juilliard the as "toughest to get into" for *The Princeton Review Student Access Guide to the Best 309 Colleges.* One possible approach to examining Juilliard's history might be to compare the administrations of presidents who would have been admitted to the School as students—Damrosch, Hutcheson, and Mennin—with those who would not have passed the auditions—Noble, Erskine, Schuman, and Polisi.

In the Drama and Dance Divisions, the yield (the percentage of those accepted who then attend) is 88 percent, 86 percent, or even 96 percent. In Music, one of every four who is accepted goes elsewhere, a yield of 75 percent. Students do not attend Juilliard for many reasons. They may have been offered a job, or fear competition or living in New York City, or be prohibited by life circumstances or financial considerations. In 1993, for example, tuition was $10,650 and fees were $600. (By 1998 tuituion had risen to $15,200.) Those wishing to live in dormitories and receive board were charged an additional $5,900 for a double room to $7,200 for a single, bringing the 1993 total to around $18,000. Yet only ninety-two of more than eight hundred students receive a full-tuition scholarship or more. The average Juilliard scholarship is nearly $6,000, which still left a cost of $12,000.

Money is also an issue for faculty. The lack of job security at Juilliard combined with the low salaries limits the administration's ability to recruit and keep faculty. Despite 20–25 percent increases during the 1990s, average faculty salaries were still not in line with those at universities, a fact the board's chair acknowledged in 1997. Two aspects of academic life, however, have never applied at Juilliard: mandatory retirement and tenure. Classical musicians are famously long-lived. Juilliard has benefited by hiring faculty who have retired from universities. To evaluate the lack of tenure is more problematic, but the fact remains that at Juilliard it is difficult to fire a popular teacher.

Polisi's ideas about the School found a sympathetic outlet in a *New York Times* article in 1993 by William Grimes that heralded "a new Juilliard."[28] The author called Juilliard "the most prestigious conservatory in the United States, and perhaps in the world" and noted that graduates account for 20 percent of the musicians in the five major American orchestras and half of those in the New York Philharmonic. Calling the School before Polisi's arrival "tough and grim, elitist and insular," Grimes reported that "most of its students toiled away in full confidence that the jobs were out there." However accurate the first part of that statement may be, the second was incorrect. Most students during Mennin's tenure were pragmatists and only too aware of how difficult it was to get a job in music.

Grimes also pointed to a recent crisis in government and corporate support for the arts, the near-collapse of musical education in the primary and secondary schools, and a shrinking marketplace for classical musicians. Perhaps related to that were the facts that the audience for classical music is declining in numbers as it ages and music education in secondary schools had suffered a severe setback with the tax revolt of the late 1970s. Proposition 13 in California and Proposition 2½ in Massachusetts had decimated public school music education in those states. Some schools no longer had even marching bands, much less orchestras and choruses. The effect on music schools in the United States was long-established: Fewer qualified American students apply, and more highly trained foreign students take their places.

Yet Grimes had a few facts wrong. His report that 90 percent of those accepted chose to attend Juilliard is contradicted by that year's annual report, which gave 75 percent, a figure that had increased to 80 percent by 1996. The claim that the endowment tripled from $96 million to $250 million in eight years was also incorrect. As acting president, Waldrop had calculated the 1983 figure to be $180 million. Polisi and the development director, Lynne Rudkin, deserve credit for an increase of $70 million by 1993. By 1997 the endowment totaled $305 million. Likewise, assertions that there had never been a student council and that the *Juilliard Journal* was the School's first student newspaper were untrue as well. *The Baton, Stretto, Harmonics,* and *Dynamics,* in addition to various student councils, all preceded Schuman and Mennin. The *Juilliard Journal* is not run by students but rather edited by professionals.

The School had told Grimes that before Polisi there had been no housing-referral information, psychological counseling, or advisors for incoming students. On the contrary, all were provided by the previous administration, although not to the highly staffed degree they are now. In 1990 the School could boast that "five years ago, the Administration began to develop an innovative on-site mental health facility. Today, this facility is the only comprehensive psychological service within an independent performing arts institution."[29] The service takes into account "the developmental sacrifices of performing arts students, the unique time demands that students must learn to negotiate, and the emotional costs of their chosen profession." Among the problems treated are substance abuse and addictions, sexual abuse, cultural conflicts, performance anxiety, and preoccupations with body, body image, and eating.

Many problems of Juilliard students are typical of students their age. Other issues, however, are specific to lives of performing artists. Self-doubt and low self-esteem are often discussed. The School offered students who sought help up to fifteen free individual sessions. Demand for mental health services became so urgent that the staff was augmented to include Elma Kanefield, Dr. Robert Berson, Dr. Arthur Rudy (who had counselled students for thirteen years before the service was inaugurated), Dr. Cheryl Walters, and Betsy McCallister.

The Mennin administration was generally perceived as providing little support to students traversing the difficult transition from student to professional life. Some floundered, not knowing what to do at auditions (unless teachers had been savvy enough to tell them), how to apply for jobs, or how to deal with a myriad of other issues where practical knowledge would have been useful. There was no career counseling, and students felt they were on their own to cast about for a professional opportunity. End-of-the-year juries were always traumatic for some, and those graduating and leaving the School felt even more adrift. Psychological problems that did occur often appeared just after graduation, when students felt especially lost and vulnerable at leaving the relatively secure environment of Juilliard. Unlike the faculty, the "real world" was indifferent to the graduates, and they soon missed the musical life and level of playing at the School.

Under Polisi, various efforts were begun to help students gain knowledge about the professional world. One, "On Beyond Juilliard," was a year-long, two-hour weekly seminar for sixty singers, who experienced mock auditions and were advised by various managers and agents on the dos and don'ts of auditioning. David Lloyd, the opera director, spent the next year concentrating on summer programs and festivals or opera centers, and prominent managers were invited to address the students. In addition, classes on performance demeanor, often decried by the faculty, were finally held.

An organist, David Friddle, has described his reaction to other students upon entering Juilliard in 1983. He had "expected to find an equally large community of compassionate, caring individuals. In reality, however, nothing could have been further from the truth. . . . I was not prepared for the level of arrogance and (what I now know to be false) self-confidence floating around, indiscriminately wounding those newcomers who dared to cross its path. The facts were these: People were not so nice here; they were frequently unfriendly; and they only rarely smiled in the halls."[30] In his final year as a student, Friddle had decided to "bare it all" by discussing the chronically bad social life in the *Juilliard Journal*. It was possible, he stressed, to learn to live in New York City, with all its problems, older students could help newer ones, and a social life was essential "in this atmosphere of obsessive/compulsive work behavior." Friddle decried "negative competition" and urged students to take advantage of the school's three parties a year and meet people.

In "A Musical Call to Arms" (1994), Polisi outlined his view of the artistic and cultural situation. "Many in the music field sense a prevailing malaise about music in America today," he began.[31] He also accounted for why musical values had declined in the financially insecure 1970s and the debt-ridden economic revival of the 1980s. Urban problems had led to a disregard of the arts in schools; multicultural influences questioned the Eurocentric focus of classical arts and the value of art in American education; and popular culture seemed to foster a shortened attention span. Polisi mentioned MTV, which he thought could make classical music seem boring.

Polisi felt that "the single occurrence that exposed the erosion of the American artistic environment was the Mapplethorpe controversy. This event allowed demagoguery and sheer ignorance of the role of the arts in American society to be triumphant over artistic and educational traditions that had prevailed in America for most of this century."[32] The controversy also weakened the National Endowment for the Arts. Polisi contrasted the highly successful U.S. conservatory and college music department programs with the music programs being abandoned in secondary education. In New York City, where he had gone to school, for example, only 5–8 percent of the elementary and junior high schools had music teachers on staff; of that percentage, most were supported by Parents' Association funds rather than the Board of Education; and although the state mandated that 10 percent of instructional time be spent on arts education, New York City and Buffalo were exempt from that statute.

In non-urban areas the music environment was more positive but not indicative of the future, observed Polisi. He accused music education departments of graduating incompetent teachers and lowering standards in order to keep enrollments up. Polisi wanted music programs to encourage serious performers to teach yet was unwilling to restore music education at Juilliard. Finally, he wrote, "The concept that the arts can enhance the quality of life of our citizenry through its positive force must be re-introduced to the collective American psyche"—a tall order.[33]

Skepticism and resistance toward Polisi's new ideas for Juilliard among the traditional faculty was strong, as the MAP controversy showed. Music had historically been taught as a series of private lessons whose dynamics and emphases seemed immune to change. The faculty possessed both impressive pedagogical lineages and successful students, which gave them credibility. It was difficult, for example, to persuade Joseph Fuchs, who had entered the IMA in 1906 and taught at Juilliard until he was ninety-seven, that the School should change its emphasis. Whether faculty will ever subscribe to James Allen's statement remains to be seen. "We could," he said, "go on as we did in the past, but the conservatory is a nineteenth-century invention, and the lives of people are not the same anymore. The pristine ivory tower where students came to refine their gifts and go off to become a star—that's over."[34]

~

In the 1980s the Lincoln Center board assessed its successes and failures. Mostly evident was its success: "It had become truly a citadel of culture in the heart of the city."[35] But all ten constituents were clamoring for more space. Juilliard students had been in the same situation since 1905: They had no place to live on campus. Nearly 150 of them lived at the 63rd Street YMCA, an unpleasant environment. In November 1989 they met to express grievances and consider staging protests. One drama student described the unsanitary conditions as "almost unlivable."[36]

The dormitory idea came up again. Polisi reported that "participants [in a colloquium planning meeting] strongly agreed that Juilliard needs to continue to create an atmosphere of trust and safety for all students, always providing for them an environment in which to grow, to learn, and to question."[37] The administration had viewed a dormitory as part of an environment that would make student life easier and more comfortable, a notion that would have made Peter Mennin wonder in disbelief. Some alumni, such as Patti LuPone, would have agreed with Mennin; she thought having a dormitory would make life too easy for students. Juilliard also needed living quarters for visiting artist-teachers who did not live in New York.

The Lincoln Center board set up a new building committee under the direction of board member Frederick P. Rose, a real estate devel-

oper, and sought to discover the feasibility and cost of expanding Lincoln Center. The remaining portion of the High School of Commerce,
recently closed, still stood on Juilliard's block, as did a firehouse and the
Good Shepherd–Faith Church. During the 1960s the city had promised John D. Rockefeller 3rd that Lincoln Center could buy the old high
school property whenever the building became available (chapter 7).
The opportunity finally presented itself; it would now cost $3.5 million.

One idea was to add to the existing building, but study showed that
its foundation would not support additional floors. The committee also
concluded after many months of debate that the cost of a building large
enough for their needs was beyond Lincoln Center's fund-raising ability. Still, they could exercise their option to purchase the vacant lot,
between the School and the firehouse, that occupies the southeast corner of Sixty-sixth Street and Amsterdam Avenue. That would result in
a large parcel of land. Brendan Gill has described the airy and fantastic
prospects that New York's peculiar development laws provided:

> The size of the building, or buildings, that the city's zoning laws
> would permit on the site would be greatly increased if the center were
> to buy from the city the air rights above the firehouse and add to
> them air rights above the Juilliard building which had remained
> unexploited at the time of its construction. A deal might perhaps be
> struck with a private developer, who would pay part of the cost of a
> not-for-profit institutional building on one part of the site as a reward
> for being allowed to build a very-much-for-profit residential sky-
> scraper on another part of the site.
>
> And then an even more attractive refinement of this proposal
> emerged from the committee's deliberations—a feat of real-estate
> sleight of hand so ingenious as to approach the metaphysical. [De-
> vised by Gordon Davis and Henry Hart Rice,] the suggested
> refinement was to plan three buildings on the site instead of two: a so-
> called base building, which would include ten floors of labyrinthally
> interlocking institutional spaces, and, springing from the top of this
> base, two towers—one providing eighteen stories of dormitory space
> for the School of American Ballet and the Juilliard, and the other pro-
> viding forty-five stories of condominium apartments.[38]

The developer would be given the right to use the address Three
Lincoln Center. The enterprise would be confined to an envelope of air
rights that began sixteen stories above ground. The developer would
hold title to air and could build a castle in the air. Lincoln Center was
to get the money that the developer would pay for the right to build, a
sum expected to cover much of the cost of the base building and the

dormitory tower. In return, Lincoln Center would guide the project through the New York City uniform land use review process.

Fortuitously for Lincoln Center, the project was devised in 1985 when the real estate market was heating up under the laissez-faire policies of Reaganism. In October fifty real estate concerns submitted bids, and by January 1986 there were five finalists. The winner was the Stillman Group, one of the country's sixty largest developers. Architects were Davis, Brody, and Associates and Abramovitz, Harris, and Kingsland. The Lincoln Center project, however, was the "boldest and most complicated" that the firm had ever undertaken. The Stillman Group paid approximately $50 million for the right to build Three Lincoln Center, one-third of the cost of the base building and dormitories. Frederick Rose undertook to raise the remaining $100 million.

The September 1986 *Juilliard Journal* excitedly announced "It's a 'Go!'" on its front page: "Dormitory Project Wins Final City Approval." An arduous negotiation process that involved students and staff had begun the previous April. Local Community Board Number 7 had voted down the proposal in May, but the vote did not have the authority to stop the project. James Allen spoke to the committee and explained that the dormitory was an urgent necessity for students. Polisi argued that Juilliard needed it to ensure its survival because "without a dorm Juilliard will not be able to attract the best students."[39] Students also spoke.

But the neighborhood did not want a sixty-story tower in its already congested environs. After much negotiating, the City Planning Commission voted approval on July 9. At yet another public hearing in August, Polisi, alumnus Marvin Hamlisch, and student Larry Green testified on behalf of Juilliard. The Board of Estimate then endorsed the project unanimously. Negotiations reduced the size of the apartment tower, however, thereby reducing the price of the air rights and necessitating that Juilliard raise more of the money itself. Construction might begin as early as January 1987 and was estimated to take three years. Anyone remembering the delays in building Juilliard at Lincoln Center had cause to wonder whether the tower would be built within the budget (originally $85 million but then $100 million) or on time.

The neighborhood around Lincoln Center had changed during the 1970s and 1980s as numerous skyscrapers cropped up across Broadway and in the surrounding area. Students and faculty were most affected at the loss of establishments on the block from 66th to 67th Street between Broadway and Columbus Avenue: Chipp's Pub, a bar serving Italian food; McGlade's, the lunchtime hangout of the Pre-College Division faculty; John's Coffee Shop, virtually everyone's hangout; and the

Cinema Studio 1 and 2 movie theater. The owners of those businesses had no commercial rent control. Most of the buildings on the block were demolished in 1990, and it is now the site of a high-rise. In 1995 Tower Records, directly across Sixty-sixth Street, closed, and that building was also razed and another erected.

Between the symbolic groundbreaking for the Lincoln Center Building on November 10, 1987, and the spring of 1990, Rose helped raise $85 million. Present at the groundbreaking were Joseph Polisi; Mrs. John D. Rockefeller 3rd; George Weissman, chair of the Lincoln Center board; and Nathan Leventhal, president of Lincoln Center. For the next three years the sounds of blasting were heard directly west of Juilliard; even final examinations were interrupted by construction sounds.

At a reception on June 11, 1990, it was announced that the largest single contribution would come from Frederick and Sandra Rose: $15 million. The base building would be named the Samuel B. and David Rose Building after Rose's father and uncle. "I wanted to keep the gift anonymous as long as possible," Rose said. "I would have felt embarrassed prodding people into giving to a building that would eventually bear my family's name. Now that the building is almost finished and we have only a few million dollars left to raise, I feel much less worried about it."[40] Referred to simply as the Rose Building, it was completed only a year late but $67 million over the original budget. The $152 million project—of which Juilliard's board raised one-quarter of the cost ($38 million) for one-quarter of the cubic feet—may well be board president June Larkin's and Joseph Polisi's greatest contribution to the School.

The Rose Building is separated from Juilliard by a driveway between Sixty-fifth and Sixty-sixth Streets. The firehouse is inconspicuously encapsulated within the new building. The Rose Building is sheathed in Minnesota limestone, and Gill wrote that "against the backdrop of the shadowy, dark brick striped vastness of Three Lincoln Center the dormitory tower appears agreeably domestic in scale." Gill also praised the main lobby on the third floor and its approach:

> [It is] reached by way of that daring architectural gesture which I see as radically improving not only the Juilliard building but the rest of Lincoln Center as well; to wit, an open-air promenade, four hundred and fifty feet long, beginning at the top of the flight of stairs affixed to the Broadway side of the Juilliard building (and belatedly providing those

OPPOSITE: Rose Building and Three Lincoln Center. The architects were Davis, Brody and Associates/Abramovitz Harris Kingsland.
(Henry Grossman, photo from The Juilliard School)

palatial steps with a worthy reason to exist), proceeding through a hollowed-out segment of the Juilliard, whose cantilevered upper stories partly shelter it from the weather, and ending in the Rose Building.

Architectural gestures on the scale of the promenade are rare, and are therefore well worth our attention; they are especially rare and especially gratifying when, as in the present instance, the architects have succeeded in creating an exhilarating new space within the framework of a defective old one. . . . The blundering placement of the entrance to the Juilliard in the spooky street-level twilight under the Sixty-fifth Street bridge is now remedied. . . . the Sixty-fifth Street bridge, whose deck, hitherto little used, has now become a terracelike extension of the promenade. Nearly half as long as the promenade and paved with handsome pinkish granite blocks, in its present incarnation how much more than a mere overpass it is![41]

Lincoln Center and Juilliard triumphed, gaining more space in an architecturally distinctive building. By the time both of the new towers were complete, however, Three Lincoln Center had fallen victim to the New York real estate market recession of the early 1990s. The developers offered some apartments for rent, hoping to ride it out; in 1990 the price for a condominium ranged from $282,000 to $3 million.

The residence hall was named in 1992 after IMA alumnus Meredith Willson. The composer of *The Music Man* and *The Unsinkable Molly Brown* was honored by his wife, Rosemary Willson, who donated a special grant. Willson's name appears on the Rose Building in lettering that will be seen on Broadway permanently. The dormitory—occupying the seventeenth through twenty-eighth floors—provides twenty-four-hour security, in-house laundry facilities, twenty-two practice rooms, a swimming pool, a typing and computer room, and television rooms. Each floor has four suites, with seven or eight students to a suite. Each suite has five bedrooms (two singles and three doubles or two doubles and three singles), a large living-room area, and two and a half bathrooms. Four studio apartments and two two-bedroom apartments are reserved for faculty and visiting artists. By 1995 the distribution of students had settled. The seventeenth floor is the quiet floor; the eighteenth and nineteenth floors are smoking floors; the twentieth is an all-female floor; the twenty-second is for graduate students; the twenty-fifth is a no-alcohol floor; and the twenty-eighth is for students over twenty.

When the residence life team finally uttered the code words "the avocados are ripe!" that meant that more than three hundred students could move into the residence hall. The "avocados" had been variously described as ripening and as falling off trees, and on October 19, 1990, the fateful words were finally uttered. Laurie Carter, director of student affairs, lived at the YMCA during this period and organized the move.

By November the *Juilliard Journal* could report that "the effects of that social life are already in evidence—new friendships and a bracing camaraderie born of the shared experience of living together and of the activities and support network provided by the residence life staff and Residence Assistants. Juilliard students can now enjoy a sense of belonging as never before."[42] As one former drama student, now a faculty member, described it: "My first-year students already know more musicians and dancers than I or most of my classmates knew when we graduated. The immediate benefit of this communication is a slight easing of pressure which develops from spending twelve hours a day with the same group of fifteen or twenty students."[43] The dream of all past presidents of Juilliard had finally been achieved.

After the Rose Building's cafeteria opened in 1991, the administration commandeered the former cafeteria space at Juilliard. During the summer of 1992 the former student lounge, faculty cafeteria, student cafeteria, and two bathrooms were demolished and subdivided into offices, including space for the Pre-College Division and the Music Advancement Program as well as a computer center for students. Other changes on the second floor meant replacing the familiar orange carpeting, redoing the ceiling, painting the walls, placing plants and photographs in the hallways, and sprucing up the hallways to the president's and dean's offices.

Those windowed hallways now look down upon a brightly lit lobby rather than on the kept-dark former "marble area" referred to colloquially as "Aïda's tomb." The lobby, which opened in October 1991, was a gift of June Larkin. The main entrance was moved from 66th Street, up one floor and to 65th Street; now the School faces Lincoln Center rather than turns its back on it. (This means that the address changed from 144 West Sixty-sixth Street to 60 Lincoln Center Plaza.) Underneath the new lobby, on the old lobby floor, is a new performing and lecture space, Morse Hall.

One unintended result of the new carpeting and paint during the summer of 1993 was confusion as people exited elevators. The building had been simple to negotiate. The street level flooring was dark gray marble; the first floor was marked by the red-carpeted lobby of Paul Hall; the orange-carpeted floor was the second (offices and cafeteria); the third floor (the Dance Division and orchestral rehearsals) was covered by black linoleum; the bright yellow carpet was on the fourth floor (practice rooms and the Drama Division); and burgundy carpeting marked the fifth floor (classrooms, lessons, and library). Now the carpeting on all floors was the same color—gray—and it is necessary to look at the lighted number above the elevator doors to determine the floor. (A fourth elevator, ghostlike, has never operated; its closed doors sit mysteriously next to the other three on all ten floors.) The labyrinth on the fifth floor was further confused because the red doors were painted black and nearly half the room numbers were changed. A faculty lounge, the first at the Lincoln Center building, was created from the lobby in front of the library. Fuschi says, "The faculty lounge is the best thing they did!"

In March 1989 Juilliard, Columbia, and Barnard announced a collaboration in their programs that would allow Juilliard students to earn a degree from both schools in five years. It was a similar collaboration to those already in place between Peabody and Johns Hopkins and between New England Conservatory and Tufts.

From January 1991 until August 1992 all Lincoln Center's constituents joined forces and celebrated a single composer: Mozart, on the bicentennial of his death. Each Mozart composition was performed. The musicological advisor to the enormous project was Juilliard graduate and faculty member Neal Zaslaw. The event also marked the first time that Lincoln Center's performing groups shared a stage.

On February 15, 1992, William Schuman died. Polisi wrote of him, "Once in a great while a person comes upon the scene with such an all-encompassing positive presence that the world changes in ways never imagined. So it was with William Schuman who, in a bit more than eighty years, helped America and the world to better appreciate the performing arts through his compositions, his vision and his abiding belief in the goodness of the human spirit."[44] The obituary in the *New York Times* reported that Schuman had studied with Roy Harris at Juilliard, although it failed to mention that he had attended the Juilliard Summer School.[45]

For eight years Schuman had again influenced affairs at Juilliard, but an era was over and numerous changes took place at Juilliard in 1992, the year Kevin Kline gave a hilarious and truthful commencement address. Not only did Michael Langham leave the Drama Division but Muriel Topaz was also pushed out of the Dance Division, causing great dismay among dance students. In addition, James Sloan Allen became provost and dean. The L&M program was again revisited and revised.

During the summer of 1994 Polisi and the trustees developed a "formal yet flexible plan for Juilliard's future" and presented a draft of the proposal to students and alumni in September 1994. The plan was to be refined and then put into effect in May 1995. The administration and board considered that the world had changed enough since 1970s that future financial support for the arts was unclear. In addition they were concerned about a decline in music in public schools, especially those in urban areas. As Polisi and the trustees envisioned it, the School's mission had four parts:

1. Juilliard's central mission is to educate talented musicians, dancers, and actors so that they may achieve the highest artistic standards as well as become leaders in their profession, and to help them to become thoughtful, confident, and responsible adults.

2. Juilliard should make every effort to provide students with the emotional, social, professional and educational skills necessary for them to embark on successful careers and productive lives as artists, leaders, and citizens.

3. Juilliard should continue to elevate its high educational and artistic standards while also inculcating in students a sense of their own professional responsibilities for enhancing the classical arts in America and around the world.

4. Juilliard should take an active role in shaping the future of the classical arts, both by intensifying its internal commitment to artistic education and by reaching beyond its doors to help the classical arts thrive anew throughout the world, and especially in the United States.[46]

(Graduate Peter Schickele had noted humorously in 1980 that "it is my belief that Juilliard was founded expressly for the purpose of insuring that there would be no more P.D.Q. Bachs.")[47]

Each of five broad categories in the long-range plan received proposals. For the first category, educational and artistic programs, was a proposal for the School to "extend the Juilliard education beyond simply technical training." Another stab was made at reducing the enrollment, 770 in 1994, to about 740. For the second category, external programs relating to educational outreach, the proposal concentrated on minority recruitment, the Music Advancement Program, and the Gluck and Morse programs (for Juilliard students to teach a half day a week at a local elementary or secondary school). Under the third category, student life and financial aid, the ideal was to be able to provide full scholarships for all those in financial need, although there are no plans to provide tuition for all accepted students. Those who can afford to pay will pay. Concerning the plan's fourth category—faculty development, governance, and compensation—the report said, "For Juilliard to exercise the kind of cultural leadership that will be required in the next century, the faculty will have to be fully committed to the School's mission, and the School will have to more vigorously support the faculty." That meant "adjusted compensation and more secure contractual arrangements."[48] A proposed pay increase for the staff was part of the fifth category, administrative staff support and physical plant needs. At most arts institutions, as at Juilliard, however, the upper administration pays itself considerably more than faculty or performers. The Boston Symphony Orchestra manager, for example, makes about $260,000 a year, whereas the BSO concertmaster earns about $170,000; at the New England Conservatory, the president makes just under $150,000, while the faculty earn a fraction of that.

In 1994 Mary Rodgers Guettel, the daughter of Richard Rodgers, replaced June Noble Larkin as chair of the twenty-five-member board. Rodgers had not wanted his daughter to study at Juilliard, as he had done at the IMA. She did compose, however, and wrote *Davy Jones' Locker*, a children's musical, in 1959. That same year she wrote the score for *Once upon a Mattress* and later wrote several successful children's books. Guettel has described the challenge facing Juilliard students: "A conservatory is no longer a wonderful gilded cage where people just get to practice twelve hours a day and then have an acclaimed debut somewhere. Our graduates, and the rest of the world, must realize that unless we go out of our way to expose kids to the arts, we will have no audiences in the future." She maintains that "we need better rounded musicians."[49]

Those musicians, the Juilliard board and administration feels, will have to become advocates for the arts, and Juilliard students have indeed begun to exhibit renewed political consciousness. At 5:30 A.M. on March 14, 1995, for example, forty "surprisingly awake" students traveled to Washington, D.C., for Arts Advocacy Day and to lobby Congress for the National Endowment for the Arts. Among them were Karen Elliott Smith, Kevin Cobb, and Carol Rodland; Andrew Thomas, director of the Pre-College Division, also lobbied. The responses they received exactly paralleled those of government officials a century earlier, when conservatories were seeking state support (chapter 1). Rodland wrote, "Some of my Juilliard colleagues did not, unfortunately, have such pleasant encounters with their representatives [as she had had with New Jersey Senator Bill Bradley]. The large New York contingent, for example, had a distressing meeting with a poorly informed aide from Republican Senator Alfonse d'Amato's office. A friend from Texas said she felt like an ineffective 'speck of dust' as she attempted to lobby, because her representatives flatly refused to consider any support whatsoever for the endowments."[50]

Juilliard's iconic reputation continues to grow. One measure has been that from 1990 to 1994 *U.S. News and World Report* named the School as the best of the forty-three schools specializing in the arts. (In 1997, however, it dropped below the Eastman School of Music.) The eternal battle between traditionalists who keep the past alive both in repertoire and teaching methods and progressives who try to foresee and accommodate the future is still waged. But the desire to perform has never abated. If Frank Damrosch could return to Juilliard, he would likely find it both familiar and changed. Yet he would recognize the talent and determination of faculty and students.

The Institute of Musical Art, the Juilliard Graduate School, the Juilliard School of Music, and The Juilliard School all overcame numerous hurdles during their sometimes strife-torn history. Juilliard survived so well because of its talented students, dedicated faculty, enlightened patrons, and strong leadership. It prospered because all of those people believed in something bigger than themselves.

NOTES

INTRODUCTION

1. Keller, "Juilliard School," 628. The entry perpetuates a long-held exaggeration by incorrectly stating the original endowment as $20 million (see chapter 3 of this volume).

2. Kingsbury, *Music, Talent, and Performance*, 19. Faculty, students, administrators, and even the school itself are given pseudonyms in this anthropological study.

3. Kogan's *Nothing but the Best: The Struggle for Perfection at The Juilliard School* provides a vivid, novelistic picture of the personal pressures Juilliard students undergo.

4. Nettl, *Heartland Excursions*, 46.

5. Kingsbury, *Music, Talent, and Performance*, 57.

6. Fitzpatrick, *The Music Conservatory in America*, an excellent study of early conservatories, includes lengthy chapters on Curtis, Eastman, and the IMA.

7. McPherson and Klein, *Measure by Measure*. The quotation comes from the advertising for this lavishly illustrated but undocumented book. The authors are members of the conservatory's liberal arts faculty.

CHAPTER 1: *The Founding Fathers*

1. Cooke, "The Advent of Endowed Institutions," 57.

2. Martin, *The Damrosch Dynasty: America's First Family of Music*.

3. Note that brother-in-law David Mannes's autobiography is entitled *Music Is My Faith*.

4. Hughes, "Rafael Joseffy's Contribution to Piano Technic," 349–64.

5. Unfortunately, her name is not mentioned in Damrosch, *Institute of Musical Art*, 2–3. Most of the graduating class of eighteen were female.

6. Frank Damrosch to Hetty Damrosch (lacking the first page but clearly July 1901), Damrosch–Tee Van Collection, box 2, Library of Congress.

7. Frank Damrosch to Hetty Damrosch, July 9, 1901, Damrosch–Tee Van Collection, box 2, Library of Congress.

8. Andrew Carnegie to Hetty Damrosch, July 16, [1902], Damrosch–Tee Van Collection, box 3, Library of Congress. The letter is quoted in Martin, *The Damrosch Dynasty*, 226.

9. For more on Loeb, see Olmstead, "The Toll of Idealism," 233–62.

10. See Chernow, *The Warburgs*, for biographical information on the family and on the two Warburgs who became board members of the school.

11. Interview with Anita Warburg, March 17, 1993, New York City.

12. Warburg, *Reminiscences of a Long Life*, 19.

13. Damrosch, *Institute of Musical Art*, 6–7.

14. Loeb, *A Memorial*, 8; see also Olmstead, "The Toll of Idealism."

15. Birmingham, *"Our Crowd."*

16. James Paul Warburg, manuscript history, 45. A look at the repertoire that Loeb played as an amateur reveals a considerable level of advancement.

17. Spalding, *Music at Harvard*, 38.

18. Loeb, *A Memorial*, 20.

19. Birmingham, *"Our Crowd,"* 254.

20. James Loeb to Frank Damrosch, typed letter signed [hereafter, tls], March 16, 1900, Damrosch–Tee Van Collection, Library of Congress.

21. Birmingham, *"Our Crowd,"* 211.

22. A bitter rivalry broke out in the 1880s between newcomer Leopold Damrosch, founder and conductor of the Oratorio Society of New York, and the more established conductor Theodore Thomas. Thomas used his influence to prevent or delay Damrosch's touring orchestra from playing in concert halls, each competed for players from the other's orchestra, and their rivalry for important premieres was intense. To escape the Damrosch-Thomas feud and strike out on his own, in 1879 Frank Damrosch decided to quit music and left New York for Denver. There he found a job selling hats and was working for a wholesale liquor business when he was asked to play the organ at the Congregational church.

Loeb's father's firm landed in the middle of a Wall Street scandal. In 1899 J. P. Morgan, James J. Hill, and Edward Harriman (financed by Schiff and Kahn at Kuhn, Loeb) caused a Wall Street panic over shares of the Northern Pacific Railroad Company. To the sensitive James Loeb, who did not want to be a banker in the first place, such a public scene must have frayed his already delicate nerves and bolstered his resolve to leave the firm, which he did in 1901. He may also have felt responsibility as well as guilt over the number of ruined families his father's company had caused.

23. Lectures, Recitals, and General Occasions, October 1905–June 1906, 1:68, Juilliard Archives.

24. Warburg, "The Testimonial Dinner to Frank Damrosch."

25. Damrosch, *Institute of Musical Art*, 5–6. Loeb's letter came six months later, however. James Loeb to Frank Damrosch, autograph letter signed [hereafter, als], March 14, 1904, Office of the President, General Administrative Records, 1904–38, box 1, folders 5–6, Juilliard Archives. It includes a three-page memorandum about founding the school. Loeb would get to name a majority of the trustees for twenty years, a condition later forgotten. Loyal to the end, Damrosch never mentions Loeb's bouts with depression.

26. Cooke, "Making a Modern Conservatory of Music," 101.

27. Damrosch, *Proceedings of the Music Teachers National Association* (1906), 14–15.

28. Freundlich, "Convocation Address, October 10, 1962," 51–52.

29. Translated and quoted in Reich, "Women as Musicians," 145.

30. The letter to Edward D. Adams, an early IMA trustee, was written on September 4, 1904, and is quoted in full in Damrosch, *Institute of Musical Art*, 7–10.

31. Paul Warburg to James Loeb, telegram, January 3, 1905, Office of the President, General Administrative Records, 1904–38, box 1, folders 5–6, Juilliard Archives.

32. Damrosch, *Institute of Musical Art*, 11.

33. Ibid., 25.

34. Ibid., 26.

35. Stebbins and Stebbins, *Frank Damrosch*, 213.

36. James Loeb to Frank Damrosch, als, January 7, 1905, Office of the President, General Administrative Records, 1904–38, box 1, folders 5–6, Juilliard Archives.

37. Damrosch, *Institute of Musical Art*, 28.

38. Catalog of the Institute of Musical Art, 1905. This prospectus was printed in subsequent catalogs.

39. Lectures, Recitals, and General Occasions, 1905–30, 1:11, Juilliard Archives. The speech is reproduced in Damrosch, *Institute of Musical Art*, 56–59.

40. Damrosch, *Institute of Musical Art*, 62.

41. Sang-Collins quoted in *The Baton* 5 (January 1926): 53.

42. The graduates were Fannie C. Amidon, Mrs. Thomas M. Balliet, Cleophe Donovan, Josephine Herron, Georgetta M. Hollis, Claire L. Kuhn, Nellie V. V. Munger, and Anna Cecile O'Brien.

43. Tick, "Passed Away Is the Piano Girl," 333.

44. Cooke, "The Advent of Endowed Institutions," 57.

CHAPTER 2: *The Institute of Musical Art*

1. *Rules for the Guidance and Instruction of Students*, 10.

2. Interview with Joseph Fuchs, October 13, 1993, New York City.

3. *Rules for the Guidance and Instruction of Students*, 1926, n.p.; Yurka, *Bohemian Girl*.

4. IMA catalog, 1919–20, 10, 11.

5. IMA faculty handbook, 1920.

6. Kinkeldey, "Waldo Selden Pratt," 162–74.

7. Ives, *Memos*, 5–6. Obsessed with effeminacy in music, Ives wrote, "[Henderson's] ears, for fifty years or so, have been massaged over and over and over again so nice by the same sweet, consonant, evenly repeated sequences and rhythms, and all the soft processes in art 85 percent emasculated, that when he says 'There is no great music in America,' one begins to have a conviction that that is the best indication that there *is* some great music in America."

8. See Thompson, "An American School of Criticism," 428–39. Henderson recommended Aldrich to succeed him on the *Times*. See also Crowthers, "Interesting Incidents of a Distinguished Career," 3. Henderson committed suicide in 1937.

9. Lectures, Recitals, and General Occasions, 1914–15, Juilliard Archives.

10. "The Institute's Rachmaninoff Reception," 8.

11. Lectures, Recitals, and General Occasions, 1906–7, Juilliard Archives.

12. Damrosch, unpublished appendix to *Institute of Musical Art*, 522, typescript, Juilliard Archives.

13. Lectures, Recitals, and General Occasions, 1908–9, Juilliard Archives.

14. Theodorowicz was assistant concertmaster of the Boston Symphony Orchestra for thirty-seven years. He also formed a quartet in Boston, and his students included Walter Piston and Harry Ellis Dickson.

15. Damrosch, *Institute of Musical Art*, 79.

16. IMA board meeting minutes, October 23, 1907, vol. 1, 50–51, Juilliard Archives.

17. Danek, "Kneisel Quartet."

18. Damrosch, *Institute of Musical Art*, 211–12.

19. Ibid., 212.

20. Interview with Joseph Fuchs, October 13, 1993, New York City.

21. "Interview with Franz Kneisel."

22. Damrosch, *Institute of Musical Art*, 213.

23. Ibid., 28.

24. Wittstein, "Percy Goetschius," 1.

25. Bersohn, "An Imaginary Interview with Dr. Goetschius," 11.

26. Saylor, "Henry Cowell."

27. IMA catalog 1916, 28, 29.

28. Perlis, "Leo Ornstein." Paderewski had advised Bertha Tapper to study with Lechetizky in Vienna.

29. James Loeb to Frank Damrosch, als, July 17, 1911, Juilliard Archives.

30. Loesser, *Men, Women and Pianos.*

31. IMA board meeting minutes, April 27, 1910, vol. 1, 88, Juilliard Archives.

32. Harris, "The Occupation of Musicians in the United States," 304.

33. Birmingham, *Real Lace*, 155.

34. Damrosch, *Institute of Musical Art*, 81.

35. Frank Damrosch to James Loeb, carbon copy [hereafter, cc], September 21, 1915, Office of the President, General Administrative Records, 1904–38, box 1, folders 5–6, Juilliard Archives.

36. James Loeb to Frank Damrosch, als, September 20, 1909, Juilliard Archives.

37. James Loeb to Frank Damrosch, als, January 20, 1910, Juilliard Archives.

38. James Loeb to Frank Damrosch, als, July 2, 1910, Juilliard Archives.

39. Barber, ed., *New York Architect*, contains a description of the building.

40. The speeches are reproduced in Damrosch's *Institute of Musical Art*, 125ff.

41. Lectures, Recitals, and General Occasions, 1910–11, Juilliard Archives. For a history of architecture in Morningside Heights and of the IMA and JGS buildings, see Dolkart, *Morningside Heights*, 257–66.

42. Reproduced in Damrosch, *Institute of Musical Art*, 139–42 (emphasis added). This slight condescension was even more startling given Spalding's actions the previous summer. Aware of the construction of a building in New York designed specifically for music, Spalding had sought out Loeb in Bavaria. There he hinted for funds to build a music building at Harvard. Loeb generously agreed on the spot, and in 1914 the Music Building, including Paine Hall, was completed. Loeb wished to remain anonymous, which explained why Spalding did not mention his bequest to Harvard in his speech

at the IMA. No such stricture governed his history of Harvard's music department, however, where he neglects to mention the building of the IMA, his attendance at its dedication ceremony, or the proposed affiliation expressed in this speech. Loeb never saw the Harvard building he and the Warburgs had built for $105,000. A plaque on an interior wall on the stairway now acknowledges his generosity. Spalding, *Music at Harvard*, 26.

43. Damrosch, *Institute of Musical Art*, 143–44.

44. Stebbins and Stebbins, *Frank Damrosch*, 218; original speech in Lectures, Recitals, and General Occasions, 1910–1911, Juilliard Archives.

45. Olmstead, "The Toll of Idealism."

46. The portrait of Loeb, donated by his three sisters and in the School's library, shows him wearing his red Cambridge academic robes.

47. James Loeb to Frank Damrosch, als, May 19, 1909, Juilliard Archives.

48. James Loeb to Frank Damrosch, als, November 24, 1909, Juilliard Archives.

49. *New York Tribune*, April 23, 1911, quoted in Damrosch, *Institute of Musical Art*, 162. Gatti-Casazza (1868–1940) did not attend any board meetings. Hertz (1872–1942), Mahler's principal partner directing German operas in Vienna, became conductor of the San Francisco Symphony.

50. Ibid., 163.

51. Kolodin, *The Metropolitan Opera*, 138.

52. Frank Damrosch to James Loeb, tls, May 31, 1909, Juilliard Archives.

53. IMA catalog, vol. 5, 1909–10.

54. James Loeb to Frank Damrosch, als, December 7, 1911, Juilliard Archives.

55. Letter cited in IMA board meeting minutes, November 1909, vol. 1, 81–82, Juilliard Archives.

56. James Loeb to Frank Damrosch, als, June 29, 1909, and tls, June 22, 1909, Juilliard Archives.

57. IMA catalog 1916–17, 10.

58. Lectures, Recitals, and General Occasions, 1909–10, Juilliard Archives.

59. Lectures, Recitals, and General Occasions, 1910–11, Juilliard Archives.

60. Ibid.

61. Lectures, Recitals, and General Occasions, 1913–14, Juilliard Archives.

62. The talented Barlow (1892–1982), a Harvard graduate who studied piano with Dethier and Friskin, was pulled out of the IMA in mid-year by his father, who "decided it would be well for him to earn his own living" at the Greenwich Settlement (student card for Samuel Barlow, Juillard Archives). His *Mon ami Pierrot* was the first American opera heard at the Opéra-Comique. Barlow wrote about the connection between art and politics in *The Astonished Muse* (1961).

63. Crowthers, "Les Frères Dethier," 4.

64. Mann wrote a memorial to his teacher: "Edouard Dethier, 1885–1962," 6.

65. Damrosch, unpublished appendix to *Institute of Musical Art*, 10, typescript, Juilliard Archives.

66. IMA board meeting minutes, April 13, 1919, vol. 1, 145, Juilliard Archives. This stipulation may indicate the problem with Ganz's teaching: He was too busy concertizing.

67. Swift destroyed Gershwin's letters to her and does not discuss her relationship with him in her autobiography. She married three times.

68. See Pescatello, *Charles Seeger.* They are the parents of Pete Seeger. Seeger's second wife was the composer Ruth Crawford.

69. Damrosch, *Institute of Musical Art*, 186.

70. Frank Damrosch to James Loeb, cc, November 4, 1914, Juilliard Archives.

71. Letz retired from Juilliard in 1963 and died in November 1969 at eighty-three.

72. Martin, *The Damrosch Dynasty*, 250. Perhaps to placate their doubters, in 1918 Walter Damrosch published a harmonized and orchestrated version of "The Star-Spangled Banner."

73. Martin, *The Damrosch Dynasty*, 251; Stebbins and Stebbins, *Frank Damrosch*, 220–25.

74. Lowens, "L'Affaire Muck"; Tischler, "One Hundred Percent Americanism."

75. Danek, "Kneisel Quartet."

76. Stebbins and Stebbins, *Frank Damrosch*, 225.

77. Damrosch, *Institute of Musical Art*, 182.

78. Lectures, Recitals, and General Occasions, 1918–19, Juilliard Archives.

79. See Olmstead, "The Toll of Idealism." They were married on May 22, 1921, in St. Moritz, Switzerland. Schiff had died on September 25, 1920.

80. Frank Damrosch to James Loeb, cc, January 16, 1923, Juilliard Archives.

81. Rodgers, *Musical Stages*, 44–47.

82. *The Baton* reprinted the *Times* review, listed who was in the audience, and printed a cast list and a two-page review by "I. B. Anonymous."

83. Rodgers, *Musical Stages*, 46. Rodgers's daughter, Mary Rodgers Guettel, is chair of Juilliard's board.

84. Damrosch, unpublished appendix to *Institute of Musical Art*, 18, typescript, Juilliard Archives.

85. Lectures, Recitals, and General Occasions, 1915–16, Juilliard Archives. All commencement addresses from the IMA graduations through 1926 are given in Damrosch, unpublished appendix to *Institute of Musical Art*, 319–534, typescript, Juilliard Archives.

CHAPTER 3: *The Juilliard Graduate School*

1. IMA board meeting minutes, 1920–27, vol. 2, 11, Juilliard Archives.

2. "Gives $5,000,000 to Advance Music."

3. "Otto H. Kahn Sees in Gift a Great Recognition of Music."

4. For Kahn, see "Juilliard Bequest Praised by Kahn"; for Bodanzky, see "Bodanzky Praises Fund"; and for Stransky, see "Stransky Discusses Juilliard Bequest to Music." Kahn saw the mission of art to end social unrest; Bodanzky hoped the bequest would aid a national conservatory; and

Stransky suggested "a sort of 'super school' for the best pupils of other conservatories." He even suggested a faculty: Rachmaninoff for piano and Leopold Auer, Ševčík, and Marteau for violin.

5. One of the numerous places this claim appears is Crowthers, "To The Glory of Music," 3. The more time that elapsed since 1919, the larger the sum was reported to be. The Foundation Library Center records the original endowment of the Juilliard Musical Foundation at $13,460,508, giving as its source Kiger's *Operating Principles of the Larger Foundations*, 124. The lack of record-keeping by the Foundation makes it impossible to determine the exact amount, although this figure is impressive in its specificity. Eugene Noble advertised a sum of $12,707,730.15; see Key, *Pierre Key's Music Yearbook*, 298.

6. One ancestor was Laurent Juilhard du Jarry (1685–1730), an ecclesiastic, poet, and orator.

7. This persecution was the reason the Huguenot parents of Eben Tourjée, founder of the New England Conservatory, fled France for the United States in the 1830s.

8. Lunney, *Kelley, Drye and Warren*. Some sources list him as having been born in Canton, Ohio.

9. It was located at 65 Worth Street, later moved to 70 Worth Street and 19–23 Thomas Street, and eventually settled at 40 Worth Street, the largest building in the area. In January 1925 it moved to the new American Radiator Company building at 40 West 40th Street.

10. Walton, *Tomahawks to Textiles*, 107.

11. "Augustus D. Juilliard"; Shaw, "Augustus D. Juilliard"; "A. D. Juilliard, Dry Goods Man, Capitalist, Dies."

12. Helen Juilliard was born on November 16, 1847, and died on April 2, 1916; her portrait hangs at the School.

13. Taubman, *Opera—Front and Back*, 265.

14. *Juilliard v. Greenman, U.S. Supreme Court Reports* 110–13, 4Sct122; 28 LawEd 204ff.

15. U.S. Congressional Hearings Supplement, House Committee on Ways and Means, March 8, 1886, 427–29.

16. Augustus D. Juilliard's will, Juilliard Archives; a copy of this passage is also in the Metropolitan Opera Archives.

17. Juilliard also gave $100,000 each to his brother, two sisters, the American Museum of Natural History, the New York Orthopedic Dispensary and Hospital, the Society of the New York Hospital, the Lincoln Hospital and Home, the Tuxedo Hospital, the New York Society for the Prevention of Cruelty to Children, St. John's Guild, and to trusts established for other relatives.

18. Obituaries of Frederick A. Juilliard in *New York Herald Tribune* and *New York Times*, June 30, 1937.

19. John Perry (d. 1951), a friend of Juilliard's and the principal tax lawyer in the firm of Kelley, Drye and Warren (still the School's legal representatives) drew up and witnessed the will.

20. James N. Wallace Obituary, *New York Times*, October 12, 1919, 22:3.

21. Editorial, *New York Times*, June 28, 1919, sec. 4, 5:1.

22. James N. Wallace Obituary.

23. George Davison served as a JMF trustee until 1948. He was a trustee of Wesleyan from 1912 until his death in 1953. One of the university's greatest benefactors, he donated the Davison Rare Book Room to their library. He is described as a "crashing bore." See Brayer, *George Eastman*, 212–13.

24. Augustus D. Juilliard's will, 18, Juilliard Archives. Had the corporation not been originated in the lifetimes of Frederick Juilliard or Robert Westaway (Juilliard's partner and treasurer of the A. D. Juilliard Company), the entire sum would have been given to the American Museum of Natural History and to St. John's Guild of New York and there would never have been a school named Juilliard.

25. Sellers, *Dickinson College*, 319.

26. Ibid.

27. "Juilliard Chief Answers Criticism"; also quoted in *New York Morning Telegraph*, September 16, 1927. This latter newspaper took particular umbrage to Noble and actively campaigned against him and for a more efficient use of Juilliard's funds.

28. *The Wesleyan Alumnus* (October 1920), 13. The source of the quotation is not given.

29. "Juilliard Millions Now Aiding Music."

30. Charles H. Meltzer to the Editor, *New York Times*, December 17, 1922, sec. 7, 4:3.

31. "$1,000,000 Interest Is Won by Juilliard Estate Heirs."

32. The Juilliard estate was finally settled in April 1925 at $15,795,892 (not counting the money for the JMF). The entire estate was appraised at $25,848,746. In May the taxes on it amounted to $441,066. The $13,000,000 given to charities was exempt from taxation. "Except for the estate of the late E. H. Harriman, railroad magnate, the Juilliard fortune was the largest ever appraised in Orange County." "Juilliard Tax $441,066."

33. "Explains Juilliard Fund to Aid Music."

34. Ibid.

35. Erskine, *My Life in Music*, 53.

36. IMA board meeting minutes, 1920–27, December 1921, vol. 2, 16b, Juilliard Archives.

37. Damrosch, *Institute of Musical Art*, 189–90.

38. Ibid., 191–92. The idea is reminiscent of Damrosch's earlier performances incorporating thousands of singers.

39. A few years after the affiliation, William Schuman earned a B.S. at Teachers College at Columbia University. He never stated that he had either applied to or attended the IMA.

40. IMA board meeting minutes, 1920–27, 1925, vol. 2, 36b, Juilliard Archives.

41. Frank Damrosch to James Loeb, cc, February 17, 1925, Juilliard Archives.

42. Berezowsky, *Duet with Nicky*, 16–17.

43. James Loeb to Frank Damrosch, tls, March 27, 1923, Juilliard Archives.

44. Later, as an investment, it bought buildings at 123–131 East 84th Street containing forty six- and seven-room apartments. The nine-story buildings were foreclosed in 1942.

45. Between 1880 and 1884 William H. Vanderbilt had built a pair of famous houses on Fifth Avenue between 51st and 52nd streets. His son, William Kissam Vanderbilt, built a chateau on the north side of Fifth Avenue and 52nd street. The JMF purchase of the guest house was not a wise investment. After standing empty in the 1930s, which provoked more public criticism of the Foundation, it became an annex to CBS radio for fifty years until it was sold to the Duane Reade Company in 1988.

46. Marcella Sembrich's studio was on the third floor; the Lhevinnes' piano studio, a former drawing room, was on the second. But Ernest Hutcheson and Carl Friedberg regularly scheduled classes in their homes.

47. "One Hundred Fellowships for Music Pupils."

48. Editorial, *New York Times*, June 23, 1924, 20:5.

49. See Brayer, *George Eastman*.

50. Damrosch, *Institute of Musical Art*, 198–99.

51. Frank Damrosch to James Loeb, cc, June 6, 1924, Juilliard Archives. Harold Bauer was one who refused Noble.

52. Flesch, *Memoires*, 334–35, 351.

53. James Loeb to Frank Damrosch, tls, September 21, 1924, Juilliard Archives. This postscript is handwritten.

54. Bellamann, "Some Conspicuous American Musical Needs," is the third article in the series.

55. Bellamann's novels include *The Upward Pass, Crescendo, The Richest Woman in Town, The Gray Man Walks,* and his best-known, *Kings Row.* He also translated Dante's *Divina Commedia* and Brahms's songs into English.

56. H.O.O., "Juilliard Foundation Plans Explained."

57. "Twelve Noted Musicians Juilliard Teachers."

58. Erskine, *My Life in Music*, 74, 75.

59. Stokowski, *An American Musician's Story*, 174–75.

60. Miller, "Marcella Sembrich."

61. Owen, *A Recollection of Marcella Sembrich*, 55, 66.

62. *An Outline of the Life and Career of Madame Marcella Sembrich.*

63. Schoen-René, *America's Musical Inheritance.* In her book Schoen-René praises Noble without reservation.

64. Damrosch, *Institute of Musical Art*, 204–5; Erskine, *My Life in Music*, 53.

65. The entire list, along with the students' hometowns, is given in "Juilliard Fellows in Music Chosen." The majority are female musicians.

66. "Results of Juilliard Fellowships."

67. "Fifty-one Win Juilliard Music Fellowships."

68. Noss, *A History of the Yale School of Music*, 128. This inference may not be the sole one; Noble was loath to commit the money to anyone and wished to dole it out personally.

69. Damrosch, *Institute of Musical Art*, 201.

70. Ibid., 198.

71. See Bradley, "The Necessity of Standardization in Music Education." Damrosch and the others were interested in 1924.

72. Neumeyer, "A History of the National Association of Schools of Music," 43.

73. "Subjects for Discussion in New York Art Circles."

74. Damrosch, *Institute of Musical Art*, 204–5.

75. "Juilliard Awards in Music Won by Forty-nine." The article notes that the year's full one hundred fellowships had been awarded.

76. Banner, *A Passionate Preference*. Giannini brought Howard Aibel and Olegna Fuschi from Juilliard to the faculty. Peters studied with Alexander Siloti from 1925 to 1933.

77. "Juilliard Foundation Advisory Board Out."

78. "The Juilliard Advisors." Consistently described as shy, Bliss overcame her upbringing, which dictated that the only times a lady's name should appear in a newspaper was at birth, marriage, and death.

79. One of the many places this statement was reprinted was in *"Musical Digest* Submits Questionnaire."

80. Erskine, *The Memory of Certain Persons*, 371.

81. Martin, *The Damrosch Dynasty*, 297.

82. Stebbins and Stebbins, *Frank Damrosch*, 236.

83. Ibid., 238; see also Martin, *The Damrosch Dynasty*, 301.

84. Erskine, *My Life in Music*, 72.

85. "Juilliard Trustees Plan Music Centre."

86. Interview with Joseph Fuchs, October 13, 1993; Schwartz, *Great Masters of the Violin*, 420.

87. Key's first article, "Juilliard Musical Foundation Faces Propitious Moment for Advancement," appeared on September 28, 1926. Subsequent articles (all with large headlines on page one) appeared in the October 5, October 12, October 19, and November 2 issues. The headlines of the December 7 issue trumpeted Bradley's resignation. Key had been educated at the Chicago Musical College and been a music critic in Chicago, where he had no doubt known Bradley.

88. P. V. Key to John Erskine, tls, September 13, 1927, Presidents' Records, box 5, folder 5, Juilliard Archives.

89. "Music Foundation Policies Attacked."

90. The secretary of state's letter appears in *"Musical Digest* Submits Questionnaire."

91. Erskine, *My Life in Music*, 55–56. The pen is not in the Juilliard Archives.

92. Peabody (1849–1931) was a lawyer who was president of the Mutual Life Insurance Company and a trustee of the Astor estate. He had been in the newspapers frequently during the 1920s as the result of various investigations into insurance dealings.

93. "Juilliard Foundation Work Is Criticized."

94. *"Musical Digest* Submits Questionnaire."

95. "Juilliard Secretary E. A. Noble Wields Supreme Authority."

96. Key, "Nation's Daily Press and Music Leaders Voice Opinions on Juilliard Foundation," 10.

97. Ibid.

98. Key, "Testimony is Conclusive," 9.

99. Martin, *Causes and Conflicts*, 280.

100. "Regents Approve Juilliard School."

101. "Music Foundation Defends Its Policy."

102. "Education Director Bradley Resigns."

103. "K. M. Bradley Quits Juilliard School."

104. Because of the JMF's lack of administrative record-keeping, no minutes of board meetings and no records of students or faculty survive in the Juilliard Archives. The JGS scrapbooks in the archives do not contain the many newspaper articles about the controversy surrounding the Foundation or the School.

105. "K. M. Bradley Quits Juilliard School."

106. "Bradley Charges Chaotic Situation." Bradley retired from music altogether in 1934, twenty years before his death.

107. Ibid.

108. "Juilliard Chief Answers Criticism."

109. Key, Editorial.

110. The name of the student is not given.

111. *Brooklyn Eagle*, March 25, 1934.

112. "Act to Reorganize Juilliard School."

113. "Juilliard Foundation Changes Are Forecast."

114. "Hutcheson to Head the Juilliard Fund."

115. Erskine, *My Life in Music*, 58.

116. Ibid., 72. The letter is dated March 20, 1928.

117. Damrosch, *Institute of Musical Art*, 221.

118. Rice, "A Tribute to Frank Damrosch," 133.

CHAPTER 4: *The Juilliard School of Music*

1. See Bull, *The Immortal Ernest Hutcheson.*

2. Kirkpatrick, "Ernest Hutcheson," 13.

3. Hutcheson, *A Musical Guide to the Richard Wagner* Ring of the Niebelung. Hutcheson's *The Literature of the Piano* was first published in Great Britain in 1948 by Alfred A. Knopf and reprinted with revisions by Rudolph Ganz in 1958, 1969, and 1974. The book traverses the repertoire from Bach to Brahms (with brief paragraphs about contemporary composers) and stresses the use of Urtext editions.

4. Kirkpatrick, "Ernest Hutcheson," 10–13.

5. Erskine, *My Life in Music*, 39–40.

6. Ibid., 31.

7. Interview with Anna Crouse, February 21, 1997, New York City.

8. Erskine, *The Memory of Certain Persons*, 371.

9. Hutcheson, "Why Study Abroad?"

10. Frank Damrosch, speaking at the twenty-fifth anniversary of the IMA in 1930, in Damrosch, unpublished appendix to *Institute of Musical Art*, 202a, typescript, Juilliard Archives.

11. Kirkpatrick, "Ernest Hutcheson," 10–13.

12. *Musical Leader*, September 15, 1932.

13. Kirkpatrick, "Ernest Hutcheson," 13.

14. John Erskine Obituary, *New York Times*, June 3, 1951, 92:1.

15. Rubin, *The Making of Middlebrow Culture*, 169. Rubin analyzes Erskine's contribution to the dissemination of literature to a wider audience.

16. Crowthers, "John Erskine."

17. Erskine, *The Private Life of Helen of Troy.*

18. Other books included *Selections from the Idylls of the King, A Pageant in Honor of Roger Bacon, The Moral Obligation to Be Intelligent, The Shadowed Hour,* and *Sonata and Other Poems.* Essays included *The Literary Discipline, The Enchanted Garden, Prohibition and Christianity, The Delight of Great Books.* Erskine was editor of *Contemporary War Poems, Intepretations of Literature, Appreciations of Poetry, Life and Literature, Talks to Writers, Books and Habits,* and *Pre-Raphaelite and other Poets.* He also wrote a history of the Philharmonic, *The Philharmonic Society of New York.*

19. Rubin, *The Making of Middlebrow Culture*, 180.

20. Smith, "Profiles."

21. Erskine, "The Juilliard Policy in Operation."

22. Erskine, "Is There a Career in Music?" 9.

23. Ibid., 10, 18, 19.

24. Erskine, *The Memory of Certain Persons*, 374.

25. Erskine, *My Life in Music*, 262. The other three autobiographies are *My Life as a Teacher,* "My Life as a Writer" (a draft), and *The Memory of Certain Persons.*

26. Erskine, *The Influence of Women.*

27. Nin, *The Early Diaries of Anaïs Nin*, vol. 4. Nin referred to Adelene Pychon as "Lilith."

28. Rhoda Erskine (1893–1934) died of an embolism at age thirty-nine. She had coached Sergei Rachmaninoff's children.

29. Martin, *The Damrosch Dynasty*, 302.

30. Irving Weil, *New York Journal*, December 3, 1928.

31. Richard L. Stokes, *New York World*, December 2, 1928. The reviews appear in Erskine's six volumes of scrapbooks in the Juilliard Archives.

32. Quoted by Ruth Crawford in an unpublished memoir (ca. 1930), Seeger Estate, Music Division, Library of Congress. Tick, "Charles Ives and Gender Ideology," 104.

33. Paul Warburg to John Erskine, April 3, 1930, Presidents' Records, box 2, folder 1, Juilliard Archives. See Potter, "Success in High Society."

34. "In 1927, the Juilliard Foundation purchased the three-story residential structure on the corner of Broadway and 122nd Street, and the Hudson-Grant View, a six-story apartment house at 122 Claremont Avenue (John C. Watson, 1908). In 1928, a small vacant lot on Broadway was purchased, as well as the Lincoln at 130 Claremont Avenue (John Hauser, 1908). In 1929, the foundation bought two additional six-story apartment buildings, the Buckingham and the Hazelton Court at 3089 and 3099 Broadway (both Neville and Bagge, 1907). The Institute of Musical Art already owned two small parcels on Broadway just north of 122nd Street." Dolkart, *Morningside Heights*, 442–43.

35. Erskine, *The Memory of Certain Persons*, 371.

36. Ibid., 371–72.

37. Kirkpatrick, "A Tone Poem in Color," 13–16. Quotations describing the building are taken from this source.

38. Like the school at whose celebration it was premiered, Prokofiev's Sinfonietta had a labored history. He had written it as a conservatory student in 1909 on hearing Rimsky-Korsakov's Sinfonietta, Opus 31. It was first performed in 1915, a year after its reworking, but that version did not satisfy the

composer, who rewrote it again in 1929. The work presaged Prokofiev's neo-classical style, but Koussevitzky called it a "pleasant nonentity."

39. Erskine, *My Life in Music*, 100–101.

40. Ibid., 120. Goettlicher continued as orchestral librarian at Juilliard and at Chautauqua for more than thirty years; he accompanied the Juilliard Orchestra to Europe in 1958 and died in 1964.

41. Kirkpatrick, "A Tone Poem in Color."

42. Erskine, *My Life in Music*, 119.

43. Kirkpatrick, "A Tone Poem in Color."

44. Ibid.

45. Erskine, *My Life in Music*, 134.

46. Arnold Schoenberg to Ernest Hutcheson, tls, November 14, 1933, Schoenberg Collection, Library of Congress.

47. Glenn Gould–Gertrud Schoenberg, recorded interview, Los Angeles, March 8, 1962, transcript, 4, Arnold Schoenberg Institute. This explanation does not ring true. Many fine European conservatories have the word *school* in their title (for example, Scuola Cantorum), including where Schoenberg himself had taught—the Berlin Hochschule für Musik. Yet the Schoenbergs may have thought that "school" in English was not the equivalent of "scuola" or "schule."

48. Schoenberg's letters are in the Arnold Schoenberg Institute; those by Hutcheson are found in the Library of Congress. None of this correspondence is in the Juilliard Archives, the result of house-cleaning during the William Schuman years.

49. Ernest Hutcheson to Arnold Schoenberg, telegram, October 5, 22, 1934, Library of Congress; Arnold Schoenberg to Ernest Hutcheson, draft, ca. October 1934, Arnold Schoenberg Institute.

50. Arnold Schoenberg to Ernest Hutcheson, tls, October 3, 1934, Arnold Schoenberg Institute, published in part in *Arnold Schoenberg Letters*, ed. Stein, 190.

51. "Schoenberg to Join Juilliard's Faculty."

52. Arnold Schoenberg to Ernest Hutcheson, cc, March 28, 1935 [in German], Arnold Schoenberg Institute, translated and published in part in *Arnold Schoenberg Letters*, ed. Stein, 193.

53. Arnold Schoenberg to Ernest Hutcheson, cc, June 11, 1935 [in German], Arnold Schoenberg Institute, also in *Arnold Schoenberg Letters*, ed. Stein, 194.

54. Kirkpatrick, "Institute News: Student Activities."

55. Freundlich, "Piu mosso."

56. *Dynamics*, November 9, 1934, 63.

57. Frank Damrosch to Martha Halbwachs, cc, n.d., Presidents' Records, box 2, folder 5, Juilliard Archives.

58. Erskine quoted in *Dynamics*, April 3, 1935, 135.

59. Letters from the Faculty to John Erskine, Presidents' Records, box 3, folder 9, Juilliard Archives.

60. Stokowski, *An American Musician's Story*, 181.

61. Kline, *Olga Samaroff Stokowski*, 144.

62. Samaroff, *An American Musician's Story*, 192–93.

63. Ibid., 177.

64. Ibid., 184.

65. Smith, *Master Pianist.*

66. Ibid., 98.

67. Ibid., 103.

68. Siloti, *Remembering Franz Liszt,* 338–75.

69. Erskine, *My Life in Music,* 106.

70. Wallace, *A Century of Music-Making.*

71. Ibid., 216.

72. Ibid., 191.

73. Spalding's autobiography, *Rise to Follow,* does not mention the twelve years he taught at Juilliard (chapter 6).

74. For more on Spalding and Persinger, see Schwarz, *Great Masters of the Violin.*

75. Stebbins and Stebbins, *Frank Damrosch,* 245.

76. Damrosch, unpublished appendix to *Institute of Musical Art,* typescript, Juilliard Archives.

77. Kolodin, "A Pioneer Passes."

CHAPTER 5: *Opera and Orchestra*

1. Interview with Bernstein June 2, 1953, in McNaughton, "Albert Stoessel," 334.

2. Ibid., 350.

3. Erskine, *My Life in Music,* 451.

4. Downes, "Music," October 4, 1931.

5. The opera was published "for the Juilliard Musical Foundation" by C. C. Birchard and Company in Boston in 1933.

6. "Insists Opera Get Juilliard Subsidy"; "Singers Intensify Opera Fund Drive."

7. Erskine, *My Life in Music,* 152.

8. Quoted in "Music" in *Time* magazine, which ran photographs of Erskine and Augustus D. Juilliard and mentioned that Erskine "spoke out of turn" in 1933 during the Met's campaign but now (in 1935) "wisely kept his counsel."

9. John Erskine to Allen Wardwell, cc plus draft version, March 27, 1933, Presidents' Records, box 2, folder 5, Juilliard Archives.

10. Erskine, *My Life in Music,* 148; Kolodin, *The Metropolitan Opera,* 477–79.

11. "Opera Accepts Juilliard Terms."

12. Erskine, *My Life in Music,* 151.

13. Downes, "Music," December 15, 1935.

14. Ernest Hutcheson to John Erskine, January 3, 1938, Presidents' Records, box 1, folder 7, Juilliard Archives.

15. Antheil, *Bad Boy of Music,* 253.

16. Thomson, "Music."

17. Kiesler, *Ten Years of American Opera Design,* New York Public Library for the Performing Arts.

18. Thomson, "The Gluck Case."

19. "Opera School Presentations Mark Composers League Twentieth Anniversary."

20. McNaughton, *Albert Stoessel*, 358.

21. Ibid., 360.

22. "Juilliard Orchestra Delights Throng."

23. McNaughton, *Albert Stoessel*, 344.

24. Interview with Mark Schubart, September 9, 1994, New York City.

25. Juilliard School of Music catalog, 1935–36, 2.

26. Interview with Frances Schuman, April 16, 1994, New York City.

27. McNaughton, *Albert Stoessel*, iii, iv.

28. "Stoessel Falls to Stage and Dies Conducting Arts Academy Fete"; Howard, *Our American Music*, 482, quoted in McNaughton, *Albert Stoessel*, 3.

29. Wolfram, Editorial.

30. Margaret McGill attended the IMA from 1907 to 1915, a student of Madeleine Walther.

31. Interview with Anne Brown, *New York World Telegram*, January 9, 1936.

32. Sherrock, "The Inquiring Reporter."

33. Oscar Wagner, minutes of the faculty meeting, October 15, 1940, Juilliard Archives.

34. Wedge, "Message from Dean Wedge."

35. Hutcheson, "A Message to Our Boys in Service."

36. Dorothy Crowthers, IMA faculty minutes, 1939–44, Juilliard Archives.

37. Ernest Hutcheson, IMA faculty minutes, 1939–44, February 9, 1944, Juilliard Archives.

CHAPTER 6: *New Blood*

1. Erskine, *My Life in Music*, 254.

2. Interview with William Schuman, Oral History, American Music, Yale University School of Music, 19, interviews conducted by Vivian Perlis, 1977. (Hereafter cited as Schuman interview, Yale Oral History.)

3. Schuman interview, Yale Oral History, 32.

4. Loesser, *A Most Remarkable Fella*, 96. These were Schuman's, Frances Schuman's, and Susan Loesser's observations about her uncle Arthur; Frank Loesser never said anything against Arthur and strove for his approval.

5. Schreiber and Persichetti, *William Schuman*, 7. The authors divide the book: Persichetti writes about the music, and Schreiber about the life. Schreiber, a professional writer and not a musicologist, is best known for her book *Sybil*, about a woman supposedly suffering from Multi-Personality Disorder. She relies entirely on Schuman's version of events, many of which would be difficult to document. The book was published by the firm Schuman headed at the time.

6. Schreiber and Persichetti, *William Schuman*, 8.

7. Dewey, *Art as Experience*. The book grew from a series of lectures Dewey gave in 1931 at Harvard University's Department of Philosophy. It barely mentions music.

8. For more on Dewey, see Ryan, *John Dewey and the High Tide of American Liberalism.*

9. Schreiber and Persichetti, *William Schuman*, 13.

10. The peripatetic Harris and his wife taught at the Summer School again in the summer of 1937; by 1941 he had been replaced on that faculty by JGS graduate Vittorio Giannini.

11. William Schuman, interview for the Lincoln Center Archives, July 10, 1990, 90, interviews conducted by Sharon Zane.

12. Copland, "Scores and Records," 245–46.

13. Schreiber and Persichetti, *William Schuman*, 19.

14. Schuman interview, Yale Oral History, 229.

15. Erskine, *My Life in Music*, 254.

16. Schuman interview, Yale Oral History, 347.

17. Another version of the story, in addition to Schuman's in the Yale Oral History, 345, appears in "William Schuman," iv.

18. Schuman interview, Yale Oral History, 346.

19. Ibid.; Schreiber and Persichetti, *William Schuman*, 30.

20. Frankenstein, "American Composers," 27.

21. Schreiber and Persichetti, *William Schuman*, 37, 39, 42.

22. Schuman interview, Yale Oral History, 360.

23. Ibid., 381.

24. Parmenter, "Juilliard School Shuts Down Its Summer Session."

25. Schuman interview, Yale Oral History, 358.

26. Ibid., 359. Calling him Dean Wagner, and then correcting himself, betrays his status as a former student.

27. Rudolf, *The Grammar of Conducting.*

28. Mark Schubart, interview for the Lincoln Center Archives, December 20, 1991, 26, conducted by Sharon Zane.

29. Schuman interview, Yale Oral History, 368.

30. Smith, *Master Pianist*, 104–5.

31. Ibid.; the original is in Presidents' Records, box 15, folder 18, Juilliard Archives.

32. Schuman interview, Yale Oral History, 350.

33. Wallace, *A Century of Music-Making*, 262.

34. William Schuman to Henry Fusner, March 21, 1947, Presidents' Records, box 15, folder 18, Juilliard Archives.

35. Muriel Kerr to William Schuman, March 18, 1950, Presidents' Records, box 16, folder 6, Juilliard Archves.

36. William Schuman to Ernest Hutcheson, June 14, 1946, Presidents' Records, box 15, folder 18, Juilliard Archives.

37. There are no letters from Schuman to Schoenberg at the Arnold Schoenberg Institute.

38. Albert Spalding to William Schuman, January 8, 1946, Presidents' Records, box 15, folder 18, Juilliard Archives.

39. William Schuman, personal memorandum, November 4, 1949, Presidents' Records, box 16, folder 6, Juilliard Archives.

40. Jacobi died on October 25, 1952.

41. "Report on Administration-Faculty-Student Relations at the Juilliard School of Music," Presidents' Records, box 1, folder 3, Juilliard Archives.

The report is signed by composition students Henry Nagorka and Gerard Jaffe, pianists Herbert Melnick and Geraldine Agress, pianist and music education major Henry E. Ziegler, and violinists Rosalyn Furlonge and Rosemary H. Smith, all members of the psychology and sociology classes taught by Jay Wright.

42. *Stretto* did, however, publish such timeless articles as "Are Singers Musicians?" and "Are Oboists Crazy?"

43. Curriculum report on the 1946–47 Teacher Training Program, Presidents' Records, box 4, folder 9, Juilliard Archives.

44. Juilliard School of Music catalog, 1947–50, 56.

45. Schuman, Yale Oral History, 368–69.

46. Worden, "About People." Worden was John Erskine's wife.

47. Glass, *Music by Philip Glass*, 136.

48. Schuman interview, Yale Oral History, 370.

49. Gay, *The Juilliard String Quartet*, 7.

50. Ibid., 8.

51. Joel Smirnoff to the author, December 27, 1995.

52. Thomson, "'Theory' at Juilliard."

53. Schuman, "On Teaching the Literature and Materials of Music."

54. Ibid., 161.

55. Ibid., 162–63.

56. Ibid., 168.

57. *The Evaluation Report for the Commission on Institutions of Higher Education of the Middle States Association of Colleges and Secondary Schools*, December 4–7, 1955, 10.

58. Ibid., 12.

59. Schuman and Goldman, "Introduction," 15–16.

60. Eyer, "Juilliard L and M Report," 146.

61. An example is Lowell, "The Juilliard Report on Teaching the Literature and Materials of Music," 250.

62. Hardy and Fish, *Music Literature: Homophony;* Hardy and Fish, *Music Literature: Polyphony.*

63. Schuman interview, Yale Oral History, 376.

64. Smith, "The Economic Situation of the Performer," 13.

65. Baumol and Bowen, *Performing Arts*, 209. See also Hart, *Orpheus in the New World* (Hart is a former manager of the Juilliard Orchestra).

66. Letter signed "Composition Students at Juilliard," May 1957, Dean's Records, box 33, folder 4, "Misc. C," Juilliard Archives.

67. Chasins, *The Van Cliburn Legend*, 42.

68. Ibid., 48; see also Reich, *Van Cliburn*, 40–73.

69. Chasins, *The Van Cliburn Legend*, 93–94; Wallace, *A Century of Music Making*, 284.

70. William Schuman to Van Cliburn, telegram, May 19, 1958, Presidents' Records, box 2, folder 16, Juilliard Archives.

71. Chasins, *Van Cliburn Legend*, 17.

72. Ibid., 138.

73. Since the late 1940s Juilliard has maintained three orchestras, and their names have changed. In 1947 they were called the Juilliard Orchestra, the Juilliard Chamber Orchestra, and the Juilliard Training Orchestra.

In 1949 the second two orchestras were known as Orchestra II and Orchestra III, which later had their names changed to the Juilliard Theater Orchestra and the Juilliard Philharmonia. In the 1970s the first orchestra was known as the Concert Orchestra, a name that returned to the "Juilliard Orchestra" in the late 1980s. During that same period, the Theater Orchestra became the Juilliard Symphony. The number of players in each orchestra has stayed constant at about one hundred. During the 1950s and 1960s, the orchestras gave seven annual concerts, a number that began to increase significantly in 1968.

74. "Juilliard Orchestra Tour—1958," 6.

75. Taubman, "On Coming Home."

76. Presidents' Records, box 9, folder 7, 17, Juilliard Archives.

77. "William Schuman."

78. W. McNeil Lowry, interview for Lincoln Center Archives, March 19, 1991, 76, 132, conducted by Sharon Zane.

79. Frank Loesser to William Schuman, August 18, 1965, quoted in Loesser, *A Most Remarkable Fella*, 263.

80. Schreiber and Persichetti, *William Schuman*, 42.

81. Interview with Frances Schuman, April 19, 1994, New York City.

82. "William Schuman Elected President," 8.

CHAPTER 7: *Lincoln Center*

1. Martin, *Lincoln Center*, 10.

2. Ibid., 11.

3. Young, *Lincoln Center*.

4. Martin, *Lincoln Center*, 14.

5. Pace, "Charles M. Spofford Is Dead."

6. Martin, *Lincoln Center*, 14. Perhaps it is not so strange, when wealth and power are concentrated in the hands of a few men.

7. Ibid., 17.

8. Young, *Lincoln Center*, 42–43.

9. Gill, "The Sky Line," 57.

10. W. McNeil Lowry, interview for the Lincoln Center Archives, January 11, 1991, 46, conducted by Sharon Zane.

11. Mennin, "Convocation," 1. All articles in the *Juilliard News Bulletin*, Mennin's replacement for the more scholarly *Juilliard Review*, are unsigned. The *Bulletin* is businesslike and has no contributions from students.

12. Young, *Lincoln Center*, 25.

13. Edgar B. Young, interview for the Lincoln Center archives, August 14, 1990, 130, conducted by Sharon Zane.

14. Grutzner, "Lincoln Square Project May Include Music and Stage Schools."

15. Mark Schubart, interview for the Lincoln Center Archives, December 20, 1991, 35, conducted by Sharon Zane.

16. Young, *Lincoln Center*, 55.

17. "Center School Is Envisioned as Providing Internships to Promising Young Artists."

18. Interview with Mark Schubart, September 9, 1994, New York City.

19. Minutes and Reports of the Board of Trustees, December 7, 1956, box 2, folder 3, Juilliard Archives.

20. Schonberg, "Juilliard to Move to Lincoln Square." Mennin considered four possible new names: Juilliard School, The Juilliard School, Juilliard School of the Performing Arts, and Juilliard School for the Performing Arts. In deference to the Dance and Drama Divisions, the School dropped "of Music" from its name in 1969. For more than three decades, however, journalists and others have not adjusted to the "new" name. The Juilliard School is still frequently—and incorrectly—referred to as the Juilliard School of Music.

21. Waldrop, "The Juilliard Story," 44. The entire issue of *Musical America* is devoted to Lincoln Center. Included are two photographs of models for the building that differ considerably from the finished product.

22. Anthony Bliss, interview for the Lincoln Center Archives, June 4, 1991, 114, conducted by Sharon Zane.

23. Ibid., 116.

24. Edgar Young, interview for the Lincoln Center Archives, October 11, 1990, 204, conducted by Sharon Zane.

25. Young, *Lincoln Center*, 88.

26. Young, *Lincoln Center*, 121.

27. Ibid., 130.

28. Schwarz, "The Juilliard School," 121.

29. Kihss, "Arts Center Costs Hits 131 Million."

30. W. McNeil Lowry, interview for Lincoln Center Archives, January 14, 1991, 94, conducted by Sharon Zane.

31. Schumach, "Seven Injured as Floor Collapses."

32. "Juilliard to Move to Lincoln Square."

33. Young, *Lincoln Center*, 248. Schuman may have had a proprietary feeling about the Carnegie money, which had come to the School while he was president. Nevertheless, Mennin's case had seemed clearcut. In "Arts Center Gets Grant of $500,000," the *New York Times* announced that "the $500,000, which will be used for scholarships and other assistance to young artists, will be administered by the Juilliard School of Music." Schuman is also quoted in the article to this effect.

34. Schwarz, "The Juilliard School," 121–30.

35. Interview with Gideon Waldrop, June 7, 1995, New York City; *Juilliard School Bulletin*, 1973–74, 17.

36. Alice Tully, interview for the Lincoln Center Archives, January 8, 1991, 14, conducted by Sharon Zane.

37. He was the son of Czar Nicholas's surgeon general. A fellow student of Jascha Heifetz, Paul was giving concerts in Russia at the age of eleven. He fought the Germans in World War I, was captured, escaped, and came to the United States by way of Japan. In Texas he struck it rich as an oilman and became friends with both Presidents Kennedy and Johnson. His sympathy for young artists trying to find acceptance in America led him to donate money for the hall.

38. Georganne Mennin, interview for the Lincoln Center Archives, December 3, 1992, 23–24, conducted by Sharon Zane.

39. Hart, "The Juilliard School Building."

40. Schonberg, Drye, Mennin, and Bernstein all quoted in Martin, *Lincoln Center*, 155, 156, 160.

41. Hellman, "Juilliard Faces Reality"; Hayes, "The History of The Juilliard School," 123.

42. Schonberg, "Taj Mahal of Music."

43. Gill, "The Sky Line," 58–59.

44. Mennin, "Commencement Address."

45. Edgar Young, interview for the Lincoln Center Archives, June 11, 1990, 336, conducted by Sharon Zane.

46. Schuman, "The New Establishment," 8; also quoted in Young, *Lincoln Center*, 283.

47. Young, *Lincoln Center*, 284.

48. Ibid., 284.

49. Ibid., 293.

50. Shepard, "Schuman Quiting Lincoln Center Post."

51. Rouse, *William Schuman Documentary*, 26.

52. Schonberg, "Juilliard Program Symbolizes a Decade."

53. Gould, "No, They're Only a Fad," 1.

54. Rouse, *William Schuman Documentary*, 23.

55. Young, *Lincoln Center*, 276.

56. Schuman, "William Schuman Protests."

57. Mayer, "Are the Trying Times Just Beginning?"

58. Mayer, "William Schuman Protests."

59. Mark Schubart, interview for the Lincoln Center Archives, December 20, 1991, 54, conducted by Sharon Zane.

CHAPTER 8: *Dancers' Training*

1. José Limón, untitled speech, February 8, 1972, Presidents' Records, box 28, folder 2, Juilliard Archives.

2. Soares, "Martha Hill."

3. Brockway, *Bennington College*, 125.

4. Soares, "Remembering Martha Hill," 8.

5. Faith Reyher Jackson, quoted in Brockway, *Bennington College*, 133.

6. Gloria Eksergian, quoted in Brockway, *Bennington College*, 127.

7. Soares, "Martha Hill," 4.

8. Ibid.

9. Kriegsman, *Modern Dance in America*, xii, xiii. As early as the 1960s, Hill and Shelly planned to write a history of the famous Bennington summer school. Not only did Hill never produce the book but she also restricted access to materials sought by other authors.

10. Soares, "Remembering Martha Hill," 9.

11. Soares, "Martha Hill," 4.

12. June Dunbar, interview for the Lincoln Center Archives, July 22, 1993, 12, conducted by Sharon Zane.

13. Interview with Muriel Topaz, July 6, 1995, Aspen, Colorado. Many of Graham's own dancers had previously studied ballet; Erick Hawkins was an early example.

14. Dance faculty contracts, Juilliard Archives.

15. "Choreography is Copyrighted for First Time."

16. "A Vital Experiment in Dance Education," 14.

17. Margaret Lloyd's description from the *Christian Science Monitor* is quoted in Soares, *Louis Horst*, 181; ibid., 182 (Doris Rudko quotation).

18. Taylor, *Private Domain*, 43, reprinted in Taylor, "Paul Taylor's Juilliard Days," 4, 5. Taylor weaves fact and fiction in his autobiography.

19. Agnes de Mille to F. Taylor Jones, quoted in *The Evaluation Report for the Commission on Institutions of Higher Education of the Middle States Association of Colleges and Secondary Schools*, December 4–7, 1955, 13.

20. Taylor, "Paul Taylor's Juilliard Days," 4, 5.

21. Gray, "Martha Graham, Teacher."

22. Cohen, ed., *Doris Humphrey*, 208.

23. Warren, *Anna Sokolow*, 173–79 (quotations on 177).

24. Ibid., 177.

25. Sabin, "Juilliard at the Crossroads."

26. Peter Mennin to Martha Hill, February 6, 1964, Presidents' Records, box 27, folder 9, "Dance Department," Juilliard Archives.

27. Schuman, "Foreword," 3.

28. Perlmutter, *Shadowplay*, 236.

29. Sirpa Tepper, quoted in ibid., 234.

30. Martha Graham, quoted in ibid., 242.

31. Interview with Muriel Topaz, July 6, 1995, Aspen, Colorado. David Diamond, however, has asserted that AIDS is taking its toll most in the Dance Division.

32. de Mille, *Martha*, 413.

33. Pischl, "Touring with the Juilliard Dance Department."

34. Barnes, "Dance."

35. Unsigned letter to Peter Mennin, Presidents' Records, box 28, folder 3, Juilliard Archives. Terrorists are not expected to be good spellers.

36. Minutes and Reports of the Board of Trustees, December 7, 1956, box 2, folder 3, Juilliard Archives. The extent of the sellout of the department was so great that Edgar Young, a participant in almost all Lincoln Center negotiations, implies in his authoritative history of Lincoln Center that before the move there was no Dance Department at all at Juilliard.

37. Sabin, "Juilliard at the Crossroads," 35; Deborah Jowitt is quoted on page 35 of the same article.

38. Gideon Waldrop, memorandum, March 29, 1968, Presidents' Records, box 28, folder 2, Juilliard Archives.

39. Sabin, "Juilliard at the Crossroads," 34.

40. Siegel, Editorial, 4. The American Dance Theatre was an attempt to create a modern dance company that would do diverse repertoire. José Limón and his company were its basis. They gave only one season at the New York State Theater in the mid-1960s and then folded.

41. Siegel, Editorial.

42. Turnbaugh, "Another Round to the Bad Guys."

43. de Mille and Bowers, Letter to the Editor; Turnbaugh, "Good Guys vs. Bad Guys at Lincoln Center," 51. Letters to Peter Mennin are in Presidents' Records, box 28, folder 2, Juilliard Archives. See, too, Sabin, "Juilliard at the Crossroads," on the dim prospects for the Dance Department.

44. Commanday, "The Squeeze-Out at the Juilliard."
45. "School of Ballet to Join Juilliard."
46. Commanday, "The Squeeze-Out at the Juilliard."
47. Interview with Muriel Topaz, July 6, 1995, Aspen, Colorado.
48. Commanday, "The Squeeze-Out at the Juilliard."
49. Ibid.
50. Interview with Muriel Topaz, July 6, 1995, Aspen, Colorado.
51. Commanday, "The Squeeze-Out at the Juilliard."
52. Interview with Muriel Topaz, July 6, 1995, Aspen, Colorado.
53. Peter Mennin to Martha Hill, memorandum, January 19, 1971, Presidents' General Administrative Records, box 28, folder 3, Juilliard Archives.
54. Sabin, "Juilliard at the Crossroads," 78.

CHAPTER 9: *Dramatic Progress*

1. Saint-Denis, *Training for the Theatre*. Peter Mennin was responsible for getting a Ford Foundation grant for Saint-Denis to write this book. Passages from the unpublished version of the Saint-Denis "bible" are sprinkled throughout Houseman's *Final Dress*.
2. Saint-Denis, *Training for the Theatre*, 66.
3. Samuels, "New Views on New School."
4. Saint-Denis, *Training for the Theatre*, 68, 66.
5. Robert Whitehead to George Woods, tls, March 4, 1961, Dean's Records, box 1, folder 11, Juilliard Archives.
6. William Schuman to Robert Whitehead, tls, March 9, 1961, Dean's Records, box 1, folder 11, Juilliard Archives.
7. Saint-Denis to Mennin, Presidents' Records, box 34, folder 4, Juilliard Archives. An original member of the 1930s' Group Theater, Meisner died in 1997 at the age of ninety-one. Meisner's students included Gregory Peck, Diane Keaton, and Robert Duvall and directors Sidney Lumet and Sydney Pollack.
8. Saint-Denis, *Training for the Theatre*, 71.
9. Houseman, *Run-Through;* Houseman, *Front and Center;* Houseman, *Final Dress;* Houseman, *Entertainers and the Entertained;* and Houseman, *Unfinished Business*.
10. Houseman, *Final Dress*, 300–301.
11. W. McNeil Lowry, interview for the Lincoln Center Archives, March 19, 1991, 120, 122, conducted by Sharon Zane.
12. Young, *Lincoln Center*, 245.
13. Esterow, "Attack by Bing on Schuman."
14. Young, *Lincoln Center*, 245.
15. Esterow, "Lincoln Center Loses Whitehead."
16. Ibid.
17. Quoted in Young, *Lincoln Center*, 246.
18. "Inside Job," 74.
19. Kolodin, *Newark Star-Ledger*, January 24, 1965. This experience did not change Schuman's mind about the press and Juilliard. In the mid-1980s he called the development director to assert that the School did not need advertising and should not advertise.

20. Whitehead, and possibly his wife, Zoe Caldwell, still harbors a grudge against Schuman.

21. Kupferberg, "The Mess at Lincoln Center," 4. The New York City Ballet's relationship with Lincoln Center is discussed in chapter 8.

22. Kupferberg, "The Mess at Lincoln Center," 6; Esterow, "Attack by Bing on Schuman."

23. Young, *Lincoln Center*, 246.

24. Kupferberg, "The Mess at Lincoln Center," 7.

25. Martin, *Lincoln Center*, 158.

26. Esterow, "Attack by Bing on Schuman."

27. Houseman, *Final Dress*, 311.

28. Houseman, "Convocation Address, October 4, 1967," 4–6.

29. Houseman, *Final Dress*, 323.

30. Ibid., 324.

31. Ibid., 330. Georganne Mennin objects to the "Sinuous Sicilian" appellation and says that no one had ever called her husband that. That Mennin blamed Schuman's international festivals for any depletion of Juilliard drama funds has little basis in fact but is consistent with his attitude toward Schuman.

32. Also quoted in *Twenty-five Years of Drama at The Juilliard School.*

33. Houseman, *Final Dress*, 331.

34. John Houseman to Peter Mennin, tl, January 19, 1968, Presidents' Records, box 35, folder 2, Juilliard Archives.

35. Excerpts from this diary fill pages 347–402 of *Final Dress*.

36. Subsequent faculty included Norman Aytron, B.H. Barry, Michael Howard, Elizabeth Keen, Jane Kosminksy, Pierre Lefèvre, Gene Lesser, Timothy Monich, Eve Shapiro, John Stix, Harold Stone, Boris Tumarin, John West, and Robert Williams.

37. Houseman, *Final Dress*, 349.

38. Ibid., 354.

39. Ibid., 338.

40. Ibid., 338.

41. Ibid., 339.

42. Ibid., 341.

43. The remaining students were Naomi Chandler, Michael Darden, Nancy Farolino, Thomas Foster, Estelle Galvan, Charles Gerber, Sam Greenbaum, Paul Kreshka, Kathy Light, Spain Logue, Sandra Ann Morgan, Nancy Nichols, Debra Oliver, Ellen O'Mara, Lawrence Reiman, Beverly Ross, Nicholas Schatzki, and Peter Schifter. Of the thirty-six, only three sought B.S. degrees, four, diplomas, and the rest sought B.F.A. degrees.

44. Houseman, *Final Dress*, 379.

45. Ibid., 400.

46. Skinner wrote a classic text, *Speak with Distinction*.

47. Gussow, "Repertory and Recipes."

48. Martin, *Lincoln Center*, 159.

49. The goals for each year are outlined under the categories "technique and imagination," "body," "voice/diction," "speech/language," "improvisation," "interpretation," and "background." Saint-Denis, *Training for the Theatre*, 88–99.

50. Samuels, "New Views on New School."

51. Houseman, *Final Dress*, 480.

52. Ibid., 488.

53. Ibid., 514.

54. Ibid., 501.

55. Glenna Syse, quoted in Klemesrud, "Togetherness Is the Acting Company."

56. W. McNeil Lowry, interview for the Lincoln Center Archives, March 19, 1991, 126, conducted by Sharon Zane.

57. Calta, "Schneider Gets Post at Juilliard."

58. Shelton, "Alan Schneider"; see also Kellman, "Alan Schneider."

59. Schneider, *Entrances*, xiv. The volume was the first of what was to have been a series and covers the period until 1966, before Schneider's arrival at Juilliard.

60. Corry, "Broadway."

61. Wilson, "A.C.T. Does 'Boff Biz' in San Francisco."

62. Alan Schneider to Clive Barnes, tls, February 22, 1978, Presidents' Records, box 32, folder 5, Juilliard Archives. The next day, Schneider wrote a second draft that does not include this paragraph.

63. Wriston Locklair to Alan Schneider, memorandum, December 9, 1976, Presidents' Records, box 34, folder 7, Juilliard Archives.

64. Gussow, "Alan Schneider Resigns."

65. W. McNeil Lowry, interview for the Lincoln Center Archives, March 19, 1991, 1990, 127, conducted by Sharon Zane.

66. Margot Harley, interview for the Lincoln Center Archives, March 13, 1992, 15, conducted by Sharon Zane.

67. Gerard, "Juilliard Drama School, at Twenty."

68. Rainey, "Acting Conservatories."

69. Margot Harley, interview for the Lincoln Center Archives, March 13, 1992, 44, conducted by Sharon Zane.

70. *Twenty-five Years of Drama at The Juilliard School.*

71. Michael Kahn, quoted in Singer, "Playwrights Begin a New Direction."

72. Interview with Michael Kahn, September 19, 1994.

73. *Twenty-five Years of Drama at The Juilliard School.*

74. John Guare, quoted in "John Guare Bridges School and Theater."

75. Interview with Anna Crouse, February 21, 1997, New York City; interview with Margot Harley, July 24, 1997; Houseman, *Final Dress*, 248.

76. At Juilliard, Williams performed the roles of Tarkington in *Look Homeward Angel*, Nonno in *Night of the Iguana*, Tybalt and Friar Laurence in *Romeo and Juliet*, Bottom in *Midsummer Night's Dream*, Luka in *The Lower Depths*, and Robin Starveling/Mustardseed/Moon in *Midsummer's Night Dream*. He shared the role of Dr. Stockmann in *The Enemy of the People* with Kelsey Grammer.

77. Meisler, "He Wasn't Most Likely to Succeed." At Juilliard, La Salle performed the roles of John Buchanan in act 1 of *Summer and Smoke*, Stanhope in *Journey's End*, Yermolay Lopakhin in *Cherry Orchard*, and Faker Englund in *Room Service*.

78. Another of Group I's members wrote about the experience; see Quinn, "A Master Teacher."

79. Meisler, "He Wasn't Most Likely to Succeed." This was in 1982; the administration was Michael Langham and Peter Mennin.

80. Saint-Denis, *Training for the Theatre*, 73.

81. Margot Harley, interview for the Lincoln Center Archives, March 13, 1992, 14, conducted by Sharon Zane; interview with Gideon Waldrop, June 7, 1995, New York City.

82. Margot Harley, interview for the Lincoln Center Archives, March 13, 1992, 14, conducted by Sharon Zane.

83. Gerard, "Juilliard Drama School, at Twenty."

CHAPTER 10: *The Juilliard School*

1. Hellman, "Juilliard Faces Reality."

2. Peter Mennin, quoted in Hellman, "Juilliard Faces Reality," 50.

3. Georganne Mennin, interview for the Lincoln Center Archives, December 3, 1992, 3–4, conducted by Sharon Zane.

4. "U.S. Composers in a Bright Era." The nine composers were Peter Mennin, Alan Hovhaness, Samuel Barber, Leonard Bernstein, Aaron Copland, Roger Sessions, Robert Kurka, Harold Shapero, and Leon Kirchner.

5. "Music," 45.

6. "Peter Mennin named President of Juilliard School."

7. Georganne Mennin, interview for the Lincoln Center Archives, December 3, 1992, 12, conducted by Sharon Zane.

8. His brother composed at a slower rate than did Mennin and in other media. Louis Mennini wrote two chamber operas during the 1950s and two symphonies in the 1960s; he produced more chamber music than did his brother. Perhaps not surprisingly, Louis also pursued administration. He served as dean of the School of Music at the North Carolina School of the Arts (1965–71) and was chair of the music department at Mercyhurst College in his hometown of Erie, where in 1973 he founded the D'Angelo School of Music and D'Angelo Young Artist Competition. In 1983 Louis Mennini founded the Virginia School of the Arts in Lynchburg and served as its head until retirement in 1988.

9. Peter Mennin, "Juilliard Master Plan," manuscript in possession of Georganne Mennin.

10. Harold C. Schonberg, quoted in Holland, "Peter Mennin, Juilliard President and Prolific Composer, Dies."

11. Interview with Jacob Druckman, July 6, 1995, Aspen, Colorado; June Dunbar, interview for the Lincoln Center Archives, June 22, 1993, 19, conducted by Sharon Zane.

12. Interview with Jacob Druckman, July 6, 1995, Aspen, Colorado. In his Yale Oral History interview, Schuman, unasked, expresses discomfort at length.

13. Goldberg, "Fears and Pitfalls of Young Composers"; Georganne Mennin, interview for the Lincoln Center Archives, December 3, 1992, 4, conducted by Sharon Zane.

14. Georganne Mennin, interview for the Lincoln Center Archives, December 3, 1992, 37, conducted by Sharon Zane.

15. Schiff, *The Music of Elliott Carter;* Olmstead, *Roger Sessions and His Music;* Olmstead, *Conversations with Roger Sessions;* Olmstead, *The Correspondence of Roger Sessions;* Machlis, *The Enjoyment of Music.* Machlis also wrote *American Composers of Our Time, Introduction to Contemporary Music, Lisa's Boy,* and *Stefan in Love* (two novels).

16. Galamian, *Principles of Violin Playing and Teaching;* Galamian, *Contemporary Violin Technique.*

17. Glass, *Music by Philip Glass,* 14. Glass went to Paris to study with Nadia Boulanger. `

18. Interview with Steve Reich, November 22, 1994, conducted by Andrew Cook, New York, revised July 28, 1997.

19. *Juilliard News Bulletin* 5 (1966–67).

20. Page, "Juilliard Stages Its First Reunion."

21. All reviews quoted in *Juilliard News Bulletin* 22, no. 6 (1984): n.p.

22. W. McNeil Lowry, interview for the Lincoln Center Archives, March 19, 1991, 129, conducted by Sharon Zane.

23. Copy of telegram dated May 5, 1970, Presidents' Records, box 95, folder 1, Juilliard Archives.

24. Mennin speech, May 11, 1970, [heavily edited], Presidents' Records, box 95, folder 1, Juilliard Archives.

25. Interview with Anna Crouse, February 21, 1997, New York City. Crouse resigned from the board because of disagreements with Mennin about the Drama Division. Later, she rejoined.

26. Mayer, "Are the Trying Times Just Beginning?" 17, 20.

27. Taubman, "Eight Music Schools Seek a Survival Plan."

28. Kogan, *Nothing but the Best: The Struggle for Perfection at The Juilliard School,* 3, 47, 48.

29. Interview with Gideon Waldrop, June 7, 1995, New York City.

30. Robin McCabe, quoted in Ruttencutter, *Pianist's Progress,* 27, 39, 82.

31. Kogan, *Nothing but the Best: The Struggle for Perfection at The Juilliard School,* 86.

32. Ardoin, ed., *Callas at Juilliard.* None of the twenty-five student singers is identified by name.

33. Robin McCabe, quoted in Ruttencutter, *Pianist's Progress,* 82.

34. Hughes, "Music: Pavarotti 'Teaches' TV 'Class.'"

35. Heindenry, *Theirs Was the Kingdom,* a biography of Lila and DeWitt Wallace, does not mention her connection with Juilliard.

36. Mayer, *One Hundred Years of Grand Opera,* 315.

37. Boutwell, "The New Man at the Met." "Music to My Ears" states that Mennin was the only American of prominence given serious consideration for the Met spot. Gentele had just begun his duties in June.

38. "The Big Met Bears a Metlet." "Juilliard said many things, all of which could be translated as go away and leave us alone. It is revealing no secret that the relationship between the Metropolitan Opera and the Juilliard School was not one of Christian joy during that period." The Minimet, which was a series of chamber operas performed by younger artists, gave only two programs at the Mitzi Newhouse Theater.

39. Interview with Olegna Fuschi, February 19, 1995, New York City; subsequent quotations from Fuschi are taken from this interview.

40. Interview with Gideon Waldrop, June 7, 1995, New York City.

41. Interview with Michael White, February 20, 1995, New York City.

42. Mennin, "A Look to the Future."

43. Interview with Gideon Waldrop, June 7, 1995, New York City.

44. "Ivan Galamian, Faculty Member for Thirty-five Years, Dies at Age Seventy-eight."

45. Holland, "Peter Mennin, Juilliard President and Prolific Composer, Dies at Sixty"; "Milestones."

46. *Peter Mennin.*

CHAPTER 11: *Juilliard in the Postmodern World*

1. W. McNeil Lowry, interview for the Lincoln Center Archives, March 19, 1991, 131, conducted by Sharon Zane.

2. Tretick, "The Personal Side of President Polisi," 3.

3. Kamen, who had enrolled in 1965 and left without receiving a degree in the fall of 1968, studied with Melvin Kaplan. He was awarded a diploma in February 1994 by Polisi.

4. Tretick, "The Personal Side of President Polisi."

5. To cite only one example of a more dispassionate view of American music history, the editors of *The New Grove Twentieth-Century American Masters* list ten American composers as the "American masters." Schuman is not among them. They include Charles Ives, John Cage, Henry Cowell, Roger Sessions, Samuel Barber, Aaron Copland, Leonard Bernstein, Elliott Carter, Virgil Thomson, and George Gershwin.

6. Polisi, "To the Faculty."

7. Ibid.

8. "Meanwhile, college and university administrators nationally have given themselves pay increases higher than the average American or the academic faculty have gotten." Marcus, "Ripped Off!" 58.

9. Interview with Joseph Polisi, January 10, 1996, New York City.

10. Interview with Gideon Waldrop, June 7, 1995, New York City.

11. Allen wrote *The Romance of Commerce and Culture: Capitalism, Modernism, and the Chicago-Aspen Crusade for Cultural Reform.*

12. Interview with Stephen Clapp, March 24, 1997, New York City.

13. White, "Vincent Persichetti." Persichetti wrote an influential harmony book: *Twentieth-Century Harmony.*

14. Dawe, "Literature and Materials Curriculum Is Changing."

15. Turner, "Recognizing the Maxwell and Muriel Gluck Fellowship Program."

16. Letter to the Members of the Board of Directors, March 5, 1994, tls, attachment with 137 signatures. Courtesy of Cindy Liou Chen.

17. Interview with Olegna Fuschi, February 19, 1995, New York City.

18. "The Sound of Music," *Sixty Minutes*, May 8, 1994, CBS television.

19. Richard and Cindy Liou, tls, May 10, 1994, to Marti Galavic-Palmer of CBS. Among other questions, they asked, "Why did you not investigate whether the tremendous amount of money being thrown at MAP by the Juilliard administration is being truly well spent?"

20. Brustein, "Culture by Coercion." Brustein is artistic director of the American Repertory Theatre in Cambridge, Massachusetts.

21. Davis, *Miles*, 58–59, 74.

22. Ishii and Moon, "On Racism." Ishii studied from 1988 to 1991 with James Chambers, Ranier DeIntinis, and Julie Landsman. Moon was a student of Julius Baker (1988–92).

23. Dubois, "Focus on Juilliard Concerto Competitions."

24. Eugenia Zukerman, quoted in Kozinn, "Women in Music Pause to Assess Their Status."

25. Interview with with Janet Kessin, March 22, 1995, New York City. Kessin came to Juilliard from Carnegie Hall.

26. Interview with Mary Gray, June 8, 1995, New York City.

27. Ibid.

28. Grimes, "A New Juilliard."

29. Kanefield, "Juilliard's Psychological Services."

30. Friddle, "The Juilliard 'Dis-ease.'"

31. Polisi, "A Musical Call to Arms."

32. Ibid., 4.

33. Ibid.

34. James Sloan Allen, quoted in Grimes, "A New Juilliard."

35. Gill, "The Sky Line," 59.

36. Vogel, "A Letter to the Editor."

37. Polisi, "Convocation to Open School Year."

38. Gill, "The Sky Line," 59–60.

39. "Dormitory Project Wins Final Approval."

40. Gill, "The Sky Line," 60.

41. Ibid., 60–61. The terrace functions somewhat as a "campus" for Juilliard.

42. "The Curtain Rises on Residence Life at Juilliard."

43. Zito, "Reflections from the Other Side of the Desk."

44. Polisi, "Juilliard President Emeritus Dies."

45. Lambert, "William Schuman Is Dead at Eighty-one." Ironically, he became the beneficiary of the Juilliard Summer School, the same Summer School he abolished because people could say they had gone to Juilliard by attending it.

46. Polisi, "Toward the Twenty-first Century."

47. Collins, "At Juilliard's Seventy-fifth Jubilee."

48. Polisi, "Toward the Twenty-first Century."

49. Rubinsky, "New Chairman Realizes an Old Dream"; Interview with Mary Rodgers Guettel, May 2, 1997, New York City.

50. Rodland, "Juilliard Students Become Lobbyists."

BIBLIOGRAPHY

Interviews Conducted by the Author

(t): tape-recorded
James Sloan Allen, June 6, 1995, New York
Mary Ellin Barrett, February 20, 1995, New York (t)
Stephen Clapp, March 24, 1997, New York (t)
Carole Convissor, September 9, 1994, New York
Anna Crouse, February 21, 1997, New York (t)
Jacob Druckman, July 6, 1995, Aspen, Colorado (t)
Joseph Fuchs, October 13, 1993, New York (t)
Olegna Fuschi, February 19, 1995, New York (t)
Mary Gray, June 8, 1995, New York (t)
Mary Rodgers Guettel, May 2, 1997, New York (t)
Gordon Hardy, June 28, 1995, Aspen, Colorado
Margot Harley, July 24, 1997, New York (by telephone)
Michael Kahn, September 19, 1994, New York (by telephone)
Janet Kessin, March 22, 1995, New York (t)
Allan Kozinn, November 3, 1995, New York
Eric Kutz, February 21, 1997, New York (t)
Georganne Mennin, November 4, 1995, New York
Constance Mensch, January 10, 1996, New York
Joseph Polisi, January 10, 1996, New York (t)
Mark Schubart, September 9, 1994, New York (t)
Frances Schuman, April 16, 1994, New York (t)
Muriel Topaz, July 6, 1995, Aspen, Colorado (t)
Gideon Waldrop, June 7, November 3, 1995, New York (t)
Anita Warburg, March 17, 1993, New York
Michael White, Febrary 20, 1995, New York
Stanley Wolfe, January 13, 1994, New York

*Interviews Conducted for Lincoln Center Archives
by Sharon Zane (all New York)*

Anthony Bliss, June 4, 1991
June Dunbar, July 22, 1993
Margot Harley, March 13, 1992
W. McNeil Lowry, January 11, March 19, 1991

Georganne Mennin, December 3, 1992
Mark Schubart, December 20, 1990
William Schuman, July 10, 1991
Alice Tully, January 8, 1991
Edgar Young, August 14, October 11, 1990

Books and Articles

"Act to Reorganize Juilliard School." *New York Times*, May 19, 1927, 8:5.

"A. D. Juilliard, Dry Goods Man, Capitalist, Dies." *New York Tribune*, April 26, 1919, 14.

Allen, Frederick Lewis. *The Big Change: America Transforms Itself, 1900–1950.* New York: Harper and Row, 1952.

Allen, James Sloan. *The Romance of Commerce and Culture: Capitalism, Modernism, and the Chicago-Aspen Crusade for Cultural Reform.* Chicago: University of Chicago Press, 1983.

Antheil, George. *Bad Boy of Music.* Garden City: Doubleday, Doran, 1945.

Ardoin, John, ed. *Callas at Juilliard: The Master Classes.* New York: Knopf, 1987.

"Arts Center Gets Grant of $500,000." *New York Times*, November 26, 1958, 31:8.

"Augustus D. Juilliard." *The National Cyclopedia of American Biography.* Vol. 28, 173. New York: James T. White, 1966.

Auletta, Ken. *Greed and Glory on Wall Street: The Fall of the House of Lehman.* New York: Random House, 1986.

Banner, Leslie. *A Passionate Preference: The Story of the North Carolina School of the Arts.* Winston-Salem: North Carolina School of the Arts Foundation, 1987.

Barber, Donn, ed. *New York Architect* 4 (November 1910).

Barlow, Samuel. *The Astonished Muse.* New York: John Day, 1961.

Barnes, Clive. "Dance: Variety at School." *New York Times*, March 15, 1966, 32:2.

Baumol, William J., and William G. Bowen. *Performing Arts, the Economic Dilemma: A Study of Problems Common to Theater, Music, and Dance.* Cambridge: MIT Press, 1966.

Bellamann, Henry. "Some Conspicuous American Musical Needs." *Musical Digest*, October 26, 1926, 4.

Berezowsky, Alice. *Duet with Nicky.* Philadelphia: J. B. Lippincott, 1943.

Bersohn, Robert. "An Imaginary Interview with Dr. Goetschius on the Subject of the 'Moderns.'" *The Baton* 2 (October 1922): 11.

Birmingham, Stephen. *"Our Crowd": The Great Jewish Families of New York.* New York: Harper and Row, 1967.

———. *Real Lace.* New York: Harper and Row, 1973.

"Bodansky Praises Fund." *New York Times*, July 7, 1919, 18:2.

Bork, Robert H. "Political Activities of Colleges and Universities: Some Policy and Legal Implications." Presented at the American Enterprise Institute for Public Policy Research, October 7, 1970.

Boutwell, Jane P. "The New Man at the Met." *New York Times Magazine*, September 12, 1971, 130.

Bowers, Faubion. Letter to the Editor. *New York Magazine* 1, no. 11 (1968).
"Bradley Charges Chaotic Situation at Juilliard School." *Musical America*, December 9, 1926, 1ff.
Bradley, Kenneth M. "The Necessity of Standardization in Music Education." *Musical Observer* 24 (September 1925): 13–14.
Brayer, Elizabeth. *George Eastman: A Biography*. Baltimore: Johns Hopkins University Press, 1996.
Brockway, Thomas P. *Bennington College: In the Beginning*. Bennington: Bennington College Press, 1981.
Brustein, Robert. "Culture by Coercion." *New York Times*, November 29, 1994, A25.
Bull, Inez. *The Immortal Ernest Hutcheson: A Biography*. Elmira: Elmira Quality Printers, 1993.
Calta, Louis. "Schneider Gets Post at Juilliard." *New York Times*, February 17, 1976, 38:1.
Caning, Peter. *American Dreamers: The Wallaces and* Reader's Digest: *An Insider's Story*. New York: Simon and Schuster, 1996.
"Center School Is Envisioned as Providing Internships to Promising Young Artists." *New York Times*, July 23, 1956, 25:3.
Chasins, Abram, with Villa Stiles. *The Van Cliburn Legend*. Garden City: Doubleday, 1959.
Chazin-Bennahum, Judith. *The Ballets of Antony Tudor: Studies in Psyche and Satire*. New York: Oxford University Press, 1994.
Chernow, Ron. *The Warburgs: The Twentieth-Century Odyssey of a Remarkable Jewish Family*. New York: Random House, 1993.
"Choreography Is Copyrighted for First Time." *New York Herald Tribune*, March 14, 1952.
Cochran, Thomas C., and William Miller. *The Age of Enterprise: A Social History of Industrial America*. Rev. ed. New York: Harper and Row, 1942.
Cohen, Selma Jeanne, ed. *Doris Humphrey: An Artist First*. Middletown: Wesleyan University Press, 1972.
Collins, Glenn. "At Juilliard's Seventy-fifth Jubilee, a Harmony of Gratitude." *New York Times*, December 19, 1980, sec. 2, 8:5.
Commanday, Robert. "The Squeeze-Out at the Juilliard." *San Francisco Examiner and Chronicle*, October 27, 1968.
Cooke, James Francis. "The Advent of Endowed Institutions in America." *Etude* 24 (February 1906): 58.
———. "Making a Modern Conservatory of Music." *Etude* 24 (March 1906): 101.
Copland, Aaron. "Scores and Records." *Modern Music* 15 (May–June 1938): 245–46.
Corry, John. "Broadway." *New York Times*, December 31, 1976, C2:4.
Crowthers, Dorothy. "Les Frères Dethier." *The Baton* 1 (May 1922): 4.
———. "Interesting Incidents of a Distinguished Career." *The Baton* 7 (May 1928): 3.
———. "John Erskine: A Portrait of Our President." *The Baton* 11 (November–December 1931): 25.
———. "To the Glory of Music." *The Baton* 11 (November–December 1931): 3.

"The Curtain Rises on Residence Life at Juilliard." *Juilliard Journal* 7 (November 1990): 7.

Damrosch, Frank. *Institute of Musical Art 1905–1926.* New York: Juilliard School of Music, 1936.

———. *Proceedings of the Music Teachers National Association* (1906), 14–15.

Damrosch, Walter. "'The Star-Spangled Banner': A Standardized Version of the Melody." New York: Schirmer, 1918.

Danek, Victor B. "A Historical Study of the Kneisel Quartet." Mus.Ed.D., Indiana University, 1962.

Davis, Miles, with Quincy Troupe. *Miles: The Autobiography of Miles Davis.* New York: Simon and Schuster, 1989.

Dawe, Jonathan. "Literature and Materials Curriculum Is Changing." *Juilliard Journal* 9 (December 1993–January 1994): 4.

de Mille, Agnes. Letter to the Editor. *New York Magazine* 1, no. 11 (1968).

———. *Martha: The Life and Works of Martha Graham.* New York: Random House, 1956.

Dewey, John. *Art as Experience.* New York: Minton Balch, 1934.

Dolkart, Andrew S. *Morningside Heights: A History of Its Architecture and Development.* New York: Columbia University Press, 1998.

"Dormitory Project Wins Final Approval." *Juilliard Journal* 1 (May 1986): 1.

Downes, Olin. "Music." *New York Times,* December 15, 1935, sec. 7, 17:1, sec. 9, 9:1.

———. "Music." *New York Times,* October 4, 1931, sec. 8, 8:1.

Dubois, Susan. "Focus on Juilliard Concerto Competitions." *Juilliard Journal* 9 (April 1994): 5.

Editorial. *New York Times,* June 23, 1924, 20:5.

Erskine, John. *The Influence of Women—and Its Cure.* Indianapolis: Bobbs-Merrill, 1936.

———. *Is There a Career in Music?* New York: Juilliard School of Music, 1929.

———. "The Juilliard Policy in Operation Throughout the Country." *The Baton* 11 (November–December 1931): 5.

———. *The Memory of Certain Persons.* Philadelphia: J. B. Lippincott Company, 1947.

———. "My Life in Literature." N.p., n.d.

———. *My Life in Music.* New York: William Morrow, 1950.

———. *My Life as a Teacher.* Philadelphia: J. B. Lippincott, 1948.

———. *The Philharmonic Society of New York: Its First Hundred Years.* New York: Macmillan, 1943.

———. *The Private Life of Helen of Troy.* Indianapolis: Bobbs-Merrill, 1925.

———, and Louis Greunberg. *Jack and the Beanstalk.* Boston: C. C. Brichard, 1933.

Esterow, Milton. "Attack by Bing on Schuman over Attempted Hiring Reveals New Controversy at Lincoln Center." *New York Times,* December 5, 1964, 1:5.

———. "Lincoln Center Loses Whitehead." *New York Times,* December 8, 1964, 1:1.

Evaluation Report for the Commission on Institutions of Higher Education of the

Middle States Association of Colleges and Secondary Schools, December 4–7, 1955.

Everett, Carole J. *The Performing Arts Major's Guide.* New Jersey: Prentice-Hall, 1992.

"Explains Juilliard Fund to Aid Music." *New York Times,* February 27, 1923, 10:1.

Eyer, Ronald. "Juilliard L and M Report." *Musical America,* February 15, 1954, 146.

"Fifty-one Win Juilliard Music Fellowships." *New York Times,* July 6, 1925, 12:1.

Fish, Arnold, and Norman Lloyd. *Fundamentals of Sight Singing and Ear Training.* New York: Dodd, Mead, 1967.

Fitzpatrick, Edward John, Jr. *The Music Conservatory in America.* Boston University: DMA, 1963.

Fleishman, Ed. "Familiar Juilliard Haunts Must Close." *Juilliard Journal* 5 (February 1990): 7.

Flesch, Carl. *The Memoires of Carl Flesch,* trans. Hans Keller. London: Rockliff, 1957.

"For a Music Conservatory." *New York Times,* April 30, 1919, 9.

"440 Students Lose U.S. Funds for Role in Campus Outbreaks." *New York Times,* October 14, 1970, 31:1.

Frankenstein, Alfred. "American Composers: xxii, William Schuman." *Modern Music* 22 (December 1944): 27.

Freundlich, Irwin. "Convocation Address, October 10, 1962." *Juilliard Review Annual (1962–63):* 51–52.

———. "Piu mosso." *Dynamics,* March 24, 1934, 7.

Friddle, David. "The Juilliard 'Dis-ease'; or, Does It Really Have to Be This Way?" *Juilliard Journal* 2 (November 1986): 8.

Galamian, Ivan, with E. Green. *Principles of Violin Playing and Teaching.* Englewood Cliffs: Prentice-Hall, 1962. 2d rev. ed., 1985.

Galamian, Ivan, with Frederick Neumann. *Contemporary Violin Technique.* 2d rev. 2 vols. New York: Galaxy Music, 1966.

Gay, Harriet. *The Juilliard String Quartet.* New York: Vantage Press, 1974.

Gerard, Jeremy, "Juilliard Drama School at Twenty, Stresses Versatility." *New York Times,* April 19, 1988, sec. 3, 15:1.

Gill, Brendan. "The Sky Line: Improving Lincoln Center." *The New Yorker,* August 19, 1991, 57–61.

"Gives $5,000,000 to Advance Music." *New York Times,* June 27, 1919, 1:2.

Glass, Philip. *Music by Philip Glass.* Edited and with supplementary material by Robert T. Jones. New York: Harper and Row, 1987.

Glenn Gould–Gertrud Schoenberg. Recorded interview, Los Angeles, March 8, 1962. Transcript, 4. Arnold Schoenberg Institute.

Goldberg, Albert. "Fears and Pitfalls of Young Composers." *Los Angeles Times,* May 21, 1961.

Gould, Glenn. "No, They're Only a Fad." *New York Times,* November 23, 1969, arts section, 1.

Gray, Diane. "Martha Graham, Teacher." *Juilliard Journal* 6 (May 1991): 5.

Grimes, William. "A New Juilliard for a More Challenging Era." *New York*

Times, June 2, 1993, C15–16. Reprinted in *Juilliard Journal* 9 (September 1993): 3, 12.

Grutzner, Charles. "Lincoln Square Project May Include Music and Stage Schools." *New York Times*, February 14, 1956, 1:3.

Guide to the Juilliard School Archives. New York: Juilliard School, 1992.

Gussow, Mel. "Alan Schneider Resigns as Head of the Juilliard Theater Center." *New York Times*, March 3, 1979, 14:5.

———. "Juilliard Company: A School for Stars." *New York Times*, December 16, 1971, 72:1.

———. "Repertory and Recipes All in a Juilliard Actor's Study." *New York Times*, February 1, 1972, 28:1.

H.O.O. "Juilliard Foundation Plans Explained." *Musical Courier*, August 7, 1924, 15.

Hajdu, David. *Lush Life: A Biography of Billy Strayhorn.* New York: Farrar Straus Giroux, 1996.

Hardy, Gordon, and Arnold Fish. *Music Literature: Homophony.* New York: Dodd, Mead, 1963.

———. *Music Literature: Polyphony.* New York: Dodd, Mead, 1970.

Harris, Henry J. "The Occupation of Musicians in the United States." *Musical Quarterly* 1 (April 1915): 304.

Hart, Philip. "The Juilliard School Building: An Architectural Description." *Juilliard News Bulletin* 7 (October-November 1969–70): 31.

———. *Orpheus in the New World: The Symphony Orchestra as an American Cultural Institution.* New York: W. W. Norton, 1973.

Hayes, Marie Therese. "The History of the Juilliard School from Its Inception to 1973." M.M. diss., Catholic University of America, 1974.

Heindenry, John. *Theirs Was the Kingdom; Lila and DeWitt Wallace and the Story of the* Reader's Digest. New York: W. W. Norton, 1993.

Hellman, Peter. "Juilliard Faces Reality." *New York Magazine*, April 21, 1969, 49.

Holland, Bernard. "Peter Mennin, Juilliard President and Prolific Composer, Dies at Sixty." *New York Times*, June 18, 1983, 11:1.

Houseman, John. "Convocation Address, October 4, 1967." *Juilliard Review Annual (1967–68):* 4–6.

———. *Entertainers and the Entertained: Essays on Theater, Film, and Television.* New York: Simon and Schuster, 1986.

———. *Final Dress.* New York: Simon and Schuster, 1983.

———. *Front and Center.* New York: Simon and Schuster, 1979.

———. *Run-Through: A Memoir.* New York: Simon and Schuster, 1972.

———. *Unfinished Business: A Memoir.* Chicago: Chatto and Windus, 1986.

Howard, John Tasker. *Our American Music.* New York: Thomas Y. Crowell, 1946.

Hughes, Allen. "Music: Pavarotti 'Teaches' TV 'Class.'" *New York Times*, January 13, 1979, 16:1.

Hughes, Edwin. "Rafael Joseffy's Contribution to Piano Technic." *Musical Quarterly* 2 (July 1916): 349–64.

Hunt, Marilyn. "Benjamin Harkarvy: Return of the Prodigal Mentor." *Dance Magazine* (April 1992): 52–56. Reprinted in *Juilliard Journal* 8 (September 1992): 4.

Hutcheson, Ernest. *The Literature of the Piano*. New York: Alfred A. Knopf, 1948. Revised by Rudolph Ganz, 1958, 1969, 1974.

——. "A Message to Our Boys in Service." *IMA News*, January 23, 1942.

——. *A Musical Guide to the Richard Wagner* Ring of the Niebelung. New York: Simon and Schuster, 1940. Reprint, 1972.

Hutcheson, Irmgart. "Why Study Abroad?" *Musical America* 54 (August 1934): 14.

"Hutcheson Heads the Juilliard Fund." *New York Times*, July 16, 1927, 10:8.

"Inside Job." *Newsweek*, December 21, 1964, 74–75.

"Insists Opera Get Juilliard Subsidy." *New York Times*, March 2, 1933, 15:1.

"The Institute's Rachmaninoff Reception." *The Baton* 4 (Spring 1925): 8.

Ishii, Michael, and Emma Moon. "On Racism." *Juilliard Journal* 5 (May 1989): 6.

"Ivan Galamian, Faculty Member for Thirty-five Years, Dies at Age Seventy-eight." *Juilliard News Bulletin* 20 (October–November 1981): 1.

Ives, Charles. *Memos*. Edited by John Kirkpatrick. New York: W. W. Norton, 1972.

"John Guare Bridges School and Theater." *Juilliard Journal* 8 (April 1993): 1.

"José Limón Dies at Age of Sixty-four; Juilliard Presents Memorial." *Juilliard News Bulletin* 11, nos. 1–2 (1972–73): 2.

"The Juilliard Advisors" [letter to the editor]. *New York Times*, November 25, 1925, 20:6.

"Juilliard Awards in Music Won by Forty-nine." *New York Times*, October 26, 1925, 25:1.

"Juilliard Bequest Praised by Kahn." *New York Times*, July 1, 1919, 19:1.

"Juilliard Chief Answers Criticism." *New York Times*, January 21, 1927, 12:2.

"Juilliard Fellows in Music Chosen." *New York Times*, December 29, 1924, 8:1.

"Juilliard Foundation Advisory Board Out; Say They Resigned; Secretary Denies It." *New York Times*, November 23, 1925, 1:2.

"Juilliard Foundation Changes Are Forecast." *New York Times*, July 15, 1927, 6:4.

"Juilliard Foundation Work Is Criticized." *New York Times*, October 3, 1926, 2:5.

"Juilliard Millions Now Aiding Music." *New York Times*, December 12, 1922, 22:3.

"Juilliard to Move to Lincoln Square." *Juilliard Review* [alumni supplement], Spring 1957, 3.

"Juilliard Musical Fund Receives $10,000,000." *New York Times*, February 23, 1923, 16:1.

"Juilliard Orchestra Delights Throng." *New York Times*, May 5, 1928, 11:2.

"Juilliard Orchestra Tour—1958—Excerpts from the Press." *Juilliard Review* 5 (Fall 1958): 6.

"Juilliard Tax $441,066." *New York Times*, May 9, 1925, 21:3.

"Juilliard Trustees Plan Music Centre." *New York Times*, January 25, 1926, 1:5.

Kanefield, Elma. "Juilliard's Psychological Services Reflections from the Fifth Year." *Juilliard Journal* 6 (December 1990–January 1991): 9.

Keller, James M. "Juilliard School." In *The Encyclopedia of New York City*. New Haven: Yale University Press, 1995.

Kellman, Barnet. "Alan Schneider: The Director's Career." *Theatre Quarterly* 3 (July–September 1973): 23–37.

Key, Pierre. Editorial. *Musical Digest*, December 7, 1926, 4.

———. "Education Director Bradley Resigns Post with the Juilliard Foundation." *Musical Digest*, December 7, 1926, 1.

———. "Juilliard Musical Foundation Faces Propitious Moment for Advancement." *Musical Digest*, September 28, 1926, 1–3.

———. "Juilliard Secretary E. A. Noble Wields Supreme Authority in Graduate School." *Musical Digest*, October 12, 1926, 1–2, 23.

———. "*Musical Digest* Submits Questionnaire to the Juilliard Foundation Trustees." *Musical Digest*, October 5, 1926, 1–3, 16.

———. "Nation's Daily Press and Music Leaders Voice Opinions on Juilliard Foundation." *Musical Digest*, October 19, 1926, 1.

———. *Pierre Key's Music Yearbook, 1925–26*. New York: Pierre Key, 1925.

———. "Testimony Is Conclusive on the Needs for Bettering the Juilliard Foundation." *Musical Digest*, November 2, 1926, 1, 9.

Key, Susan. "'Sweet Melody over Silent Wave': Depression-Era Radio and the American Composer." Ph.D. diss., University of Maryland, College Park, 1995.

Kiesler, Frederick. *Ten Years of American Opera Design*. New York Public Library for the Performing Arts Collection, 1941.

Kiger, Joseph. *Operating Principles of the Larger Foundations*. New York: Sage Publications, 1954.

Kihss, Peter. "Arts Center Cost Hits 131 Million." *New York Times*, May 25, 1960, 28:3.

Kingsbury, Henry. *Music, Talent, and Performance: A Conservatory Cultural System*. Philadelphia: Temple University Press, 1988.

Kinkeldey, Otto. "Waldo Selden Pratt." *Musical Quarterly* 26 (April 1940): 162–74.

Kirkpatrick, Albert. "Ernest Hutcheson." *The Baton* 11 (January 1932): 10–13.

———. "Institute News: Student Activities." *The Baton* 11 (March 1932): 9.

———. "A Tone Poem in Color with the New Building as Theme." *The Baton* 11 (November–December 1931): 13–16.

Klemesrud, Judy. "Togetherness Is the Acting Company." *New York Times*, October 26, 1975, sec. 2, 5:1.

Kline, Donna Staley. *Olga Samaroff Stokowski: An American Virtuoso on the World Stage*. College Station: Texas A&M University Press, 1996.

"K. M. Bradley Quits Juilliard School." *New York Times*, December 3, 1926, 13:1.

Kneisel, Franz. "Interview with Franz Kneisel." *The Baton* 3 (February 1922): 1–4.

Kogan, Judith. *Nothing but the Best: The Struggle for Perfection at the Juilliard School*. New York: Random House, 1987.

Kolodin, Irving. *The Metropolitan Opera*. New York: A. A. Knopf, 1966.

————. *The Metropolitan Opera, 1883–1939.* New York: Oxford University Press, 1940.

————. "A Pioneer Passes." *New York Sun*, October 30, 1937.

Koner, Pauline. *Solitary Song.* Durham: Duke University Press, 1989.

Kozinn, Allan. "Women in Music Pause to Assess Their Status." *New York Times*, October 22, 1988, 11:4.

Kriegsman, Sali Ann. *Modern Dance in America: The Bennington Years.* Boston: G. K. Hall, 1981.

Kupferberg, Herbert. "The Mess at Lincoln Center." *Sunday Herald Tribune Magazine*, December 27, 1964, 4–7.

Lambert, Bruce. "William Schuman Is Dead at Eighty-one; Noted Composer Headed Juilliard." *New York Times*, February 16, 1992, 48. Reprinted as *"The New York Times* Recounts Mr. Schuman's Life." *Juilliard Journal* 7 (March 1992): 3.

Loeb, James. *A Memorial: Our Father, 1829–1929.* Munich: privately printed, June 1929.

Loesser, Arthur. *Men, Women and Pianos: A Social History.* New York: Simon and Schuster, 1954.

Loesser, Susan. *A Most Remarkable Fella: Frank Loesser and the Guys and Dolls in His Life—A Portrait by His Daughter.* New York: Donald I. Fine, 1993.

Longy-Miquelle, Renée. *Principles of Music Theory.* Boston: E. C. Schirmer, 1925.

Lowell, John H. "The Juilliard Report on Teaching the Literature and Materials of Music." *Musical Quarterly* 40 (April 1954): 250.

Lowens, Irving. "L'Affaire Muck: A Study in War Hysteria (1917–18)." *Musicology* 1 (1947): 274ff.

Lunney, Robert M. *Kelley Drye and Warren: An Informal History, 1836–1984.* New York: Kelley Drye and Warren, 1985.

Machlis, Joseph. *American Composers of Our Time.* New York: Thomas Y. Crowell, 1963.

————. *The Enjoyment of Music: an Introduction to Perceptive Listening.* 5th ed. New York: W. W. Norton, 1984.

————. *Introduction to Contemporary Music.* New York: W. W. Norton, 1979.

————. *Lisa's Boy.* New York: W. W. Norton, 1982.

————. *Stefan in Love: A Novel.* New York: W. W. Norton, 1991.

Mann, Robert. "Edouard Dethier, 1885–1962." *Juilliard Review* 9 (Spring 1962): 6.

Mannes, David. *Music Is My Faith.* New York: Norton, 1938. Reprint. New York: Da Capo Press, 1978.

Marcus, Jon. "Ripped Off! Inside the Higher Education Racket." *Boston Magazine* 89 (November 1997): 54–59, 104–10.

Martin, George. *Causes and Conflicts: The Centennial History of the Association of the Bar of the City of New York, 1870–1970.* Boston: Houghton Mifflin, 1970.

————. *The Damrosch Dynasty; America's First Family of Music.* Boston: Houghton Mifflin, 1983.

Martin, Ralph G. *Lincoln Center for the Performing Arts.* Englewood Cliffs: Prentice-Hall, 1971.

Mayer, Martin. "Are the Trying Times Just Beginning?" *New York Times*, September 28, 1969, sec. 2, 17:1.

———. *One Hundred Years of Grand Opera*. New York: Simon and Schuster, 1983.

———. "William Schuman Protests a 'Completely False History.'" [Mr. Mayer Replies.] *New York Times*, October 26, 1969, sec. 2, 29:2.

McCoy, Donald R. *Coming of Age: The United States during the 1920s and 1930s*. Middlesex, England: Penguin Books, 1973.

McNaughton, Charles David. "Albert Stoessel: American Musician." Ph.D. diss, New York University, 1957.

McPherson, Bruce, and James A. Klein. *Measure by Measure: A History of New England Conservatory from 1867*. Boston: New England Conservatory, 1995.

Meisler, Andy. "He Wasn't Most Likely to Succeed, but He Is Now." *New York Times*, November 6, 1994, sec. 2, 30:1.

Meltzer, Charles H. Letter to the Editor. *New York Times*, December 17, 1922, sec. 7, 4:3.

Mennin, Peter. "Commencement Address." *Juilliard News Bulletin* 7 (May 1969): 2–4.

———. "Convocation." *Juilliard News Bulletin* 4 (November 1965), 1.

———. "A Look to the Future." *Juilliard News Bulletin* 7, nos. 1–2 (1969–70): 21.

Miller, Philip Lieson. "Marcella Sembrich." In *The New Grove Dictionary of American Music*, edited by Stanley Sadie and H. Wiley Hitchcock. Vol. 4, 187. New York: Macmillan, 1986.

"Milestones." *Time*, June 27, 1983, 76.

"Music." *Time*, June 22, 1962, 45.

"Music Foundation Defends Its Policy." *New York Times*, November 23, 1926, 11:4.

"Music Foundation Policies Attacked." *New York Times*, September 29, 1926, 12:1.

"Music to My Ears." *Saturday Review*, December 26, 1970, 34.

Nettl, Bruno. *Heartland Excursions: Ethnomusicological Reflections on Schools of Music*. Urbana: University of Illinois Press, 1995.

Neumeyer, Carl Melvin. "A History of the National Association of Schools of Music." D.Mus.Ed. diss., Indiana University, 1954.

Nin, Anaïs. *The Early Diaries of Anaïs Nin, 1927–31*. Vol. 4. New York: Harcourt, Brace, Jovanovich, 1985.

Noss, Luther. *A History of the Yale School of Music, 1855–1970*. New Haven: Yale School of Music, 1984.

O'Connor, John J. "Juilliard: Beyond the Sound of Music." *The Wall Street Journal*, January 13, 1969.

Olmstead, Andrea. *Conversations with Roger Sessions*. Boston: Northeastern University Press, 1987.

———. *The Correspondence of Roger Sessions*. Boston: Northeastern University Press, 1992.

———. "Frank Damrosch and the Institute of Musical Art." *Juilliard Journal* 9 (February 1994): 1ff.

———. "A Glimpse into Juilliard's History Examines Role of James Loeb." *Juilliard Journal* 9 (November 1993): 1ff.

———. *Roger Sessions and His Music*. Ann Arbor: UMI Research Press, 1985.

———. "The Toll of Idealism: James Loeb—Musician, Classicist, Philanthropist." *Journal of Musicology* 14 (Spring 1996): 233–62.

"One Hundred Fellowships for Music Pupils." *New York Times*, June 22, 1924, 22:1.

"$1,000,000 Interest Is Won by Juilliard Estate Heirs." *New York Times*, December 28, 1923, 17:2.

"Opera Accepts Juilliard Terms; Witherspoon (an American) to Succeed Gatti." *New York Times*, March 7, 1935, 1:4.

"Opera School Presentations Mark Composers League Twentieth Anniversary." *New York Times*, December 10, 1942, 33:4.

"Otto H. Kahn Sees in Gift a Great Recognition of Music." *Musical America*, July 5, 1919, 1, 4.

An Outline of the Life and Career of Madame Marcella Sembrich. Sembrich Memorial Association, 1945.

Owen, H. Goddard. *A Recollection of Marcella Sembrich*. New York: Marcella Sembrich Memorial Association, 1950. Rev. ed. New York: Marcella Sembrich Memorial Association, 1982.

Pace, Eric. "Charles M. Spofford Is Dead at Eighty-eight; Furnished Idea for Lincoln Center." *New York Times*, March 25, 1991, B10:2.

Page, Tim. "Juilliard Stages Its First Reunion." *New York Times*, October 13, 1984, sec. 1, 13:4.

Parmenter, Ross. "Juilliard School Shuts Down Its Summer Session as Country Schools Take Over." *New York Times*, July 4, 1954, sec. 2, 7:3.

———. "Lincoln Square Plan Developing toward World Cultural Center." *New York Times*, July 23, 1956, 1:1, 25.

Perlis, Vivian. "Leo Ornstein." In *The New Grove Dictionary of American Music*, edited by Stanley Sadie and H. Wiley Hitchcock. Vol. 3, 452. New York: Macmillan, 1986.

Perlmutter, Donna. *Shadowplay: The Life of Antony Tudor*. New York: Viking, 1991.

Persichetti, Vincent. *Twentieth-Century Harmony: Creative Aspects and Practice*. New York: W. W. Norton, 1961.

Pescatello, Ann M. *Charles Seeger: A Life in American Music*. Pittsburgh: University of Pittsburgh Press, 1992.

Peter Mennin: The Composer Draws His Own Profile with Original Prose. Aspen Music Festival memorial brochure, 1983.

"Peter Mennin Named President of Juilliard School of Music." *New York Times*, June 11, 1962, 1:1.

Pischl, A. J. "Touring with the Juilliard Dance Department." *Juilliard Annual Review (1963–64):* 40.

Polisi, Joseph. "Convocation to Open School Year on Note of Tradition." *Juilliard Journal* 11 (September 1995): 1.

———. "Juilliard President Emeritus Dies." *Juilliard Journal* 7 (March 1992): 1.

———. "A Musical Call to Arms." *Juilliard Journal* 9 (February 1994): 1.

———. "President Polisi Addresses Society's Questioning of the Importance of the Performing Arts." *Juilliard Journal* 9 (September 1993): 3, 6.

———. "To the Faculty." *Juilliard Bulletin* 23 (October 1984): 3–4.

———. "Toward the Twenty-first Century: Juilliard Faces Its Future." *Juilliard Journal* 10 (September 1994): 3, 10, 11.

Potter, Tully. "Success in High Society." *The Strad* 108 (February 1997): 154–61.

Quinn, Kathleen. "A Master Teacher in Act I at Juilliard." *New York Times*, November 6, 1988, sec. 2, 8:5.

Rainey, David. "Acting Conservatories—Are They Offering Adequate Training?" *Juilliard Journal* 3 (May 1988): 4.

"Regents Approve Juilliard School." *New York Times*, November 14, 1926, 13:1.

Reich, Howard. *Van Cliburn*. Nashville: Thomas Nelson Publishers, 1993.

Reich, Nancy B. "Women as Musicians: A Question of Class." In *Musicology and Difference: Gender and Sexuality in Music Scholarship*, edited by Ruth A. Solie. Pages 125–46. Berkeley: University of California Press, 1993.

———. "Women and the Music Conservatory." In *Aflame with Music: One Hundred Years of Music at the University of Melbourne*. Melbourne: University of Melbourne, 1995.

"Results of Juilliard Fellowships—Educational Purposes and Problems." *New York Times*, June 7, 1925, 5:1.

Rice, Edwin T. "A Tribute to Frank Damrosch." *Musical Quarterly* 25 (April 1939): 129–34.

Riker, Charles. *The Eastman School of Music: Its First Quarter Century (1921–1946)*. Rochester: University of Rochester Press, 1948.

Rodgers, Richard. *Musical Stages: An Autobiography*. New York: Random House, 1975. Reprint. New York: Da Capo Press, 1995.

Rodland, Carol. "Juilliard Students Become Lobbyists for a Day." *Juilliard Journal* 10 (April 1995): 8.

Rouse, Christopher. *William Schuman Documentary*. New York: G. Schirmer, 1980.

Rubin, Joan S. *The Making of Middlebrow Culture*. Chapel Hill: University of North Carolina Press, 1992.

Rubinsky, Jane. "New Chairman Realizes an Old Dream: Getting to Juilliard." *Juilliard Journal* 10 (September 1994): 13.

Rudolf, Max. *The Grammar of Conducting: A Comprehensive Guide to Baton Technique and Interpretation*. New York: Schirmer Books, 1950.

Rules for the Guidance and Instruction of Students. Institute of Musical Art, 1907.

Ruttencutter, Helen Drees. *Pianist's Progress*. New York: Thomas Y. Crowell, 1979.

Ryan, Alan. *John Dewey and the High Tide of American Liberalism*. New York: W. W. Norton, 1996.

Sabin, Robert. "Juilliard at the Crossroads." *Dance Magazine* (July 1968): 33–39, 76–79.

Saint-Denis, Michel. *Training for the Theatre: Premises and Promises*. Edited by Suria Saint-Denis. New York: Theatre Arts Books, 1982.

Samuels, Gertrude. "New Views on New School." *New York Times*, April 5, 1959, sec. 2, 3:1.

Saylor, Bruce. "Henry Cowell." In *The New Grove Dictionary of Music and Musicians*, edited by Stanley Sadie. Vol. 5, 9. New York: Macmillan Press, 1980.

Schiff, David. *The Music of Elliott Carter*. London: Eulenberg, 1983. 2d rev. ed. Ithaca: Cornell University Press, 1998.

Schneider, Alan. *Entrances: An American Director's Journey*. New York: Viking, 1986.

Schoenberg, Arnold. *Arnold Schoenberg Letters*. Edited by Erwin Stein, translated by Eithne Wilkins and Ernest Kaiser. Berkeley: University of California Press, 1964.

Schonberg, Harold C. "The Big Met Bears a Metlet." *New York Times*, February 18, 1973, D:17.

———. "Juilliard to Move to Lincoln Square and Add Training in the Drama." *New York Times*, February 7, 1957, 1.

———. "Juilliard Program Symbolizes a Decade." *New York Times*, October 27, 1969, 57:1.

———. "Taj Mahal of Music." *New York Times*, October 3, 1969, 47:2.

"Schoenberg to Join Juilliard's Faculty." *New York Times*, February 14, 1935, 23:7.

Schoen-René, Anna Eugénie. *America's Musical Inheritance; Memories and Reminiscences*. New York: G. P. Putnam's Sons, 1941.

"School of Ballet to Join Juilliard." *New York Times*, November 2, 1965, 27:2.

Schreiber, Flora Rheta, and Vincent Persichetti. *William Schuman*. New York: G. Schirmer, 1954.

Schumach, Murray. "Seven Injured as Floor Collapses at New Juilliard School in Lincoln Center." *New York Times*, March 10, 1967, 1:6.

Schuman, William. "Foreword." *Dance Perspectives 16 (Composer/Choreographer)*. 1963.

———. "The New Establishment." Presented at the Conference on the Performing Arts: Their Economic Problems, December 8–9, 1966, Princeton University.

———. "On Teaching the Literature and Materials of Music." *Musical Quarterly* 34 (April 1948): 155–68.

———. "William Schuman Protests a 'Completely False History'" [letter to the editor]. *New York Times*, October 26, 1969, sec. 2, 29:2.

Schuman, William, and Richard Franko Goldman. "Introduction." *The Juilliard Report on Teaching the Literature and Materials of Music*. New York: W. W. Norton, 1953.

Schwarz, Boris. *Great Masters of the Violin: From Corelli and Vivaldi to Stern, Zukerman and Perlman*. New York: Simon and Schuster, 1983.

Schwarz, Mildred F. "The Juilliard School." *Architectural Record* 147 (January 1970): 121–30.

Sellers, Charles Coleman. *Dickinson College: A History*. Middletown: Wesleyan University Press, 1973.

Shaw, W. B. "Augustus D. Juilliard." In *Dictionary of American Biography*. Vol. 5, 244. New York: Scribner's, 1932.

Shelton, Lewis E. "Alan Schneider." In *Theatrical Directors: A Biographical*

Dictionary, edited by J. W. Frick and Stephen M. Vadillo. Page 357. Westport: Greenwood Press, 1994.

Shepard, Richard F. "Schumann Quiting Lincoln Center Post." *New York Times*, December 5, 1968, 1:4.

Sherrock, Irene E. "The Inquiring Reporter." *IMA News*, March 31, 1942.

Siegel, Marcia B. *Days on Earth: The Dance of Doris Humphrey.* New Haven: Yale University Press, 1987.

———. Editorial. *Dance Scope* 3 (Fall 1966): 1–4.

Siloti, Alexander. *Remembering Franz Liszt.* Introduction by Mark Grant. New York: Limelight Editions, 1987.

Singer, Blair. "Playwrights Begin a New Direction." *Juilliard Journal* 10 (December 1994–January 1995): 4.

"Singers Intensify Opera Fund Drive." *New York Times*, March 5, 1933, sec. 2, 1:2.

Skinner, Edith. *Speak with Distinction.* Revised, with material added by Timothy Monich and Lilene Mansell. New York: Applause Theatre Book Publishers, 1990.

Smith, Helena Huntington. "Profiles: Professor's Progress." *The New Yorker*, December 10, 1927, 28.

Smith, Julia. *Master Pianist: The Career and Teaching of Carl Friedberg.* New York: Philosophical Library, 1963.

Smith, S. Stephenson. "The Economic Situation of the Performer." *Juilliard Review* 2 (Fall 1955): 13.

Soares, Janet Mansfield. *Louis Horst: Musician in a Dancer's World.* Durham: Duke University Press, 1992.

———. "Martha Hill: 'With the Future in Mind.'" *Juilliard Journal* 2 (April 1987): 4–5.

———. "Remembering Martha Hill, Juilliard's Dance Legend." *Juilliard Journal* 12 (September 1996): 8–9.

"The Sound of Music." *Sixty Minutes*, CBS television. May 8, 1994.

Spalding, Albert. *Rise to Follow.* New York: Henry Holt, 1943.

Spalding, Walter Raymond. *Music at Harvard: A Historical Review of Men and Events.* New York: Coward-McCann, 1935.

Stebbins, Lucy Poate, and Richard Poate Stebbins. *Frank Damrosch: Let the People Sing.* Durham: Duke University Press, 1945.

"Stoessel Falls to Stage and Dies Conducting Arts Academy Fete." *New York Times*, May 13, 1943, 1:2.

Stokowski, Olga Samaroff. *An American Musician's Story.* New York: W. W. Norton, 1939.

"Stransky Discusses Juilliard Bequest to Music." *New York Times*, August 10, 1919, sec. 4, 5:2.

"Subjects of Discussion in New York Art Circles." *New York Times*, October 18, 1925, sec. 9, 13:1.

Taubman, Howard. "Eight Music Schools Seek a Survival Plan." *New York Times*, January 20, 1970, 48:1.

———. "Juilliard Opens $36–Million Fund Drive." *New York Times*, September 13, 1971, 44:1.

———. "On Coming Home." *New York Times*, September 14, 1958, sec. 2, 11:1.

———. *Opera—Front and Back*. New York: Charles Scribners' Sons, 1938.

Taylor, Paul. "Paul Taylor's Juilliard Days." *Juilliard Journal* 3 (October 1987): 4–5.

———. *Private Domain*. New York: Alfred A. Knopf, 1987.

Thompson, Oscar. "An American School of Criticism: The Legacy Left by W. J. Henderson, Richard Aldrich, and Their Colleagues of the Old Guard." *Musical Quarterly* 23 (October 1937): 428–39.

Thomson, Virgil. "The Gluck Case." *New York Herald Tribune*, March 8, 1942, sec. 6, 6:1.

———. "Music." *New York Herald Tribune*, December 12, 1940, 27:1.

———. "'Theory' at Juilliard." *New York Herald Tribune*, May 18, 1947, sec. 5, 6:1.

Tick, Judith. "Charles Ives and Gender Ideology." In *Musicology and Difference: Gender and Sexuality in Music Scholarship*, edited by Ruth A. Solie. Pages 83–107. Berkeley: University of California Press, 1993.

———. "Passed Away Is the Piano Girl: Changes in American Musical Life, 1870–1900." In *Women Making Music: The Western Art Tradition, 1150–1950*, edited by Jane Bowers and Judith Tick. Pages 325–48. Urbana: University of Illinois Press, 1986.

Tischler, Barbara L. "One Hundred Percent Americanism and Music in Boston during World War I." *American Music* 4 (Summer 1986): 164–76.

Tretick, Drew. "The Personal Side of President Polisi." *Juilliard Journal* 2 (February 1987): 3.

Turnbaugh, Douglas. "Another Round to the Bad Guys." *New York Magazine*, July 15, 1968.

———. "Good Guys vs. Bad Guys at Lincoln Center." *New York Magazine*, May 20, 1968, 51.

Turner, Stephen. "Recognizing the Maxwell and Muriel Gluck Fellowship Program in Its Fifth Year." *Juilliard Journal* 9 (December 1993–January 1994): 5.

"Twelve Noted Musicians Juilliard Teachers." *New York Times*, October 5, 1924, 26:2.

Twenty-five Years of Drama at The Juilliard School. Program book and video, gala celebration, April 25, 1994.

"U.S. Composers in a Bright Era." *Life Magazine*, May 21, 1956, 141ff.

U.S. Congress, House. Congressional Hearings Supplement, House Committee on Ways and Means, March 8, 1886, 427–29.

U.S. Supreme Court Reports 110–13. 4Sct122; 28LawEd204, *Juilliard v. Greenman*.

"A Vital Experiment in Dance Education." *Musical America*, April 15, 1951, 14.

Vogel, Carlo. "A Letter to the Editor." *Juilliard Journal* 5 (December 1989–January 1990): 8.

Waldrop, Gideon. "The Juilliard Story." *Musical America* 82 (September 1962): 44.

Wallace, Robert K. *A Century of Music-Making: The Lives of Josef and Rosina Lhevinne*. Bloomington: Indiana University Press, 1976.

Walton, Frank L. *Tomahawks to Textiles: The Fabulous Story of Worth Street*. New York: Appleton-Century-Crofts, 1953.

Warburg, Frieda Schiff. *Reminiscences of a Long Life*. New York: privately printed, 1956.

Warburg, Paul. "The Testimonial Dinner to Frank Damrosch." *The Baton* 5 (February 1926): 4–5.

Warren, Larry. *Anna Sokolow: The Rebelious Spirit*. Princeton: Princeton Book Company, 1991.

Wedge, George. "Message from Dean Wedge." *IMA News*, December 17, 1941.

The Wesleyan Alumnus (October 1920): 13.

White, Michael. "Vincent Persichetti: Portrait of a Teacher." *Juilliard Journal* 8 (May 1993): 8.

"William Schuman." Special insert to *Juilliard Journal* 7 (April 1992): 4.

"William Schuman Elected President of Lincoln Center." *Juilliard Review* 8 (Fall 1961): 8.

"Will Present *Helen Retires*." *New York Times*, June 16, 1933, 20:1.

Wilson, Edwin. "A.C.T. Does 'Boff Biz' in San Francisco." *Wall Street Journal*, January 19, 1977, 16:4.

Wittstein, Hyman. "Percy Goetschius." *The Baton* 1 (March 1922): 1.

Wolfram, Victor. "Editorial." *Harmonics*, January 1939, 2.

Worden, Helen. "About People." *New York Herald Tribune*, December 6, 1948, 19:6.

Young, Edgar B. *Lincoln Center: The Building of an Institution*. New York: New York University Press, 1980.

Yurka, Blanche. *Bohemian Girl: Blanche Yurka's Theatrical Life*. Athens: Ohio University Press, 1970.

Zito, Ralph. "Reflections from the Other Side of the Desk." *Juilliard Journal* 8 (March 1993): 3.

INDEX

117, 121, 122, 125, 129, 130, 133, 192

ANDREA OLMSTEAD taught music history at The Juilliard School from 1972 to 1980. Formerly a violinist, she played in the New York Youth Symphony and the National Orchestral Association. Since 1981 she has been coordinator of the Department of Music History at The Boston Conservatory and is chair of the master's degree program in music history.

She has held several residencies, both as a writer at the Virginia Center for the Creative Arts and as a visiting scholar at the American Academy in Rome. The author of numerous articles, reviews, and liner notes, she has also written three books: *Roger Sessions and His Music* (1985), *Conversations with Roger Sessions* (1987), and *The Correspondence of Roger Sessions* (1992). She lives in Boston with her husband, composer and pianist Larry Bell.

Typeset in 10/13.5 Adobe Janson
with Janson display
Designed by Copenhaver Cumpston
Composed by Jim Proefrock
at the University of Illinois Press
Manufactured by Cushing-Malloy, Inc.